Aug 16, 1945

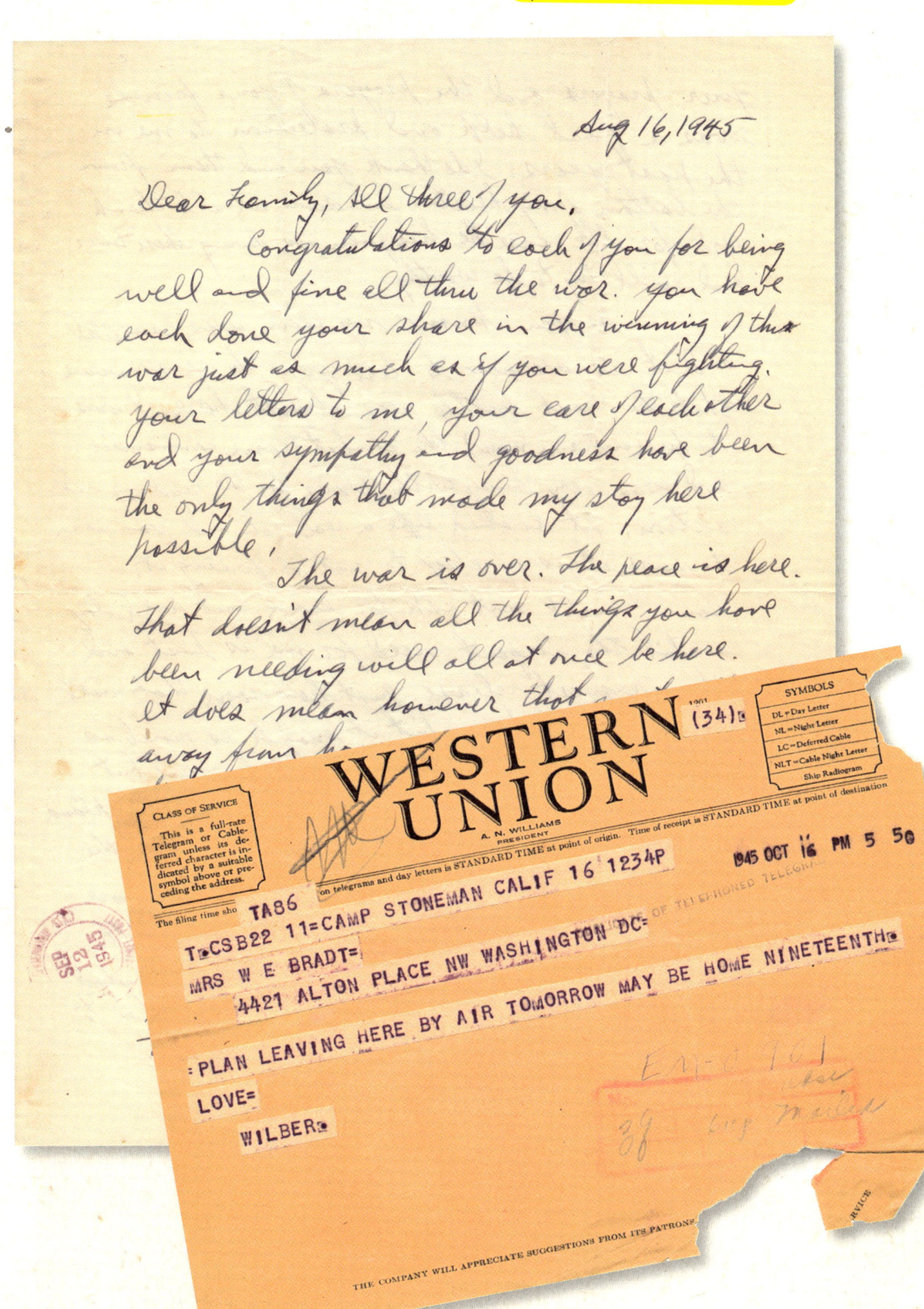

Dear Family, All three of you,

Congratulations to each of you for being well and fine all thru the war. You have each done your share in the winning of this war just as much as if you were fighting. Your letters to me, your care of each other and your sympathy and goodness have been the only things that made my stay here possible.

The war is over. The peace is here. That doesn't mean all the things you have been needing will all at once be here. It does mean however that

---

WESTERN UNION

A. N. WILLIAMS, PRESIDENT

1945 OCT 16 PM 5 50

TA86
T.CSB22 11=CAMP STONEMAN CALIF 16 1234P

MRS W E BRADT=
4421 ALTON PLACE NW WASHINGTON DC=

=PLAN LEAVING HERE BY AIR TOMORROW MAY BE HOME NINETEENTH LOVE=

WILBER

VICTORY AND HOMECOMING

WILBER'S WAR

WILBER'S WAR TRILOGY
Citizen Soldier (Book 1)
Combat and New Life (Book 2)
Victory and Homecoming (Book 3)

BOOK 3

VICTORY AND HOMECOMING

WILBER'S WAR

An American Family's Journey through World War II

Hale Bradt

Victory and Homecoming
Book 3 of the *Wilber's War* Trilogy:
An American Family's Journey through World War II
www.wilberswar.com

Copyright © 2016 by Hale Bradt

Van Dorn Books
P.O. Box 8836, Salem, MA 01971
www.vandornbooks.com

All rights reserved. This book may not be reproduced in part or whole without the express written permission of the publisher. For permission to reproduce any material from the book, kindly contact the publisher at the address above or through info@vandornbooks.com

For information about bulk sales,
please contact the publisher at info@vandornbooks.com

Every effort has been made to trace and credit accurate copyright ownership of the visual material used in this book. Errors or omissions will be corrected in subsequent editions provided notification is made in writing to the publisher at the address above.
Book Editor: Frances B. King, HistoryKeep.com
Book design: Lisa Carta Design, lisacartadesign@gmail.com
Typefaces: Minion, Chaparral Pro
Book and case front-cover images: U.S. Army
Back-cover images: Bradt family
Printed by Friesens, Canada, http://www.friesens.com

Wilber's War (the trilogy)
ISBN 978-0-9908544-0-1
Library of Congress Control Number: 2014922173

Limited First Edition

The individual books (if separated from the set)
ISBN (Book 1, Citizen Soldier): 978-0-9908544-1-8
ISBN (Book 2, Combat and New Life): 978-0-9908544-2-5
ISBN (Book 3, Victory and Homecoming): 978-0-9908544-3-2
Library of Congress Control Numbers:
Book 1 (Citizen Soldier): 2014922166
Book 2 (Combat and New Life): 2014922168
Book 3 (Victory and Homecoming): 2014922167

In memory of Wilber and Norma
And for Valerie and Abby
—this is their story too

CONTENTS

Preface		*xiii*
Maps and Charts		*xvii*

PART I Combat, New Guinea

1	*I'm back on the Jap business again* At sea and Aitape, New Guinea, July–September, 1944	3
2	*Running on and off ships* Aitape, September–November, 1944	23
3	*You can be sure we'll take care of Mother* Aitape, November–December, 1944	45

PART II Final battles, Luzon

4	*Some minutes are worth more than years of living* At sea en route to Luzon, December 1944–January 1945	69
5	*I'm not sure just what the Lord got* Central plains combat, January–February, 1945	95
6	*Send along the blue letters and don't worry about them* Guimba and Mabalacat; Rehabilitation and combat reserve, February–March, 1945	115
7	*Things were tight for awhile* Shimbu Line combat, March–April, 1945	127
8	*We are in mud to our ears* Ipo Dam combat, May 1945	147
9	*I am again wearing the crossed rifles* Wrap-up operations, May–June, 1945	161
10	*Your old man now commands a regiment* Camp La Croix, Cabanatuan, July–August, 1945	171
11	*So it's over. Well! I think I'll go sit under that tree* Camp LaCroix, August–September, 1945	189

PART III Interlude 1983, Luzon

12 *Laguna de Bay and Corregidor* — *201*
    May 1–6, 1983

13 *Hacienda Cinco, San Fabian, and American Cemetery* — *213*
    May 3–6, 1983

PART IV Japan and home

14 *Tokyo and Yokohama are ruins* — *225*
    Kumagaya, Japan, September 1945

15 *My heart rests in your dear hands* — *237*
    At sea and Washington, D.C., September–December, 1945

PART V Epilog

16 *I have never known such deep despair and ill health* — *263*
    Washington, D.C., December 1945–June 1947

17 *I think we might grow to love each other. Don't you?* — *281*
    Midwest and East Coast, 1947–1984

18 *Reflections* — *293*
    Salem, Massachusetts, 2014

Acknowledgments — *303*

Bibliography — *307*

Index — *311*

FIGURES

CHARTS

Chart 1. Bradt, Sparlin, and Bourjaily families xix
Chart 2. Organization of 43rd Infantry Division, 1944–1945......... xx

MAPS

Map 1. Pacific areas controlled by combatants xxii
Map 2. Pacific command areas and voyages xxiii
Map 3. Eastern New Guinea......................................xxiv
Map 4. Aitape coastline.. xxv
Map 5. Convoy track en route Luzon xxvi
Map 6. Luzon, Japanese defensive zones xxvii
Map 7. Luzon, locations of 43rd Division actions................ xxviii
Map 8. Landing beaches of Sixth Army, Lingayen Gulf............xxix
Map 9. Landing beaches, 43rd Division, Lingayen Gulf xxx
Map 10. First day's advances on Luzon........................xxxi
Map 11. Hill 200 enveloped by 103rd RCT xxxii
Map 12. Capture of Pozorrubio................................. xxxiii
Map 13. Teresa–Bosoboso River region xxxiv
Map 14. Drive of 103rd RCT to Lumban xxxv
Map 15. Ipo Dam attack plan................................. xxxvi
Map 16. Manila Bay..xxxvii
Map 17. Kyushu, Japan, Olympic landing sites xxxviii
Map 18. Artillery plan, Shibushi Bay xxxix

ILLUSTRATIONS

PART I Combat, New Guinea

Envelope addressed by Wilber................................. 15
Valerie, Hale, and Norma splashing in lake....................... 24
Wilber and Captain Burns, Aitape 25
Howitzer (105-mm) firing at Aitape............................ 26
Truck being pulled from surf, Aitape 29
Pontoon bridge, Aitape.. 29
Knife made for Wilber, sketch of............................... 42
Norma, portrait of... 49
Hale and Valerie, portraits of.................................. 50
Native choir at Christmas...................................... 60

ILLUSTRATIONS Continued

PART II Final battles, Luzon, P.I.

USS Fayette (APA-43)	71
Amphibious vehicles being loaded, Aitape	74
Menu on USS Fayette, New Year's Day	80
Combat belt, sketched by Wilber	89
American fleet at Lingayen Gulf	93
LCVPs heading for beach, Lingayen Gulf	93
Troops unloading supplies on beach	94
Wilber's first letter after Luzon landing	97
Troops wading through stream, San Fabian	98
Troops taking cover behind amtrac	98
San Fabian, Municipal Hall	99
Generals Wing and Swift	99
Guerilla rescue, sketch of	101
Colonel Oseth and Filipino, Manaoag	102
Japanese 12-inch howitzer, Luzon	107
Antipolo, Luzon, damage to	129
Observation post on Hill 600	130
Gen. Wing, Col. Cleland, and prisoner	130
Signal crew and monkey, Tanay	132
Terrain on march to Mabitac	133
Troops of 103rd RCT clearing roadblock	134
Wilber's letter from Lumban bridge	135
Lumban bridge and tank, 1945	137
Filipino pro-Japanese Makapilis	139
Generals Wing and Krueger	143
Col. Marcus Agustin, guerilla commander	149
Long Tom six-inch gun manned by Filipinos	149
Trucks in mud and rain, Ipo Dam action	153
Japanese prisoners eating, Ipo Dam area	155
Japanese officers' underground quarters	156
Message center, 43rd Division, Bulacan	156
Ipo Dam, aerial view	157
Guests at dinner hosted by Col. Sheng	169
Wilber Bradt as executive of 172nd RCT	173
Gale at age about 20 months	174
Generals Wing and Barker, Cabanatuan	177
General Wing decorating Wilber	182
Wilber's letter at end of war	190

PART III Interlude 1983, Luzon

Bridge at Lumban and Hale 1983 202
Boysie Florendo and old man, Lumban 203
Wooden pilings of old Lumban bridge........................... 203
Jeepneys at Cuyapo 205
Liberation celebration, Pakil 206
Historic plaque, San Ildefonso, Tanay......................... 207
San Ildefonso de Toledo church, Tanay 208
Base theater, ruined, Corregidor 210
Coastal gun, 12-inch, Corregidor 210
Malinta tunnel, Corregidor 211
Mrs. José Dacquel, Cuyapo..................................... 212
Portico remnant of old home, Guimba........................... 215
Lt. Heidelberger as army private 1941–42 218
Manila American Cemetery, rows of crosses..................... 219
Heidelberger grave and Hale, Manila Cemetery 219

PART IV Japan and Home

Shibushi Bay, Kyushu, Japan, with Hale 232
USS Gen. John Pope, arrival, San Francisco 239
Troops on USS Gen. Pope 239
Wilber and Capt. Reddy on USS Gen. Pope 240
General Wing, portrait, gift to Wilber 241
Telegram announcing expected arrival home 242
Wilber's letter of November 27, 1945 253
List of souvenir Christmas gifts.............................. 257
News clipping, Wilber's death 258

PART V Epilog

Stoney Sparlin in navy uniform................................ 265
Letter typed by Stoney to his mother 269
Hale, bicycle, and Gale 273
Monte Bourjaily holding Gale 274
Grandmother Terkman Bourjaily and Gale........................ 274
Hale and an upside down Gale 274
Gale standing and smiling, ca. 1946 275
Hale with campers, Grace Boys Camp 277
Bradt-Bourjaily family 1952................................... 283

Hale's Model A, Grafton, WV, 1952 288
Hale and his grandmother Bradt, 1952. 289
Bradt-Bourjaily family ca. 1978. 295
Norma at piano 1985. 297
Norma and Valerie 1985. 297
Mary Bradt Higgins, Versailles 1987. 298
Wilber's three siblings 1987 298
Hale, Mary, and covered bridge 1987 299
Wilber's granddaughters (Hale's daughters). 302
Wilber's grandsons (Valerie's sons) 302

Preface

This is the third and final volume of *Wilber's War*.

The first, *Citizen Soldier,* began with the untimely death of my father, Lt. Col. Wilber E. Bradt, a highly decorated army officer, shortly after his return home from the Pacific Theater at the end of World War II. It then looked back at Wilber and his wife Norma, at their Indiana and Washington State origins, their marriage in 1927, and the births of two children, me in 1930, and my sister Valerie in 1932.

After earning his PhD in chemistry, Wilber held positions as a chemistry professor in both Washington State and Ohio (Cincinnati) before becoming head of the chemistry department at the University of Maine. The family persevered through the Great Depression of the 1930s, the threats of world war, the call-up of Wilber's national guard unit in February 1941, and his successful efforts to qualify for active duty. Then came his training at camps in Florida and Mississippi, and Norma's move with Valerie and me to New York City where she could advance her piano and writing skills. Wilber's unit, the 43rd Infantry Division, left San Francisco on October 1, 1942, for New Zealand, the beginning of a three-year Pacific saga that took Wilber to New Caledonia, to Guadalcanal, and then to the front lines in the Russell Islands where he experienced torpedo-plane and bombing attacks. At home, Norma's life was upended when she found herself pregnant through a liaison with a family friend while Wilber was overseas. She chose to keep the pregnancy a secret from all but that friend and his mother.

The second volume, *Combat and New Life*, carried Wilber through three phases of intense combat over three months in the New Georgia group of the Solomon Islands, a decompression period of defensive duty in the Solomons, and finally rehabilitation and retraining in New Zealand. Many aspects of Wilber's combat experiences surfaced in his letters during these latter phases. Army life after intense combat was interesting in its own right. In New Zealand, the troops enjoyed Kiwi hospitality, toured the country, made poignant romantic connections, and endured rigorous training in freezing temperatures.

VICTORY AND HOMECOMING

At home, while Wilber was facing his first combat, Norma put her children in summer camps followed by boarding schools so they would remain unaware of her pregnancy. The birth of baby Gale in October 1943, its aftermath, and our independent lives (Norma's, Valerie's, and mine) all became part of the saga. It was America in the midst of war.

At the end of the school year (June 1944), Norma reunited the family in Bangor, Maine, our prewar hometown, but left baby Gale in Washington, D.C., with her father. Bangor was the home base of the artillery unit that Wilber commanded (the 152nd Field Artillery Battalion), and was only a few miles from the University of Maine where he had taught chemistry before the war. The town was full of his academic and military associates or their families. Norma had chosen to resume her prewar role of mother and proper faculty and military wife, but without her infant daughter.

On July 7, 1944, Wilber's unit, the 43rd Infantry Division, set sail from Auckland, New Zealand, to head off a Japanese threat in New Guinea.

This final volume, *Victory and Homecoming*, follows Norma as she attempts to normalize her life. It also accompanies Wilber through combat in New Guinea, the massive invasion of Luzon in the Philippines, the extended combat and his medal winning exploits there, the occupation of Japan, and finally his return home, his untimely death, and its aftereffects.

The story is presented largely through contemporaneous photographs and letters. It also includes my own efforts to uncover and understand the story through interviews, archival searches, and visits to the Pacific sites where Wilber had camped and fought.

Wilber's prose constitutes about 50% of the material in this trilogy, which in turn is only about 40% of the material available in his extant letters. Entire letters have been omitted without indication, but a deletion within a letter is indicated with an ellipsis. Detailed editing of the letters was very light, with inconsistencies in Wilber's impromptu style retained. Material [in square brackets] is mine. In large part, it is Wilber's writing that carries forward this story of combat and its aftermath.

As the 43rd Division sailed for New Guinea in July 1944, Japan still controlled large areas of the Pacific Ocean and Asia. (Map 1; charts and maps follow this preface.) The advance up the New Guinea coast toward the Philippines was one part of the two-pronged Allied westward advance toward, ultimately, Japan. The other was an island-hopping campaign that had begun the previous November with landings in the Gilbert Islands and later the Marshall Islands. The next jump, to the Mariana Islands, occurred with the June 15, 1944, landings on Saipan, which was secured on July 9. Tinian and Guam fell two weeks later. The naval Battle of the Philippine Sea and the associated "Marianas Turkey Shoot" in June gave the Allies air and sea control of the Mariana Islands thus ensuring victory on Saipan. In the process, the air arm of the Japanese fleet was decimated.

Elsewhere, the Allies had landed on the beaches of Normandy, France, on June 6 and were on the march in Russia, Poland, Italy, and on the India-Burma front; but the advances were episodic and costly. The hedgerows of Normandy greatly hindered progress there. Italy had surrendered the previous September (1943), but the Germans had moved in to oppose the Allied advance up the Italian boot with strong defensive lines. The two Axis powers (Japan and Germany) remained strong and were determined to delay their defeat by exacting the greatest possible price from the Allies in the hope of an unexpected "act of God" that would favor them or at least lead to more favorable peace terms. The Allies were demanding unconditional surrender, a hard pill for the Axis countries to swallow.

MAPS & CHARTS

Maps and Charts

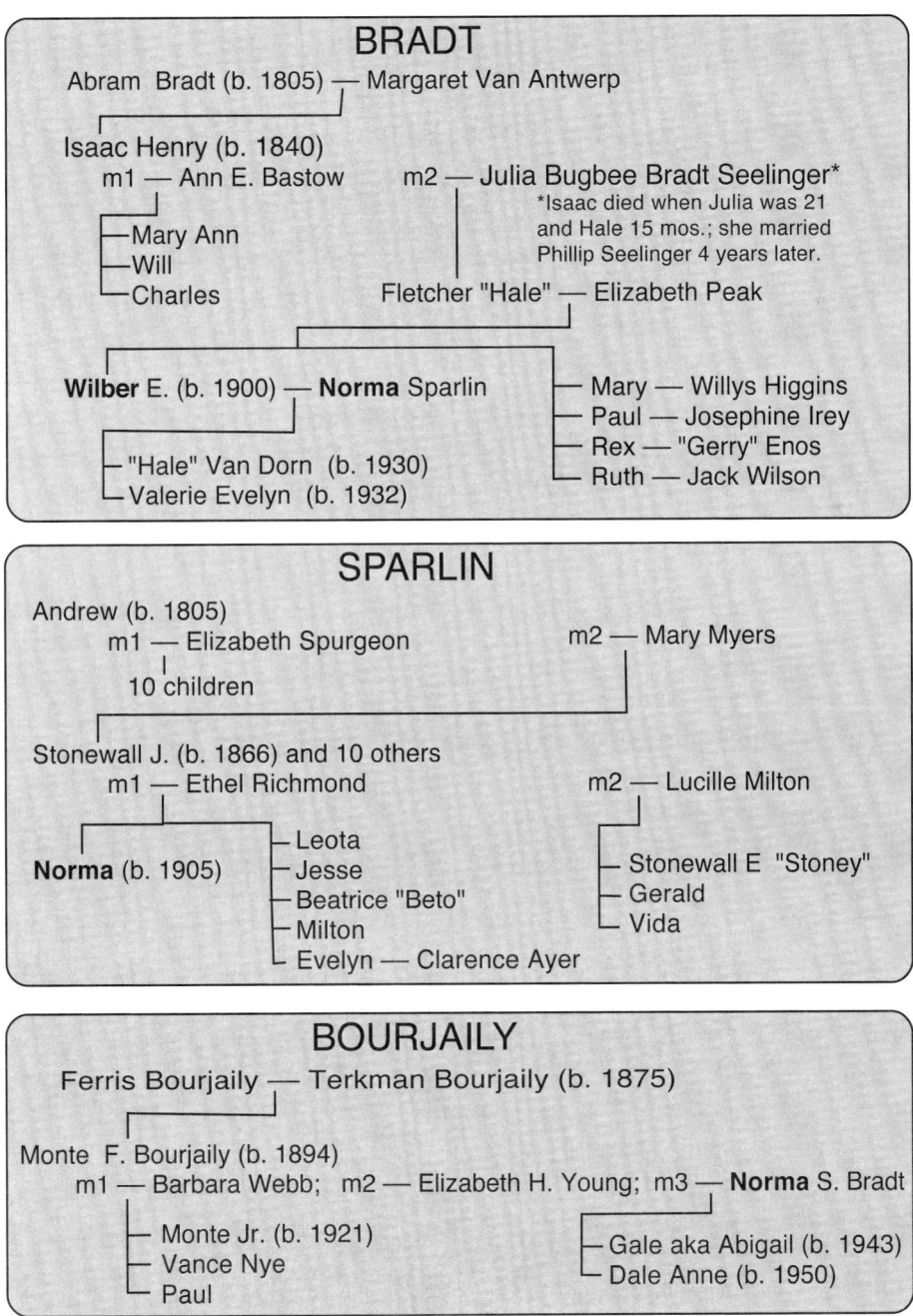

Chart 1. *The Bradt, Sparlin, and Bourjaily families.*

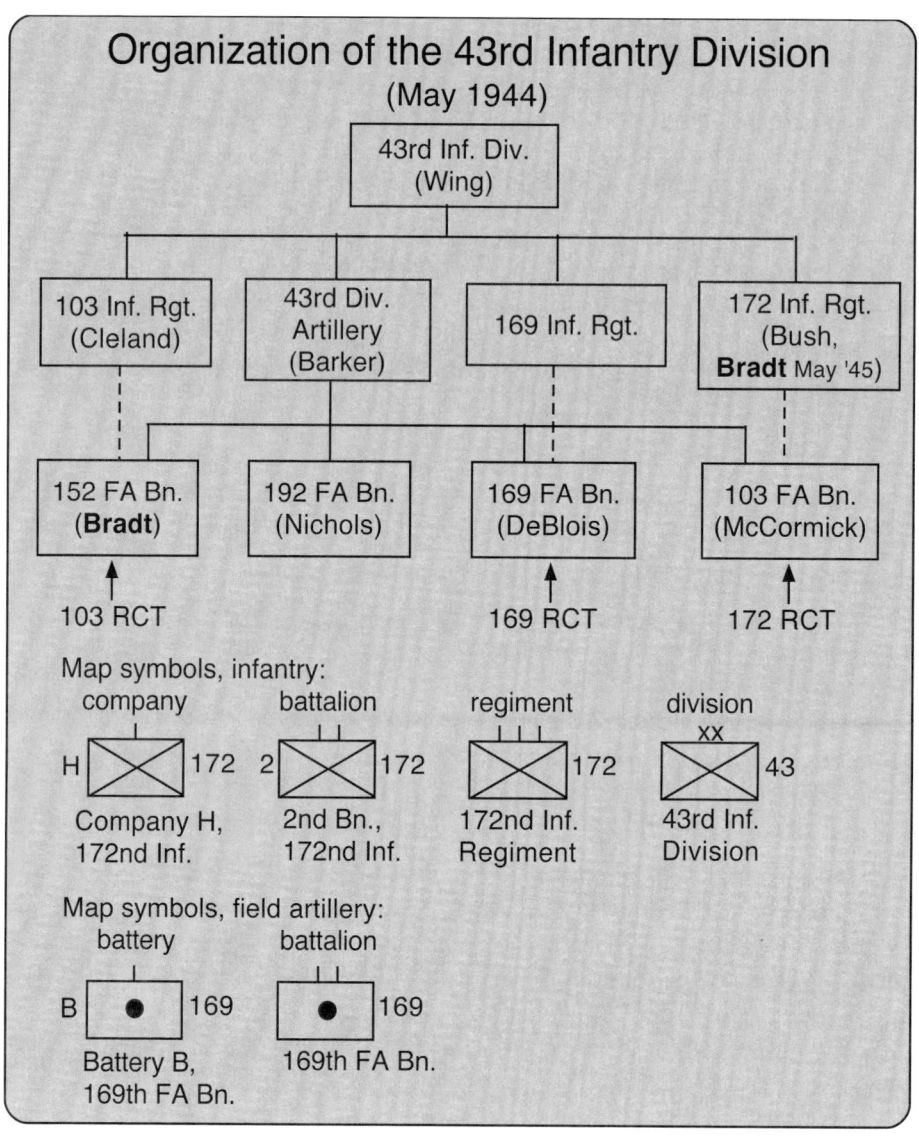

Chart 2. Organization and commanders of the 43rd Infantry Division, 1944–1945.

1. The commanding officers (C.O.) shown are those in command during the New Guinea and Philippine actions who were mentioned in Wilber's letters.

2. The division (Div.) had numerous other supporting elements.

3. The three "light" field artillery (FA) battalions (103rd, 152nd, and 169th) had 105-mm (4-inch) howitzers, which had a range of about five miles. The "medium" battalion (192nd FA) had 155-mm (6-inch) howitzers, which had a greater range.

4. A field artillery battalion consisted of about 500 men and 12 howitzers divided into three batteries (A, B, C) of four howitzers each and a headquarters battery.

5. An infantry regiment (Inf. Rgt.) consisted of three infantry battalions, 1st Bn., 2nd Bn., and 3rd Bn., each with about 500 men in four companies, designated A, B, C, and D in the 1st Bn., E–H in the 2nd Bn., and I, K, L, M in the 3rd Bn.

6. The four artillery battalions were under the command of General Barker, but could be assigned to regimental combat teams (RCT), which could operate independently of one another. The three light artillery battalions were normally assigned to the infantry regiments shown (dashed lines), but assignments could vary. The medium artillery battalion was reserved for general support where needed.

7. The National Guard origins of these units were:
Connecticut: 169 Inf. and 192 FA.
Maine: 152 FA and 103 Inf.
Rhode Island: 103 FA and 169 FA.
Vermont: 172 Inf.

8. Army officer ranks in ascending order in 1943 were: 2nd lieutenant (Lt.), 1st Lt., captain (Capt.), major (Maj.), lieutenant colonel (Lt. Col.), colonel, brigadier general (one-star insignia), major general (two stars), lieutenant general (three stars), and general (four stars). A five-star rank, General of the Army, was reactivated in late 1944.

VICTORY AND HOMECOMING

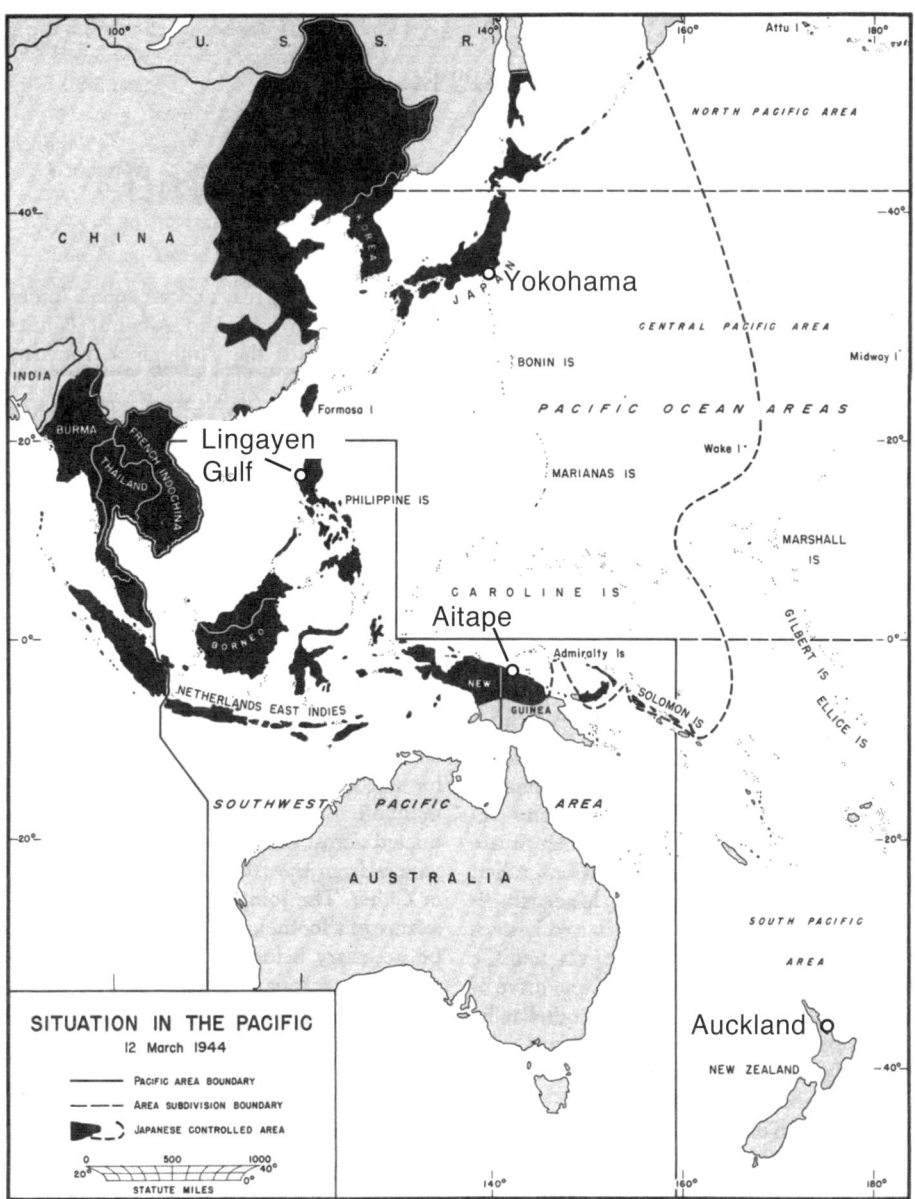

Map 1. Pacific areas controlled by Japanese (black and to left of dashed line) and the Allies, March 1944. The Allies had begun a march toward the Philippines along the north New Guinea coast and by sea via the Gilbert, Marshall, and Mariana Islands. American B29 bombers could reach Japan from the Marianas, which were invaded on June 15, 1944. In July 1944, the 43rd Division sailed from Auckland, New Zealand, to Aitape on the north coast of New Guinea. In January 1945, it landed at Lingayen Gulf, Luzon, Philippine Islands, and in September 1945 at Yokohama, Japan. [MAP: V. BROOKS, IN SMITH, *APPROACH*, MAP 1, P. 2]

Maps and Charts

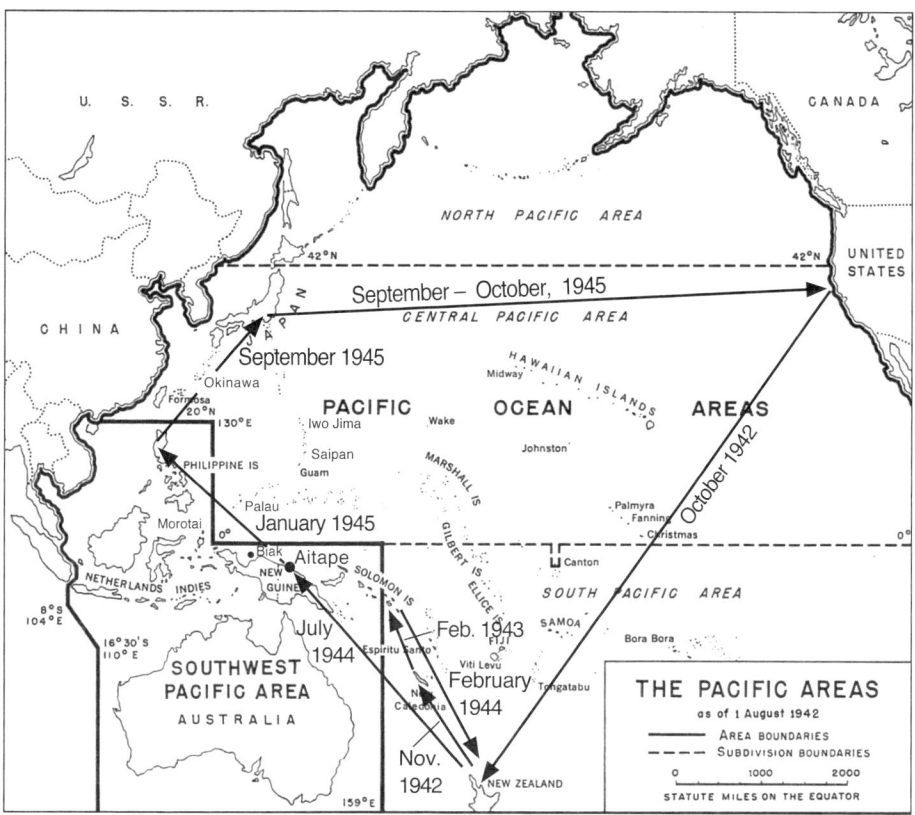

Map 2. The eight long sea voyages (black lines with arrowheads and dates) the 43rd Division made in the Pacific Ocean during three years overseas. Three additional (overnight) voyages were made within the Solomon Islands. Also delineated are the four military command areas of the Pacific Theater. The North, Central, and South Pacific Areas were the domain of the U.S. Navy (Admiral Chester Nimitz), and the Southwest Pacific Area, the domain of the U.S. Army (General Douglas MacArthur). [UNDERLYING MAP: R. JOHNSTONE, IN MILLER, *CARTWHEEL*, MAP 2, P. 3]

VICTORY AND HOMECOMING

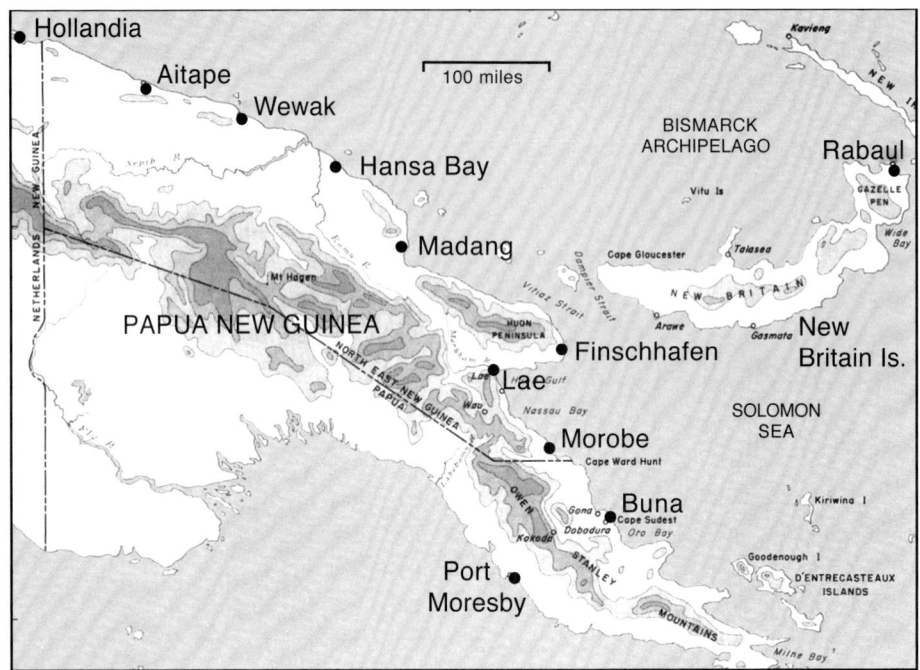

Map 3. Eastern New Guinea. The Allies landed at Hollandia and Aitape in April 1944, bypassing the Japanese 18th Army at Hansa Bay and Wewak. The 43rd Division arrived at Aitape July 17, 1944, to help hold the line against Japanese moving westward. The Allies, by this time, held the coast southeast of Madang (center) and had rendered ineffective the major Japanese naval and air base, Rabaul (far right) [UNDERLYING MAP: MILLER, CARTWHEEL, MAP 3, P. 23]

Maps and Charts

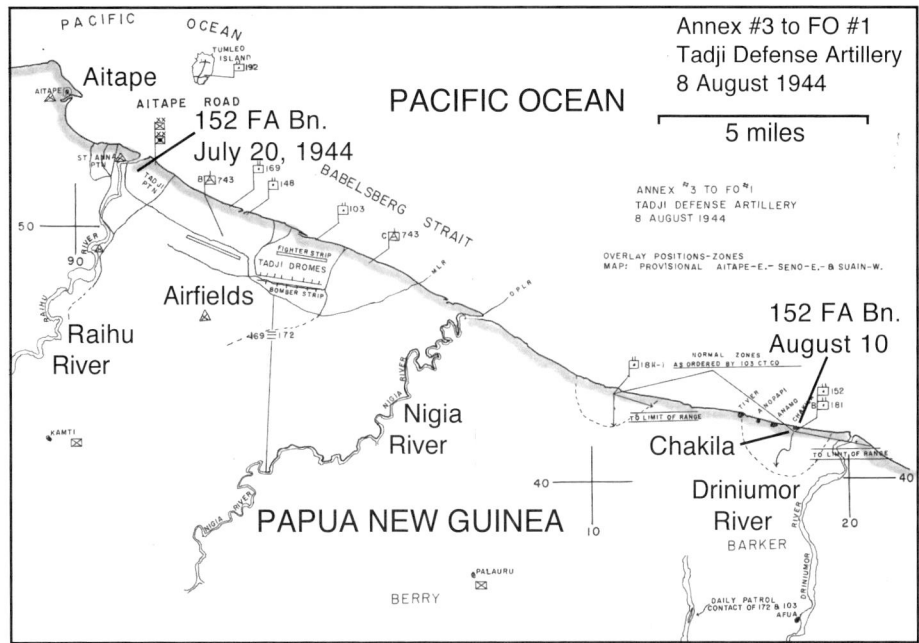

Map 4. Artillery map of the Aitape area of New Guinea, August 8, 1944. The 152nd Field Artillery Battalion, Wilber's outfit, was initially located at the mouth of the Raihu River (to left) where it could defend the Tadji airfields and later it was at the Driniumor River to the southeast. The Japanese were mostly to the east of the Driniumor. Wilber spent a lot of time being driven between the two locations, a straight-line distance of about 18 miles. Yakamul is six miles east of the Driniumor on the coast. [SEE MAP IV OF SMITH, APPROACH; UNDERLYING MAP: BARKER, P. 132]

VICTORY AND HOMECOMING

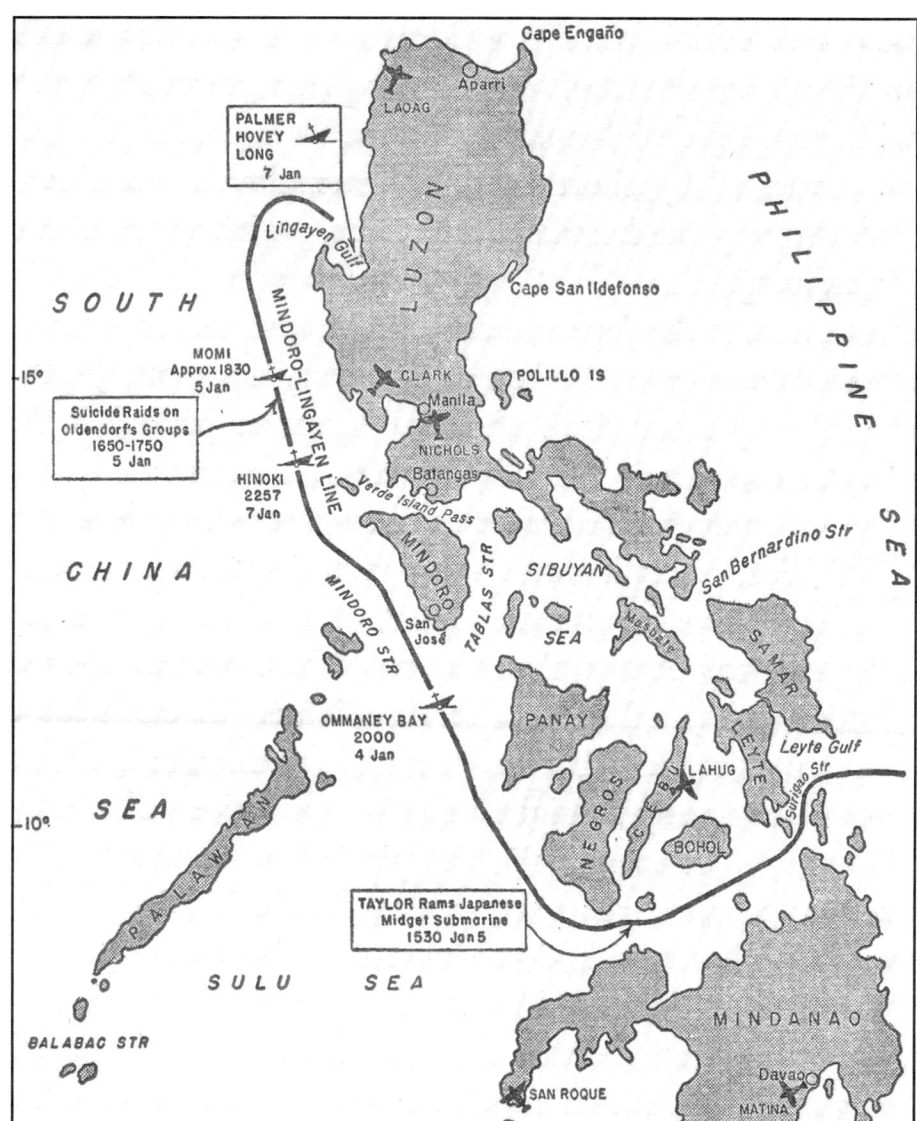

Map 5. Philippine Islands showing the principal Japanese airfields and the track of the attacking Allied convoys heading toward Lingayen Gulf in early January 1945. The U.S. Bombardment Force arrived three days before the troopships and took heavy losses from kamikaze (suicide plane) attacks. The full east-west width of Mindanao (lower right) is about 300 miles. The convoy could travel about 200 miles in a 24-hour day.
[MAP: MORISON, V. XIII, P. 100]

Maps and Charts

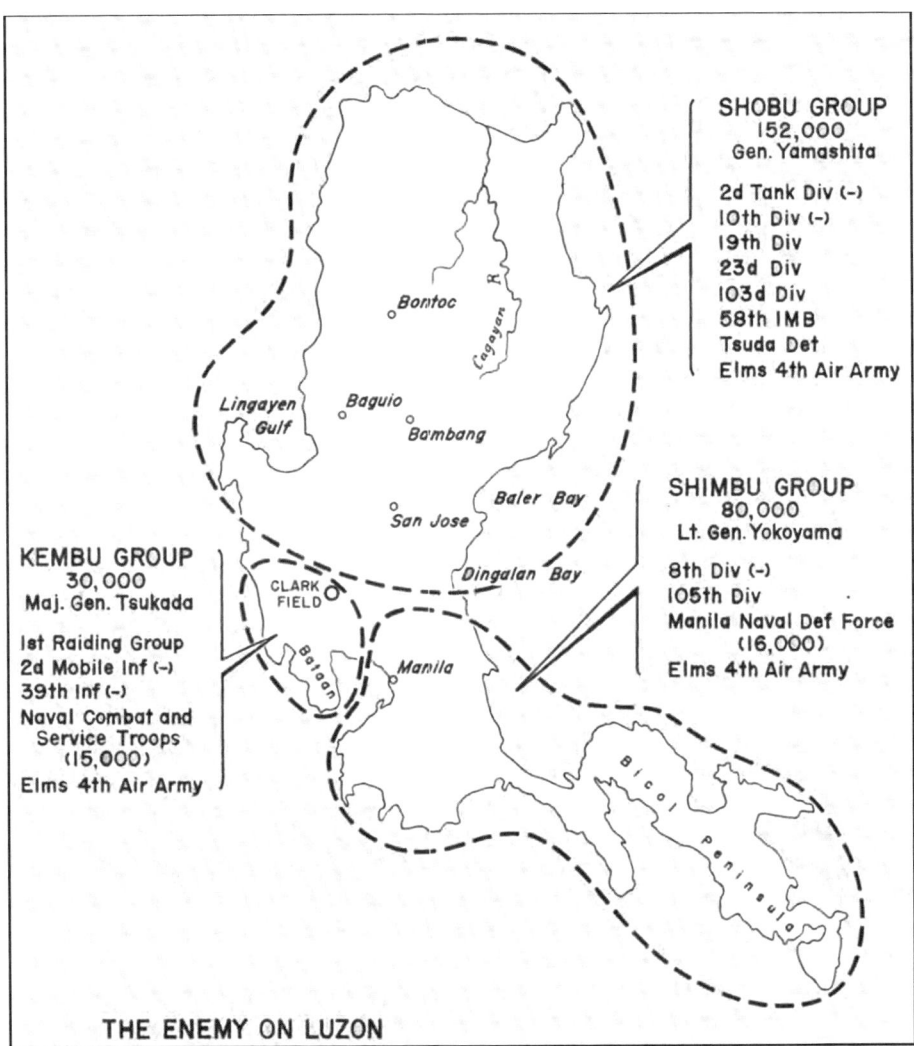

Map 6. *The enemy on Luzon, divided into three groups in well defended positions. The strategic goal was to delay for as long as possible the inevitable American conquest of Luzon.* [MAP: SMITH, TRIUMPH, MAP 3, P. 95]

VICTORY AND HOMECOMING

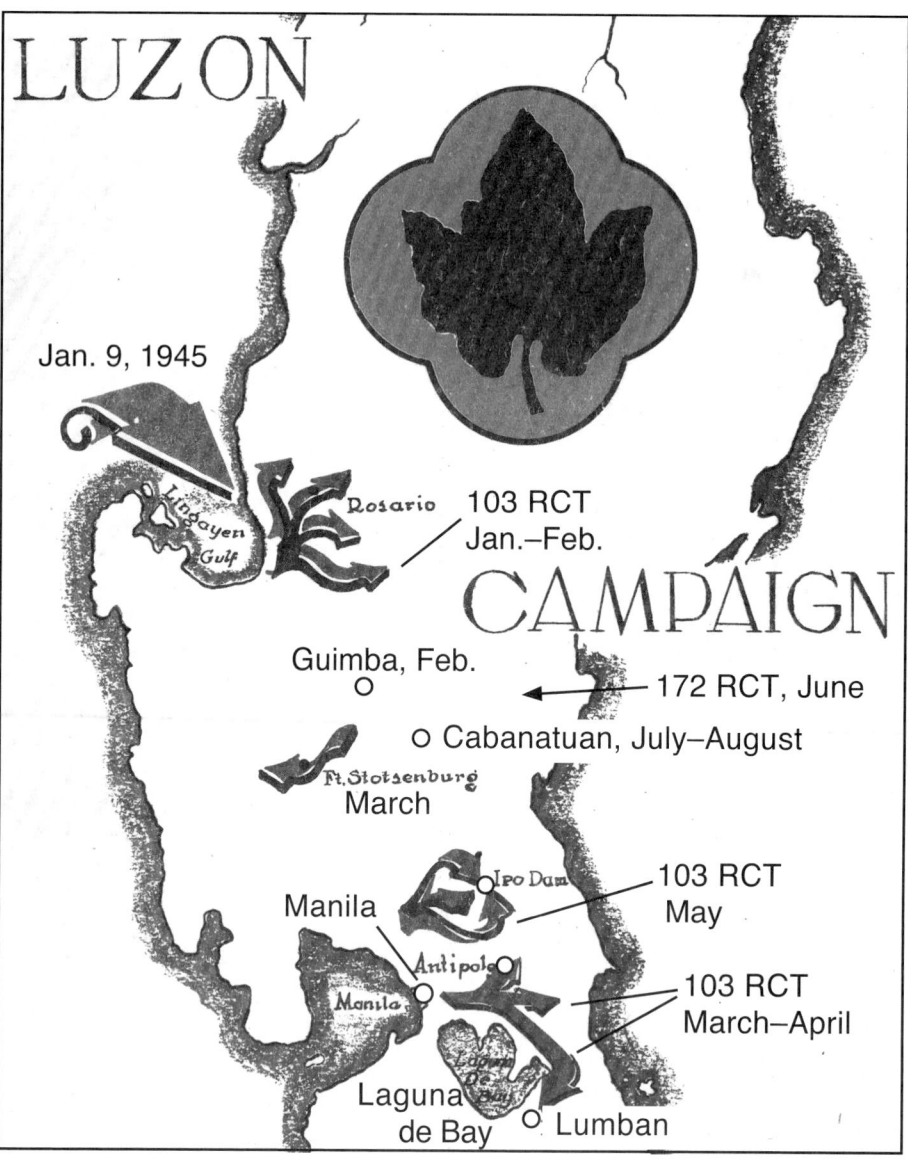

Map 7. Four actions (groups of broad arrows) of the 43rd Infantry Division on Luzon, Philippine Islands, as shown on the cover of the 43rd's report of its actions in Luzon. These actions occurred in sequence from north to south, except that the Ipo Dam action followed the Antipolo-Lumban action. The actions, locations, and action dates for the units Wilber was with are indicated. The 103rd RCT was held in reserve for the Fort Stotsenburg action. The maple leaf insignia (top center) was the emblem of the 43rd Division. [UNDERLYING MAP: HIST, RPT. LUZON CAMPAIGN, 43RD DIV., COVER].

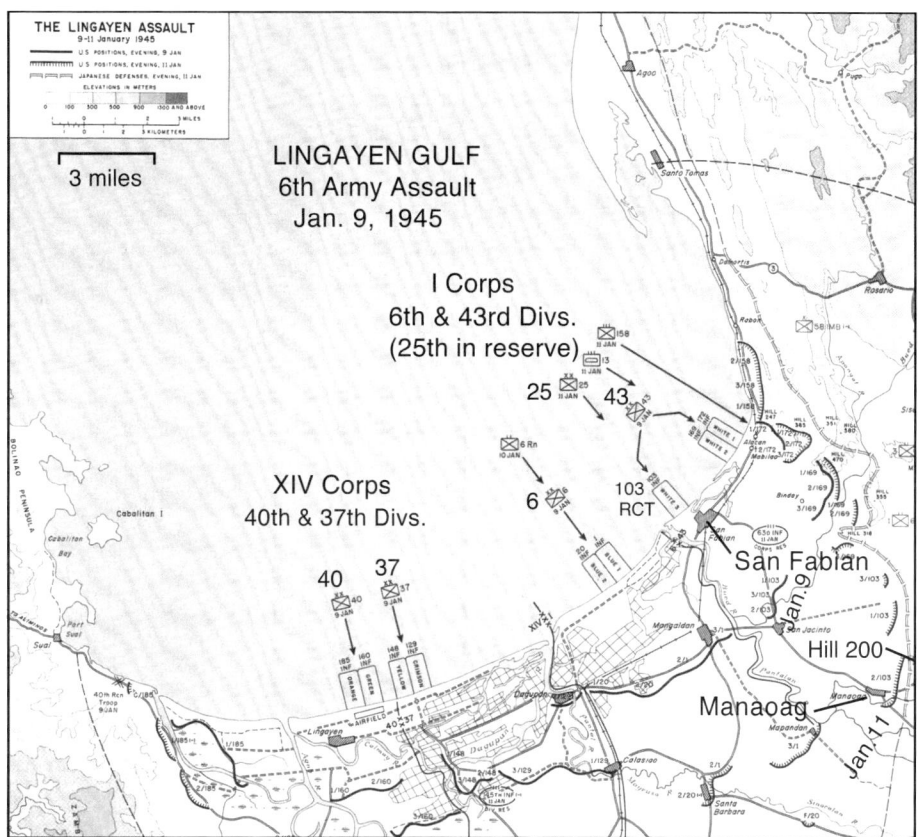

Map 8. Sixth Army assault on Luzon at Lingayen Gulf on January 9, 1945. Four divisions (40th, 37th, 6th, and 43rd) made the first landings. The 43rd Division landed at the upper right with mountainous terrain to its left (our right). The 103rd Regimental Combat Team, which included Wilber's 152nd Field Artillery Battalion, landed at San Fabian. The 25th Division, which included the 161st Infantry Regiment from Washington State (Wilber's unit in the early 1930s), was held in reserve and landed a couple of days later. The indicated landing sites extended over 18 miles. The lines of advance of the 103rd RCT for January 9 and 11 are labeled. Hill 200, just off the map beyond Manaoag, was the first day's objective. It had not been taken on the 11th, was bypassed, and was finally taken on January 17. (These features are shown more clearly on the following maps.) The Japanese did not oppose the landings on the beaches but put up a strong delaying defense in the surrounding hills and mountains. [UNDERLYING MAP: SMITH, *TRIUMPH*, MAP I CROPPED]

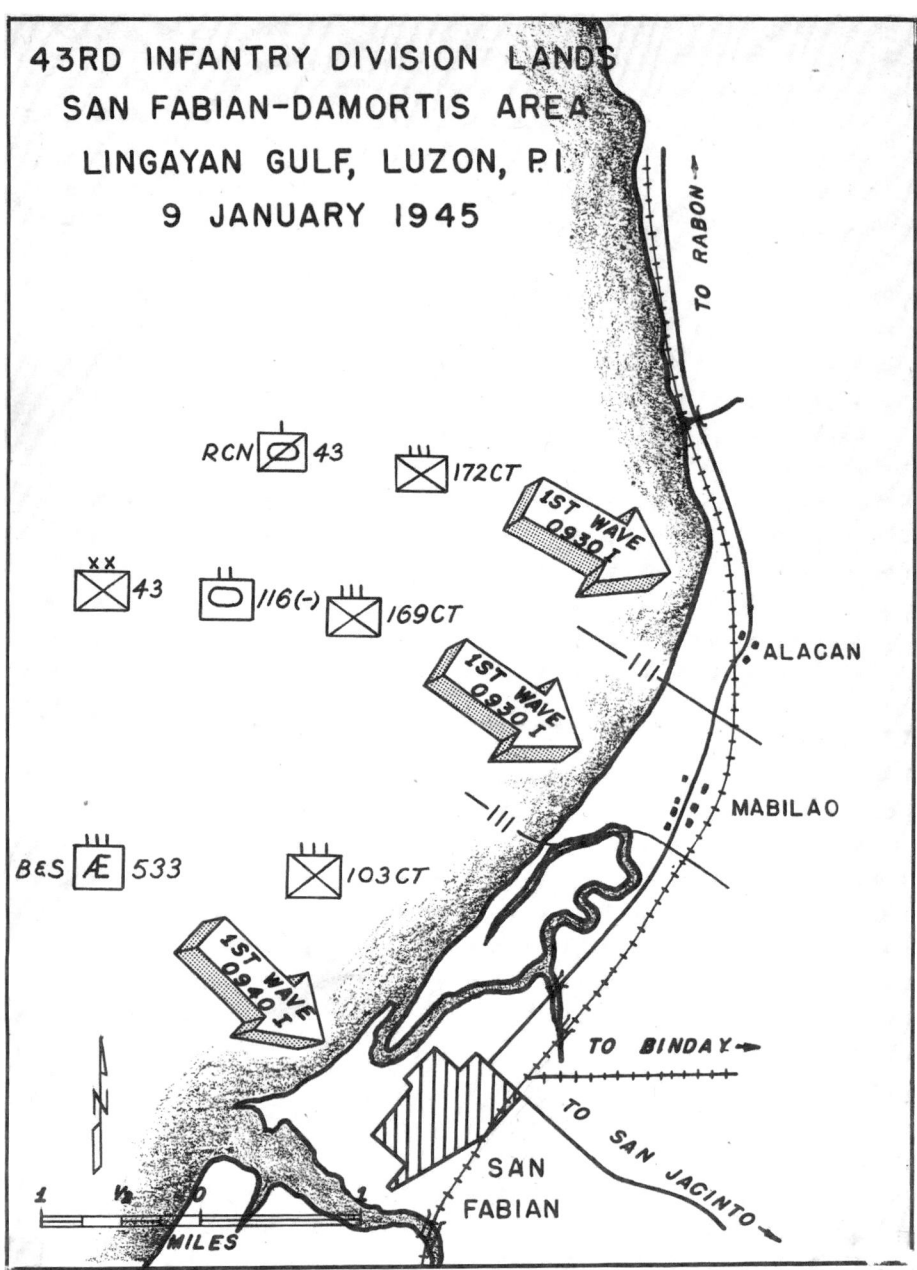

Map 9. Landings of the three regimental combat teams (RCT) of the 43rd Division (172nd, 169th, and 103rd) on January 9, 1945. Wilber landed with the 103rd, right behind the first wave at San Fabian on what was called White Beach 3. [MAP: HIST. RPT. LUZON, 43RD DIV., SKETCH 1]

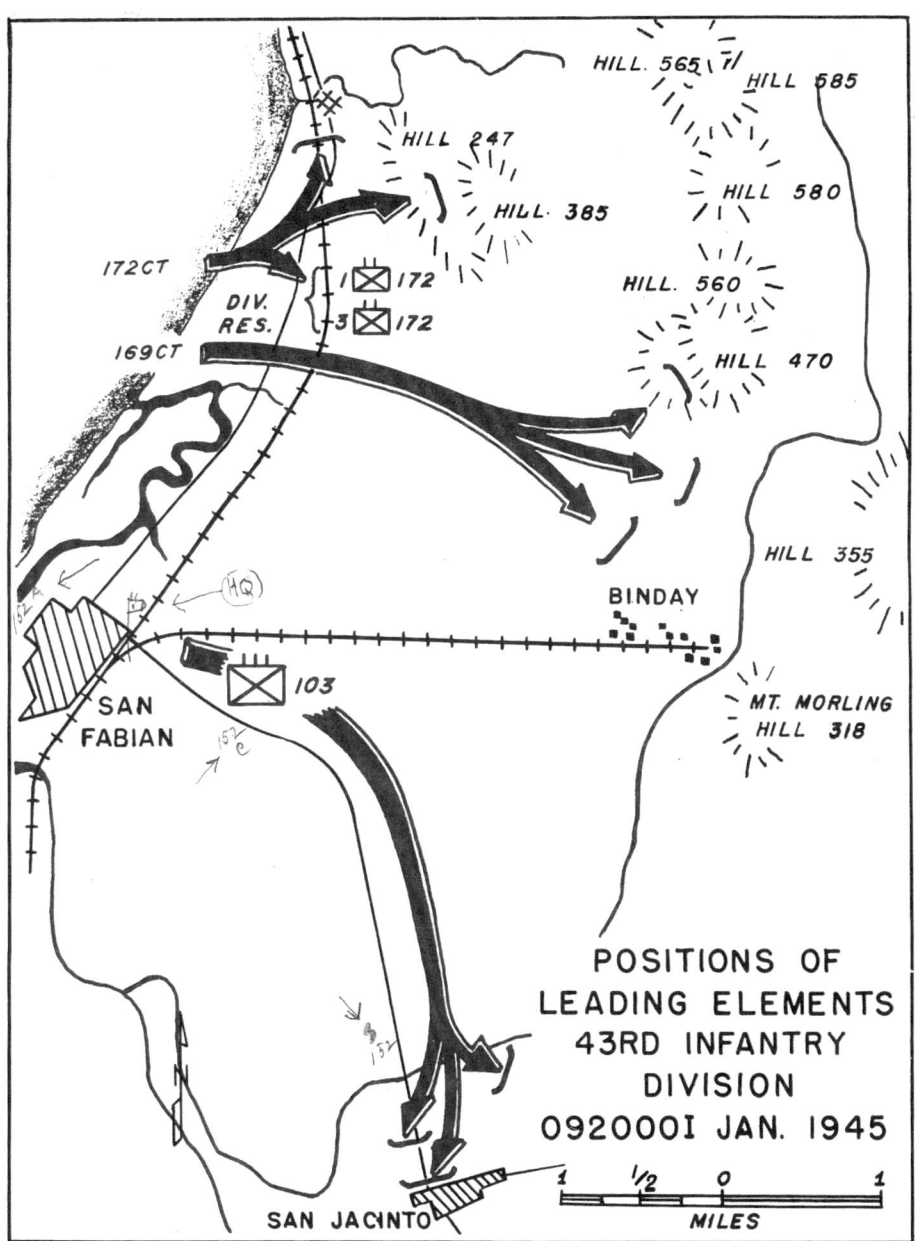

Map 10. Advances by the 43rd Division during the first day on Luzon. Wilber's artillery, the 152 Field Artillery Battalion, supported the 103rd Infantry RCT, which drove southeasterly toward San Jacinto. Wilber marked in pencil the positions of his battalion headquarters with a flag symbol (at San Fabian) and the three batteries, "152 A," etc. (I added small arrows to point out his markings.) Battery A was located just off the beach in front of San Fabian and was the first to fire. [MAP: HIST. RPT. LUZON, 43RD DIV., SKETCH 2]

VICTORY AND HOMECOMING

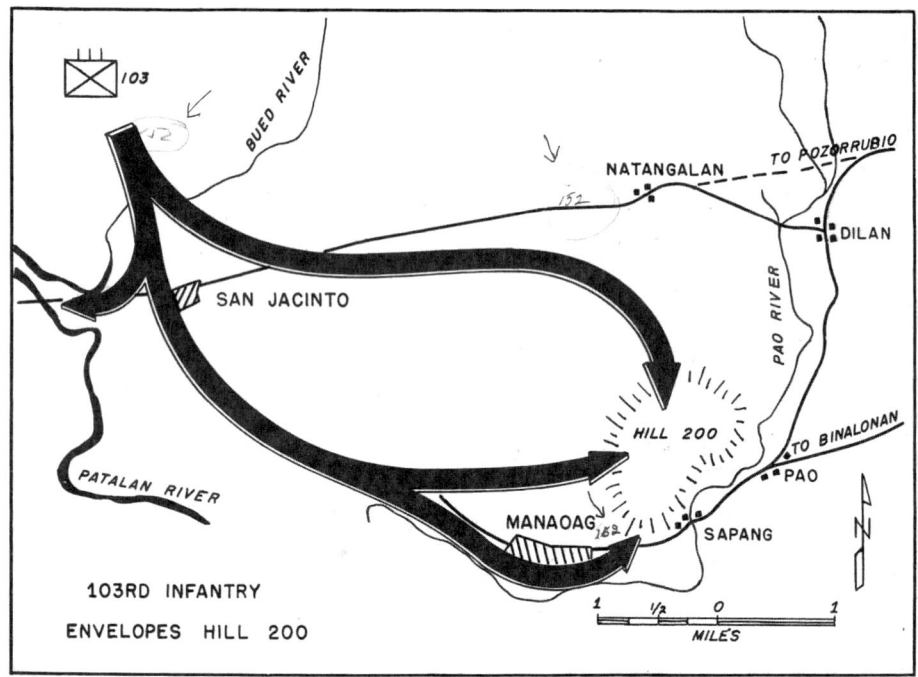

Map 11. Attack on Hill 200 by the 103rd RCT, January 11 and 12, 1945. It was not secured until January 17. Manaoag is where Wilber helped rescue the wounded Filipino guerilla for which he was awarded a cluster in lieu of a second Silver Star. Again, Wilber marked the locations of his batteries with "152." [REFERENCE: *HIST. 103RD INF. RGT. JAN.-MAY, 1945*, PP. 10, 13, 19. MAP: *HIST. RPT. LUZON, 43RD DIV.*, SKETCH 6]

Maps and Charts

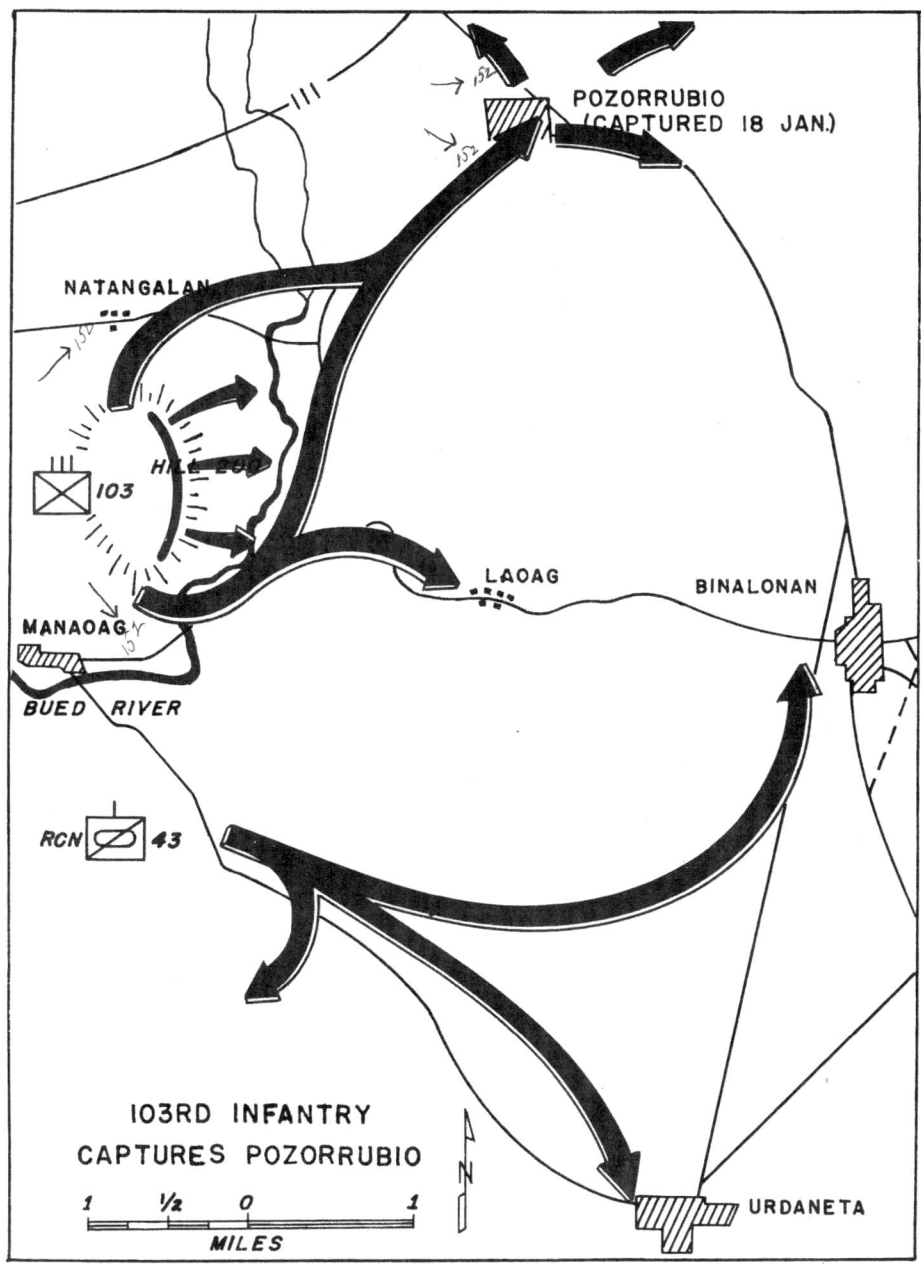

Map 12. Capture of Pozorrubio. Hill 200 is shown at left center (label obscured); Hill 600 (not shown) is north of Pozorrubio. Hill 600 is where Wilber did the forward artillery spotting that merited him the Silver Star. Wilber's "152" notations indicated locations occupied by his three artillery batteries for varying durations. [MAP: HIST. RPT. LUZON, 43RD DIV., SKETCH 7]

VICTORY AND HOMECOMING

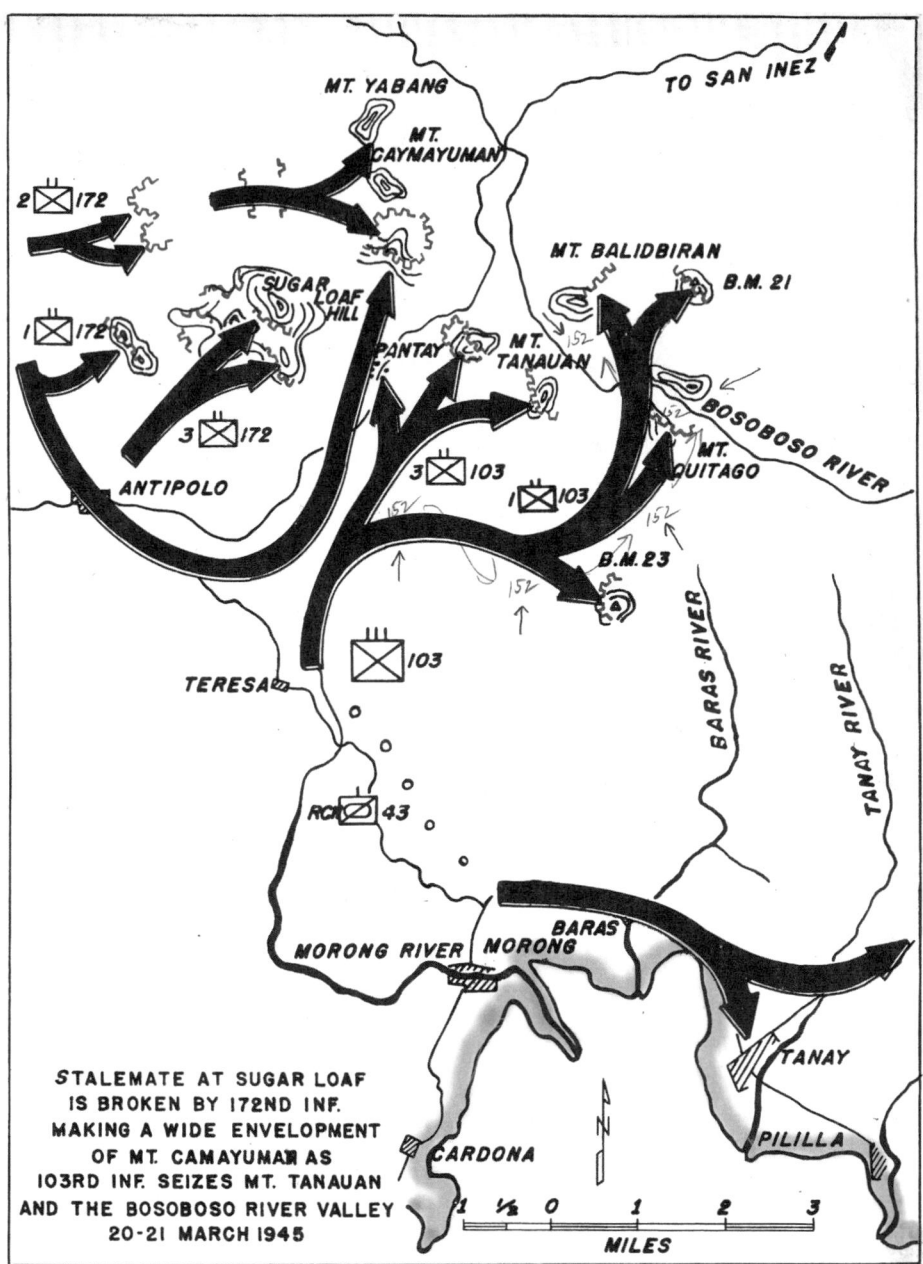

Map 13. Teresa-Bosoboso River region. The 103rd RCT drove to Mts. Tanauan and Balidbiran with support of the 152nd Field Artillery. Wilber marked the several positions of his artillery units. The lake Laguna de Bay (lower right) and Antipolo (middle left) are labeled on Map 7; Tanay and Pililla (lower right) are shown on Map 14 (upper left).
[MAP: *HIST. RPT. LUZON, 43RD DIV.*, SKETCH 14]

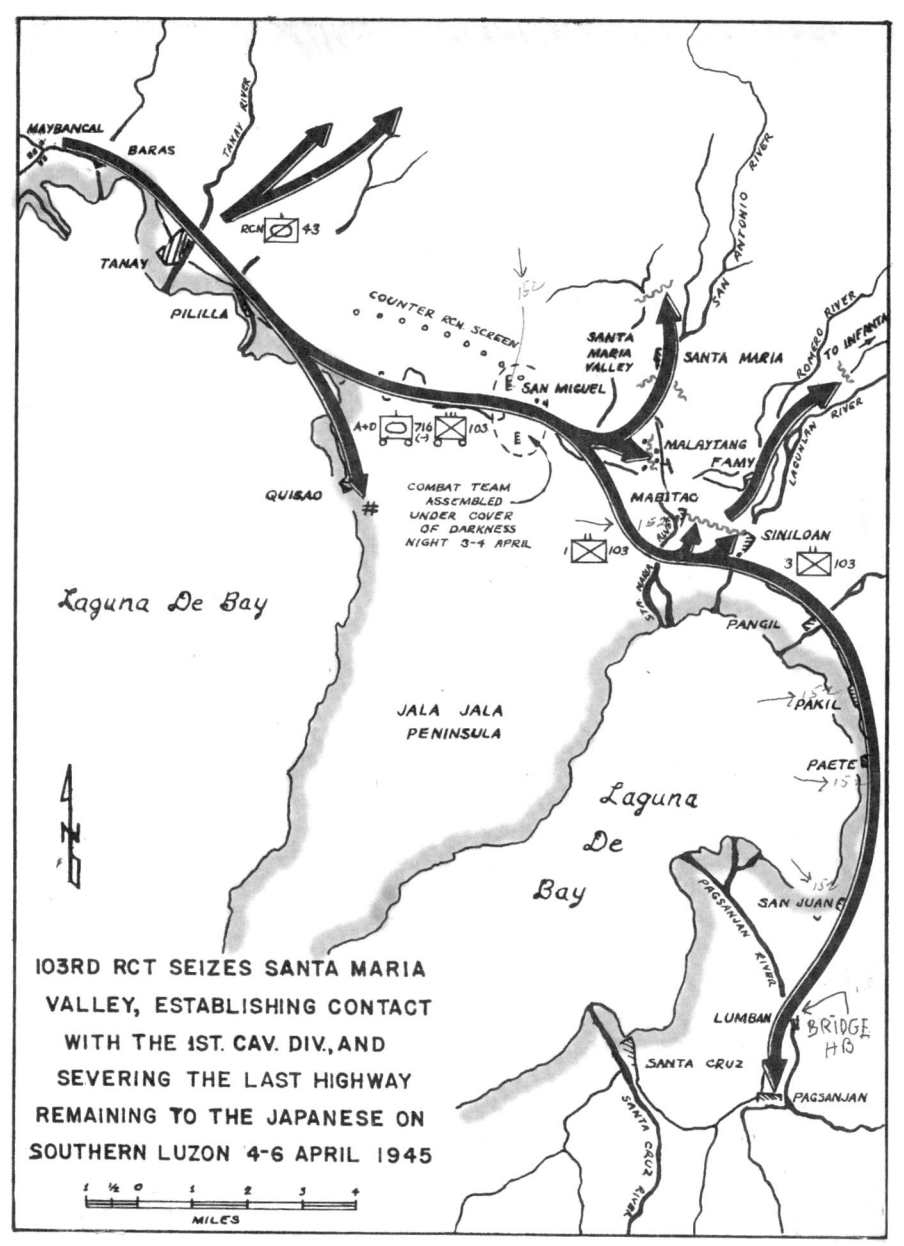

Map 14. The drive of the 103rd RCT across the Jala Jala Peninsula and down the eastern shore of Laguna de Bay to Lumban and Pagsanjan (lower right), April 4–6, 1945. The positions of Wilber's artillery are indicated (small arrows and "152"). Wilber's actions in the capture of the bridge (labeled by me) over the Pagsanjan River at Lumban earned him a second cluster for his Silver Star. The First Cavalry Division was driving toward Pagsanjan from the south. The large lake, Laguna de Bay, is also seen on Maps 7 and 13. The full length of the distance scale (lower left) is five miles. [MAP: HIST. RPT. LUZON, 43RD DIV., SKETCH 15]

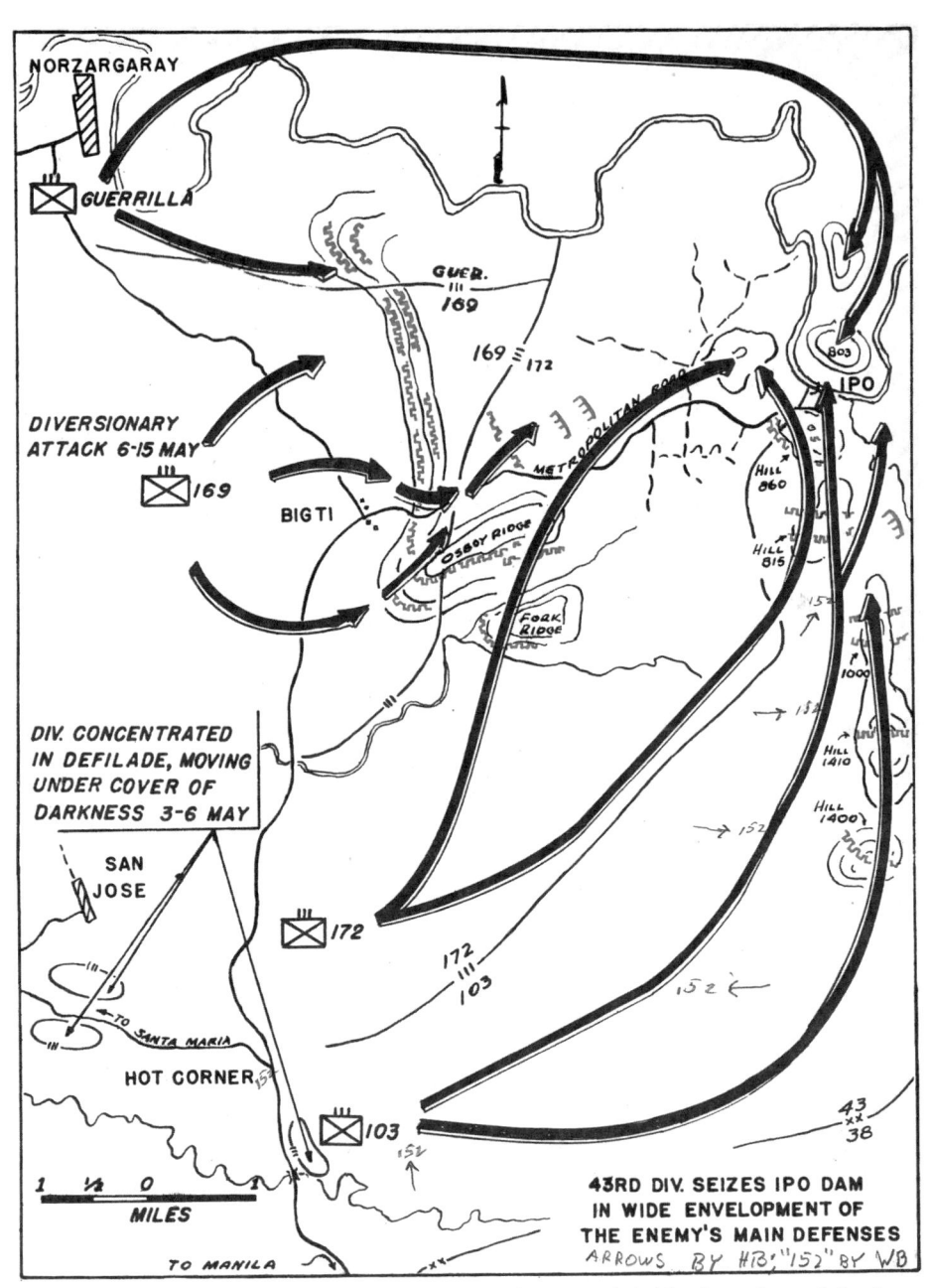

Map 15. Attack by the 43rd Division on Ipo Dam (upper right). The frontal attack by the 169th RCT on the main Japanese defenses was a diversion. The main thrust was from the south over mountainous terrain by the 172nd and 103rd RCTs. Again, Wilber noted where he placed batteries of his artillery unit, the 152nd Field Artillery. These thrusts are also shown on Map 7. [MAP: HIST. RPT. LUZON, 43RD DIV., SKETCH 16]

Maps and Charts

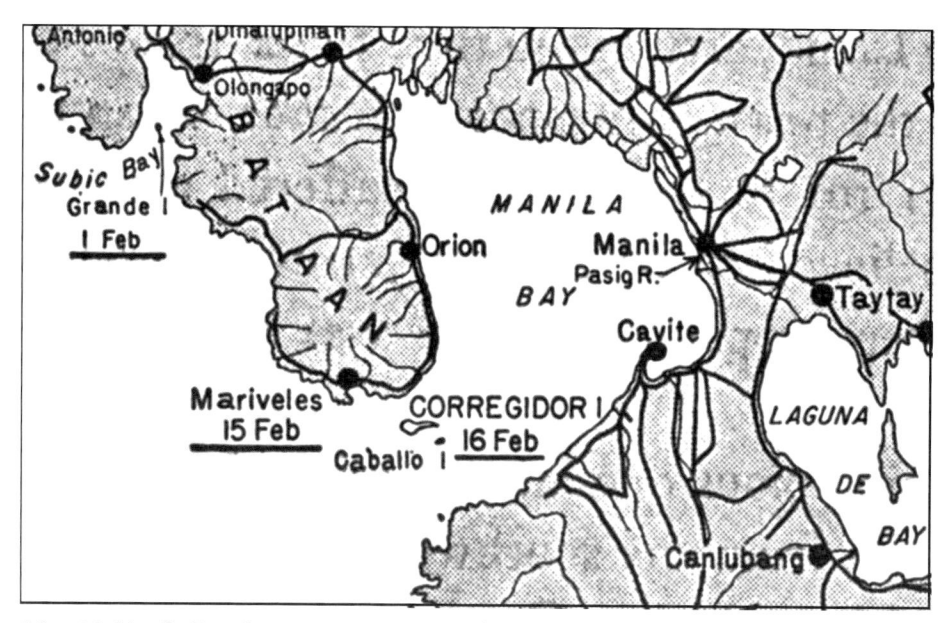

Map 16. Manila Bay showing Bataan peninsula, Manila, and Corregidor Island, which protected the mouth of the harbor, and also Laguna de Bay (lower right). Bataan and Corregidor were the last bastions held by the Americans before they capitulated to the Japanese in April and May of 1942. The dates shown here are of Allied actions in 1945. The distance from Corregidor to Manila is 28 miles. [MAP: ADAPTED FROM MORISON, V. XIII, P. 190]

VICTORY AND HOMECOMING

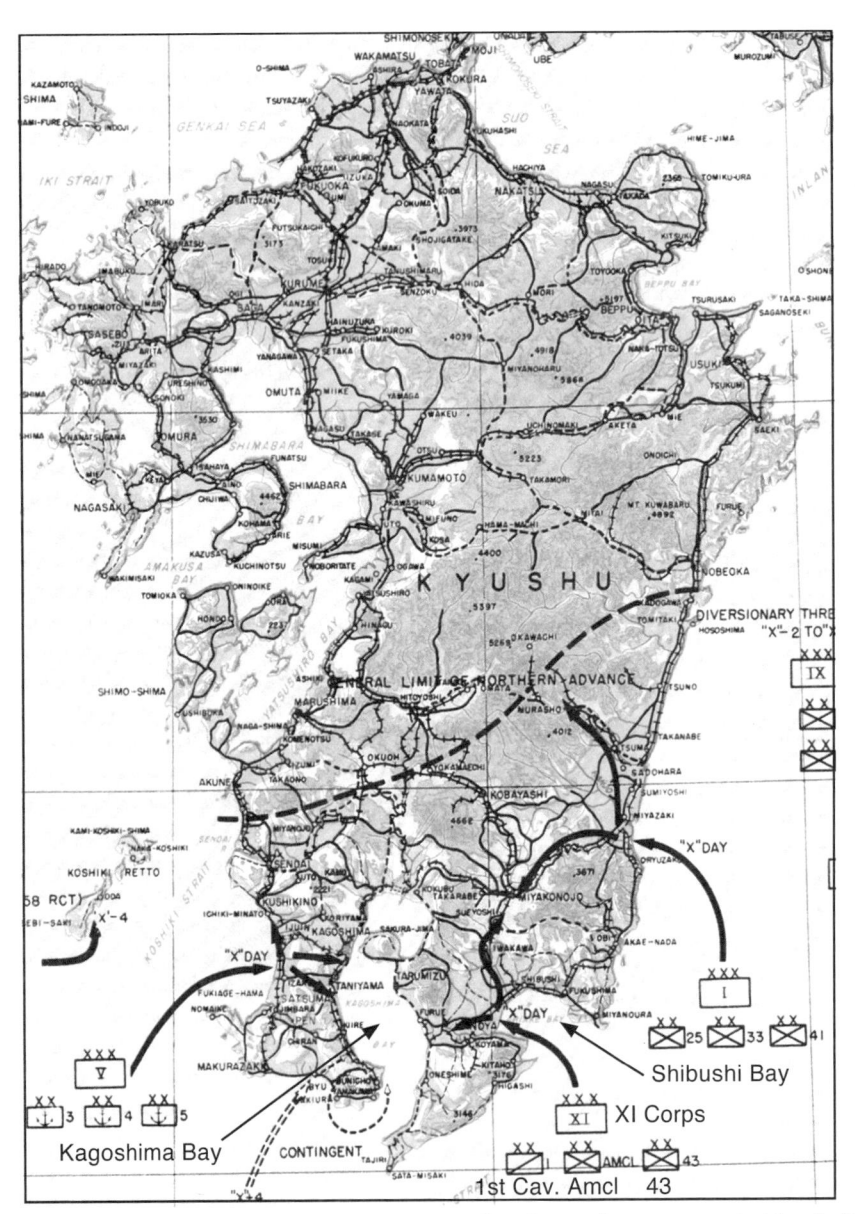

Map 17. Operation Olympic landings on Kyushu, the southernmost main island of Japan. On "X" day, scheduled for November 1, two army corps (I and XI) and one marine corps (V Corps) would land at the indicated points with the objective of securing Japanese airfields and establishing a base area to support landings in the vicinity of Tokyo on Honshu four months later. Other units would follow as needed. The 43rd Division was in the XI Corps and would land at Shibushi Bay (lower right). The 1st Cavalry Division and the Americal Division were also in XI Corps. The Americans would limit their advance in Kyushu to the area below the heavy dashed line. [MAP: REPORTS OF GENERAL MACARTHUR, V. 1, MAP 118, P. 413]

Maps and Charts

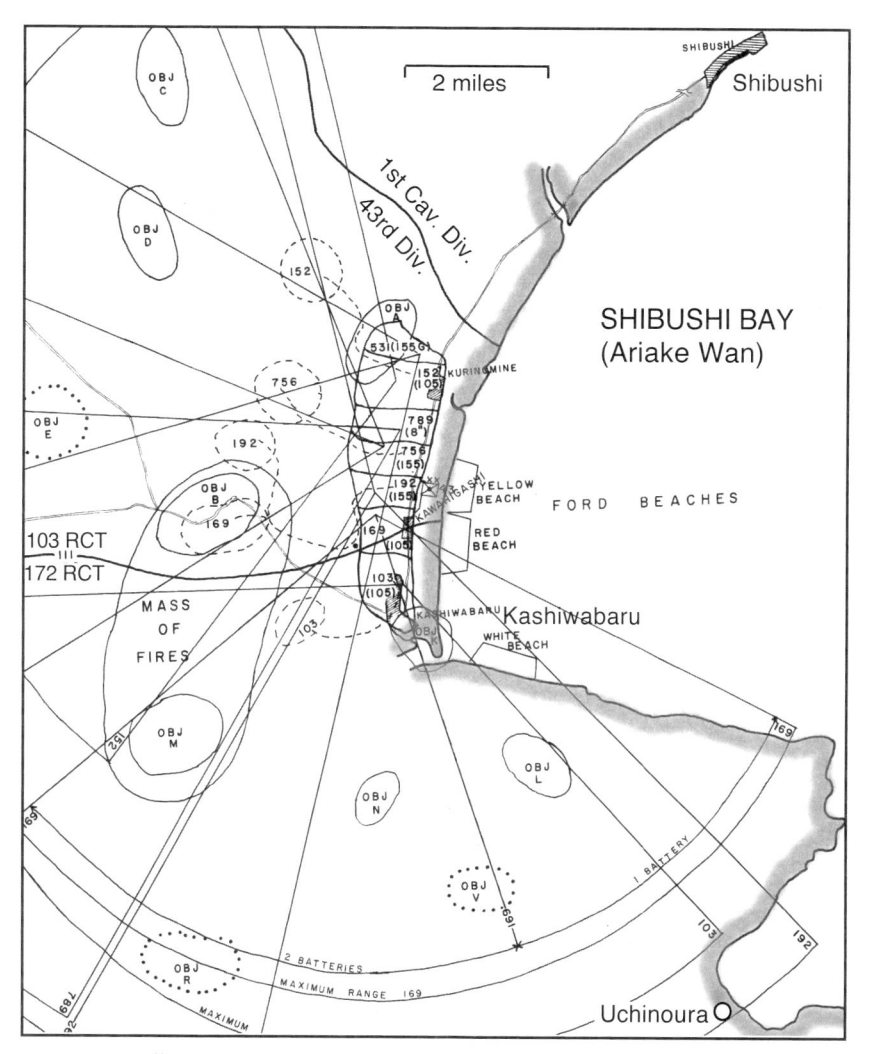

Map 18. Artillery Plan of the Shibushi Bay landing area, dated August 5, 1945, showing positions of the 43rd Division artillery units, areas accessible to their howitzers, and objectives (firing targets). The invasion was scheduled for November 1, 1945. The 43rd Division was to land on the southern end of the long beach. The zone of the 172nd Regimental Combat Team commanded by Wilber was the entire lower part of this figure. The 103rd RCT was to be to its right (boundary line, center left), and the First Cavalry Division would be to the north on the 43rd's right. (Earlier plans had the 43rd's and 1st Cavalry's positions reversed.) The mountains in the 172nd zone (objectives L and N) reached to 2660 feet in altitude. Wilber wrote that "my regiment was given the point considered most critical to the success of the division action. That meant we couldn't take our time but would have to drive thru anything we met the costly way." [letter 9/20/45] Uchinoura (lower right) is the town where I stayed on my 1983 visit to the nearby rocket launch facility (south of the town). The town would have been within range of the division's artillery! [UNDERLYING MAP: BARKER, P. 231]

PART I

COMBAT, NEW GUINEA

AITAPE, NEW GUINEA
JULY—SEPTEMBER, 1944

★ ★ ★

1

"I'm back on the Jap business again"

At sea and Aitape, New Guinea
July–September, 1944

It had been nine months since the men of the 43rd Division had last seen combat. They were now, on July 8, 1944, en route from New Zealand in the midst of winter to the warmer climes of New Guinea (Map 2), in theory refreshed, trained, and fully staffed. Despite the presence of many replacements who had never heard a shot fired in battle, the division was a seasoned professional outfit. Nevertheless, the veterans still carried with them the psychological effects of the three months of intense combat in New Georgia (Solomon Islands) the previous year.

At this time, Norma, Valerie and I, aged 38, 12, and 13 respectively, were together again at our prewar home at 204 Broadway, Bangor, Maine. Valerie and I remained unaware of Norma's baby (Gale) who was with the baby's father, Monte Bourjaily, and his mother in Washington, D.C. We probably traveled to Bangor from our New Jersey boarding schools by train. I felt responsible now as the "man" of the family for seeing that all of our luggage was still with us as we departed, arrived, or changed trains. Opening and getting settled in our Bangor home likely entailed a lot of hard work, but Norma was adept at quickly turning an inhospitable dwelling into a warm inviting home. It was to be a relatively relaxed summer for Valerie and me; we awaited the September school opening with no significant commitments other than helping around the house. I recall long hours reading on the porch. My violin practicing and lessons, totally neglected during my year in boarding school, may have resumed that summer.

My memories of life in Bangor that year are rich with varied experiences. I enjoyed the freedom a bicycle gave me for the first time since our summer in Hattiesburg, Mississippi, two years earlier. I bicycled the three-quarter-mile distance to Garland Street Junior High School (now the Cohen School) with scores of other students, as did Valerie. And I continued my riding all winter, through snow and ice, much to my Bangor friends' amazement. I became adept at repairing my bike and learned the hard way that one does not take apart the coaster brake with its multitude of tiny parts and ball bearings on a grassy lawn!

My friend Bob Butler and I would ride our bikes into the countryside and shoot at crows with our .22 rifles. We never hit one, but we were more successful with rats in the city dump. I joined a Boy Scout troop and was the second most senior scout, having advanced to First Class at St. Bernard's (boarding) School the previous year. There was no adult scoutmaster, because many qualified men were off at war. The scout senior to me, a high school student and a Star Scout, acted as scoutmaster and I as assistant scoutmaster. We did our best to provide meaningful activities for the dozen or so troop members throughout that year.

I took my schoolwork, including algebra and French, seriously but not overly so. I played in the school orchestra. We played loud marches with great gusto and little precision. All in all, it was a year that gave me the freedom to spread my wings a bit.

I became enamored of at least two girls that year, but I was still barely able to muster the nerve to ask Sue Chase out to the movie matinee for the only date I had that entire year, and that was a bust romantically because another of her admirers came along with us!

Meanwhile, the coming year was to be a challenge for Wilber as he faced combat again and also for Norma as she resumed the "proper" life in Bangor with her two children, but without little Gale, now eight months old. Unfortunately she had not fully imagined how painful this abandonment of her little daughter would be. She was determined to put her life back into the Wilber camp and to put her "transgression" behind her.

x · o · ø · o · x

CHAPTER 1   *I'm back on the Jap business again*

The USAT Sea Devil carried Wilber and his troops from Auckland, New Zealand, to Aitape, New Guinea, a voyage of ten days. Aitape is about midway along the north coast of New Guinea (Map 3). Earlier, on April 22, American units had landed at Aitape and at Hollandia 120 miles farther west. The landings were a complete surprise to the Japanese; the airfields at both locations were captured with little organized resistance. This was a major step in the western march of the Americans along the New Guinea coast because it bypassed Hansa Bay and Wewak, which were still held by the Japanese.

Hollandia was the more important target, but the airfield at Aitape provided air cover to the Hollandia area, and American forces at Aitape would serve as a buffer against attacks by the bypassed 18th Japanese army to the east. Indications in June that the Japanese were moving westward and hence threatening Aitape led to the July 7 embarkation of the 43rd Division in Auckland for Aitape.

The next day, Wilber wrote to his family from shipboard.

[USAT SEA DEVIL] JULY 8, 1944
Dear Norma, Valerie + Hale — Another day is done. The weather is still cloudy but is warmer. Almost no one (I've seen no one) is seasick. The boys are pretty fair sailors now and the mild weather is helping them get their sea legs again.

Today I took another shot [inoculation] in the arm. I'm pretty well perforated now and should be immune to anything except homesickness. Of course you realize my arm is a bit lame but it really isn't any trouble, no fever or headache this time.

We are on the way to [New Guinea] and are to be under [MacArthur]. I understand we will be able to say we are there after arrival so by the time this letter is mailed it should be OK. If not I'll censor out the [N.G.] part [he did.]. I'm glad to go there instead of to [Nimitz] because we will be under army and not navy control. That may be better for the men.…

> The bracketed names and places were written and later aggressively obliterated by Wilber; I infer them here from the context. The drive up the New Guinea north coast was under the command of Gen. Douglas MacArthur, while the navy under Admiral Nimitz controlled the advance in the Central Pacific.

Today we had our first formal inspection of the ship. I inspect accompanied by the ATS Captain. Things were pretty well cleaned up and well organized. The feeding is one of the difficult problems, and trouble comes from poor routes for mess lines, men going thru twice and some of the last running short on food and trouble with schedules. It doesn't help much either to always have a different and inexperienced officer in charge of the mess. Ours is learning but painfully.

I'm sitting on the "Boat deck" which is the top one. Below it is the "Promenade deck" and below that is the "Weather deck." Those are the three top decks. The others are inside the ship proper. The sea is very blue with fleecy clouds in the sky. We passed another ship today but didn't find out who she was. The sun is warm. This is my first day without a sweater and jacket.

DeBlois is nearby. He has just gotten two pictures of Madeline, one smiling + one she liked. I told him I had been promised one too. I love you all very much. Please have a "Round + Round" [holding hands] for me. — XXXOOO Wilber

Major René L. DeBlois, formerly Wilber's executive officer, had assumed command of the 169th Field Artillery Battalion, Wilber's former outfit. Wilber was now commanding officer of the 152nd Field Artillery Battalion, his old Bangor, Maine, outfit. The 169th and 152nd were two of the four field artillery (FA) battalions of the 43rd Infantry Division, a New England National Guard outfit (Chart 2).

x · o · ø · o · x

Three days later, Wilber continued his shipboard story.

JULY 11, 12, 1944

Dear Norma + Hale + Valerie — This is morning now and a soft breeze blows and it promises to be a hot day. I've enjoyed the heat and the freedom at night from all the blankets I used a week ago. Our men have pretty well adapted themselves to the ship's routine. The kitchen is pretty well organized mainly because I put [Capt. Donald L.] Mushik in there a day or so ago, and most of the big gamblers have learned to control their ambitions. It stopped quite suddenly when I confiscated about $75.00 [roughly $1,000 in today's dollars]. I turned it over to their Bn. C.O.s [battalion commanding officers] as a gift for their company funds. The inspection yesterday showed a spick + span ship. As the boys say, if we are here long enough, we will clean up every ship in the Pacific.… — XXXOOO Wilber

It's still July 12, in the late evening. The Skipper says we have covered over two thousand miles so far. This afternoon it rained quite a lot and I spent a couple of hours in my bunk. My stateroom is really quite comfortable and I've spent about two hours in a nap each day since we were settled. I haven't been eating lunch so that is the time I select so I won't see the others eat. As a result my belt is losing a little of that steak and eggs tightness.…

CHAPTER 1   *I'm back on the Jap business again*

Dearest, since I'm going back to the jungle, packages are in order again at your convenience. This is a request for lobster, mustard, oysters, cheese, coca cola syrup, olives and any other items that do not cost ration coupons and that might make good sandwiches. (No Vienna sausage please.) Don't go to any trouble, but if you have any suggestions, I'll send a request about once a month just to remind you husbands + daddies are some trouble + [and] like to be spoiled....

I do adore you. I think you are my most beautiful wife in the whole world. Some day I'll tell you all about it. — XXXOOO Wilber

x · o · ∅ · o · x

This next letter told nothing of his being on shipboard or his location so it could be mailed at Morobe, New Guinea, where the ship stopped briefly. He did drop a subtle hint, though, that he had moved northward out of the grip of the New Zealand winter. The port was described in the subsequent letter. Note that Wilber was again writing to the three of us, Mother (Norma), Valerie, and me, together; we were no longer in separate locations.

JULY 13, 1944
Dear Nana, Hale + Valerie — How are my Mainiacs? It is warm today and I'm sitting in the sun without a jacket. It's a good feeling, as you well know. Did you have breakfast in the yard today or are you all still too tired from cleaning the house + yard. How I would enjoy doing it with you. I'm wondering about the bookcase too. Did you solve the problem?

We were again living in the Bangor house we had bought in 1938 and lived in until Wilber's unit was activated in early 1941. He could, for the first time in over a year, picture our whereabouts and relish thoughts of us there.

This must be a short letter because I want to mail it today but it will assure you that everything here is under control. I've completely recovered from my cold and am feeling fine. Also that tightness about the belt is easing a little. The doctor believed in "feeding a cold" even to the extent of a midnight steak + egg dinner. Remember that treatment, for I liked it. — Love to all of you, Wilber

x · o · ∅ · o · x

VICTORY AND HOMECOMING   PART I: COMBAT, NEW GUINEA

JULY 13–14, 1944

Dearest Valerie and Nana & Hale — This is a two-day letter again. Yesterday [the 13th] I wasn't too busy but when I did have time it was very hot and I would probably only have written of the heat. It is early morning now and I'm just back from a cup of coffee and a grapefruit. It was the type the A&P used to sell for "4 for 25 cents," but good.

Yesterday marked a milestone in our voyage. At 3:00 P.M. we pulled into a port [Morobe, Map 3] that used to be famous on the MacArthur battlefront. From the map it looked like quite a place but on the ground it was just like all the others – a few plantation houses, native huts and the recent military installations. It was a pretty little place and was considered safe because we were allowed lights and showed a movie to the men on the weather deck. The mountains that we read so much about came down to the sea so we could see how rough the country [and the fighting] could be in the interior.

At midnight we moved again, going up the coast to another rendezvous point [Finschhaven; arrived 5 a.m., July 14; WB Journal]. The news today says one of the new points of Jap combat is where we are going [Aitape]. It seems the Japs are trying to break thru our lines there. Consequently we have a lot of speculation on board about the conditions we will find on arrival. I'm not worried much because my men & officers are as nearly ready as I could wish. If we don't do a lot of damage to the Japs, I'll be very much surprised. It is good to be back in action again. I was about fed up with this "rest" business.

FDR [President Franklin D. Roosevelt] has just announced he will be a candidate again. Please send me the necessary forms for voting, if I am going to be able to vote....

Yesterday I did write a letter and mailed it, hoping it would reach you only about a week after the one I mailed just as we sailed. Of course I didn't mention anything about what I was doing or where I was at the time.

Valerie this letter was especially to you. I wanted to remind you that I was still your daddy. Maybe you deserve a paddling today & I should be there to give it to you. However I expect you are too old now and never need one. How about it? I love you and N. & H. too. — Wilber

> Wilber eventually voted for the Republican candidate, Thomas Dewey. During the prewar period, Wilber was definitely an interventionist and supportive of Roosevelt in that regard, but he and his family disfavored the New Deal, which they saw as intrusive big government. He was not in favor of electing Roosevelt to a fourth term.

x · o · ø · o · x

CHAPTER 1   *I'm back on the Jap business again*

JULY 15, 16, 1944
Greetings Again — It is time again for me to talk to my family. I had the barber give me a stream-lined [very short] haircut yesterday. No Jap will be able to hold [on] to me by the hair now. The news today indicates that we may get some business with the Japs soon. It is raining today and I'm sitting in my cabin writing. In about 15 minutes I'll have to go inspect the ship....

This is my last day for this series of letters. Tomorrow [17 July] we expect to debark and soon I'll be able to mail you a letter without any news in it except about myself. These letters must wait until a month after we arrive [due to censorship rules].

> Since his candid shipboard letters could not be immediately mailed, they did not serve as a primary communication link to his family. He knew he was participating in historic events and was clearly writing for the historical record. Of course, we the recipients found them to be of great interest even though delayed.

… OK Norma, I'll not mention your arthritis to anyone. However you should realize that Norma Sparlin's knee is news in almost any letter. It puts the reader in a sympathetic (to me) frame of mind, you know. Time to stop. Good Bye. I love you. — XXXOOO Wilber

> This was the first indication of Norma's sensitivity to private matters possibly becoming public to her Bangor neighbors. Wilber was serving with many Bangor men who would write home with any juicy gossip about their commander or his wife.
>
> On July 10, one week before the arrival of the 43rd Division at Aitape, the Japanese 18th Army under Lt. Gen. Hatazo Adachi attacked westward at the Driniumor River in the vain hope of capturing Tadji airfield 15 miles to the west (near Aitape, Map 4) and thus acquiring American food supplies. It broke through one segment of the U.S. lines but was driven back. Subsequent sporadic fighting took place well into August.
>
> The Japanese had been isolated from their supply lines for some time and the surviving men in the Aitape area had exhausted their food supplies and were suffering "increasingly heavy casualties from combat, starvation and disease; they had no artillery support and could obtain none." [Smith, *Approach*," p. 195]

x·o·ø·o·x

The USAT Sea Devil arrived at Aitape at 11 a.m. on July 17, and the battalion was ashore at 3 p.m.; it had posted guards in the battalion area by 6 p.m. [152nd FA Journal]. This was an extremely busy time for Wilber, one that he recalled much later in a letter to his father. "For example, once I was told to be firing in 48 hours and all my men, ammunition (300 tons) and equipment (__ tons) [sic] were still in the holds of a transport." [letter 11/3/44]

Wilber wrote his first letter from shore that day and, so he could mail it immediately, said only that he was back with the coconut trees. He probably was at Tadji Plantation at the mouth of the Raihu River where the battalion was initially stationed.

[AITAPE] JULY 17, 1944

Dear Sweet Wife — Last night I was recalling how lovely you were when you came to Hattiesburg [Mississippi]. Did I ever tell you that you were so beautiful that evening it almost hurt to look at you? It did. It was nice to see the children too and I will always remember that day as one of my "forever" days. You were tired but so sweet and after the children were in bed, it was a dream come true to be with you and to hold you close to me.…

I hope you + the children have gotten comfortably settled in Bangor without too much work. Somehow I feel better about your being there than anywhere else. Scientifically I can reason that you are better off in other places, but my farmer instincts feel that you are safer on my soil. Silly? … As I have said before, I love you, the whole lot of you, and I wish you were all twins. (except Nana). — XXXOOO Wilber

x · o · ø · o · x

The next morning, on July 18, at 7:20 a.m., Wilber and other officers left to search out artillery positions, which they had selected by 9:30 a.m., at the mouth of the Raihu River. The battalion was ready to carry out emergency fires by 6:30 p.m. the next day, although the "impedimenta" of the battalion were "still coming off ships very slowly" [152nd FA Journal]. Their mission was the defense of the Tadji airfield several miles to the east. The front lines were 18 miles further east at the Driniumor River, well beyond artillery range of the 105-mm guns of the battalion. The battalion aggressively registered their guns on plotted firing positions in preparation for a defense of the airfields in case they were attacked. The battalion saw no organized combat for about three weeks. Interestingly, Wilber now revealed that he was on New Guinea.

CHAPTER 1   *I'm back on the Jap business again*

JULY 19, 1944

Dearest Nana and children — I'm back on the Jap business again. You can be sure it is a welcome change. Just now I'm sitting under a tent beside the ever-present palm tree. This palm tree is in New Guinea but it looks familiar just the same. So far I haven't fired any shots in anger but other people are, so I have hopes.

> Wilber appeared eager to get his battalion into the action! I wonder how many of his men were equally as eager.

The Bn. is doing a fine job and [I] have already made some new friends. I'll be able to tell you more details later. As you know I'm just a little busy during this phase. Don't worry, I'm in no personal hazard and am feeling fine. I love all of you and will write as I can. Good Luck. — XXXOOO Wilber

x · o · ø · o · x

JULY 25, 1944

Dearest Norma — There isn't time to answer your last two letters so this is just to tell you I still love you. Things here are going well and there is no reason to be concerned about me. I hope you aren't going to insist on worrying.

> But how could she help but worry? Had it crossed her mind that if Wilber did not return, her dilemma might be solved, at least in part? She could leave Bangor and perhaps recover her little daughter, although she would still be faced with the awkward birth date. She would also lose Wilber's continuing financial support. Had Monte offered to marry her in that event?
> Norma must have feared Wilber's wrath upon his eventual return. To this day, it chills me that she might even have hoped, subliminally, that Wilber would not return. But she and Wilber had always freely acknowledged that possibility. She surely had such thoughts and would have been terribly conflicted by them.

Apparently something I have said about your writing and music has worried you. Dearest I didn't mean to hurt you. Please know that. Also when I spoke of wanting you just to be a wife to me, I realized that is out of the question. Things will work out OK, Dear. I'll be trying to be an understanding husband when I come home.

> Wilber was becoming more realistic about his relationship to Norma. It was not to be all roses and sex.

This being apart is hard on each of us and my first prayer is that afterward we can find something as fine as we knew before the war. It's pretty hot here now but I like it better than the cold … Don't forget I love you more than anyone in the world and I think the children are just what I wanted. — XXXOOO Wilber

x·o·ø·o·x

During that summer of 1944, Valerie, age 12, rather overstepped protocol when she wrote to Wilber's immediate superior, Brig. Gen. Harold R. Barker, commander of the 43rd Division Artillery. But Barker honored her with a reply he did not share with Wilber.

Dear Valerie — I was greatly pleased to receive your note, which you enclosed in a letter to your Daddy. I know exactly how you feel about having your Daddy come home on leave and I can appreciate how much you miss him. My own daughter has written to me and has expressed the same sentiments and she doesn't see why I can't come home at least for a leave.

Rest assured that if there was any way I could give your father a leave at this time, I would do so, but your father holds a very important position in the 43rd Division Artillery and simply cannot be spared at this time. Nevertheless, it may not be too far distant when this leave can be accomplished and rest assured it will have my hearty approval.

As to keeping your dad out of a major battle, I will do my best. He is one of the bravest officers we have and it is hard to hold him back. You really should be very proud of having a father so efficient and courageous. I am sure it will only be a question of time when he will return to you safe and sound with a most enviable record.

Thank you for sending me this note and with the very kindest of regards, I remain — Sincerely, H. R. BARKER, Brigadier General, U.S.A., Commanding

x·o·ø·o·x

The following letter included a number of routine household and financial matters, most of which I have deleted in favor of Norma's concerns and Wilber's activities.

JULY 29, 1944
Hello Wife of Mine — Or are you so independent that you prefer "comrade." I've three grand long letters from you, each written when you were too tired on June 25, July 2, and 7. Thank you. I'll answer them first.…

CHAPTER 1   *I'm back on the Jap business again*

Your letter doesn't sound dreary. It sounds tired and maybe lonesome. Please remember when you feel that way that I haven't meant to be critical of you. Really I haven't thought an unloving thought of you for years. I know I have asked you to get along without a maid and that I often didn't help with the housework. I have tried tho and I had no intention of leaving the impression with you that I expect you to be an official professional success. For me you are a success. Sparlins do get so "perterbated" and my stumbling letters never seem to picture my thoughts correctly. In fact most of my difficulties started in my letters.

Just yesterday I got a strong letter from Father because I wasn't going to vote. I never said I didn't want to vote. In fact I've been trying to find out how I can vote. However, if I try to tell him that I never thought any such thing, I'll probably only graduate from the "Non-Voters League" to the "Liars Club." Such a war! Just as insurance, don't take this letter too seriously. It too is probably a miscarriage.

… Your declaration of independence is noted, but I'm not much worried and I'll try not to demand too many wifely duties of you when I return. If that is the way you really want it, I'll try to be Ok about things.

> Norma was insisting on her independence, even though she had returned to her "former" quite constrained life. She was not free of society's expectations.

… Don't be concerned about the shaver. It does work and I use it frequently except when I'm too sweaty. Hale's tooth situation noted. I think those baby teeth need to come out. Re Valerie's, I'll leave it to you. It would probably defer [her] interest in dates [with boys] for a while to wear braces.

I was out on an infantry patrol today and am pretty tired tonight. It wasn't dangerous so don't be worried about me. René DeBlois was wounded yesterday. He caught a bomb fragment in the fleshy part of his leg just above the knee. They aren't removing the piece now but it did not reach the bone so isn't considered critical. I went over to see him in the hospital yesterday + today. He is quite cheerful but says being C.O. of the 169th has some aspects he doesn't care about. I wrote Madeleine that when René said it wasn't serious, he was being accurate.

> DeBlois was referring, in his "some aspects he doesn't care about," to the fact that Wilber, as the former commanding officer of the 169th Field Artillery Battalion, had also been wounded by a bomb fragment, in July 1943. In the 1980s, it occurred to me that there were no Japanese aircraft in the Aitape area when DeBlois was wounded, so I asked Wilber's former subordinate, Capt. Howard Brown, then a retired colonel, about the bomb. He said it was a

practice bomb or bomblet dropped by a U.S. plane for target practice! Friendly fire was a consistent threat as Wilber, in a rare admission, then revealed:

We get in the news a lot but this, so far, is a pretty sedate battle for me. I've only been scared once and that was by our own mortars.

If I can do some outstanding job here, perhaps I can have a leave home someday. You know I'm trying to do my best all the time but often the [result] is mediocre and almost routine in character. However the end of the war is coming nearer more rapidly every week. Keep the corners up [the smiles] and remember that when I am home, it will be for a long time. — XXXOOO Wilber

Wilber was trying to keep his own "corners up."

x · o · ø · o · x

The last few letters above were to Norma alone, though she probably shared parts with Valerie and me. This next was to me alone.

AUGUST 9, 1944
Dear Son Hale — The box of letter paper [stationery] came yesterday and was in very good shape. I still have a little of this 169 paper left so am using it first. Thank you so much. It is really a pleasure to write on it and I am proud to send it to my friends.…

The previous year, in my New Jersey boarding school, I had worked in the print shop and on two occasions had printed up letterhead stationery for him with his name, unit number, and address. The first set had had his old unit number (169th FA Bn) on it. The gift served well his penchant for letter writing.

We are moving closer to the Japs [at Driniumor River] so we will be in better range. We ran a bit short of Japs where we were firing. Our new place is a beautiful beach where the breeze is good nearly all the time. No mosquitoes and no neighbors, except a stray Jap now and then, all goes for a good home.

We are the first Bn. of the [43rd] Div. Arty to see action on New Guinea. It looks as if it were [will be] much easier than Munda was. The men are sure glad to be firing again, and so am I.

… I'm pretty safe now so don't let the girls worry. — Your father, Wilber

On August 10, the 152nd Field Artillery Battalion moved about 18 miles east to Chakila, New Guinea, (Map 4) at the mouth of the Driniumor River

CHAPTER 1   *I'm back on the Jap business again*

Envelope addressed to Wilber's father Hale. This was from the second batch of stationery I had set up and printed in the St. Bernard's School print shop. It had the requested modifications: the return address on the front of the envelope and his then-current unit (152 F. A. Bn.). Wilber's signature indicated he had self-censored the letter. The six-cent stamp bought airmail transit within the U.S. Although the Bradt farm was in Versailles, it was on a Dillsboro postal route.

as part of the artillery "Covering Force" for the combat along the river and eastward of it. [152nd FA Journal; Barker, p. 131]. That same day the battalion was assigned to provide direct support to the 126th Infantry of the 32nd Division and, on August 13, it began support of its usual partner, the 103rd Infantry of the 43rd Division. The battalion gave artillery support to aggressive patrolling east of the Driniumor River, which encountered pockets of resistance. Forward observer and liaison parties from the artillery battalion accompanied these patrols and brought artillery fires onto Japanese strong points. Small aircraft were also used to carry out artillery observations. [152nd FA History]

x·o·ø·o·x

Two days after the move to the Driniumor River, Wilber wrote to Norma.

[ON DRINIUMOR RIVER] 12 AUG. 1944
Dear Wife — I like to write "Dear Wife" since it is you whom I have for a Dear Wife. This is a very, very hot day. I am in my C.P. with a canteen beside me and with the

perspiration running down my face + arms in rivulets. A radio [message] just came in that Maj. Fish is bringing a prisoner of war back from the front lines. Since he was S-3 in New Georgia, this was his first trip to the front lines. I imagine he will have gotten quite a kick out of his initiation.

> Major Waldo H. Fish was executive officer of the 152nd Field Artillery Battalion, second in command under Wilber.

We have been attached to another division temporarily so I'm dealing with new generals and colonels. It's always interesting to be with other units and to learn their methods. Their Div. Arty. Commander has checked me on many details and finally said he hoped I didn't mind for he didn't know what kind of a Bn. I had, but as soon as he knew, he would leave me alone. He has kept his word and is leaving us alone now.

I went up front to see Mushik this morning and he looked the most contented that I've noticed since New Georgia. We are accusing him and [Capt. Thomas A.] DeWolfe for getting us into this action because they asked me for permission to visit the front lines. I said, "No," but three hours later we were ordered into action.

[Note on side of page:] Don't worry about this combat. It's really tame. Numerous Japs are surrendering. WB

Fish just came in with his prisoner and he was his prisoner that he captured himself. The whole Bn. is thrilled about it. This is probably the first Jap ever captured by an artillery major. Fish said the Jap was bathing in the ocean and was wearing a loin cloth and carrying a grenade. He looked at Major Fish and threw the grenade out into the ocean. He had a can of our rations and came up to Fish holding his hand out and grabbed and shook vigorously Maj. Fish's hand. Then he offered Maj. Fish a cracker out of the can. When Fish declined, he took a bite and looked like it was very good and ran his hand up + down in front of his stomach as if it were a big fat one. Next he took some Jap rations out of a cloth he had on the beach and smelled it, then made an awful face and threw it toward the Jap lines.

Fish put him in the car and started off and the Jap began to sing. He bowed and bowed toward the Jap lines, held his arms up to the sun and looked at it, and whenever he passed U.S. soldiers he waved and waved at them. Next he tried to choke himself by pulling his rag tight around his throat. He pulled it so tight his tongue and eyes stuck out but when Fish didn't seem to mind he decided not to commit suicide. Later he kept looking very inquiringly at Fish and drawing his finger across his throat, apparently wondering if he was to be killed that way. Waldo gave him some more food and he relaxed and started to feel around the leggings on one of Waldo's two men. The man slapped him across the thigh and he caught on OK and stopped. We call Waldo "Bring' em Alive Fish." He is sure being kidded a lot....

CHAPTER 1   *I'm back on the Jap business again*

Aug 15 — … I can easily see why you would need a rest after Lamoine. You are always so conscientious about doing your share. That was one of the reasons I loved you in 1927 and why I love you even more today.

Is it hot in Washington? It was a good idea to have a [medical] check-up. I'll want to make a thorough one too when I get home. I didn't and won't be writing about you to anyone. When I write to other people it is hard not to talk about the person I think the nicest in the world. However I'll try.…

Aug. 17 — … Don't work too hard on the house and do not try to put the upper storm windows in. Get a good strong man to do it.… — Good Luck + XXXOOO Wilber

> Mother, Valerie, and I had made a day visit to the summer cottage of University of Maine friends at the shore in Lamoine, Maine (near Bar Harbor).
>
> Norma apparently visited Washington, D.C., in late July, almost certainly to see baby Gale and possibly also for a medical checkup. Was affection for Monte part of the visit? Possibly yes, or possibly not at all; it is impossible to know.

x · o · ø · o · x

> Wilber's next letter to me enhanced our view of his life on the Driniumor River.

AUGUST 20, 1944

Dear Son — My battalion is in position on a nice beach, and when we are not firing, the men who are not busy go in swimming. There hasn't been much action for us altho we have worked in three different divisions [43rd, 32nd, and 31st; WB Journal]. You know me – just being helpful.

I've been into the jungle several times and am getting pretty well oriented. There are mountains not far inland and I went up there yesterday. Two Japs were captured and a couple shot while I was there. The two captured ones were physically exhausted and all thru fighting.

Capt. DeWolfe fell the other day from a tree and fractured a vertebra. He will recover OK but may be sent home (to U.S.) for his hospitalization. Maj. [Samuel F.] Pierson said if that happened we should put a sign on the tree he fell from, "This way to the U.S." with an arrow pointing up the tree; then another sign at the right limb, "Let go here."

The natives here are small and quite black. They, tho men, wear a cloth about the size of two towels which they wrap around their waist. Some wear plain ones (they look like skirts) and some wear bright red or blue. I've never seen a green one. Perhaps they don't care for it. They often wear red or yellow flowers in their hair and sometimes a green bit of some plant. Their sense of beauty is surprising and they are likable little people. Their houses are built of palm fronds and small poles.... — Good Luck and love to you and Valerie and Norma from Wilber XXXOOO

Sam Pierson, a Princeton arts graduate, was the battalion S-3 (training and plans) officer under Wilber, a critical position third in the line of command after the commander and executive officer.

x·o·ø·o·x

By this time, the Japanese 18th Army, initially consisting of some 50,000 men, had endured thousands of casualties and had ceased to be an effective force. On August 25, the Aitape operation was declared ended by Lt. Gen. Walter Krueger, commander of the Sixth Army, of which the 43rd Division was a part [Smith, ibid, p. 204].

The Japanese survivors retreated eastward toward Wewak and eventually into the mountains south of Wewak (Map 3). (After the surrender of Japan in August 1945, General Adachi and the few thousand surviving soldiers surrendered to Australian forces. Adachi was convicted of war crimes and sentenced to life imprisonment. On April 27, 1947, he committed suicide [Smith, p. 205].) This hiatus gave Wilber time to write several letters, one to me with grim news, passed on rather lightly.

AUGUST 31, 1944
Dear Son — ... This isn't a bad war here for I've seen a lot more dead Japs than wounded Americans. However two of my best friends were killed, so it is still a war with all its bad aspects.

... I'll write to Father and ask him to lend the Legion of Merit medal to you for a while. I gave it to him, but I know you and Valerie and Norma would like to see it. After you have had it for a few weeks, please send it back to Father. I hope you don't mind that I gave it to him, for it did seem to please him. Don't take any wooden nickels. — Your father, Wilber

Who were those two "best friends" who were killed? On August 7, five officers and nine enlisted men of the 2nd Battalion, 169th Infantry, were killed or fatally wounded and another 11 were wounded by misplaced mortar rounds fired by the battalion's own mortar company! The next day

CHAPTER 1   *I'm back on the Jap business again*

U.S. artillery (not of the 43rd Division) mistakenly fired upon U.S. troops of another battalion in the same "TED" force." The TED force was carrying out a nine-day probe behind enemy lines through thick, hilly jungle when these tragic events took place. The wounded had to be carried on jungle trails for two days before they could reach medical treatment [Smith, p. 199; Higgins, p. 39.] The deceased officers of the 169th Infantry surely included Wilber's two friends. Wilber had worked directly with the 169th Infantry Regiment in the Munda campaign. A vivid first-hand account of this tragic event is in Ockenden, Chapters 19 and 20. The senselessness of those losses surely affected Wilber and many others deeply.

x · o · ø · o · x

Grasshoppers were a favorite of Valerie's; on one of our visits to Indiana, our grandmother Elizabeth Bradt had taught her how to catch them with her bare hand. She loved it even though they expelled a green goo (blood) when caught; I was repelled by it. Wilber may have had her interest in grasshoppers in mind in this letter.

AUGUST 31, 1944
Hello there Valerie — Your very nice letter came yesterday and I enjoyed every word of it.…

The other day I was up in my [artillery observation] plane and flew along the coast and over the jungle. It was very interesting and pretty. They call these planes "grasshoppers" because they fly so low and seem to just hop along over the trees.

My position is on a beautiful sandy beach, and I swim whenever I can. During the day the sun is too hot but in the evening it is quite nice. At least we can clean up every once in a while. I think of you and wish we could be swimming together. Don't worry too much about my getting home. This war is going to be over some of these days and I'll be back. I love you, Dearest. — Wilber

x · o · ø · o · x

Wilber continued his monthly correspondence with his father, F. Hale, a retired Indiana teacher now living with his wife Elizabeth in his newly built, asbestos-shingled home on his Versailles, Indiana, farm. The house still lacked finishing details within. Wilber wrote of how an Indiana connection had helped move the war along.

VICTORY AND HOMECOMING   PART I: COMBAT, NEW GUINEA

AUGUST 31, 1944

Dear Father — I'm much relieved to hear your report on your and Mother's health. Please don't try to cover up anything for a morale effect on me. To feel that I wasn't given a true picture would immediately cause me much concern. I'm sure you appreciate that and would act accordingly.

… My Bn. saw more service here than any other Arty Bn, but we didn't see anything as stiff as the Munda affair. I doubt if we ever will.

An Inf. Bn. [of the 32nd Division] that we supported here a few days [August 11–13] was a bit disgusted that they didn't have their own artillery. However I found the Bn. C.O. came from Bedford [Indiana, about 100 miles down Rt. 50 from the Bradt farm in Versailles] so everything was OK. After the job was over, their artillery commander gave us a commendation so he [the Bedford native] must have been well satisfied. Must stop. — Love, Wilber

x · o · ø · o · x

SEPT. 2, 1944

Dear Wife — … It must be beautiful in Maine now. I'd like so much to share it with you. The news from Europe is so good today that I'm really encouraged to think I may better my original five-year estimate. Germany is surely tottering and only a miracle can delay her collapse now. Then we should have a lot of company over here and things will really roll along.

It looks now as if we have wound up the recent action and thank God no battle casualties in my battalion this time. We are moving into our administrative camp [at Aitape] with only a rather casual tactical mission. Maybe we can get cleaned up now and do a little training. Really I don't think I'll ever see as tough action as in the [Solomon] Islands. So don't worry about me. I've three major battles to my credit [Guadalcanal, Northern Solomons, and New Guinea] and am in good health + spirits.

I love you all and will be remembering our [honeymoon] days at L[ake] Louise and Sicamous. Would you by any chance remember too? — Your husband Wilber

> Wilber would eventually merit four campaign (battle) stars on his Asiatic-Pacific ribbon, the fourth being for Luzon, the Philippines.
>
> On September 2, the 152nd Field Artillery Battalion ceased its support of the 103rd Infantry and the next day returned to Aitape, probably to Tadji Plantation. The division was to be primed with intensive training for the next advance. With combat over, Wilber had no difficulty finding poetic and humorous aspects of life at Aitape.

CHAPTER 1   *I'm back on the Jap business again*

The Allied armies had finally broken free of Normandy in early August and were rushing across France toward Germany. They were soon to be joined by troops that had landed on the south coast of France on August 15. They entered Paris on August 23.

On September 15, landings at Morotai (Indonesia) west of New Guinea and at Peleliu in the Palau Islands (Map 2) would bring the Americans to the doorstep of the Philippines. The decision to invade Peleliu remains controversial to this day because of its questionable strategic value and its high casualty rate. In Europe, the Russians began an offensive in the north, also on September 15, which led to the capture of Riga on the Baltic coast on October 13 and the encirclement and isolation of the German Army Group North.

2

"Running on and off ships"

Aitape
September–November, 1944

With the end of action in Aitape, three months of training commenced. The division was scheduled to participate in the November 1 Mindanao invasion (on this most southern major Philippine island; Map 5) to secure airfields in support of the move into Leyte (also in the Philippines). On September 15, that operation was canceled and MacArthur was directed by the Joint Chiefs in Washington to proceed directly to Leyte on October 20. The 43rd did not participate in that operation, though for a time it appeared to be a possibility. In late December, the 43rd Division would depart for the invasion of the main Philippine island of Luzon.

In this period, Wilber's letters became shorter and more direct. He tended to write larger with more space between the lines and to complete a letter when the page (both sides) was filled. His writing became more routine, but no less dramatic.

SEPT. 6, 1944
Dearest Wife + Children — It is my personal opinion that our most recent combat has reached the "shadow boxing" stage. Business is very slack and we are back to routine training and the ever-present business of counting shirts, shoes, bolts and nuts.…

Please have a fine time at Lucerne. I'd like a cottage there someday. Would you like that? I've been afraid that you + the children would find the work on the house too hard. You certainly are planning well on its upkeep. I knew you would.

Norma rented a cottage on Phillips Lake, in Lucerne, Maine, some 15 miles outside Bangor for a week or two that summer. I find it surprising that she would take the trouble to do this, given the work needed to fix up the Bangor house. She would get into her head the idea that something would be good for her children and then would just go ahead and do it. I do not remember how we got ourselves and our stuff out there; we had no car during the entire time Wilber was in the service. The cottage was quite rudimentary and not very welcoming, but Norma quickly made it a comfortable home, hopefully with some help from Valerie and me.

I've been reading Plato recently and will send it to you when I've finished it. Any of the things I send along will not mean I didn't enjoy them but that I am reducing my luggage. I know that in our next action, I must be traveling light....

Today I sit on a General Court. That spoils a long record for I've been on the Court Board for over a year without ever being present at a trial. There are some advantages to being the C.O. who is always stationed on some remote location [like Ondonga]....

Give the children a big hug for me. I am still your very adoring husband. — XXXOOO Wilber

x·o·ø·o·x

Valerie (left), me, and Norma (foreground) splashing in lake, summer 1944, probably at Lucerne, Maine. [PHOTO: BRADT FAMILY]

SEPT. 16, 1944

Dear Son of Mine — It is fairly cool tonight and I am sitting in my tent with Major Fish. He is working on his radio and I have a Nestles choc. bar. I'll use the last piece for bait in my rat trap. We have caught five this week but decided not to eat them as the Japs sometimes do.

Today we had a big inspection with both [Maj. Gen. Leonard F.]Wing [commander, 43rd Division] and General Barker officiating. The 152d really did a magnificent job, and both W. & B. were very complimentary. I doubt if any other unit here has done as well in their inspections. I wish you could have seen our trucks and tractors all clean and fresh paint, lined up in a perfect line.

I'm enclosing some pictures of Capt. [Frank J.] Burns and myself taken by an army photographer from a point on the front during the recent scrap here. We were adjusting artillery fire in the edge of the jungle shown in the background. My holster is the left handed one [your] Aunt Ruth sent me. I've since given it away

Wilber (left) and Capt. Frank J. Burns adjusting artillery fires in New Guinea [letter 9/16/44]. [PHOTO: PROBABLY U.S. ARMY SIGNAL CORPS]

A 105-mm howitzer of the 152nd Field Artillery Battalion (Wilber's unit) firing "over the American perimeter," Aitape, New Guinea, August 4, 1944. [PHOTO: U.S. ARMY SIGNAL CORPS. SC 267974]

because I nearly lost my pistol twice from it. You can tell that this wasn't a very dangerous place by the fact that I was not wearing a helmet. I'm very particular about that when the Japs are shooting my way....

I went fishing the other day and caught — nothing. BUT I got dumped out by the surf and really was soaked. Fun! — I love you. Your father, Wilber

x·o·ø·o·x

Penciled notations on this letter by Norma suggest she was not in Bangor sometime after receiving it. She may have been visiting little Gale in Washington, D.C., perhaps for her first birthday on October 29.

SEPT. 20, 1944
Dear Norma — ... The other day I went to the G-2 office to ask if it was safe for me to go to Y— [probably Yakamul, about six miles east of the Driniumor on the coast]. They gave me the horse laugh and said, "Why do you ask? In New Georgia you went where you pleased without even telling where you had been." I seem to have some very loyal + inaccurate friends. – It was safe + I'm back OK. I still love you. — Wilber.

CHAPTER 2   *Running on and off ships*

x · o · ø · o · x

It may have been during Norma's absence that October that I became entranced by the young woman who stayed in our Bangor home to watch over Valerie and me. She was in her early twenties; I do not remember her name. She was newly married and her husband was away in the army. I was not quite 14. Early on she asked me if I could dance and, as I had had a few lessons at St. Bernard's School, we danced a number of times to music on the radio. She would put her head on my shoulder—I was quite tall—and she was probably dreaming of other people and times. I liked her and to please her I enthusiastically did chores such as cleaning up the back yard when asked. I chatted animatedly with her during intermission at a school concert (in which I participated) as if she were my date; my violin stand below the stage was next to her front row audience seat. At home, we had conversations that covered a number of intimate topics. I was definitely smitten. I learned from her (verbally only) about the hymen and that her birth control apparatus was at her home where her mother could keep a watchful eye on it. I heard from her, for the first time, the old story that if a newly married couple put a penny in a jar each time they made love the first year of their marriage and thereafter removed a penny each time for the rest of their lives, they would never empty the jar.

Fortunately, or regrettably I sometimes think, she drew the line at further intimacies. I once suggested that we change into our pajamas and dance in them, but she wasn't buying that. One evening, just after Norma's return, she and Norma were having a wrap-up conversation when I came downstairs in my pajamas and bathrobe to join the conversation. Seeing me on the stairs, Mother sent me right back up. Later she severely chastised me for "tempting" a young woman by showing up in pajamas. I didn't realize I had been playing the tempter, and certainly did not, then or ever, volunteer to my mother any information about dancing and intimate conversations.

I do wonder if my life might have taken an entirely different path had the relationship gone further. Perhaps the fact that it did not was a contributing factor to my relatively stable and productive life. I also speculate on how Norma's adulterous experience and subsequent anguish could have led directly, through her trip to Washington, to similar anguish for this young woman, whose husband was also off at war.

x · o · ø · o · x

VICTORY AND HOMECOMING   PART I: COMBAT, NEW GUINEA

As usual, Wilber's monthly letter to his father revealed practicalities of the war that he may not have shared with his immediate family.

SEPTEMBER 25, 1944
Dear Father — We have had a strenuous but not particularly hazardous month. A little local combat broke out in my area and we heard a few rifle bullets go by too close, but all in all it was pretty mild. The battalion did a good job, rushed back from the perimeter and spent a period in amphibious training (running on and off ships) with all our equipment and vehicles. Next Gen. Wing inspected us with the assistance of several inspection (Technical) teams. For our showing we received an official commendation. Next we went back on the perimeter, and now the Sixth Army is inspecting us. You see what I mean by strenuous.... — Love, Wilber

Inspections and training could be as strenuous as combat! "Running on and off ships with all our equipment and vehicles" even once would have been a major undertaking and not without danger. The ships were anchored well off the beach, accessible only by small boats. Getting aboard required booms and winches for cargo and climbing nets for soldiers.

x·o·ø·o·x

However, Wilber did share with Norma the effects of training but also the occasional entertainment.

OCT. 1, 1944
Hello Lovely Wife — On my anniversary [October 1, two years after leaving San Francisco], I received three letters from you (Sept 18, 19, 20)....
Rotation is now a fact with us. Because of my decorations and large amount of service in the "Forward Areas," I have a very high priority....
Last week the Bn. was down on a once prominent river [Driniumor for training; Barker, p. 134], and I commuted between my rear and forward headquarters, 26 miles each way along a beach. It kept me pretty busy so I did not write you for several days.

He was probably commuting from the Tadji Plantation area (from the mouth of the Raihu River eastward to his battalion at the Driniumor River, 18 miles as the crow flies) or possibly to the Yakamul area (another six miles) where their firing targets could have been.

Vehicle being retrieved from the surf by a "cat" at Aitape, New Guinea, July 27, 1944. It had tried to ford the outlet of a river between the 32nd Division headquarters and the front lines. Wilber described a similar incident in his letter of October 1, 1944. [PHOTO: U.S. ARMY SIGNAL CORPS, SC 267910]

U.S. troops crossing a pontoon bridge over the Driniumor River, near Aitape, constructed by 43rd Division engineers to accommodate the rising tide, August 1, 1944. [PHOTO: U.S. ARMY SIGNAL CORPS, SC 267950]

Once the river came up fast and caught two of our vehicles. About ten of us had to carry a cable out to the truck thru a raging torrent. I haven't had so much fun for a long time. We could get to about 8 feet from the truck then the current would sweep us off our feet and down the river. About a dozen of us made the trip before we got a man on the truck and a few more before we got the cable across. Pierson grabbed a log as he headed for the ocean but Lt. Lanier sailed by and grabbed his arm and pulled him off again. I got involved with some rapids and bounced around quite a bit going clear under a couple of times and finally gave up trying to walk and swam out. After I got ashore I discovered I was still wearing my helmet liner and didn't even have the strap under my chin. We [got] the trucks out + had a lot of fun. Some of the men seemed quite surprised to find me in the river with them. Maybe they expected me to be shouting from the bank. Good Night Lover, I'm your most special husband. Keep the corners up. — XXXOOO Wilber

Wilber, the battalion commander, had a grand time being one of the boys. As a college letterman swimmer, he was in his element.

x·o·ø·o·x

Wilber again turned to serious advice for me, his son, this time on dating. In Bangor, I was already quite taken by my new female classmates, having been in boys' schools the previous three years; this was undoubtedly amplified by a 13-year-old's hormonal surge. He could see this in my letters, but in his efforts to be a good father, he may well have misjudged my mental state and overestimated my very limited social activities. He was blunt and direct in his advice.

OCT. 8, 1944

Dear Son — In several of your letters you have mentioned interest in girls. I am very glad for you to like girls and to be with them but it begins to look as if you were going a bit to extremes. This year you have never mentioned any boy friend in your letters.

You are making a mistake to start dates at this age. You will some day want to ask some girl to marry you. That means you will want to be able to earn enough to give her a home and take care of her when she isn't well. Now is the time for you to work on that end of the problem. You must try to be in a position to be free to make love to that girl when you and she are ready to marry.

This love business is pretty closely tied up with sex, and sex is the expression of one of the strongest instincts existing – that to mate and reproduce. It is not something to play with except for keeps. There is a lot of talk and writing about great loves, which people can't control. All those cases started by people fooling around with something they couldn't control. My rule with girls before I married Norma was "never to have dates with any girl I wouldn't be proud of as a wife and further never to make love to a girl unless I was ready to marry her." This doesn't mean that in high school I never had dates. I probably averaged one a month when a senior and half that when a junior.

> He surely intended the old meaning (until the 1950s) of "to make love," namely to woo or to court, but not the contemporary meaning, to have sexual intercourse. Recall his mention of the chasteness of his premarital courting of Norma in his letter of December 24, 1943 (Book 2): "You are a most seductive young lady, and it nearly caused your downfall more than one night." Also recall his letter to me of April 3, 1944 (Book 2): "I have never lain with any woman but Nana, and never will." He did not mention here any concern for girls' feelings, but he did in the April 3 letter.

If I were home now we could talk over this whole thing in detail but, since I won't be home before spring, I must write. Please try to read my intent into the things I write to further your best interest, not now perhaps, but for the later years.

> He did realize that mail was a poor way to have this conversation. But it may indeed have made the conversation easier, because it was not face-to-face.

Except for special occasions, I want you to stop any social twosome dates until you are in the upper two years of high school. I want you to learn to like and make a practice of choosing your recreation with either boys or mixed crowds. This doesn't mean at all that I don't want you to have girls among your friends. It does mean that I will be very disappointed to have you hanging around some girl's parlor at this stage in your life.

I must stop now and sweat a while again. It's getting dark and I hope will cool off soon. Tell the girls I'll write soon. — Your Pop, Wilber

> In fact, I did all my biking, hiking, scouting, and shooting in and around Bangor then with male friends. My dating life that year, as noted, was non-existent. Although his advice was not on target and was largely set aside, I suspect it lodged somewhere within me to my benefit in my later dating years.

x·o·ø·o·x

A week later, Wilber turned to his daughter with quite a different tone.

OCT. 15, 1944
Dear Valerie — It is Sunday afternoon now and I am sitting outside of my tent in the shade. I will list the main events of the day. 1. We caught two rats in my trap

last night. 2. Our chapel was dedicated as St. Andrews today. The men have made it quite a place. 3. I walked along the beach for an hour for exercise. 4. Cold lemonade for lunch. All in all, that makes a pretty nice day.

You would have enjoyed the beach. The sand is almost entirely free of gravel. The water is warm and clean with nice surf. Two or three islands show up out to sea and several ships were in sight – food for Pop probably. On the jungle side of the beach are casuarina trees that look like pines except the needle is segmented. Farther in are the sago palms, which can be split open and a starchy food like farina can be gotten. If I ever land alone in a jungle remind me to have an axe with me.

A native Melanesian just went by with a bow and arrows [with the bow being] nearly twice as long as he is tall. He grinned & showed his red teeth (stained with betel nut) and said "Lo!" and saluted. I said "Hello Boy!" and saluted also. He grinned some more and apparently considered it a very satisfactory encounter for he went on into the jungle. His shirt was blue and he had a red flower in his hair.

[General] Barker is learning to fly an airplane now [likely a Piper Cub, used for artillery observations] and is having a good time doing it. We worry about him but he doesn't. I have never seen anyone more brave than he is. All thru the fighting he is going about where Japs can shoot at him. So far they have missed him. I hope they keep on missing....

Goodbye now Little Sweet. I'll be along to see you some day not too distant. I love you — Your Daddy, Wilber

x · o · ø · o · x

OCTOBER 21, 1944

Dear Hale — ... Today we test fired three of our howitzers to be sure they were still accurate. I guess we can count on them dropping the shells where we want. We have done quite a lot of firing while here and one went out of adjustment. Of course it is pretty important to keep my guns accurate because we usually fire so close to our own friends. It is a pretty hard decision to make when the infantry wants you to fire at a target 150 yards away when you know that about five percent of your rounds are due to fall a hundred yards short of the target. The infantry like to have the artillery shells fall about forty yards away provided they don't get hit by fragments. When we fire close in, I tell the infantry commander I'm willing to do it if he wants me to do it, but that I'll kill some of his men. Then if a few fragments nick a few, they feel lucky; if no one is even hurt they think I'm wonderful. I've been very lucky in this and hope to stay so....

Goodbye now Son. I love you and hope everything is OK with you. — Your Daddy, Wilber

x · o · ø · o · x

The planned move to the Philippine island of Leyte took place on October 20, 1944, without the 43rd Division. Wilber wrote Norma the next day.

OCT. 21, 1944
Dearest Nana — Your letters of Oct 5 + 6 came a day or so ago. It is so nice to get even short letters from you. Maybe it's because I love you.

MacArthur finally decided he could go into the Philippines without my help. I felt worried for him but he seemed to make out OK in Leyte without me – most disillusioning! … The Tokyo radio commentator has annihilated the 43d again. She calls us, "the 43d Div. the Murderers of Munda." Very flattering to be remembered so long by Tokyo and so favorably!

This is Sunday, Oct. 22 and we are listening to the McArthur [sic] reports. Possibly you are listening also.…

DeBlois' Service Battery achieved a combination of renown and notoriety the other day. Three of his men stole a truck out of the motor park, speeded past one of General Wing's staff majors so fast he couldn't catch them and drove down the beach to the front lines.

That didn't mean a thing to them because the infantry had already picked up the souvenirs there, so they went on thru the U.S. Outpost line and found a new road previously not known to our troops. They drove farther into the Jap area than any of our infantry patrols have gone before or since. Finally they came to a hill and climbed it and saw a lot of Jap cooking fires all around them – "hundreds of them" so they decided "to get the h—l out of there." Just then some Japs jumped them and they killed one or two, captured a Jap Medical Captain complete with instruments + kit and a Jap Lt. of a new kind of Jap unit not yet known to U.S. G-2s [intelligence branch]. Then they loaded Jap pistols, rifles, and a saber, field glasses and other junk in the truck and came home. Results: 1. The G-2 section wants to decorate them; 2. The G-3 section [operations and security] issued orders that passes are required to get outside the main U.S. bivouac area; 3. The Div. Ordnance Officer wants to court martial them for damage to the truck; 4. The Provost Marshall wants to try them for speeding.

It's DeBlois' problem and I'm glad. I love you Sweet Heart. — Wilber

x · o · ø · o · x

VICTORY AND HOMECOMING   PART I: COMBAT, NEW GUINEA

OCT. 24, 1944
Hello Wife — It's the end of another tiring day. I worked all morning computing boat cargoes. One of the interesting aspects of any move here is not, "What do we have?" but "How much do we think we can do without?" Space on ships is critical during the first few waves that go ashore. This afternoon I studied artillery, checked on training, went out in the jungle to a position and came back panting + perspiring. It was a little consolation to find after I walked back that one of my men bet 10 to 1 that I would be walking. The other fellow thought I would hitch a ride.

The other day I sent another box home. It contained some wool uniforms, books, and a pitcher. The radio for Valerie's Christmas went in a separate box. The pitcher was one we used at the officer's mess when you + I were at [Fort] Lewis [Washington State] in 1931. In Sept. 1940 it went to California and in Dec. 1941 was on the way to the Philippines but on Dec. 7 was turned back to Hawaii. Next it showed up in Guadalcanal. I didn't see it in New Georgia but it was there, but I found it on a shelf in a N[ew] Z[ealand] camp area. The 152 [i.e., Wilber] brought it to New Guinea where it saw its third combat. I decided since I paid for it back in 1931 that I would claim it and send it to you for a present. I hope you will like it and think of Carroll [Knowles] + Don [Downen] + me when you use it.

> This pitcher was solid white porcelain with a small colored emblem of the 161st Infantry emblazoned on its side near the top edge. Wilber bought it to replace an old grapefruit juice can they had been using to serve coffee on maneuvers in Washington State. It stayed with the 161st until Wilber happened to see it in New Zealand, probably in the tent of one of his Washington State friends. It was part of our household for many of the postwar years and my sister Valerie had it after Norma died. In 1983 Valerie still had it, but it was later damaged when water froze in it, whereupon she threw it out not realizing its amazing history. I practically cried upon hearing this, and so did she when told its story. Many artifacts that illustrate this story have been lost, given away, or damaged. I think of the bent bullet that wounded Wilber, the kaori gum he sent me from New Zealand, and the telescopic gun sight from the Baanga guns. Keeping such things amid the bustle of real life is always difficult. By the time their value is appreciated, they are often lost. Stories like this one, however, help to keep the memories of them alive.

I've been reading Aristotle recently. It is the first time I've ever read him. So far, not interesting, but challenging. The copy of Plato and of Milton may interest you. I liked Plato better than Paradise Lost.

I doubt there were many other readers of such material on those New Guinea beaches!

Our OP [Observation Post] was the hottest place I've ever seen since I left home. A temperature of 110° was measured in the shade there and we weren't in the shade. I never came so near to a heat stroke in my life. However I still prefer it to mud and ice.

Oct. 27 — Last night we saw Bob Hope + Dorothy Lamour in "They Got Me Covered." It was a lot of fun and I wished you could have seen it with me.

Night before last wasn't so pleasant for me. We were firing into the jungle when the phone rang with the cheerful tidings that we had fired into some [of our] troops and wounded four. When these things happen, it is always interesting to see who has confidence in you and expects it to be an erroneous report, who just expects to make a thorough check-up to find the truth before acting, and who immediately assumes you guilty and hastens to point out that the Bn. CO is responsible. Of course the Bn. CO is responsible and he knows so many different men could make mistakes and cause things like this. He is confronted with the necessity first of determining for himself if his Bn. is guilty or innocent and next of establishing that innocence so definitely that no one can question it. That means outside officers checking the laying of the guns, the records of the fire, the charts and points of impact. These are the things that lead to exoneration or the "Board" [court martial].

So our firing stopped about 8:00 P.M. and the evidence was collected and a preliminary hearing held at about 9:30. Fortunately (Thank God for a good Bn!) I could prove all my rounds were falling at least a mile from where the men were wounded. That still left the fact that there were casualties unexplained. Since they were Allied troops [probably Australian] there were a lot of generals excited about it. I was sure glad I was in the clear this time, altho eventually something like this may land on my doorstep. The next morning it developed that the four soldiers had been trying to disassemble a dud mortar shell for souvenirs, so our Allies were no doubt glad they had been courteous the night before. Incidentally Jim Ruhlin [a fellow officer and Bangor friend from prewar days] was in a position to make things difficult for me but conducted himself most fairly. He told me afterward that he had made so many mistakes in artillery himself that he knew I might be caught by an error but that he figured the facts would settle everything. I thanked him the next day. These are the things that put grey hair on artillery commanders' head[s].

The checkup on me when Gen. Krueger [Sixth Army commanding general] said I was firing on his airport was even more thorough. Berry + Barker + Files [all of divisional artillery headquarters] were practically petrified because they couldn't conceive of Krueger [a four-star general] being even questioned. In fact

I received the impression it would be discourteous to prove that I hadn't fired on his airfield. I'm not so easily impressed and did have a personal interest in the case, so I insisted on clearing myself. Of course all this firing on targets so close to our own troops is the sort of thing that everyone just loves as long as it just clears them. There is only about fifty yards difference between being a hero and a heel. Wish me luck and don't think I haven't appreciated what I've had to date.

> General Krueger's postwar memoir mentioned this event [Krueger, p. 73]. On July 23, 1944, he had flown to Aitape from Hollandia "but [our plane] was unable to land at Tadji airdrome because of our own artillery test-firing from within the perimeter, which for lack of radio contact we could not stop." I imagine there was hell to pay and a lot of scrambling for explanations by the brass at Aitape.

Time here really flies and that gives me courage to keep on. The Nimitz-Kinkaid naval victory [naval Battle of Leyte Gulf] is on the radio. That speeds the day I'll take you in my arms, carry you upstairs, undress you, toss you on the bed and say, "There you are Mrs. B. and there you stay for the next two weeks." — XXXØØØ, Wilber

> The historic naval Battle of Leyte Gulf was a series of naval actions over several days (October 24–26). It arose from an all-out Japanese attempt with its surface fleet to defeat the Allied landings on Leyte. Allied occupation of Leyte would isolate Japan from its conquered territories and its oil supplies. Although there were serious Allied blunders and losses (three light or escort carriers, two destroyers, and one destroyer escort), Japanese naval losses were huge (four carriers, three battleships, ten cruisers, and perhaps 11 destroyers). Japan's attempt to block the invasion had clearly failed.
>
> Thereafter the surviving Japanese heavy warships were largely not deployed because of oil shortages. In this action, the Japanese first introduced suicidal "kamikaze" air attacks wherein piloted planes carrying torpedoes or bombs would strive to crash directly into Allied ships. Kamikaze attacks became a major threat to U.S. ships in later encounters.

x · o · ø · o · x

> Wilber's attention turned again to his father, with news of an earthquake, inspections, and his unit's readiness for combat. The pressure arising from preparations for the upcoming combat was intensifying.

OCT. 27, 1944
Dear Father — It's late at night and a strong breeze is making the surf thunder along the beach about 200 yards from my tent. You may have read of an earthquake some time ago. It really gave us some high waves and some installations had to move rather hurriedly. We have frequent quakes here but of course there are no buildings to fall.…

> In July 1998, a major but localized tsunami—originating from an earthquake just off the coast—struck barely 20 miles west of Aitape, and more than 2,200 people were killed. It was not clear that the armies camped on the New Guinea coastline in 1944 fully appreciated the potential danger of their locations.

This has been a strenuous month for me, but the hazards have been of the diplomatic and administrative type. We have been attached to two different Armies and made a part of two different Corps. All four of these headquarters very properly wanted to know how good we were and proceeded to deluge us with inspectors. I couldn't get a haircut without an inspector checking on the barber. We've adopted the "latest" modes in tents, truck parks, shops, dispatch systems, urinals, mess halls, [and] incinerators four times. One inspection crew liked soup so we had soup on our menus until the "stew" proponents came along.

Eventually we were so used to it, it became routine. In one battery at 1:00 A.M., the First Sergeant [called] an emergency formation to get some men on a ship. After the whistle blew, I heard a disgusted voice in the night call "Hq. Btry! Fall in for inspection" [as if the inspectors would show up at 1 A.M.].

The battalion has shown up well, and I've been able to be proud of them. They don't yet have the fire in them that the 169th did, but they do have a stubborn pride in doing things well that will carry them a long way. I'll bring the spark out when the combat gets tough. It is better I think to save that for the tight places. If they were too high now, they would slump later if combat is delayed too long.… I love you and hope everything is OK with you. — Wilber

> Wilber thought of his battalion like a sports team. He strove to bring it to peak performance at the most critical times.

x·o·ø·o·x

> Here, Wilber described the unit's chapel to 12-year-old Valerie and asked her to keep a secret. He wrote, unknowingly, on little Gale's first birthday.

OCT. 29, 1944
Dear Valerie — This is Sunday morning and I have just gotten back from church. Our chapel is called St. Andrews and the men built it. The altar is covered with red and white parachute. The flower vases are polished brass shell cases and the candlesticks are made of the same material. Seats are planks on cocoanut logs and the roof is scrap canvas. The men have planted young palms around the sides for walls and to make it prettier. I wish you could see it for it is very nice.…

There is a secret I want to tell you. Will you be sure not to tell anyone not even Hale and especially not Nana? It is about her X-mas present. It may not come in time for Christmas, so I'm sending you a picture of it to hide. If her present is late please put the picture in an envelope on the Christmas tree for her. I am relying on you so don't forget. The present is some sterling knives, forks, and spoons. She wanted some a long time ago and I had to ask her to wait then because I couldn't afford it. Since she was so nice to wait, I want to surprise her now. I hope you are as helpful to your husband someday. Goodbye, Secret Girl. I love you and hope you are being especially good. — Your Pop. Wilber

> This silverware was the Stradivari pattern by Wallace, reminiscent of a violin scroll; it is still in the family.

x·o·ø·o·x

NOV. 8, 1944
How about a little chat, Wife of Mine? — Two of your letters came today. One post dated the 25th and one the 29th Oct. They were nice letters too and I read them twice and now for the third time.

Nov. 9 — Another day is here. Last night I was so sleepy that I went to bed at seven o'clock, and this morning Waldo had a hard time waking me at a quarter of six. My back has been bothering me lately and I've not been sleeping well, but last night I had a grand sleep. The back business comes with the peep riding and I've had a lot of it recently [up and down the coast].

So we know who is the same president now. Anyway I still hold to the fact that the majority of the people should have what they want, and I find myself in the permanent minority.…

> Democratic President Franklin Delano Roosevelt had defeated Republican Thomas E. Dewey 432 to 99 in the electoral college. During World War II, the quarter-ton jeep was widely known as a peep.

I wrote a memorandum on artillery forward observers recently and was told it was the best directive seen out here yet. The F.O.s are what makes or breaks [sic] a unit in combat and was what made the 169th so outstanding. That is why I spent so much time up front. I could help them and keep them in an aggressive mood and see that they had what they needed. Besides it's more fun up there most of the time.

Nov. 11 (Armistice Day!) — This letter is getting to be a serial but I'm sure you realize that it is because I am trying to "keep all six balls in the air at once." You seem to be the seventh ball and I've dropped it a few times. Today is very comfortable so far (0800).

Last night was cool and I drove about 20 miles along the beach + thru jungle trails. Along the beach the starlight and car lights made the surf mysterious and depressive, almost ominous. The waves would come rolling in dark and seem to grow and grow in height then all at once they would break with a deep boom and thud as if they were dropping explosives to tear away the beach. The backwash of the previous wave would meet the incoming one and they appeared to struggle for supremacy. High columns of water and foam spewed up into the air as in gestures of anger and hatred. In contrast, the beach in the car lights was all silver and diamonds. The foam left by the receding wave made thousands of little bursting bubbles each one glistening like jewels. Hundreds of big and little crabs frightened by the light skated sidewise along the beach and across the beach. Each one appeared ivory white. The contrast between the beach and the sea was absolute; the one was a fairyland while the other suggested Beowulf and Neptunic strife.

On the way down to this position area to which I was going, I traveled an old jungle road. Along one side was a swamp, which occasionally became a lagoon. It was as noisy as an Indiana pond in June. The air was full of fireflies, katydids, mosquitos. Snakes were crawling across the road. We have pythons here but the ones I saw were pale green. Big green frogs hopped along in the car lights and one jumped on the radiator and rode almost a half-mile. He was a tree climbing variety because he climbed up right in the middle of the windshield and stuck on there like an incubus. (I wonder what an incubus really looks like.) Bats with wingspread up to two feet were upset by the lights and flew around the car, sometimes so close I could reach them with my hands. Fallen trees in places arched over the road and everywhere an almost solid mat of vines and palms made it an almost complete tunnel. I didn't see any Jap bones, but I knew they had been there when we fought along this trail not too long ago for I saw them then. You have no idea of all the noises of the night jungle. Ben Ames Williams [American novelist, 1889–1953] could write even more morosely in this environment than in Maine. If I'm ever left here I'll send you a series of stories for "Weird Tales," then go out on the beach and write fantasies.

> Physically the ride was an endurance contest. I'm still lame, but it was a different page in my Jungle Book. I love you Dearest. You are my own sweet wife and I'd rather be with you than in any book. — XXXOOO Wilber

These descriptions of the beach and the jungle at night are absolutely poetic.

x · o · ø · o · x

Wilber brought Norma up to date on the Waldo Fish affair. Fish, Wilber's executive officer, had had a close relationship in New Zealand with a "Margaret" (not her real name). At the time, he was married to a Rhode Island woman widely described to me as a wonderful person, and they had a son about five years old. Wilber knew and liked Margaret. During my investigations in the 1980s, I met and talked with both Waldo and Margaret, as described in Book 2.

NOV. 19, 1944
Dearest Wife — … "Margaret" will be very glad to know you have the [napkin] rings and that you like them. Her husband was killed in the early years of the war. She and one of my officers are very much in love, but the situation is complicated by the fact that the officer [Waldo Fish] is married. They are both fine people and I presume the wife is also, so I am afraid someone will be hurt. She [the wife] has shown an honest attitude in the matter (you see the officer tells me all), and I don't know why I should judge any of the parties concerned. I have tried to be disinterested but understanding in the whole thing. She [the wife] may mention some of this to you on the assumption that you would know. I suppose, in fact I know, there are a good many such situations growing out of the war. I know you will understand because of the Hoosier boy [Wilber] who, not caring for Indiana girls, goes to Washington and finds the sweetest one [Norma] in the whole world.… — Good Night Pearl Without Price. I love you Wilber

My queries in 1984 revealed that Margaret was still married in 1944 according to registry records, though she may have been separated from her husband. He had not been killed in the war; another relative had been. It seems that she had not been completely honest with Fish. Wilber's nonchalant attitude about the breakup of Fish's marriage was likely wrenching for Norma; she had invested herself totally in preserving her marriage by the move to Bangor.

x·o·ø·o·x

    Wilber again turned poetic, this time for Valerie, about the beauty of fireflies in a hibiscus hedge.

NOV. 21, 1944

Dear Sweet Valerie — It is late at night but I want to tell you of something beautiful that I saw tonight. I had been out in the jungle and was coming back in the dark. There were a few fireflies in the woods winking their lights on & off. This was nothing new for we often see them here.

    Later I came past the foundations of a house that the Japs had burned. It must have been a lovely place to live for it overlooked the ocean and had once had a beautiful garden about it. This morning I noticed the hedges along the walk and around the garden were hibiscus. Hibiscus is a beautiful red flower that the natives often wear in their hair. It grows on a pretty bush and is common in gardens in the tropics.

    Tonight as I came back in the dark I noticed a lot of fireflies in the old garden. I went down to see them and found they were collecting in the hibiscus hedge. I walked to the entrance of the old front walk and saw a real fairyland right out of Fantasia only more wonderful. There were actually hundreds of fireflies in every hibiscus shrub and the walk glittered and glowed with myriads of little flashes until it was almost light enough to read large print.

    It really looked as if each leaf was a little stage on which a little fairy was dancing with her magic wand flashing as she danced. I wished you could have been with me because we could have enjoyed it for hours together. The rows of hedge looked like Christmas trees only they had more lights.

    Good night Darling. I love you and on Thanksgiving I'll be so thankful for my dear family. — XXXOOO Wilber (Pop)

x·o·ø·o·x

    It was now Thanksgiving and Wilber wrote several letters on that theme, the first to me.

NOV. [23], 1944

Dear Son Hale — This is early Thanksgiving morning (before breakfast). I am sitting in my canvas chair with slippers on and my sox pulled up outside my pants to keep the mosquitos out. We have a lot to be thankful for this time, don't we? … I'm thankful too for good health, for good officers and men, for a chance to fight for the things for which my country is fighting, for a good tent, for my chairs, for all the

VICTORY AND HOMECOMING   PART I: COMBAT, NEW GUINEA

interesting things I've seen and done, for the beautiful things I've seen, and more than anything else for the family waiting for me in Maine.

One of my men has made me a new knife. It is the finest I've ever seen. The blade is six inches long narrow and tapered all the way to the point. The point is needle sharp and both edges are sharp. The hilt is faced with silver next to the blade and the handle is made of rings of plastic with occasional leather rings. At the base of the handle is a 1/4 inch of silver to which is soldered a Lt. Col's silver oak leaf. The plastic is colored yellow, red and blue by painting its edges and center hole before assembling it. Here is an outline of the handle [sketch]. The handle is flat so I can carry it inside my sleeve.

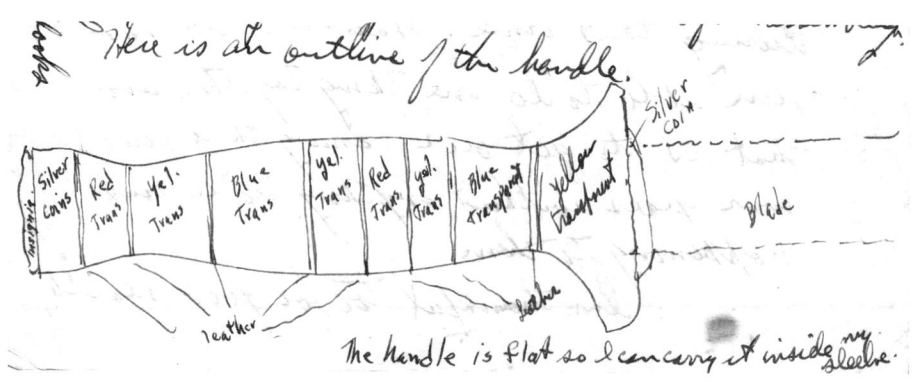

Sketch by Wilber of a knife made for him [letter 11/23/44]. The lieutenant colonel's silver maple-leaf insignia was affixed to the silver coins at the left end, which were tapered to match the shape of the insignia at the leftmost coin. The transparent rings of plastic of the handle were in different colors—the edges and center hole were painted before assembly— and were separated by pieces of leather. From the left, the labeled colors are: red, yellow, blue, yellow, red, yellow, blue, and yellow. The blade emerged from another silver coin and was razor sharp on both edges.

It's breakfast time – dried eggs, I hope. They are really good scrambled. Turkey for dinner, three months supply of beer (seven cans). It looks like a good Thanksgiving – but hot. I love you. — Your father, Wilber

I kept that knife for some time, but naturally never carried it around; it was lethal. Note in the previous two letters that the topics Wilber chose for Valerie and me tended to be gender specific, along the lines of the thinking in those days.

x·o·ø·o·x

42

THANKSGIVING DAY [NOV. 23, 1944]

Happy Thanksgiving Dearest [Norma] — We do have so many things to be thankful for and you are one of the most precious.…

Don't mention it to a soul, not even the children but I wish you would be thinking whether I should stay in the army as a profession after the war is over. Two Reg[ular] Army Generals have thought it would be possible that I wouldn't lose too much rank. It may be the best financial plan we could adopt in view of my long absence from chemistry. One of the main items to consider is whether you would be unhappy because we would be outside the inner West-Point clique. I'm thinking of it, knowing it's too early to know what the opportunities would be after the war, so don't be perturbed. I just wondered if you would like it or not. — I love you, Wilber

> Wilber was beginning to think about the postwar period, and was concerned about his competence in chemistry after a long absence from it. Did his comment about the "West Point clique" suggest that Norma would be more concerned about status than he, or was he expressing his own doubts? He was not a socializer and may have been worried about how he would fare in a more social peacetime army. Of course, such a path might not have been available to him anyway in a shrinking postwar army.

x · o · ø · o · x

NOV. 23, 1944

Dear Father — This is a little early for my Nov. letter but in these days I write when I can. We have really been busy lately. I go around with my tongue hanging out and wondering just what I'm not doing that I should be doing. Being commander actually means no escape from the responsibility. I work at it all day and dream about army and artillery at night, then wake up in the night and make notes. It's a great life, but one always has the feeling of being just one jump ahead of some mishap or omission. I'll be glad when it's over.…

Things are going well here and I have much to be thankful for today. I hope the winter isn't too severe in Indiana and that you and mother are well. Paul's wife just wrote. She and Paul are well and very exited about the expected baby. Just in case I can't write later, this is a Merry Christmas to you. — I Love you, Wilber

> The pressure was now on in full force for the unit's embarkation for its next phase of combat, a month hence. Wilber's "feeling of being one jump ahead of some mishap or omission" clearly characterized the burden of command in busy times.

On November 24, Tokyo was bombed by 111 B-29 bombers based in the recently captured Mariana Islands. The conquest of Leyte Island in the Philippines was proving to be a difficult task in the face of determined Japanese resistance in mountainous country. On December 7, an additional American division would land on the west coast at Ormoc. That quickly brought the campaign to a close, with organized Japanese resistance ending late that month.

3

"You can be sure we'll take care of Mother"

Aitape
November–December, 1944

The buildup to the invasion of Luzon in the Philippines dominated Wilber's last month in New Guinea, but he also had a new concern, placed on him by his sister Mary. On November 20, Mary had written Wilber a V-mail letter (now lost) notifying him that their father had had a heart attack on November 11 and was seriously ill. On November 25, she wrote an update. But it took two weeks or more for these letters to reach Wilber, so he would not get this latest one until early December.

SAT. A.M. – NOV 25, 1944
Dear Wilber — Glad I can give you better news about Father's condition, which though still "critical" is much improved. The fever has left him and his heart is slower and steadier and most of the fluid has left his lungs. The doctor says he is "not out of the woods" yet and can take a turn for the better or worse very quickly – in fact three of the six nights this week both Mother + I thought would be his last.

We have to be with him constantly day and night not only because of his heart but his kidney condition. I sleep from 8 P.M. – 2 A.M. + Mother from 2–8 A.M. conditions being good, and we are supposed to sleep some during the day but never seem to manage that for washings are heavy, we have many callers both day + night and then there is farm work, cooking + housework to divide between us with one always with Father. Dr. says he is better off at home than in a hospital for here he is more content + strangers being around worries him and so it is up to us. Hope all is well with you and yours. Will write as things develop. — Your sister, Mary

VICTORY AND HOMECOMING   PART I: COMBAT, NEW GUINEA

x·o·ø·o·x

NOV. 25 [1944]
Beloved [to Norma] — I've just seen [the movie] "Mark Twain" and I want to tell you how much his wife reminded me of you. You have always been so much help to me, keeping my "chin up" and showing your faith in me....

Nov. 28 — ... My back still troubles me but not seriously. I had an X-ray, which showed a slight previous injury but nothing else. The Doc. said I had a very young back so maybe it's growing pains. It only bothers me at night so I'm not concerned about it.

Did I tell you Capt. Mushik received a wire [that] his father had died very unexpectedly of heart trouble. Don is pretty badly shaken by it. It seems the family finances are in a mess too. His two brothers are in Europe and his sisters + mother aren't very capable of handling the situation. I was able to arrange for an advance to the Bn. of one officer's rotation leave for him. He will have 30 days at home, which may help. This is probably my leave he is using but it seemed the thing to do....

My arm is around you especially on those times I don't write. Don't forget. — XXXOOO Your Husband Wilber

> Wilber may have inadvertently given away the leave he could use in the event of his own father's death, but he was still unaware of his father's illness. As commander in the face of new action, it is unlikely he would have made use of it.

x·o·ø·o·x

NOV. 30, 1944
Dear Pistol Packing Mamma — Happy Birthday to you [her 39th]....

The curse of all people will be on the Germans for generations. I consider their crime much greater than Japan's because they know what they do. The Japs have never been taught, as they will be now, that a people is responsible for its ruler's crimes. No German could possibly be free of guilt for these crimes against people except those Germans who died fighting [against] the things their government furthers.... This is no way to write a birthday letter. However the more I think of these things, that much more am I convinced the individual is accountable if he does not fight evil just as much as if he actively entered into the evil. As I said before, the Japs are just uncivilized dangerous animals that must be disciplined for the good of their neighbors. They haven't known Christianity as the Germans did. Their education is just beginning. (End of Indignation)

CHAPTER 3   *You can be sure we'll take care of Mother*

Wilber was evidently referring to the Nazi death camps. The Russians had been liberating them since the previous summer—the first liberation by the American Army would not come until April 1945. He felt strongly that individual German citizens were responsible for letting the camps happen. He tacitly assumes that individual American citizens would have reacted better under similar circumstances.

On December 1, the Australian 6th Division relieved the 43rd Division at Aitape [Barker, p. 141; Williams, p. 342]. Intense preparations continued for the Luzon invasion; embarkation was just a few weeks away.

Dec. 2. — … Re the children's allowance, I had considered it their part of the family income that we might spend for non-essentials. It is certainly true tho that they should do their share of the service work of the home to be entitled to any of the extras we can have. Valerie very definitely should be doing some daily household duty.… In the same way, Hale should also have daily house + yard duties which he does for the keeping of the home.… — Love to all of you. Wilber.

Wilber's father Hale died on December 3 of heart failure. But Wilber was not even yet aware of Hale's November 11 heart attack and its continuing aftermath.

x · o · ø · o · x

DEC. 5, 1944

Dearest Wife — … Day before yesterday, [Major] Fish + I and Lt. Col. Devine (Inf) went out to dinner on a ship [USS Fayette, APA-43]. We were the guests of the Captain and the Commodore, named respectively [Capt. J. C.] Lester and [Capt. D. L.] Ryan. It was nice to eat off a linen tablecloth with silver and ice water and napkins. It was a good dinner too, fresh potatoes (fried), steak, fish, and ice cream + coffee. Both the Capt. + Commodore were regular navy men – "four stripes" which makes them equivalent to our colonels.…

I must stop now, Lover, and get to work. Don't get too cold in Maine. I'm OK and am still in love with you. — Your husband, Wilber

Devine was the executive of the 103rd Infantry, the unit usually supported by Wilber's artillery. In December 1980, Waldo Fish, Wilber's executive officer, described for me this visit to the Fayette with these words: "Bill got very drunk aboard ship with the Captain. When we got back to his tent, he simply collapsed onto his bunk and did not move. I never saw him drunk any other time." I wonder about this story because U.S. Navy ships have been dry since 1914 by U.S. Navy regulation. Did the commodore and the captain both subvert this regulation? Perhaps.

This was the ship Wilber's unit would sail on 20 days later. This visit was surely to make arrangements for their rehearsals of the Luzon amphibious landings.

x · o · ø · o · x

A formal photograph of Norma had arrived, to Wilber's great pleasure. Eight months earlier, on April 6, 1944, from a New Zealand hospital (for minor maintenance), he had requested such a photo "so you could watch me and smile at me while I work." He may already have had studio portraits of Valerie and me that were taken in Mississippi in the summer of 1942.

DEC. 7, 1944
My Lovely Beautiful Darling — Today is Christmas for me because the present I've wanted so long came today. Wife, I'd forgotten how really beautiful you are. It brings back to me all the sweetness of you and the sunshine of my life with you.

I'm so proud of you and your picture. Capt. Ackerson said, "Oh! Is that your daughter?" When I said you were my wife, he said very seriously, "Why, I would have thought she was only about twenty two," then went for his mother's picture to show me how young she looked too. Maj. Fish said "She's not your wife!" Such diplomacy! Lt. Col. Sutton said, "Is that your wife? When was that picture taken? Ask her if she will be busy on two years from Thursday?" So you see what I mean when I say it's my nicest present.... I like it too because you wore the 169th [FA] pin. [It showed the emblem or "coat of arms" of Wilber's former unit.] They will always be the Munda boys to me too. I'll always wish I might have taken them all the way. If the 152 does as well in the next big job, you could send me another photograph wearing their insignia....

Last evening I went walking along the beach as I often do. The surf was high and made wonderful music as well as a magnificent picture. Great ships were out on the horizon and I wondered how it could be I watched the sea from New Guinea when once it had seemed so strange to see it in the U.S. I wished I were Harold [Parker] Wheeler [Band Director at Washington State College in the 1930s] for I was sure he could have composed a symphony from what I saw and felt and heard last evening. Now no one else will know how beautiful and strange and unreal my beach was last evening. Chemists can't compose.

I think this chemist could, and did!

... I'm so glad I'm your husband. — Wilber XXXOOO

CHAPTER 3   *You can be sure we'll take care of Mother*

VICTORY AND HOMECOMING   PART I: COMBAT, NEW GUINEA

Studio portraits of Valerie and me, taken in 1942 in Hattiesburg, Mississippi. [PHOTO: MCVADON]

Previous page: Studio portrait of Norma Sparlin Bradt, November 1944. She was wearing the insignia pin (barely visible at bottom center) of the 169th Field Artillery Battalion that Wilber had sent her. Wilber requested a photo in April 1944 [letter 4/6/44] and was delighted to receive this one in New Guinea eight months later [letter 12/7/44]. He expressed admiration again when it resurfaced in his belongings after the Philippine landings [letters 2/26/45 and 7/15/45]. In the July 1945 letter, he wrote "Your picture and the children's pictures are looking down on me making my hut a home." [PHOTOGRAPHER: UNKNOWN]

CHAPTER 3   *You can be sure we'll take care of Mother*

x · o · ø · o · x

DEC. 7, 1944
Dear Mary [Wilber's sister] — Your V-mail of Nov. 20 just came [that Father is ill]. You can imagine that it was quite a shock to me. I had received a letter from Father written early in November and thought then he was in particularly good spirits. Of course out here we never know how much you people at home keep from us because of the morale propaganda.

> It was a tenet of the times that those at home did not write discouraging news to overseas soldiers and sailors lest the resulting demoralization would make them more vulnerable in combat.

I certainly hope you know by now that you were too pessimistic about Father's ability to recover. If he really wants to, I'm sure he has reserves, which will help him now. Your being there too, I know will give him comfort and care that will mean a lot to him. It helps me too to know you are there and I appreciate how hard it is for you.

How is Mother standing all of this? It must be terribly hard for her too. Father had given me the impression she was not so well as he was. If there is anything I can do from here for her please tell me because I doubt if she would. She may think all the past misunderstandings and troubles indicate a lack of affection on my part. I still love her as much as ever even tho I have shown it but poorly.

Thank you for writing, Mary. Please keep me informed as often as you can. In the meantime I hope and pray that Father is well on the way back to recovery. That would be the nicest Christmas possible and I wish it for you with all my heart.

I'm enclosing a note for Father and here is love and sympathy for you. — Wilber

x · o · ø · o · x

> Still unaware of his father's death on December 3, Wilber began a letter to him with an awkward attempt at humor. The elder Hale would not have been pleased by President Roosevelt's election to a fourth term.

DEC. 7, 1944
Dear Father — I'm sure you are taking the Roosevelt Reign too seriously. It would have been all right to let your beard grow until FDR was defeated but you rather went to an extreme to take to bed. After all you don't want to give the Democrats that much recognition.

Seriously tho I'm more sorry than I can tell that you are having trouble. I hope that by the time this letter reaches you that you will be back on your feet and feeling fine. Remember I'm counting on seeing you after this war and that will be some time yet.

Yesterday I ate some "cooking" bananas raw and I'm sick as a dog myself. Of course I've no one to blame but myself so all I can do is charge it up to education by experience.

Please Father take care of yourself and fight this thing thru until you are OK again. However if it is too much trouble, you can be sure we'll take care of Mother. — I love you, Wilber

> Sadly, on this, my own 14th birthday, my grandfather was no longer with us. After his death at age 73 on December 3, his wife Elizabeth carried on. During her more than 16 years of widowhood, she lived alone on the farm with her cats and chickens and maintained a large garden and fruit trees. Neighbors would look in on her frequently as would her daughter Mary who lived and worked in nearby Cincinnati. Her other children lived in Wisconsin, Warsaw (Indiana), and Washington, D.C. Neighbor Chester Henderson continued to farm the cropland for her, an arrangement begun in 1939 when he was just 19. Henderson died at 87 in 2007; his father had been Wilber's boyhood friend.
>
> Elizabeth continued reaching out to her grandchildren with chatty letters about her life on the farm and always welcomed their visits. I was never aware of any stubbornly held hurts. (She had been deeply insulted, she felt, by Wilber's sudden marriage to Norma in 1927 in a distant city without Wilber's family present; and, she had refrained from writing Wilber while he was overseas because of a spat with him and Norma about finances in February 1941, detailed in Book 1.)

x·o·ø·o·x

DEC. 9, 1944

Dear Nana — … I had a letter from Mary yesterday telling of a heart attack that Father had Nov. 11. It apparently was a very severe one and it looked as if he were going to die. On Nov. 20 he had rallied somewhat and they were beginning to be hopeful; then he had another relapse. His lungs + kidneys are making trouble and Mary isn't very optimistic. The doctor said at best he wouldn't be out of bed for 6–8 weeks but that his lungs were clearing a little.…

Wilber was far out of the loop on this because of the mail transit times. Norma surely already knew of Hale's death when Wilber wrote this. In my navy days, urgent private messages could be sent by radio over official channels. During World War II, such channels were either not available or the Bradts were not aware of them. Mary did not write to Wilber about Hale's November 11 heart attack until the 20th. This may have been due to the prohibition against sending bad news overseas, which might have done more harm than good because soldiers were then free to imagine the worst.

Did I ever tell you who my higher infantry officers are now? The regimental C.O. [103rd Infantry] is Col. Joseph [P.] Cleland, commonly called behind his back, "Uncle Joe." He is about my age but has white hair. I like him. His Exec is "Wallie" [Wally?] Devine (Lt. Col.) from Portland, Me. [The battalion commanders are:] … Altogether they make a pretty strong team and they are all front line soldiers, and they think I am too. I can just see myself running around with them scared half to death but wearing my best poker face. Anyway, it's interesting work if you can get it, and I can.

Wilber was to work closely with Colonel Cleland and his battalion commanders throughout the forthcoming Luzon campaign.

It begins to look as if Doug [MacArthur] has decided to quit fooling [around] in Leyte since he has landed at Ormoc. The U.S. Navy is surely trying to wipe out the memory of Pearl Harbor and we (the army) profit by it. I can imagine those boys at Ormoc are earning their pay now tho.… I love you and am so proud you are my wife even at long range. — Your husband, Wilber

x · o · ø · o · x

Valerie wanted to know whether her daddy "is or ain't."

DECEMBER 10, 1944
Dear Daughter — How is my Valerie this Christmas? Darling I hope it is a very fine Christmas and New Year for you. Do you remember our last one at home together [1940 in Bangor]. It was so much fun that I'll never forget it.…

You asked me "Is I is or is I ain't?" I'm still is, but of course one is never sure down here just for how long. Maybe I ain't and just don't know the difference. What do you think? It's a rather depressing idea isn't it?

The popular song went: "Is you is or is you ain't my baby?"

I'm interested that you know about our altar because something else happened to our chapel. In front of the altar is an open space, then logs for seats and behind

VICTORY AND HOMECOMING   PART I: COMBAT, NEW GUINEA

them is more room that becomes a mess hall. The men eat at tables in that end which is still under the same roof. Altogether it is a very long shed with a roof of scrap canvas. The other day one of the men had a truck loaded with radios and other important equipment, and it started to rain. He backed the truck into what was the back end of the chapel or the front end of the mess hall and left it there. A little later Fr. Tyler came by and saw it and WAS HE MAD? I was afraid to go to church today. Do you think I should turn Catholic? It might be safer.... Here is a big hugful of Love from Daddy. — Wilber

Capt. Barrett L. Tyler was killed by Japanese artillery on Luzon, March 14, 1945 [Barker, p. 173].

x·o·ø·o·x

Wilber maintained his connection to the University of Maine by writing Prof. Irwin Douglass, the acting head of the chemistry department in Wilber's absence. He was a good friend with whom Wilber shared some of his more private thoughts. In 1990, I visited Prof. Douglass in Maine and he shared with me his file of correspondence with Wilber.

DEC. 12, 1944

Dear Doug — Today we are having one of the movie-type tropical downpours....

My morale still seems to keep up to normal (for me) and only suffers twinges when I allow myself to remember I've been out here over two years now. Physically, I'm probably better off than if I were at the U. That is discouraging because it means no compensation [for disability] after the war, and I'll still have to earn a living mentally [with my mind]. I wouldn't know just what my present status is, but I've my suspicions. In fact, I've always had them, sometimes they grow almost into convictions, but let's not go into that. Psychologically, I find myself extremely unstable varying from a condition of absolute terror to that of extreme optimism, from interest to the ultimate of boredom but most of the time typified by a mottled-gray attitude. That, I think, accurately reports on the present status of one Bradt.

... One of the most encouraging things about democracy to me has been the able leaders we have found for our Army and Navy. When one considers the fact that we are a nation of amateurs in war and that none of our generals ever handled even a small army before 1940, it is almost a miracle that we have seen. I've had the privilege of knowing some of these men, and the most inspiring aspect of those to me has been the conspicuous "Average American" characteristics of each. The more I see of the "Average American" in war, and of all ranks, just that much more am I convinced of the real nobility of that individual. I'm not idealizing him for he is often a most annoying soul (I've one in the stockade now for about six most original offenses.), but he does have an invincibility of spirit that cannot be erased.

How I run on! Anyway, I hope all is well with the Douglasses as with me and I wish you a very Merry Christmas and a Grand New Year. — Your friend, Wilber Bradt

>   Here Wilber revealed more about his state of mind than he probably intended. By "status," he was apparently referring to his ability to earn a living using his mind, for example in chemistry. He referred to "suspicions" that sometimes "grow almost into convictions" that he was not up to earning such a living. The next sentence admitted that this was indeed a "psychological" problem. His depression, which we have heard about on several earlier occasions, was apparently moderate, but it was enough to prompt him to reveal this much to a professional colleague.
>
>   Resurrecting his chemistry career was clearly of concern to him. One could argue that his state of mind was normal for someone who had learned just five days earlier that his father had become mortally ill and had possibly even died. But Wilber also demonstrated that he could still see the positive side of his situation.

x·o·ø·o·x

>   Norma wrote a long, single-spaced, typed letter to Wilber's brother Rex nine days after their father had died. This was a letter that showed Norma in action: her quick defense of Wilber and her portrayal of the burdens she faced, along with her rather poor judgment about how her writings would be received. Norma was still very sensitive to the Bradts because of past confrontations and she responded defensively to perceived criticisms. She wrote from our home in Bangor, Maine.

December 12, 1944
Dear Rex — We address you, as you were kind enough to write Hale such a nice long letter about Father's ideals of duty, justice, and all. We agree that Father is one of the most remarkable men of our time. We read the letter, hoping to have news of Father's last hours, but only after Hale had first absorbed it seriously. Our bereavement was very real, too, and we hope that you received the flowers, and the letter we wrote, saying what we would have said to him or written, had the news of his illness come sooner....

>   She was clearly hurt by not having had an opportunity to communicate with Hale before his death, a point she was not shy about making.

Hale was very worried about your remark, that, due to your remaining in chemistry instead of going as a soldier, you would probably not have a job after the War. You said that you could have gone, and wanted to, but learned it was your duty to stay here in ordnance work. I am sure that you have done a very fine job and [made] a great contribution. You said of course you would not have the parades, medals, bonuses, nor all the glory of the soldier, but … etc. The children were much puzzled, as their values were suddenly assailed. If you will ponder, you will see why. You had just sent on Wilber's Legion of Merit medal. Valerie hotly contended that Daddy did not go to war for the Parades, Medals, and Bonuses. She said "Didn't Daddy get this medal for bravery?" Hale and I both said certainly yes, and I had to explain about you, and about Wilber.…

The indignation here was largely Norma's. Neither Valerie nor I would have had the sophistication to make such arguments. Rex was clearly sensitive to not being in uniform as this was widely viewed as shirking, and he had chosen words that Norma viewed as demeaning to Wilber. She quickly rose to Wilber's defense, but with a creative twist: she imputed her criticism to Valerie and me.

You said in a letter to me, at the same time as the defective shell episode, "I have this regard for you, at least as long as you are faithful to Wilber." All I want to say is, that our relationship to each other is our own affair, that I feel that Paul [Wilber's other brother] and Jo [his wife] and I have built up such a kinship, that it would survive even a possible rift with Wilber. When Wilber was on leave in New Zealand, he kept company with a young lady, and I have written to thank her for her many kindnesses to him. Four years is a long war, with the two years of the special kind of hell, which Wilber has had to endure. He has urged me to go out on dates, but I have somehow not felt the need for a rigorous social life.

Rex had cut closer to the bone than he probably realized, and we see how Norma had ingested Wilber's brief chaste encounters with Olive Madsen. They were not intimate (see Book 2), but Norma much later indicated that she believed otherwise. I doubt that Wilber ever "urged" Norma "to go out on dates," though he did express concern that, while "doing war work" (during her secret pregnancy), she seemed to have cut herself off from friends and family.

Rex, I am afraid that, in your letter, you showed no slightest conception of the sacrifices Wilber has made. His job is in just as much jeopardy as yours. He has been separated from chemistry for a long time, and does not really feel himself competent to step into his work at once. You at least have kept your peacetime skill, so I do not think that Hale should be made to feel that you are in peril of your job. Paul and Jo understand this, through frequent correspondence with Wilber, that life here in the States is not to be compared with jungle life, in foxholes and swamps much of the time, with constant hazard of one's life, with constant responsibility for the lives of others, with insects and snakes, and fevers, and jungle infections. One of the officers with Wilber had his feet nearly rotted off....

You boys should have some comprehension of our financial situation. Back of all considerations is Wilber's insurance, which, in case of any war accident, would pay us somewhat in the neighborhood of $38.00 per month for a period of time.... We were able to save, in New York and Washington, but cannot seem to do so here, with the extensive demands of this big house and fuel. There have been a great many repairs necessary, and, you boys may not realize it, but every little thing which goes wrong necessitates an outside workman and a charge of anything from $5.00 on up.... Recent roof job was $60 – Storm windows: merely put on $20.00.

This discussion was probably prompted by Rex mentioning the likelihood of the widowed Elizabeth needing financial support. This was a highly touchy subject dating from a heated difference of opinion between the Maine and Indiana Bradts in early 1941 (Book 1). Norma did not mention the government insurance payment of $10,000 that would come to her in the event that Wilber died in the service.

You may understand, from our small insurance, why I have kept in touch with work in the cities along the lines I know. I am prepared to take over in any emergency. Right now, with the housework and the children at home, I keep up my skill by writing all during mornings on radio scripts and books, I practice [piano] all each afternoon, begin cooking, etc., at 4 [P.M.] and work on until 12 at night on washing, ironing, mending, bookkeeping, etc. It is the only way I feel safe. And I do not mind it at all. There is no time to be bored and my writing and music are such joy that they compensate. The best radio programs are at night while I do my housework, so that is fun.

This gave a sense of Norma's life in Bangor that year, though it was a bit overplayed. She had indeed made a nice home for us. I remember how I loved the wonderful smell of baking Syrian (pita) bread wafting up to my bedroom late one night when I was sick and quite miserable with a painful earache.

For whatever financial assistance is needed [for Mother Bradt], I will cash one of the bonds. Or more, if necessary. The house is mortgaged, as you know. I make bi-yearly payments, with huge interest. One payment lacking, and p-f-f-f-t! – all we've put into it is gone, and I am determined to save this place for Wilber and the children....

After all this, she was, amazingly, prepared to help Elizabeth, but not without sacrifice! Perhaps I am overly critical of her. Indeed, it was probably important to inform the Bradts of her and Wilber's circumstances and challenges, lest they were to make unfounded assumptions.

A copy of this goes to Paul and I hope he sends it on to Mary and Ruth, Love to Douglas, Gerry, Connie Lou. — Our Sincerest, Norma

A copy of this letter also went to Wilber, and as expected, he was embarrassed. He knew that Norma was a much nicer person than this letter indicated. But when she felt threatened, her pianist's fingers would fly over the typewriter keyboard, and her anxieties would flow from them onto the paper. Rex, admirably, reacted with grace in a letter that he may not have mailed—it was found in his papers—in which he wrote, "you unloaded on me like a sister should on a brother." He, her brother-in-law, had granted her full sister status, at least on paper.

x·o·ø·o·x

Back in the palm groves of New Guinea, Wilber found that training for the next invasion was not without its misunderstandings.

DEC. 13, 1944
Dear Norma — Another day nearer to the end of this war and what a day. [General] Harold [Barker] came out where we were training and flew into quite a rage so I closed up the firing and ordered the unit back to camp. Boy was he mad! I wasn't any less so, but not so demonstrative if you know what I mean. He haled [sic] me over to his Hq and slapped a pamphlet in front of me and wanted to know why in __ I hadn't followed the instructions therein. My answer – "I've never seen it before." More fireworks. Big investigation of records to show where I had signed for it. Very embarrassing because they show I had never received it. Much rage at his message center. More rage at his staff, rage all around for everybody.

Next he hauls out [a] training memo and unfortunately it directed we do what we were doing. Not so noisy now. "Bradt do you have any questions?" Boy did I have questions; most important in my mind was "How long is this war going to last?" However I contented myself with, "Yes. What do I do now?" More earthquakes, blood all around, monkeys fainting and falling out of cocoanut trees. To

CHAPTER 3   *You can be sure we'll take care of Mother*

make a long story short the poor staff got a harangue on how could Bradt know what to do if no one informed him and why did he have to do all the coordinating. Lord, spare me from too much coordination. After the storm, "Now Bradt why don't you stay for dinner?" I didn't say why but I didn't stay. So went the 13th of December in New Guinea.

Waldo asked how we (Covill + I) came out, and we announced bruised but not beaten. Such is life where men are men and women are absent.…

I love you Sweet Wife. Don't take my story too seriously. I get paid for it. — Your Husband, Wilber

> I met the former Capt. Warren K. Covill at a luncheon meeting of 43rd Division veterans in March 1981 and asked him about this event. He had no memory of it. But he did tell me about his pivotal role during the sinking of the SS President Coolidge in late 1942 (Book 1). Original letters thankfully retain for us the memories of dramatic events that would otherwise be lost to time.

x · o · ø · o · x

> As Christmas and the embarkation for the Philippines approached, Wilber described for me some details of camp life in New Guinea.

DEC. 18, 1944

Dear Son — Seven more shopping days before Christmas and no shops. Think of the money I'm saving.…

It is late evening and I have had a shower and seen a movie. My shower is an oil drum up on some posts. The men fill it daily, and the staff officers and I usually shower after supper to get rid of the dust and sweat of the day. The movie was terrible, but I liked it.

… I've a new gas mask and a new entrenching tool, which is really just a baby shovel. When bombs and shells start dropping around, you ought to see me make the dirt fly.…

I must go to bed now, Son. I love you and hope 1945 will bring us together. — Your Daddy, Wilber

x · o · ø · o · x

> Wilber wrote to express concern for his mother's and sister's well being. He still did not know of his father's death. This letter was addressed to both of them, but he was thinking of Mary as he wrote.

VICTORY AND HOMECOMING   PART I: COMBAT, NEW GUINEA

Chaplains Joseph P. Monahan (directing) and John F. Connolly (standing rear left) rehearsing a native choir for Christmas Eve service of the 43rd Infantry Division, Aitape, New Guinea, December 18, 1944. [PHOTO: U.S. ARMY SIGNAL CORPS, SC 291084]

DEC. 20, 1944
Dear Mary and Mother — Your letter of Dec. 1 just came. I surely appreciate your taking time to write when I know you must be very tired and under a great strain. I hope you will continue to send just a note now and then even if I don't answer. There are times you know when it is impossible for me to send mail. If I fail to write, you must not feel that I'm not concerned about Father.

It must be very hard for you and Mother to do all the care alone. Can't you get someone to do the heavy work for you.... I know Mother never liked Norma, but Norma loves Father and would want to help. Father knows [that] Norma loves him and I don't think she would worry him. You know better than I how Mother would feel about her being there but if you think it would be OK, please write her and say you need her. That is all she will want.

I'm so glad your [Mary's] letter came when it did. Take care of yourself for your brother. — Wilber

> Wilber seemed totally out of touch here. It was wholly unrealistic to think that the Bradts would consider for even a minute inviting Norma to come and help. Loved ones tend to cluster around the dying, fending off even close friends, and Norma certainly had never reached that status in their minds. It's clear that Wilber's need to help in some way led to this

suggestion. He probably had vivid memories of Norma caring for him, Valerie, and me when we were ill. Norma was a wonderful, sympathetic, and unflagging caregiver. He felt she could be his proxy.

x · o · ø · o · x

Wilber finally did get word of his father's death, three weeks after the fact. He then took on the role of oldest son as best he could from such a distance. He wrote to his brothers and, here, to his sister and mother. He was extremely busy, with embarkation for the Philippines less than a week away.

DEC. 21, 1944
Dear Mother and Mary — I've just heard of our loss [Father's death]. Altho Mary had prepared me as kindly and conscientiously as possible, it was (is) still a terrible shock. If it is hard for me, I know it must have been so much worse for you. I wish I might be there and try to comfort you. You used to say, Mother, that my shoulders were good for crying. Spiritually I offer it [sic] to you now.

I'm so rushed at this time I can't even write long, so to business. The allotment to Father has been changed to your name. That may mean a delay of one or two months.… Money is a poor way to show my love for you and it has been the cause of several misunderstandings. Without wanting to revive any unpleasant memories, I want to repeat to you what I have always thought I had promised. At least it is what I've always wanted to do. That is to assure you that you need have no worry about being cared for. Also I want it to be as nearly the way you want it as possible. Mary I rely on you + Paul to keep me informed so I may be intelligently helpful. There must have been many expenses recently and I can surely assume from a third to a half of them, perhaps more.

To me Father, like Grandmother [Hale's mother, Julia Seelinger], will never die. They are part of my life and death has nothing to do with that. To me death is nothing to fear or regret except for those left lonely. I love you both and am so sorry you must bear this sorrow alone. Believe me, Father is OK now and I hope you two soon will be too. Wilber

[Marginal note:] I'll write you [Mother] within one or two days of the first of each month as I did to Father except when we are restricted by the tactical situation. Please do answer. — Wilber

The plea to his mother, "Please do answer," was heart rending—and this, from an outwardly tough wartime commander of 500 men! I have found no evidence that his mother Elizabeth, a prolific letter writer, ever wrote Wilber during the war as she did to her other offspring, most probably because of that 1941 financial dispute.

x · o · ø · o · x

DEC. 22, 1944

Darling Nana — Your letter about Father was the first word I had of his death. Mary had written most faithfully, kept me informed, and I tried to get word to you so you wouldn't be told poorly. I'm so sorry I didn't get a letter of Father's illness to you sooner.… I must stop now and get the six balls in the air again. Talking to you is a privilege that I have always prized and this is almost talking. I love you. Merry Christmas. Jan. 8 is Mary's birthday. Kisses to you – beautiful wife of mine. — XXXØØ Wilber

x · o · ø · o · x

DEC. 23, 1944

Dearest Norma — Just have time for a note. I think the Junior League is wonderful to be interested in my boys. It isn't possible to arrange now for someone to write each member so we are doing the next best thing. Forty of us are [each] requesting six books of the President [of the Junior League]. These will be addressed in 40 letters to her so the envelopes can be shown the P.M. [Postmaster]

Of course I've no idea how many books they have in mind and would be thankful for even fifty or one for each ten men. I'm enclosing a letter to the President for her files. You have no idea how much this means out here. I'm sure it will send some men home sane who might otherwise crack. We will pick the books up [as] our battalion personally-owned property and take as good care of them as we can.… — Love XXXOOO Wilber

The Junior League, a women's club in Bangor, Maine, had proposed that it provide books to the 152nd Field Artillery for the troops to read, probably at Norma's behest. However, nothing could be shipped to an overseas soldier unless the soldier had explicitly requested it. The postmaster had to be shown the letter with the request before the package could be mailed.

x · o · ø · o · x

Wilber had received from Norma a copy of her unfortunate letter to Rex. Did she send it to show how strongly she stood up to Rex on Wilber's behalf? Did she not see how hurtful it would be to Rex who had just lost his father? Wilber's response to it targeted beautifully and with understanding the underlying issues. He wrote on Christmas Eve.

DEC. 24, 1944

Dearest — Your letters of Dec. 8 and 12 came today. It sounds as if you and the children were on a pretty strenuous schedule. I should have enjoyed Hale's play and can just imagine how nice Valerie's Christmas Card design was....

> I have no memory of being in a play at Garland Street Junior High. I do remember playing in the school orchestra for assemblies and staged events.

Your letter to Rex disturbs me quite a bit. I'm sorry you wrote it. You must realize the people who are not in the service now are on the defensive in their own minds. It is very important that they justify to themselves their decision. I have always felt that we who were in the service could afford to be generous in this matter and had promised myself to try to remember to be so. After all, I am here because I want to be, not because I was ordered, therefore I should remember not to take myself too seriously. I'm sorry about the medal [Legion of Merit] having occasioned this trouble and wish I had not received it, if it becomes the cause of misunderstanding. Incidentally Valerie is right. The L. of M. is not given for heroism. It is for jobs well done.

> Wilber misremembered Valerie's putative comment: "Didn't Daddy get this medal for bravery?" [Norma letter 12/12/44]

Please don't feel badly, Lover. I know your motives were of the best and that it is natural to want to strike back. I love you, My Wife, and wish I could be with you now. This Christmas Eve, I'll be praying for you. Keep your courage a little longer and I'll be home to take a lot of worries off your soft white shoulders. — XXXOOO Wilber

x · o · ø · o · x

The next day, Christmas Day and the eve of his boarding ship for the invasion of Luzon, Wilber set aside all concerns about the army, his father, his widowed mother, and Norma's letter to Rex, and wrote "final" tributes to Norma, Valerie, and me. It would be a long (2,500 miles) voyage, half of which would be through Japanese waters. Despite the impotence of the

Japanese fleet, land-based Japanese planes with suicidal intent (kamikazes) were plentiful and a mortal threat. Transport ships full of soldiers were high-priority targets. Wilber knew that these could well be his last words to us.

CHRISTMAS DAY. [1944]
Dear Sweet Wife and children — Merry Christmas from New Guinea! I have had a very nice Christmas, thanks particularly to you and also a good dinner, thanks to Uncle Sam. The only thing lacking is my family and you have all seemed very near and dear to me last night + today. It is a beautiful day with sunshine and a breeze and a few fleecy white clouds in the sky. Everything is as peaceful here as a Christmas should be everywhere.

Today Hale I want to thank you for being such a young man about our home and for being as fine and honest as you are. I see so many boys here whose sons are getting in trouble at home and I know how terribly they worry because they can't be there. I predict that you will be a fine man like your grandfather. So now I wish you a very very happy New Year and know you will help others to have a happy 1945 also.

And you Valerie have made me thankful that you came [in]to my family. I'm so happy that you are controlling your temper better and that you are so helpful around the home. Your unselfishness and consideration for other people is one of things I love most about you. You are a very sweet and loveable daughter. I wish you a very wonderful new year.

And you, My Darling Wife, today I wish to offer you all my love. You have been such a dear sweet comrade all these years. I pray this Christmas you will find comfort and strength and serenity of spirit. I love you Golden Girl, more today than on any other Christmas Day. Thru next year, I'll be loving you more than in 1944. You grow into my heart each day. Your picture shows me that you are more lovely now than when we last were together. There are so few words to tell you of my love for you. I would much rather, My Queen, have my memories of you than the love of any other woman. You are truly a part of me. I know Dearest that we will have many wonderful years together, and these years apart will make each day of them precious days for me.

I heard an Australian Bag Pipe Band play the other day. It was the first time I'd ever heard the bagpipes. I wished you were here.…

Good bye now Loved Ones. I'll write again as soon as I can. — XXXOOO, Wilber

x·o·ø·o·x

Norma returned to her warmer and more engaging style in this letter to Rex's wife, Gerry. Wilber's chastisement, dated three days earlier would not yet have reached her. It was clear that she was aware of the unfortunate tone of her earlier letter. Connie was Rex and Gerry's seven-year-old daughter, and Dougie their year-old son.

Dec. 27 [1944]
Dearest Gerry [from Norma] — Your lovely box was overwhelming. I thought we had by mutual consent discontinued Christmas boxes, and we had only passed on some worn books + sea shells which W. sent to Connie. It grieves me that she may have thought it a gift box, and it was not. Your gifts were thoughtful + lovely. Please explain to Connie! The snaps were delightful. Dougie is so alert + snappy and bright – how we love him! His personality just sparkles.

Your letter was much appreciated. It wasn't necessary to give us so much assurance of your love + regard. We knew it was there, but always defend our "Papa" at the "drop of a hat." I know that Rex's work must be very important and feel that you are a most loyal wife and that your thoughts are generous to your "in-laws."

We don't want Rex and Paul to carry all the financial burden and know that Wilber will do + wants to do his full share. I know that it will worry him to have Mother alone on the farm and we shall both feel that Rex will be overburdened to keep up his own work + go there each weekend. I hope that a different arrangement will evolve.

Happy New Year to all of you – and many thanks for your thoughtful gifts. — Love to all, Norma B.

x·o·ø·o·x

On Christmas day, Wilber's stay on New Guinea came to an end. Training, including amphibious drills, had been completed, and the division embarked yet again on ships for another objective, the invasion of Luzon, the principal island of the Republic of the Philippines. Wilber's battalion boarded the USS Fayette on December 26, carried out a final rehearsal of amphibious landings on the 27th, and departed Aitape on the 28th.

The family at home celebrated Christmas in Bangor, their first there since the somber Christmas of 1940 when Europe was in flames and Wilber's departure was imminent. Unfortunately, I have no particular memory of that 1944 Christmas. But we surely had a decorated tree and presents, as was our custom.

As the 43rd Division's presence at Aitape came to an end, so too did the fighting on Leyte. This set the stage for landings on Luzon, the main island of the Philippines.

On the Western front in France, Luxembourg, and Belgium, the Allies were at Germany's borders by mid-September when their progress was slowed by stretched supply lines and German defenses. In a surprise move on December 16, the Germans carried out a major counterattack with concentrated resources in the Battle of the Bulge. The Allied lines in Belgium and Luxembourg were forced back with many casualties, but the defenders blocked the advance before the Germans could break out into open country. The Allied lines were restored by January 16. Both Allied and German losses were substantial.

On the Eastern front, the Russians had reached the Vistula River outside Warsaw by August 1. They remained there, outside Warsaw, until the end of the year, cruelly refusing to come to the aid of the Polish Home Army, which took up arms against the German occupiers (the Warsaw uprising, August 1 to October 2) but was destroyed by the Germans. The Russians also waited through the subsequent systematic razing of the historic city by the Germans. The Russians finally entered Warsaw on January 17, 1945. In the meantime, they had made substantial advances in the south on the Ukrainian front in Hungary and in the north toward the Baltic Sea. The major drive on to Berlin would begin in January 1945.

During this period, American industry was working full-tilt, providing the Pacific fleet with increasing numbers of combat vessels, aircraft, and landing craft. This output greatly exceeded Japanese production capabilities, which had peaked and were decreasing under ever-heavier stress, due to shortages of oil and raw materials. Nevertheless, the Japanese were determined to make Allied advances slow and costly.

Allied landings on the principal Philippine island of Luzon would take place on January 9, 1945. This major undertaking would be on the scale of the Normandy invasion, but launched from bases thousands of miles from the landing beaches. It was a huge undertaking, and Wilber would be an active, willing participant in that show.

PART II

FINAL BATTLES, LUZON

PHILIPPINE ISLANDS
JANUARY–SEPTEMBER, 1945

★ ★ ★

4

"Some minutes are worth more than years of living"

At sea en route to Luzon
December 1944–January 1945

The task forces soon to be heading to Luzon would eventually consist of hundreds of ships from many different locations in the South Pacific. There was no intermediate staging area. Upon arrival at Luzon's Lingayen Gulf, after voyages of thousands of miles, the soldiers would be deposited directly onto the beaches. Those in ships would reach the beaches in small landing craft carried by the ships themselves. Those in sea-going landing craft would debark directly onto the beaches. Wilber was about to begin an adventure that, as he noted, he "wouldn't miss … for anything."

Amphibious landings were complicated and dangerous as had been amply demonstrated at Normandy (France) six months earlier. The 43rd Division's own experiences at Munda, the Russells, and at Aitape demonstrated the need for preparation and practice. Rehearsals with all equipment had been carried out earlier at Aitape [letter 9/25/44 to father]. A final rehearsal just prior to departure did not involve the time-consuming unloading and reloading of heavy equipment [Morison, v. XIII, p. 97].

(Wilber explained to us after his return that one could load a landing ship for rapid off-loading so that the vehicles with howitzers in tow were ready to roll off the ship as soon as the ramp was lowered. In contrast, the ships could be loaded for maximum amounts of equipment. In this case vehicles could be raised above the deck on stacked rows of shell cases to take advantage of the increasing width of the ship with height and thus make room for another row of vehicles. Further, the towing tongues of the howitzers could be lifted into the backs of trucks to minimize the length of a truck-howitzer combination. Such steps materially extended the off-loading time. These decisions had been made at Aitape with the aid of real-sized outlines of the ships laid out on the ground.)

Wilber and about two-thirds of his unit (152nd Field Artillery Battalion) boarded the USS Fayette (APA-43) at Aitape. The other third had left a few days earlier on slower landing craft.

The 2,500-mile voyage to Luzon would be fraught with danger because the task force had to pass through waters (Surigao Strait, Mindanao Sea, Sulu Sea, and the South China Sea) that were accessible from many Japanese-held airfields (Map 5). Suicide attacks by Japanese kamikaze aircraft had been introduced in the Battle of Leyte Gulf and continued to threaten shipping there as the Leyte fighting proceeded through November into December. The Luzon convoys would surely be attacked aggressively.

The plan was for the navy to send an advance task force, the Bombardment Group, to Lingayen Gulf, Luzon, to bombard the coastal defenses, clear minefields, and attack airfields. It would arrive three days before the invasion force. It, too, would be a target for the kamikazes.

x·o·ø·o·x

Wilber wrote a series of letters during his 12-day voyage to Lingayen Gulf. He labeled each with a day number countdown to S Day, the invasion date. This countdown as the ship approached Luzon emphasized the growing tension. Wilber described the onboard planning and his personal preparations for S Day and acknowledged the growing threats to the convoy as it traveled through Japanese waters. These letters would be mailed well after the landings in accord with censorship rules. The first such letter was written the day he and his troops boarded the Fayette, 14 days before the invasion date (S-14 Day). The Fayette was still anchored off Aitape.

S-14 DAY [DEC. 26, 1944]

Dearest Nana — This is the first of a series of letters that must be mailed after it has been announced that we are in Luzon. Yesterday was spent in a final clean up of our areas and the striking of our tents. We had had our Christmas day on the [self-censored; surely the 24th]. [General] Wing had a party for the Field officers [majors, lieutenant colonels and full colonels] of the division the next day. I only stayed an hour. I think I mentioned the bagpipes before, but that was where I heard

CHAPTER 4   *Some minutes are worth more than years of living*

USS Fayette (APA-43) at unknown location. This ship carried Wilber and about two-thirds of his battalion to the Luzon landing. The others left earlier on slower craft. [PHOTO: NAVSOURCE ONLINE, WAYNE VANDERVOORT]

them. Of course, since [the] tents were down, it rained last night for the first time in a week. The men were soaked.

Today we had reveille at 0100 [1 A.M.] and at 0400 marched to the beach. I drove down and watched them come into the assembly area. At 0800 we were loaded on LCTs and taken out to the USS Fayette where we boarded by going up the nets. It was about 30 ft high and I was worried about the possibility of men falling between the two ships or falling off the net because of their heavy packs or radios. However the only accident was a fracture of a bone in one man's (not 152) foot, and the men are all well quartered now. A third of my unit left a week ago – remember I said I was busy. So the troops here are the remainder of my men less a few on other ships. Maj. Fish is on another ship. Pierson has not yet returned [from leave in the States] so he misses this show.

> Major Pierson was the training and plans officer (S-3) of the battalion. This was a key position, so he would be missed. He rejoined the 152nd Field Artillery Battalion in Luzon.

71

VICTORY AND HOMECOMING   PART II: FINAL BATTLES, LUZON

I am quartered with Col. Cleland [commander, 103rd Infantry] and Col. [I. M.] Oseth [of the War Dept.] in a very nice stateroom. There are some 80 or 90 other officers on board in a large hold. They eat in a troop mess for officers but the captain [Skipper] (J.C. Lester) directed that I eat with him. The group includes the Skipper, Commodore Ryan, Gen. [Alexander] Stark [assistant commander, 43rd Division] and the two Cols mentioned above. That means four chicken colonels (in army terms) and one general, which makes me low man on that totem pole. It is nice tho because we have nice linen, silver, Philippine cooking, and Negro waiters. Also it is an interesting group. I've no official duties on board except to be a passenger. It is my first "free" trip and I hope to get some good rest. Saw a [movie] show on board after supper.

I'll continue tomorrow but you should know how much I love you. It's a whole lot Baby and you'll hear more about that too. Good night now lover. I am starting another step toward our reunion today. Rejoice. — Wilber

> I can easily relive these shipboard scenes with Wilber, given my 18 months on the USS Diphda in the Korean conflict, and so, I hope, can the reader through these letters. Wilber was clearly motivated by a strong sense of the historic import of these events.
>
> The opportunities for African American sailors were extremely limited in the segregated U.S. Navy at that time. Many served as "mess attendants" or stewards in the officers' wardrooms (dining rooms) aboard ships. Eating while attended by black waiters and servers was, in the southern tradition, considered elegant dining. It was in this context that Wilber mentioned it. Filipinos also generally served as stewards; thus the reference to "Philippine cooking." The armed forces were desegregated by presidential order in 1948, but the officers' mess stewards on my ship in 1953–54 were all African American and Filipino. Neither Wilber nor I, nor many other Americans, appreciated the injustice inherent in this actual and, later de facto, segregation.

x·o·ø·o·x

S-13 DAY [DEC. 27, 1944]

[No salutation] — Another day has passed. We rehearsed our landing with all the assault boats going in to shore loaded with men. Of course no ammunition was fired but it was a thrill to see it. One couldn't help wondering about the boys in the boats and amphibious tractors + their future.

CHAPTER 4   *Some minutes are worth more than years of living*

I go with Col. Cleland on one of the guide ships [boats?], which will stop about a mile from shore while the assault waves go on to shore. The first wave hits the beach at "H-hour" with others each four minutes. The navy will be firing on the beach until just before H-hour. My boys are due to go in as the seventh wave (H + 28) in LSMs so Capt. DeGlow, Sgt. Oliver and I will go in by special boat at H + 15 minutes to select their routes and positions before they arrive. We are going to try to be firing before any of the other artillery reaches the shore. They come in at H + 70 minutes so we may be able to show that the 152 is still leading.

Of course my observers will be and are now with the infantry with their radios ready for us to report ready to fire. Our men are all set and morale is higher than I've ever seen. It could be we will do a real job.

It was a thrilling sight to see this immense convoy of ships all wheel into place with the big ones farthest out, all like mother hens surrounded by little boats milling about in circles waiting for the last ones to be loaded and for their starting time. In turn each bevy would suddenly straighten out into a long rank and race to the beach five miles away. We could see wave after wave following the buffalos [tracked landing vehicles] and amphibious tanks as they approached us – then as they passed us on the way to the beach. There the buffalos + tanks clamber thru the surf and up on the beach + men dash into the trees in scrambled lines. Behind them the assault boats ride into the surf, drop ramps and more men splash ashore and disappear in more hasty lines.

This is a big affair, Norma, and I wouldn't miss it for anything. Don't forget that if I don't come thru it, some minutes are worth more than years of living and such minutes are coming to us. I love you and nothing can take me away from you. No matter what happens, I'll be caring for you. — Wilber

> The thrill of participating in this huge dramatic undertaking was, as Wilber noted, well worth the ultimate price he might have to pay. It offered big adventure in pursuit of a big goal.

x · o · ø · o · x

> This next letter was the last Wilber would be able to get off the ship before it left Aitape. It was written to be censor-proof but an astute reader would notice the new "Somewhere in the S.W. Pacific" that was not found in his previous letters, along with the clear hints that he was on a ship: "seagulls wheel about" and he "played with the medicine ball," a common shipboard exercise [letter 10/17/42]. He was well aware that this could be

VICTORY AND HOMECOMING PART II: FINAL BATTLES, LUZON

Amphibious LVTs (Landing Vehicle Tracked, small tank-tracked landing vehicles also known as "amtracs") being loaded onto LSTs (note #474), Aitape, New Guinea, December 27, 1944. The foreground vessel was probably a Mark 6 Landing Craft Tank (LCT). The troops and ships, about to depart for the invasion of Luzon, Philippine Islands, carried out a final landing exercise at Aitape on this date; this photo likely showed the subsequent reloading. The task force departed the next day for the 2,500-mile voyage to Luzon, P.I.
[PHOTO: U.S. ARMY SIGNAL CORPS, SC 200008]

the last letter Norma received from him should his ship be attacked and lost en route Luzon. This was his ninth voyage of the war.

DEC. 28, 1944, SOMEWHERE IN S.W. PACIFIC

Dear Lovely Wife of Mine — This is a lovely day and I've had time to think again. Business is not so hectic as during the past weeks. And having time to relax and think and dream, means that you have been with me today. I love you so much. Every minute of our life together has been a precious jewel in my soul. Never doubt but that I love you.

The sky is very blue with white clouds chasing my worries away. Seagulls wheel about over the waves and I wonder if they will pass the word to their brothers on the Maine coast that I'm sitting musing on my great fortune – you. The sea is very green and the swell is quiet and smooth. And I love my Norma.

CHAPTER 4   *Some minutes are worth more than years of living*

There is nothing new to say to you that I have not said thousands of times. It is just, "I love you." Do you think those words will ever become monotonous to you? I hope not. Beloved, for then my heaven will have crashed. Be comforted, My Dearest, everything is well with me. I'm feeling fine and am as healthy as one could wish. You magnify the business of my back. It is nothing and is almost completely OK. No aches or pains at all. Today I played with the medicine ball with Col. Cleland + raised a good sweat.

Good night, Mother of my children. I will be dreaming of you and holding your spirit near me. Give the children a good hug for me just to remind them that [they] still have a father. Goodnight, Sweet Love. Keep them turned up at the corners for I will be wanting smiling kisses from them some day. Cheek to cheek, Darling. — Your husband, Wilber – thinks you are wonderful.

x · o · ø · o · x

And on the same day, after the Fayette was underway, he continued his countdown.

S-12 DAY. [DEC. 28, 1944]
Hello there good Looking and Far Away! — ... At 1400 today we left Aitape. It was a great sight to see all the transports move out of the anchorage, form into columns. We are the lead ship on the starboard side. One of the transports had a boat ashore so started late. The Commodore was a bit exercised and there was much flashing of signal lights to the poor Captain who blinked back most apologetically. Later his ship came steaming up along the flank, puffing smoke and perspiring foam from her bow with a big white wake behind her that suggested ocean dust. She reminded me of fat Indiana housewives who clean house frantically before church then rush off late forgetting their contribution, therefore arriving in a very snappish mood with all the rest of the family treading warily. Those were the days when the sermon was "very poor."

So My Darling, we are off on our great adventure. This 1944 was pretty easy so now we even up our account with Uncle Sam. I hope we do well and that not too many of my boys are killed. In the meantime I send my hugs + kisses to you + Valerie and a good hand on Hale's shoulder. — Wilber XXXOOO.

He hoped "not too many of [his] boys are killed." Wilber was frank about the risks; it was a grim game they played.

The 43rd Division left Aitape this date, December 28, as part of Vice Adm. Daniel E. Barbey's "San Fabian Attack Force," Task Force 78, which carried

I Corps (6th and 43rd Divisions) to Luzon. Altogether it would eventually consist of 44 transports and 137 Landing Ship Tanks as well as numerous protective escorts. [Morison, v. XIII, pp 97; see also pp 308–9] Part of Wilber's battalion had left earlier on December 17 on two (slower) LSMs (Landing Ship Mediums) [152nd FA Journal], which would later rendezvous with the larger and faster transports. The LSM was a sea-going craft of length 203.5 feet; it could carry approximately six trucks or a combination of trucks and howitzers. The LSMs probably carried the howitzers and trucks that would be offloaded directly onto the beach in the first landing waves.

Altogether, five infantry divisions and additional supporting units would be committed to the Lingayen landing: four in the initial assault and one in reserve. They were transported from 16 different Pacific bases, all but one (Noumea) previously held by the Japanese [Morison, v. XIII, p. 97]. The ships carrying these various elements would all arrive at Lingayen Gulf in the early hours of S day, January 9, 1945.

x·o·ø·o·x

S-11 DAY [DEC. 29, 1944]
Hello Sweet Wife — It is evening now and Col. Oseth and Gen. Stark and I were out on deck after supper. The moon is out and shining on the ocean as it did one night you + I watched at Sea Wall [on Mt. Desert Island, Maine]. Do you remember? I remember too how pretty you were and I still carry the snapshot of you in the bathing suit. And that reminds me to thank you again for your picture. Each time I look at it I'm more in love and more convinced you are the Princess of my dreams.…

Today I inspected the ship for Col. Cleland, napped, played with the medicine ball for exercise, read a book … and dreamed on deck of my home and family. I dreamed of you too last night very intimately too. Our meals on ship are outstanding. We have "cracking" [scrambled] eggs for breakfast and soup with dinner. Good night Wife Beautiful. Keep the song on your lips and laughter in the eyes of our children. — XXXOOO, Wilber

> "Cracking" was a childish quote from Valerie or me. Wilber referred to "intimate" dreams and then moved immediately to another topic. He was much less focused on sex than when he had sailed overseas in 1942.

x·o·ø·o·x

CHAPTER 4 *Some minutes are worth more than years of living*

S-10 DAY [DEC. 30, 1944]

Greetings Golden Girl of Mine — Today is a mixture of sun and showers (squalls in the navy). I upped at seven o'clock this morning and walked the deck for a half hour before breakfast then went in to my "cracking" eggs and bacon with iced pineapple juice. To bring my morale up still higher, the location report showed that I had passed one milestone toward which I have been working for a long time. Dearest I now am on the same side of the equator with you. Really I feel actually as if I were on the way home. Of course there is still a way to go but it is good to be back in the northern hemisphere.

After breakfast the Commodore, General Stark + Col. Cleland + Col. Oseth + I sat and talked for a time. They talked. I listened.… Next Col. Cleland and I and one of his majors then spent an hour on our plans for the landing and attack.

> Colonel Cleland was the commanding officer of the 103rd Infantry Regiment, which Wilber's 152nd Field Artillery would be supporting. Together with other supporting units, they made up the 103rd Regimental Combat Team (RCT), commanded by Cleland (Chart 2). He and Wilber would work closely together throughout the Luzon actions.

This show, Lover, is going to be the biggest affair out here yet. It is probably true that more heavy warships will participate than were used in the European invasion [at Normandy]. As I go ashore, there will be firing on that 500 yards of beach to which I go, one battleship, two (?) cruisers and several destroyers. In addition the navy will have been shelling and bombing the entire Lingayen Gulf beach areas for three days. They should have things pretty well knocked about before we land. My old friends of two divisions [25th and 37th] besides the 43d, that I supported [in New Georgia and Arundel], will be alongside again. I'll be sorry Don [Downen] isn't with them, but Petrie will [be] along a little later.

The 152 [FA Bn.] will land at H + 28 minutes. Capt. DeGlow and I will go in at H + 10 minutes to find routes away from the beach and position areas for the batteries. The other artillery comes in at H + 70, so I am very much disapproved of by DeBlois + the other commanders. However we are going to try to be firing before they land, and I think we will. At all events, if the Japs counterattack early, I'll be set. It is a gamble as to whether or not the hazard is greater close behind the naval fire or later, so we are betting the advantages will outweigh any possible increased risk. — Love, Wilber XXXOOO

> Was it due to simple chance that Wilber's battalion was scheduled for early landing or was it due to his initiative? I suspect the latter, at least in part, because of his aggressive and successful use of artillery in the Solo-

mons. Just how the landing was managed would have been up to the combat team commander, Colonel Cleland, Wilber's roommate on this ship. Wilber had sufficient opportunity on this long voyage to argue that early artillery support would be highly advantageous to the infantry and that early landing of the valuable artillery howitzers would not be unduly risky.

x · o · ø · o · x

In this next letter Wilber described, most clearly, the objectives and challenges of his unit the first day ashore; see Maps 8 and 9.

S-9 DAY [DEC. 31, 1944]

Darling — It's another day and Sunday too. I have just returned from communion service given by a fine young priest. I didn't find his name but did like his enthusiasm a great deal. This was my first communion on shipboard. One does seem a little nearer God out on the ocean. I think we must take a voyage some day on a ship where Episcopal services are available.…

This being a large operation and we being in the initial landing waves it is of course more dangerous and a lot of people will be hurt. I don't want you to be concerned about me so my prayers this morning were that you and the children will remember [that] I'm doing the thing I feel [to be the] most worthwhile that I will ever have a chance to do and know I am content. Personally I have no intention of being killed because I've still a lot of unfinished business with these Japs, so you really will have no cause for worry anyway.

We land at the town of San Fabian and take it. I put my guns in position just off the beach at S.F. and support the 103[rd Infantry] in their drive inland to take San Jacinto about four miles inland. If possible, we are to seize a hill #200, which is eight miles inland before night. That may mean fighting well into the first night. This is open country, mainly rice paddies. The open terrain should enable us to handle our artillery fire with much greater accuracy. We hope to be able to catch most of them [Japanese] before they are so close to our troops as they were in the jungle. On our left flank are some hills that overlook our zone of attack. These are in the 169 [Regimental Combat Team] zone. In case they are slow to take them [the hills], we will be under their [Japanese] observation and fire. If we are, I certainly won't consider them immune just because they are on the other side of the fence. There is a battalion of medium [155-mm] artillery [181st FA Bn; Barker, p. 148] assigned to reinforce my fires, and I plan to keep them busy covering our flanks.

The initial landing is made simultaneously by four divisions in two Corps. The XIV Corps under [Lt. Gen. Oscar W.] Griswold consists initially of the 37th and

CHAPTER 4   *Some minutes are worth more than years of living*

40th divisions. We are in the I Corps under [Lt.] Gen. [Innis P.] Swift, which consists of the 6th and 43d Divs. Other divisions are present but do not participate in the initial landings so should not be named now.

Our convoy has just been joined by some escort carriers and more destroyers. The sea is beginning to look crowded around here. So far everything is most peaceful and probably will remain so for several days yet. After we reach Leyte, I expect Jap PT boats and planes to make life a little more interesting.… Dearest we will have a wonderful time again someday. Until then my spirit will be with you. — Wilber

> As Wilber outlined the tactical situation facing him, he was reviewing it for himself. The two corps mentioned were the major elements of the Sixth Army, commanded by General Krueger whose boss was General MacArthur. Wilber's colleagues from Washington State (161st Regiment of the 25th Division) were in the Sixth Army Reserve and would be landed behind the 43rd Division at San Fabian two days after S Day.

x · o · ø · o · x

S-8 DAY [JAN. 1, 1945]

Happy New Year Nana! Happy New Year Valerie! Happy New Year Hale! — I hope you are all well and cheerful this first day of our reunion year. It's about time to plan to be reunited again and I can't think of a better plan than "Home for Christmas in '45." Do you agree? Or should I bring you out here? … Be that as it may, I am thankful we have weathered 1944 as well as we did. It has asked less of me than I expected and we (N. H. V.) are well and not in want or suffering as so many people in this world are now.

> In 1944, the 43rd Division had been in combat only in Aitape, New Guinea, and that was mostly in a defensive role. Prior to that they were in New Zealand. The combat in the Solomons ended in late 1943.

This morning's breakfast was a cheese omelet and bacon with coffee + toast. It is a good thing I'm being very conscientious about my exercise or I'd be too fat to fight. It is so nice too to start the day with table linen and bright silver. It will be still nicer when it is your table and linen and silverware. Which makes me wonder if you have your birthday-Christmas present. I can hardly wait to hear what you think of it. How I wish I might see your eyes when you open it.

> The Christmas gift Wilber had sent was a set of sterling silver flatware [letter 10/29/44]. He planned far in advance for this gift and was anxious

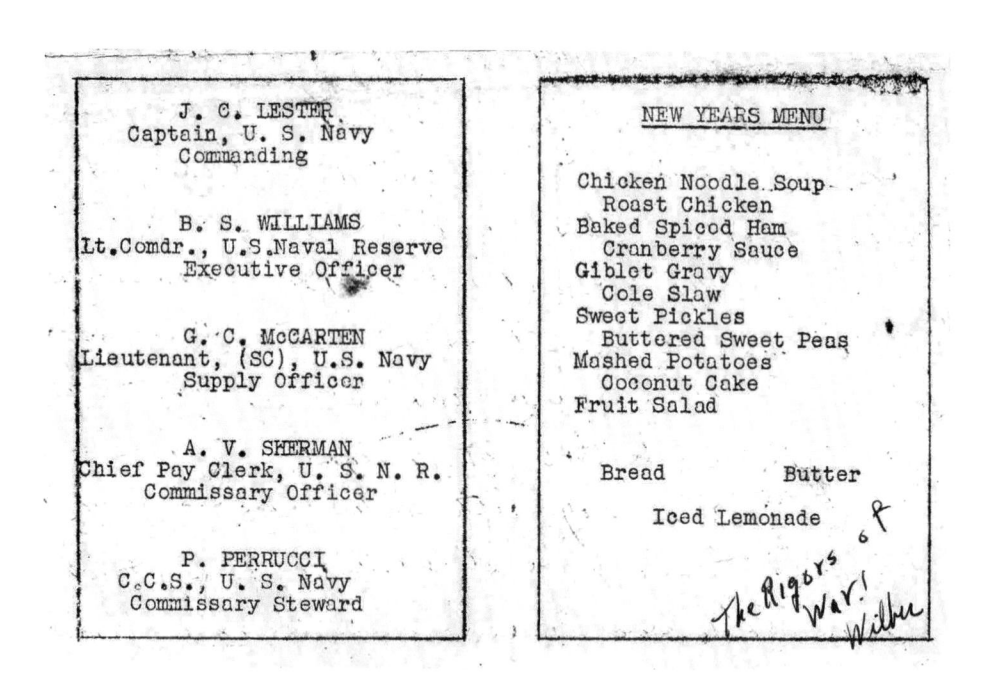

VICTORY AND HOMECOMING   PART II: FINAL BATTLES, LUZON

Shipboard menu, New Year's Day, 1945, on the USS Fayette, with Wilber's notations: "S-8 Day" and "The Rigors of War! Wilber."

that it be well received. The first page of this letter is written on the back of the ship's menu for New Year's Day.

After breakfast we studied our plan again for taking San Fabian and our advance inland. The navy backing us will shell our beach and the adjoining beach for three days before we arrive and will shell it until H-5 minutes on S-Day. Their fire will probably reach inland about five miles. There are more battleships and carriers out here than I knew the US owned....

Last night another convoy joined us and I found out that an unidentified ship is called a "skunk." These were skunks until they properly identified themselves. We went up on the bridge and watched the radar locate them while they were still miles away. We had a sub alert yesterday but it turned out to be a false alarm. Probably it was a whale. They say a lot of them have been depth bombed just to be sure.

Dear ones, I love you all and I'm so happy to have such a family. Keep your courage up this year. Take care of each other and be kind and generous to each other. No whining, no scolding, no quarrelling between brother and sister....

I do love you each and will try to be home in 1945 to stay. — Happy New Year from Wilber XXXOOO.

> Wilber was well aware that 1945 could herald the end of the war. He had long estimated that it would be a five-year effort when he was called to active duty in February 1941.

x · o · ø · o · x

The countdown continued.

S-7 [JAN. 2, 1945]

Here is that man again — Hello Wife with the lovely hands. Last night I dreamed we were back in Hattiesburg sitting on the porch in the early morning. You were so sweet and unselfish and understanding. It is certainly true that some of those hours you did not spend with me [when I was on duty or training] are hours which now give me confidence and perhaps have given me life. It would have been so easy and so wonderful to spend all my time with you then....

> Hattiesburg, Mississippi, was very special to Wilber because it was the last time he had seen Norma before shipping overseas more than two years earlier. Norma, Valerie, and I had spent the entire summer of 1942 there near his training camp (Camp Shelby); see Book 1.

VICTORY AND HOMECOMING   PART II: FINAL BATTLES, LUZON

I woke up in the middle of my dream and thought how all my life with you has been a marvelous dream, much nicer than the dreams too.… There are so many precious moments that I've shared with you in our few years together. If anything happens to me on this job, I want you to remember we had more joy together than other married people have in an ordinary lifetime. Do you remember I once told you I'd go to Hell for you? Perhaps this will be one but I take with me my knowledge of you and have no fear of what will happen. I do love you so dearly.

We have encountered four floating mines in the past 24 hours but have spotted them and had no mishaps. There have been several questionable sub contacts and they may be out ahead laying mines in our path. Most unsocial of them, isn't it?

The sea is beautiful in the night now and the moon is as bright as I've ever seen it.… I love you, Wife. Here is a kiss just behind that sweet pink ear. — XXXOOO Wilber

x·o·ø·o·x

On this next day, January 3, 1945—S-6 Day—near the Palau Islands (Map 2), Admiral Barbey's TF 78 (Wilber's convoy, the "San Fabian Attack Force") rendezvoused with two escort aircraft carriers and with the slower LSTs and LCIs ("Tractor groups") of Adm. Wilkinson's TF 79 ("Lingayen Attack Force") [Morison, v. XIII, p. 115]. Palau is about 400 miles east of Mindanao (Philippine Islands). The combined flotilla would enter Philippine waters at Surigao Strait the next day. TF 79 carried XIV Corps (37th and 40th Divisions). The faster vessels of TF 79 would enter Philippine waters after the slower TF 78 (6th and 43rd Divisions) and join TF 78 as both arrived at Lingayen Gulf. Altogether, these two attack forces consisted of 430 ships: transports, seagoing landing ships, and escorting destroyers. [Morison, v. XIII, Appendix I]

Another 164 vessels (Vice Adm. Jesse B. Oldendorf's Bombardment Force) would, as noted, arrive at Lingayen Gulf three days ahead of the transports to bombard the shore, sweep for mines, and generally clear the area. In addition, Adm. William F. Halsey's Third Fleet, east of Luzon, was available to provide carrier air support by attacking Japanese airfields and hopefully suppressing kamikaze attacks. It was a massive effort by naval, ground, and air forces. MacArthur would eventually use the equivalent of 15 divisions, including Philippine guerilla units, in the conquest of Luzon. This was by far the largest commitment of ground and service forces in the Pacific and exceeded those used in the campaigns in North Africa, Italy, or southern France, though not central Europe. [Smith, *Triumph*, p. 30]

CHAPTER 4   *Some minutes are worth more than years of living*

The four divisions of the initial assault on Lingayen Gulf did not match the scale of the Normandy landings the previous June (five infantry/armored and three airborne divisions), but they were mounted from bases thousands of miles away rather than the 100-mile width of the English Channel. The Allies in Normandy had absolute air superiority from land bases, whereas in the Philippines, kamikaze attacks were a major threat. There were an estimated 400 Japanese aircraft on Luzon with replacements available in Formosa, China, and elsewhere [Smith, ibid p. 28].

S-6 DAY [JAN. 3, 1945]
Dearest Norma — The one thing I regret the most about these voyages is the fact that you go so long without word that I am still OK. This time, Nana, I do hope you aren't being over impressed by all the Jap claims about sinking our transports. Remember I am in only one transport, not every one the Japs claim.

I think I mentioned the Jap plane over us. It was a "Betty" [Japanese bomber] and was obviously a Snooper from Palau. We expected an attack last night but none developed. Just an hour ago another Jap bomber came over us but was shot down before he could do any damage. Aside from this, the day has [been] very quiet. There are the usual "Bogey" and "Skunk" alerts but [they] are often caused by delay [by friendly planes] in putting out recognition signals.

The Palaus had been "neutralized" by the capture and subsequent use of a Japanese airbase on Peleliu and the establishment of a bomber strip on Angaur; but the largest island of the group, Babeldaob, which had a Japanese airfield, was bypassed. Despite American air dominance and frequent air raids, Japanese reconnaissance planes may still have been able to fly from there.

We are nearing the coast of the P.I.s [Philippine Islands] now and the sea is a lot more rough but no one is seasick. These men are becoming very good sailors after all these years. They really know how to enjoy a ship. Incidentally we have never been on a ship where the officers and crew did so much for the comfort of our men. I am glad because my experience on the other navy transport "American Legion" was far different. Capt. Lester has done everything he can to make us comfortable. The ship's officers have given our officers instruction on various subjects; they send over the speaker a running account of Jap attacks on us, the food is ample and well prepared, and all in all, it is outstanding cooperation in every way.

Did I tell you we anticipate that Japs will use [poisonous] gas on Luzon? We go ashore with masks just in case. I'm sure glad we got out of the jungle before this came up. Of course it probably is just a precaution and the Japs will be too smart to start it. We are in much better shape for gas war than they are and they probably know it.... — Love Wilber

> Wilber was referring to the scourge of poisonous gas, which was used extensively in World War I, but never in World War II. The U.S. refrained from using it, but was prepared to retaliate with it if the enemy introduced it.

x · o · ø · o · x

> The afternoon of January 4, Task Force 78 entered Leyte Gulf (Map 5) and was joined by a Close Covering Group of four cruisers and eight destroyers. The combined convoy now extended over 40 miles and was in range of numerous Japanese airfields.

S-5 DAY [JAN. 4, 1945]

Hello again Dearest — Another quiet day has half passed. We can see Leyte now and all is still well. Today I checked over my equipment and refitted my straps and belts. Uncle Sam sure loads one down and the added gas mask didn't help any.

The plan now is that I will go ashore at H + 4 minutes, behind the first two waves. That is a little early because the infantry will not yet have cleared the areas to which I want to go. However it is probably as safe ashore as sitting in a boat 400 yards out. Anyway I'll know which was the better in a few more days.

> Note that Wilber's planned landing time had been advancing in his letters, from H + 15 minutes to H + 10 to H + 4! Since Wilber and Cleland would land in the same boat, they were likely convincing each other that earlier was better, if not safer. In fact, Wilber landed at H + 15, possibly because his coxswain had difficulty identifying the proper beach (see below).

Our weather has been marvelous. Not even a hint of a storm. Today it is cool and the sea is as blue as I've ever seen it. Another convoy has joined us so the ships extend beyond the horizon even when I'm on the flying or signal bridge. Last night we passed over the Philippine Deep, which is the deepest place in the world. It is over six miles deep. However the top of it didn't look any different from the rest of the ocean.

This morning we had shirred eggs and toast for breakfast and at noon macaroni and meatballs. The food here spoils us and it is hard not to gain weight. However I'm exercising daily and seem to be quite fit.

Dear Nana, I love you and think of you so much. Your spirit seems so close to mine. How did I ever succeed in persuading you to be my wife? It still is beyond

CHAPTER 4 *Some minutes are worth more than years of living*

my understanding. However one thing is certain – I have been a most fortunate individual. You have made my life so full and so wonderful.… Good-bye now, I will carry you upstairs again when I'm home. — Love, Wilber

x · o · ø · o · x

S-5 DAY [JAN. 4, 1945]
Beloved — This is my second letter today. I've been thinking of how loveable and how beautiful you are and how good it would be to hold you in my arms. You have always been so generous of yourself to me and so responsive to my caresses. I thank you for each of those wonderful hours, Dear Heart. I remember the smoothness of your cheeks + the perfume of your hair.

Then too I have been thinking of the joy of coming home to you in the evenings. Your kisses and welcome were always such a help for a tired and perhaps discouraged man. It was always so comforting to sit in your kitchen before supper and to listen to your footsteps and to know I was in your home and heart too. In the evenings you used to play [piano] while I studied and maybe lie on the couch with the firelight on your face. You will never know, for I cannot tell you how much life with you has meant to me. Whether or not I have taken care of you well enough, only time will establish. I wonder at times like this if I should have saved more of material things for you. What I can be sure I leave with you is the fact that, since I met you, no other woman has entered my life. I've never touched another nor made love to another because my knowledge of you has been completely perfect.… — XXXOOO Wilber

> Here again was Wilber's frank admission that he was sometimes a "discouraged man" combined with memories of his homecoming after dealing with often intractable problems at the university. Here also was another voluntary profession of Wilber's sexual loyalty to Norma. During this voyage, since he could receive no letters, he seemed disconnected from the details of our lives in Bangor, Maine, where we were in the deep of winter. He was focused solely on the ongoing drama, the upcoming invasion, and an idealized Norma.

x · o · ø · o · x

On the night of Jan. 4–5, the convoy passed through Surigao Strait. [Morison, v. XIII, p. 115]. Thus began the most dangerous portion of the voyage westward along the northern coast of Mindanao (Mindanao Sea) and then up the west side of the Philippines for some 500 miles. They would pass by many Japanese airfields. Fortunately for this convoy, the Japanese were devoting their attention to the U.S. Bombardment Group, which would reach Lingayen Gulf the next day. Would the Japanese then turn their attention toward the transports of Wilber's convoy in those final four days? Substantial losses due to kamikaze attacks, a new and dangerous threat, could jeopardize the entire operation. The senior commanders were surely holding their collective breath.

S-4 DAY [JAN. 5, 1945]

Dear Wife — Another day has passed in peace and quiet. More convoys have joined us and more warships for escorts have appeared. So far it has been a surprisingly uneventful voyage. The next four days may however be a bit more interesting because we are now running the gauntlet within easy reach of scores of Jap airfields.

Last night and today we are winding our way thru the P.I.s and will soon swing up the west coast of Luzon to our destination. We just passed a fairly high mountain and have been continuously in sight of land all morning. The islands are green with forest in places, with grasslands in others. Occasionally rough ridges and rock outcrops predominate. Along the shore are scattered white houses.

Our supper last night was lamb with mint sauce and was surely good. This morning I ate scrambled eggs and toast and good coffee. Do you remember us loitering over an extra slice and cup some breakfasts? I certainly do.

After supper I went up on the bridge for an hour and watched the ships slide by the islands as quietly as shadows. It is fascinating to watch there and hear the orders for changes in course come in over the radio, followed by our own captain's orders to his ship. The lookouts continually report logs, lights, unidentified objects and give [the] location of each. A ship's officer reports the fact that some ship is out of formation and the commodore issues orders to them to correct their course. From the radar come reports of "skunks" and "bogies," then general quarters is sounded and all guns manned with all troops below.

Each evening we attend lectures (with slides) on airplane identification. He is really a good instructor and even I am learning to recognize more Jap planes. Today it is my turn to inspect ship and that is a very warm job [very hot below decks]. It is my second time and I certainly can't object because I have had [to make] daily inspections on my last three voyages.

Everything out here is under control and I love each one of you. — Wilber XXXOOO

CHAPTER 4   *Some minutes are worth more than years of living*

x · o · ø · o · x

S-4 DAY [JAN. 5, 1945; 2ND LETTER]

Sweet Heart — I'm just down from the bridge where Col. Cleland + I were working up a sweat with the medicine ball. It was 4:30 in the afternoon and the sun was out + felt good on the skin. I was wearing slippers and shorts. I am also the proud owner of a new haircut or should I say shearing for the barber left little padding for my helmet.

While we were there (bridge) a Jap [midget] sub fired two torpedoes at one of our escort ships, but missed. Then a destroyer [USS Taylor] fired a couple of salvos at the sub and stepped on the gas and rammed it. The job was finished by the destroyer dropping some depth charges on the sub. The bow of the destroyer was only slightly damaged. As one of the soldiers said, "The navy is sure on the job," with all the air of approving their policy. So we proceed thru the gauntlet safe and undisturbed but interested.

This voyage has been such a fine rest, Lover, I feel much more ready for action than when we went into New Georgia or New Guinea. For example this afternoon I slept from one to three o'clock and read another hour.... Today I inspected the ship again and found that the men have learned what needs to be done. — Love, Wilber

 The Japanese torpedoes had been fired at the cruiser USS Boise, which carried Gen. MacArthur. On the evening of January 5, fifteen Japanese planes flew over the convoy, but did not take note of it. [Morison, v. XIII, p. 115]

x · o · ø · o · x

 On January 6, before dawn, the Bombardment Group arrived in Lingayen Gulf. The kamikaze attacks they had been experiencing en route since January 3 intensified, and on this day, 11 ships were damaged and the minesweeper USS Long was sunk. It was the worst day for the U.S. Navy since November 30, 1942, at Guadalcanal. In contrast, the transports still en route had a quiet time. At 9:10 p.m. on January 6, Admiral Oldendorf in a message to his superior (Adm. Kinkaid) stated that if the transports suffered similar treatment on S Day, the troops "might be slaughtered before they could land." [Morison, v. XIII, pp. 110, 111, 116]

VICTORY AND HOMECOMING   PART II: FINAL BATTLES, LUZON

S-3 DAY [JAN. 6, 1945]
Hello There Nana — Pop is still here. We are now finishing a very quiet day. There were only two events furnished by the Sons of Togo – one, some planes and two, a sub. The sub is still lurking outside in the dark, but I trust a lot of destroyers have an ear turned his way. The planes looked and went home.

Hale + Valerie, I've passed thru the Mindanao Sea, the Sulu Sea and am now in the China Sea. I think I'll look in the morning to see if "The sun comes up like thunder." Don't you think you should all sing "On the Road to Mandalay" for me? We are the first transports to see the China Sea since Dec. 7, 1941 and I'm quite proud to be here. I wish you could see all these ships spread so thickly and so far across the ocean. Each one carries our flag so proudly and the flag looks so glad to be going about where it wants and not retreating from the Japs any more.

All day today, Adm. Halsey has been bombarding and bombing the beaches where I will land. Our mine sweepers have gone into Lingayen Gulf and swept out the mines. They carried our flag too and I'm sure they had a hard and dangerous time. Now Halsey can go in close for shelling the Japs there. I hope he does a good job and knowing Halsey I am sure he will. This will go on until ten minutes before our first troops land.

I love you all, Hale, Valerie and Nana. Don't worry about the possibilities here. I expect to keep my head down at the right times and I think my battalion can out shoot any three Jap artillery battalions. — Your (husband) (father), Wilber

> The refrain of Kipling's poem "Mandalay" is "On the road to Mandalay, where the flyin' fishes play, An' the dawn comes up like thunder outer China 'crost the Bay!"
> It was Oldendorf's Bombardment Group, not Halsey's Third Fleet, that was clearing Lingayen Gulf and the landing beaches. The Third Fleet was east of Luzon providing air cover and assaulting Japanese airfields.

x·o·ø·o·x

At daybreak January 7, the convoy was passing through Mindoro Strait [Morison, v. XIII, p. 116], which brought it adjacent to Luzon. In the early morning, a Japanese bomb splashed near the cruiser, the USS Boise, that carried MacArthur.

S-2 DAY [JAN. 7, 1945; 4 P.M.]
Sweet Wife — This is just a note congratulating you on the fact that you still have a husband. The Japs have showed up for a look at us but so far haven't been much

CHAPTER 4   *Some minutes are worth more than years of living*

trouble. Again it has been a lovely day and I've enjoyed every minute of it (It's 4:00 P.M.).

Alexander has put gas-repelling ointment on my shoes. I've packed my cottons, manuals and extra sox in my jungle pack to be brought ashore by one of my officers who comes ashore later in the day. My knife is razor sharp, my compass checked, my gas mask waterproofed. Extra sox, handkerchief and toilet paper are wrapped in my rubber sack, my pistol is loaded, clips are full of ammo, my aid kit is complete, my canteen full, and pencils in my pocket. I've put my maps in my helmet, my notebook in a waterproof case and hung all this junk on my person. For rations I'm carrying a chocolate bar. I can get more from the Bn. [battalion] later. My belt looks like this.

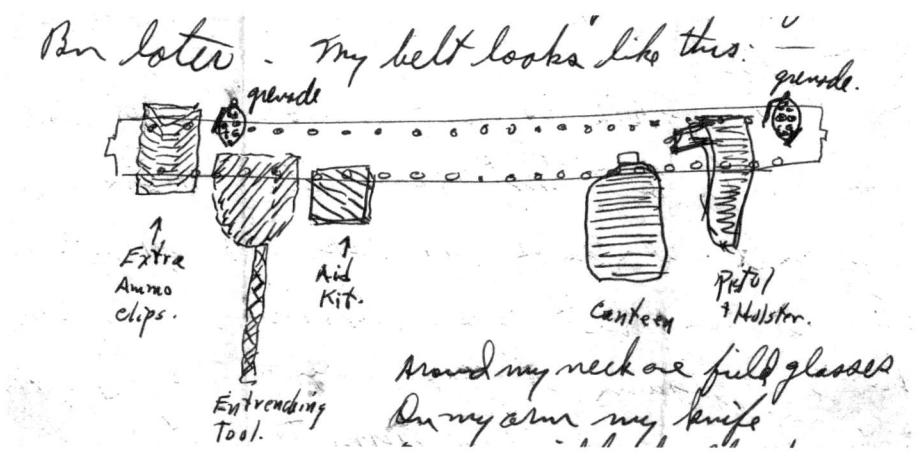

Wilber's sketch of the combat belt he would wear during the Luzon landings. The items noted were, from left: extra ammo clips, grenade, entrenching tool, aid kit, canteen, pistol & holster, grenade. [LETTER 1/7/45, S-2 DAY]

Around my neck are field glasses. On my arm, my knife. Over my right shoulder the gas mask. This is known as traveling light.

> What a checklist! Wilber's acknowledgment of the dangers ahead did not extend to fatalism. He was simply taking the steps he deemed necessary to ensure his personal safety and his ability to function effectively.

It has been a long time since I've been able to mail you a letter and I know you are worrying.… Day after Tomorrow I'll leave a letter with the skipper reporting myself OK.… Afterward when I'm ashore I'll mail a letter as soon as possible letting you know how I'm progressing. In the gaps between letters, I'll be loving all of you and dreaming of the days when we will see peace together. — I love you, Wilber XXXOOO

Again, this was for history; Norma would not get this explanation until well after the operation had transpired.

x·o·ø·o·x

During the night of January 7–8, the convoy passed Manila Bay; at daybreak, the escort carriers accompanying the transports were attacked by kamikazes and at 7:51 a.m. one crashed into the USS Kadashan Bay; at 7:55 a.m. another crashed into the transport USS Callaway killing 29 sailors but none of the 1,188 army troops aboard [Morison, v. XIII, p. 117]. Wilber did not mention the latter two incidents, possibly due to censorship.

This was S-1 Day; the quiet apprehension aboard those transports would have been palpable.

S-1 DAY [JAN. 8, 1945; 9:15 A.M.]

Dear Norma and Hale and Valerie — It is 0915 of the day before the big day and all is well. In the last 24 hours we have been alerted and placed at "General Quarters" several times.…

One of our LSTs [LST-912] was attacked yesterday [at dusk] and was bombed (which missed); then she shot down the Jap. Two other Jap planes went splash without any hits on our ships all day. Last night [at 9:00 p.m.] our escort caught a large Jap destroyer or light cruiser trying to get in reach of us. Four of our ships blew him [her] out of the water in about ten minutes. It was quite a sight. Our ships fired star shells over and beyond the Jap so she stood out like a sore thumb. Then the[y] proceeded to pour salvo after salvo into her. In a few minutes the radio reported her dead in the water and that they (our ships) were closing in. In a minute or two there [were] three terrific explosions after which she sank [at 10:55 p.m.].

It was interesting how the show started. First the radar spotted a "skunk;" [then, when] attempts to get a recognition signal from her failed, one destroyer requested and received permission to investigate. She steamed off into the dark and soon reported "Skunk identified as Jap. Request permission to fire star shell." Permission was granted so she fired 20 or more star shells. Then the other ships joined her + that was the last chapter.

We had poached eggs on toast for breakfast this morning and I remembered your neat and sweet breakfasts. Goodbye now Lover. I'll write again today if anything happens. — Love, Wilber XXXOOO

A kamikaze had crash-dived into LST-912, killing four men but only slightly damaging the ship. Again Wilber did not mention the damage or losses.

CHAPTER 4   *Some minutes are worth more than years of living*

The "destroyer or light cruiser" was a small Japanese destroyer escort, the Hinoki, trying to escape from Manila Bay when it inadvertently encountered the huge convoy [Morison, v. XIII, p. 116]. To the crew of perhaps 200 on the Hinoki, their ship was their home and workplace and their fellow crewmembers were their family. In moments, that was all destroyed. I am sure this was not lost on the soldiers and sailors who witnessed it, but Wilber's quick transition from "last chapter" to "poached eggs" does not show it; he was in combat mode.

x·o·ø·o·x

In the early hours of January 9, the ships turned south into Lingayen Gulf, and all the transports of both task forces were in position by 7 a.m.

This next letter, written shortly before Wilber debarked would be mailed immediately and did not include any reference to what he was doing. In the heading, he even suggested that he was still in the Southwest Pacific, with no hint at all that he was then in the Northwest Pacific.

JAN. 9, 1945; SOMEWHERE IN SW PAC.
Dear Nana — This is just a note to tell you I am well and as busy as usual if not more so. It is too bad I haven't been able to write you for the last two weeks but so it goes. You may be sure I have often thought of you, in fact have written some letters to be mailed later when censorship regulations will permit.

I can imagine how cold you are now and how you worry about the fuel bills. Take care of your and the children's health. Keep your courage up and don't worry about Pop.

It is lovely weather today and you would enjoy being here so much. I wish you might share the beauty with me. — Good bye now. I love you all, Wilber

x·o·ø·o·x

Wilber did go ashore at Lingayen Gulf as planned. He did not write a continuous narrative about the landings, but we got snippets of those moments in later letters to his sister Mary and to me.

[LANDING AT LINGAYEN GULF; EXCERPTS]
Feb. 21, 1945 [To Mary] — The naval bombardment over our heads was certainly impressive to me – probably more so to the Japs. My landing boat got lost and I practically visited all the beaches before I could convince the skipper I knew where

I was to land. Of course the smoke of the shells covered things a lot so it was hard to keep oriented. Of course, it was a very pleasant surprise to find myself on the beach quite pale but otherwise OK.

Feb. 28, 1945 [To Mary] — Perhaps you would like to know a bit about our landing. I spent your birthday [January 8 – the day before the landings] checking equipment and plans for debarking and wondering about the next morning. My battalion was the first artillery in the division to land and I was wondering if I had been wrong in recommending that we go in early. I landed at H + 15 minutes and the Bn. came in 13 minutes later. The naval fire was a stupendous sight. I wish I could name the battleships + cruisers. The Japs were trying suicide dive tactics but I didn't have much time to gawk. One strafed the beach where I was and I sure stopped working and stuck my nose in the sand for that job. After we had our howitzers ashore and so could shoot back, everyone felt much better.

March 10, 1945 [To me] — You asked about the Luzon combat. It is hard to tell the complete story but there were special times I can mention. Of course the first thing was "S" day and our landing. The 152nd was the first artillery ashore and I think fired the first shell on Luzon. Battery "A" [four howitzers] stopped almost at the waters edge and started firing. By the time the other two were ashore I was able to put them a mile inland.

One of my bulldozers, when coming ashore from the LSM [Landing Ship Medium], ran into a shell crater where a big 16-inch naval shell had burst. One minute the driver was driving along with water just up to the seat of his pants and the next minute he was out of sight. Then he came back to the surface and swam around disgustedly looking for his tractor and found none. When he came ashore he was the maddest driver I've seen for a long time. Of course, pretty soon an LCT [Landing Craft Tank] came by and ran over the dozer pushing it still farther under. So far as I know it's still there.

> The landings were largely unopposed by Japanese ground forces, and the troopships were not damaged by air or artillery fire. There were a few successful attacks on navy ships, with modest damage and some loss of life, but generally the Japanese kamikaze effort had "shot its bolt" in its attacks on the Bombardment Group the previous days. Had the Japanese waited to attack the transports, the result could well have been disastrous.

CHAPTER 4   *Some minutes are worth more than years of living*

American fleet at Lingayen Gulf, Luzon, Philippine Islands, the day following the initial assault, January 10, 1945. The planes were of the 7th Fleet Air Sea Rescue Squadron. [U.S. ARMY SIGNAL CORPS, SC 198654-S]

Landing craft heading for the beach during the invasion of Lingayen Gulf in a photo taken from LST-22, January 9, 1945. [PHOTO: U.S. ARMY SIGNAL CORPS, SC 200007]

Troops unloading supplies and equipment at Yellow Beach, Lingayen Gulf, Luzon. January 9, 1945. Wilber landed at White Beach 3. [PHOTO: U.S. ARMY SIGNAL CORPS, SC 200969]

5

"I'm not sure just what the Lord got"
Central plains combat
January–February, 1945

The Japanese did not defend the beaches of Lingayen Gulf but had retreated to more easily fortified positions in the mountains east and north of Lingayen Gulf and on the approaches to Manila to the south. The commander of the Japanese forces on Luzon, General Tomoyuki Yamashita, commander of the 14th Area Army had 260,000 troops at his disposal, but was short on supplies and expected no reinforcements or supplies from Japan. He knew he could not prevent MacArthur's superior forces from taking Luzon. He thus determined to husband his troops in defensive positions in order to delay the inevitable outcome as long as possible.

Yamashita divided his forces into a northern "Shobu Group," a western "Kembu Group," and a southern "Shimbu Group" (Map 6). The northern (Shobu) force of 152,000 men held defensive positions in the mountains north and east of the Lingayen beachhead. The U.S. I Corps landed on the left (north) flank of the beach with the 43rd Division to the left of the 6th Division. The 43rd Division was responsible for containing the forces north of the beach; its objective was to secure a road crossing some seven miles inland, which would block the northern Japanese force from moving south to attack American forces driving southward from Lingayen Gulf toward Manila. The latter forces (XIV Corps) were precluded from moving toward Manila until I Corps secured their northern flank. The 43rd Division "had the most hazardous and difficult S-Day tasks" [Smith, p. 80].

Wilber's 152nd Field Artillery Battalion was part of the 103rd Regimental Combat Team, one of three regimental combat teams (RCTs) of the 43rd Division, the others being the 172nd and 169th. The 103rd RCT landed at St. Fabian to the right of the other two RCTs. Those two had to deal with the Japanese strong points in the mountains just north of the beachhead while the 103rd drove inland to secure towns and Japanese strong points in the hills behind the beach. This was a relatively fast-moving situation, and the artillery had to be relocated quite frequently. This was a big change from the relatively static campaigns of the Solomons and New Guinea. There, the troop movements were more localized and the moves of the field artillery less frequent.

The 43rd Division engaged in four distinct phases of combat on Luzon (Map 7). The first, following the Lingayen landing, was the containment of the northern Shobu Group east of Lingayen Gulf. This was followed by a two-week respite, February 16 to March 1, after which the 103rd RCT served as division reserve during the 43rd's assault on the Kembu Group defenses northwest of Manila, the so-called Fort Stotsenburg action. The third action was the dislodgment of the southern Shimbu Group east of Manila, and the fourth was the capture of Ipo Dam northeast of Manila. It would not be until July 1 that the 43rd Division would be relieved of combat responsibility on Luzon.

x·o·ø·o·x

Once ashore on Luzon the morning of January 9, the 103rd RCT drove southeast and by nightfall was just short of San Jacinto, about four miles beyond San Fabian (Map 10), well short of the first day's objective, Hill 200 (Map 11). (Hills were typically designated by their approximate height in feet.) By January 12, the unit had advanced, with some difficulty, another four miles to the vicinity of Manaoag and had begun the attack on Hill 200. Well-hidden enemy artillery proved to be a new challenge, and Wilber's artillery sought to destroy it without being destroyed in the process.

Wilber found a moment to rush off a few lines three days after the landings.

JAN. 12, 1945
Dearest — Am in the Philippines, am well, and having a real time. The Bn. [battalion] is doing a fine job. Don't worry about me. Tell Mrs. Averill that Roger is OK, also Bob Hussey. Both are doing a magnificent job. — Love Wilber

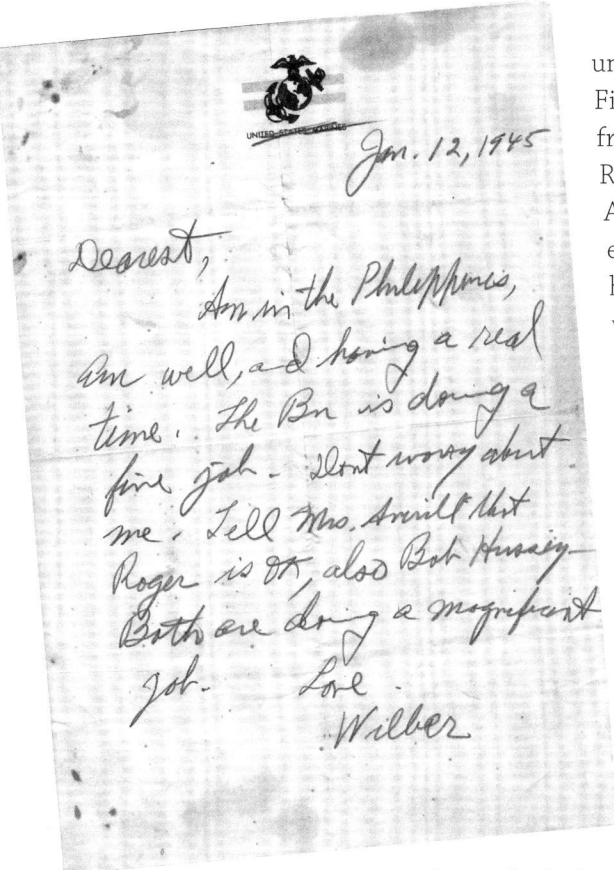

Wilber was referring to the unit he commanded, the 152nd Field Artillery Battalion, a unit from Bangor, Maine. Captains Robert S. Hussey and Roger L. Averill were battery commanders in the 152nd and both hailed from Bangor, where we were living. Both earned Silver Stars in the Luzon campaign [Barker, p. 241].

On this date, January 12, Wilber used artillery fire to rescue a wounded Filipino guerilla near Manaoag (Map 11). For this, he was awarded an oak leaf cluster for his Silver Star in lieu of a second Silver Star; the first was awarded for an event the following week, described below. (The tiny bronze cluster is worn on the ribbon suspender from which the medal hangs, or it is placed on the bar ribbon that represents the medal.) The Silver Star is awarded for "extraordinary" personal heroism and is the third highest award for valor in the face of the enemy. Wilber with some modesty discounted this distinction by telling us after the war that it was easier for officers to get medals because when an officer does what an infantry foot soldier ordinarily did, it would be considered "beyond the call of duty." The citation reads as follows:

[CITATION FOR SILVER STAR: RESCUE OF FILIPINO, JANUARY 12, 1945]
For gallantry in action against the enemy in the vicinity of Manaoag, Luzon, Philippine Islands on 12 January 1945. Colonel Bradt displayed exemplary courage and devotion to duty in assisting in the rescue of a wounded Filipino who had volunteered to guide a guerrilla patrol, under an American infantry officer, to an enemy position. Upon hearing that the party was pinned down by enemy fire from a concealed position, Colonel Bradt unhesitatingly joined a small, volunteer rescue party and proceeded to the scene, taking a field radio set to maintain contact with

VICTORY AND HOMECOMING   PART II: FINAL BATTLES, LUZON

First-wave troops of the 103rd Infantry fording a stream en route to San Fabian, January 9, 1945. Wilber's artillery was supporting the 103rd Infantry. [PHOTO: U.S. ARMY SIGNAL CORPS, SC 200017]

First-wave troops of the 103rd Infantry take cover behind an amtrac 300 yards inland from White Beach 3, Lingayen Gulf, Luzon, January 9, 1945. Wilber landed there just behind the first wave and was probably close by this action. [PHOTO: U.S. ARMY SIGNAL CORPS, SC 200019].

CHAPTER 5   *I'm not sure just what the Lord got*

San Fabian Municipal Hall damaged by bombing and naval fire, shown the day after the landings, January 10, 1945. [PHOTO: U.S. ARMY SIGNAL CORPS, SC 265235]

Maj. Gen. Leonard Wing, commander of the 43rd Division (left), conferring with I Corps Commander, Maj. Gen. Innis P. Swift (center) at the 43rd Division command post, Lingayen Gulf, January 10, 1945. [PHOTO: U.S. ARMY SIGNAL CORPS, SC 265239]

field artillery units under his command. While the wounded man, lying in an open field directly in line with enemy fire, was being rescued, Colonel Bradt personally joined in the firefight covering the rescue from an exposed position. From this very position he further directed by radio the delivery of artillery fire upon the hostile position so close to his position as to involve great personal danger to himself. Colonel Bradt's coolness under fire and his total disregard for personal safety on this occasion set an example which greatly contributed to the effectiveness of his unit." (Sect. II, G.O. #64, Hq. 43rd Div., 2 April 1945)

x·o·ø·o·x

Wilber provided us with his more personal version of this event four months later:

JUNE 1, 1945

Darling — … The Filipino affair was long before [the Lumban bridge incident] and was really a matter of saving face for Uncle Sam. I guess I had forgotten to tell you about it.

One evening [Jan. 12], just as I drove in[to] the [103rd] Inf. C.P. [command post at or near Manaoag], Wally Devine (Lt. Col. from Portland, Me.) [and executive officer of 103rd Infantry] drove out with a jeep + trailer. In it was Col. Oseth of the War Dept. and about six riflemen. Wally yelled to me "Come on." and I yelled "Where?" but he was past. So Ogden my Old Town [Maine] driver turned around and followed Wally along a winding road beside a small stream. After a mile or so we came to this sceen [sic; scene]: [sketch of the area]

Somewhere in the tall grass were the Japs with two machine guns but we didn't know where. Whenever anyone tried to get to the wounded Filipino the Japs opened up on them and had wounded several. Wally's plan was for Oseth and the six men to go to "A" [see sketch] keeping under cover. Then he with his machine gun went to behind the big tree at "B." When he opened up on the Japs they might duck long enough for two of the men at "A" to dash thru the hedge and get the wounded man out. There weren't enough of us to go in after the Japs, and it was late evening.

The signal to make the dash was Wally opening up with his M.G. I was just a bystander up to this time. Wally opened up and on the sixth round his M.G. jammed. The soldiers dashed thru the hedge. The Japs opened up on them. So we had no M.G.

Wally at "B" and the boys at "A" and I under the house at "C" opened up with what we had. My pistol scared a hog tied to a post of the house + she made a big to-do. Being afraid she would disclose my position I cut her rope and she dashed

CHAPTER 5   *I'm not sure just what the Lord got*

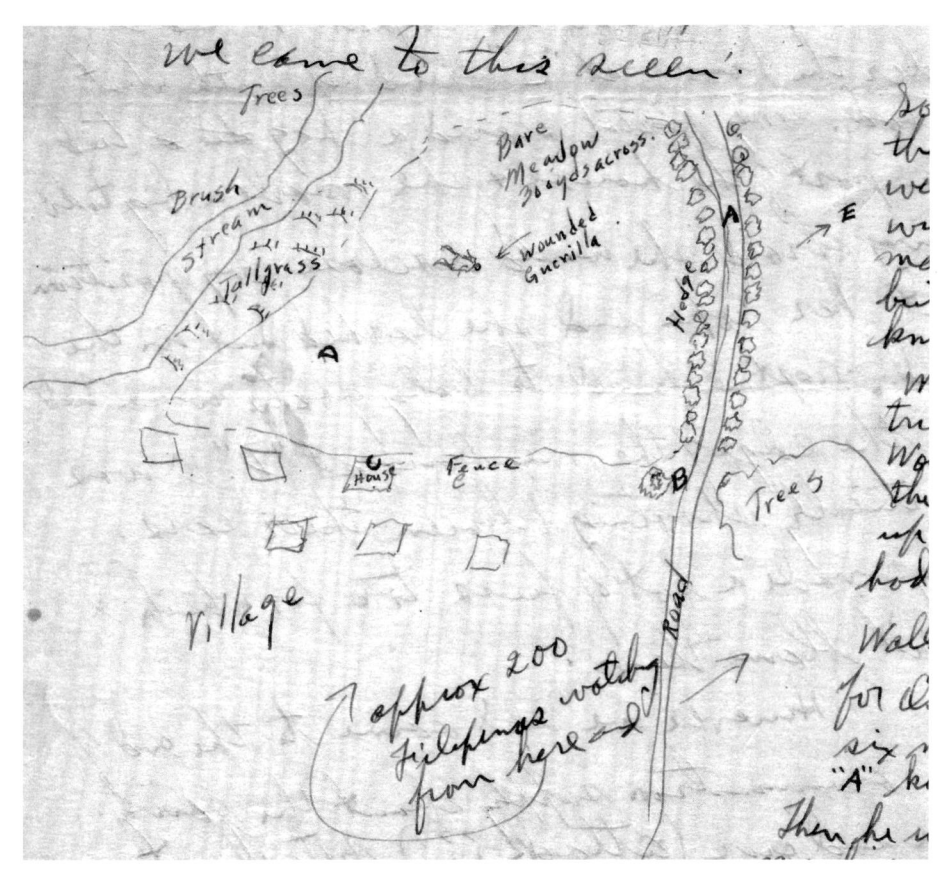

Wilber's sketch of the rescue of a wounded Filipino guerilla at Manaoag, P. I. Wilber was under a house at C (a bit left of center) and the Japanese were in the "tall grass" to the upper left. Baby goats were at D between Wilber and the Japanese, a jammed machine gun was at B, and men hoping to rescue the guerilla were at A, at upper right in road. The first artillery round landed at E as hoped [LETTER 6/1/45].

out in the field. Next I found [two] baby goats were tied in the edge of the meadow at "D." I was practically shooting between their ears. They made a lot of fuss too for which I didn't blame them.

However we all came to the end of our ammunition supply about the same time and our (attack???) petered out. Of course the Japs fired a few bursts after that so they definitely had the last word and the Filipino was still there unrescued. Also the population of the town had seen us bested, and perhaps would see us go off and leave the Japs there. It was too late to get more help.

So I proposed artillery. It was too close quarters to be safely used but I thought I might be able to do it. We made the people move back and I radioed for a trial

VICTORY AND HOMECOMING   PART II: FINAL BATTLES, LUZON

Colonel I. M. Oseth (right), director of the Infantry Board at Fort Benning, Georgia, confers with Lt. R. B. Dooley, 103rd Infantry Regiment (seated), and a Filipino in the market place at Manaoag, Luzon, January 12, 1945. On this date, in the evening, Colonels Oseth and Devine, Wilber, and about six enlisted men rescued a wounded Filipino, primarily with Wilber's artillery. Each of these three officers earned a Silver Star for this incident [letter 6/1/45]. [PHOTO: U.S. ARMY SIGNAL CORPS, SC 265265]

round. Covill radioed back "Unsafe to Fire." I thought so too, but sent back "Safe to Fire signed Bradt." When the first round came out I had everyone down but myself + Wally who never let me appear braver than him. I had to stand to see where it landed and as we heard it whistle I said to Wally, "If we read the map right, it will land across the road and if not maybe behind us on the people." Those are the hard moments in artillery.

However it landed across the road at "E." I shortened the range 100 yds, and dropped a shell just in front of the Filipino, then shortened range again and called for a volley, which fell in the grass behind the F. [Filipino] and in the stream. Then we walked volleys back + forth thru the grass + stream using high explosive shell. Each time I expected to see the F. disappear because he was within dispersion limits. One round hit a house and each volley threw fragments all around and way beyond us. We weren't hurt altho one hit my foot + Wally picked up a hot one at his feet. Next I threw in a few volleys of smoke shell and told the soldiers to go get the F.

CHAPTER 5   *I'm not sure just what the Lord got*

The Japs had left or been killed. It was too dark to go see for we were nearly out of pistol and rifle ammunition. I had two rounds left. Later (next day) the Filipinos went in, but I didn't hear what they found.

Wally + Oseth were given a Silver Star for the job. However, after that, Wally told [others] that I [had] earned his S.S. after he + O. had failed; so to balance the books + stop the talk, Col. Cleland sent my name in also.

So the prestige of Uncle Sam was still all right and the people knew then who would finally win. That I think was as important as the F.... — Your Husband Wilber

> In an earlier letter to his sister Mary on February 28, Wilber put a different slant on the rescue story: "I put the fire on the machine guns and the Lord made the shells miss the boy. So we got him out and that was another high spot. They awarded me a Silver Star for that job, but I'm not sure just what the Lord got."
>
> Wilber appreciated the symbolic value of this rescue in the first days of the American presence. When I was in Manaoag in 1983, my limited inquiries failed to locate anyone familiar with the event or its location; see the following Interlude.

x · o · ø · o · x

On January 14, the commander of an attached regiment making slow progress to the north was relieved by Gen. Wing, commander of the 43rd Division. [Smith, p. 108]

Hill 200 turned out to be a tough nut to crack—it was to have been captured on the first day of the landings. It was a series of rolling ridges easily defended by the enemy. It had been the site of an army camp even before World War II and still is today; it was finally secured on January 17. While still reducing Hill 200, the 103rd RCT had driven on to Pozorrubio, several miles further northeast.

Up to this point, maps marked by Wilber showed at least seven different positions occupied by the batteries of his battalion. There were three such batteries in the battalion (recall that a battery had about 120 men and four 105-mm howitzers). Such moves were complex affairs, entailing the movement of equipment and supplies, finding and preparing howitzer positions not easily locatable by the enemy spotters, and building earthen emplacements to protect from the shrapnel of incoming artillery shells. Also needed were accurate surveys to establish howitzer alignments and communication set-ups, among many other tasks. Early readiness to fire after a move was the sign of a well-trained outfit.

The prime mission of the battalion was to provide direct support for the 103rd Infantry. However, counter-battery fire against enemy artillery positions was an important secondary task. This was a challenge because a Japanese gun could be fired for a brief interval and then immediately retracted into its camouflaged redoubt. American howitzers were also vulnerable to artillery fire, so they had to be well placed and camouflaged. One of Wilber's jobs was to find those positions.

JAN. 16, 1945

Dearest — I've been in the Philippines now a week. During that time we have been in combat each day. Things go well with the Bn. and with me. There have been one or two close ones but nothing to worry about.

> It was OK to not worry about the "close ones" after they missed, but what about the next ones?

This is a very good change from the jungle. Altho the sun is quite hot, there is usually a cool breeze.

Just now I am sitting in the shade of a tree on a hill top watching part of the battle across the valley from me. I'm controlling the artillery fire from here. The present job is to take a hill [probably Hill 200], which the Japs hold. It is slow but we make consistent progress.

The people here are very nice and are a welcome change from the New Guinea and Solomon Island types. Our surgeon delivered a baby yesterday much to the general interest of the battalion. The Doc. is tickled to have something beside athlete's foot to treat.

Goodbye now. I love all of you. I'm OK and feeling fine. So far I've stayed out of the dog-house. In fact a Col. Oseth (a War Dept. Observer from Wash. D.C.) told one of the Inf. officers of the regiment I was the most intelligent artillery officer he had ever met. He being an Inf. officer may never have met an artilleryman before. Anyway I love you. — Wilber – Averill + Hussey OK.

x · o · ø · o · x

On January 18, Pozorrubio was captured (Map 12) and Wilber took part in some artillery spotting that he briefly described.

JAN. 19, 1945

Dear Norma, Valerie + Hale — I'm still in good shape and feeling fine. Things have been very strenuous for the Bn. and for me, but we haven't failed our infantry yet.

Last night the Japs shelled us with a six-inch gun until we plotted his flashes and swatted him with six battalion volleys. [Each of the battalion's 12 howitzers fired six times, as fast as they could reload.] We haven't heard from him since. This A.M., I ran into six Japs. There were four of us. We had a little fire fight in which we killed one and possibly another and drove the others off. I was behind an ant hill, and the nearest one was in a hedge about 20 yards away. I flattened him.

We make good progress. I love all of you. Take care of yourselves and be kind to each other for me. Goodbye Now. — XXXOOO, Wilber

> I do not know if "flattened him" meant Wilber had killed him or forced him to lie flat. On February 28, he wrote some additional detail to his sister Mary: "Another time I ran into some Japs when I was out where I had no business to be. They left when I had only two rounds left but they left (except one who couldn't) and since I had a pistol and they had rifles, I was surely relieved – another high spot."
>
> On this date, January 19, the 152nd Field Artillery Journal recorded:
> *1100: Col. Bradt, Lt. Maples, Lt. Bink, and Sgt. H. Cook in vic. of Pozorrubio had a fire fight with Jap patrol killing possible one. No injuries to themselves.*
>
> The disabling of the Japanese six-inch gun "last night" earned Wilber his first awarded Silver Star. The citation reads:

> **[CITATION FOR SILVER STAR: ARTILLERY SPOTTING, JAN. 18, 1945]**
> *For gallantry in action against the enemy on 18 January 1945 on Hill 200 [sic, Hill 600], just North of Pozorrubio, Luzon, Philippine Islands. While directing fire Colonel Bradt displayed courage and devotion to duty. For two days previous our troops, which were attacking on Hill 200 [600], had been constantly harassed by enemy fire from positions which could not be definitely located. Of his own volition, Colonel Bradt went to the most forward position in order that he might determine the location of the enemy firing positions. Although under heavy artillery fire, some of which landed only feet from him, he moved to more exposed positions from which he could better locate the enemy guns. By his deliberate coolness, courage, and utter disregard for his own safety, Colonel Bradt was able to obtain data which resulted in the destruction of the enemy positions. (Sect II, G.O. #20, Hq. 43rd Div., 7 Feb. 1945)*

> The location ("north of Pozorrubio") and the date (January 18) both strongly suggest Hill 600, not Hill 200. (See Map 12 and pullout Map II of Smith's *Triumph*.) Hill 200 had been secured on January 17 and the first approaches to Hill 600 began on that same day. Hill 600 was a strategically

VICTORY AND HOMECOMING   PART II: FINAL BATTLES, LUZON

important complex of hills that were very strongly defended by the Japanese. [Hist. Rpt. 103rd Inf. January–May 1945, pp. 10, 18.]

These two back-to-back events—the observing "last night ... as Japs shelled us" and "this A.M. ... a little firefight"—together with the Filipino rescue event of only a week earlier underscored Wilber's vulnerability. There had been and would still be other "close ones."

x·o·ø·o·x

Meanwhile, in Indiana, Wilber's mother, who had been widowed for only about six weeks, wrote to her daughter Mary and indicated that she would at last begin writing to her overseas son.

JAN. 19, 1945
My dear Daughter [Mary] — Your letter with enclosures came today. Ruth's letter was a typical Ruth letter and was good, but Wilber's letter did me a great deal of good. Now I can write him and be glad to do so....
Sat. A.M. 56° inside, 20° outside. — I love you, Elizabeth Bradt

This probably referred to Wilber's letter of December 21, 1944: "I'll write you [near] the first of each month.... Please do answer."

x·o·ø·o·x

On January 21, the division launched a coordinated attack on all fronts with advances in all sectors. The 103rd Infantry "continued its attack on Hill 600 from the east, west, and south, advancing against continuous artillery, mortar, machine gun, and rifle fire." [Historical Report, Luzon Campaign, 43rd Division. 1945, p. 13]

Further to the north, American units came under fire of huge (12-inch diameter) howitzers, one of which was captured intact. [Historical Report, Luzon, 43rd Division, p. 21]

JAN. 21, 1945
Dear Norma — I am sitting in the evening at the infantry command post. We have been digesting the day's progress and making plans for the morrow. It is nearly dark and time for me to get into my foxhole. I am still well intact and feeling fit on the 13th day of combat. In fact the only event that personally annoyed me today was

CHAPTER 5   *I'm not sure just what the Lord got*

Twelve-inch Japanese howitzer captured intact west of Rosario in the 172nd Infantry sector about February 3, 1945. The onlookers (upper right) are seated on a rail used to support a house used for camouflage. It would be rolled away when the gun was to be fired. There were two such guns camouflaged with great effort and skill. American artillery scouting planes had overflown these positions at low level numerous times without suspecting the houses covered the guns until counterbattery fire damaged the camouflage of one of them. [PHOTO: HIST. RPT., LUZON CAMPAIGN, 43RD INF. DIV., P. 21]

some Jap artillery, which I haven't found yet. They aren't dangerous, but are good cause for finding a hole. — Love Wilber

On January 22, as the 103rd Infantry continued its assault of Hill 600 and adjacent areas, an "incautious grouping of officers and enlisted men" of the 3rd Battalion of the 103rd Infantry attracted over a dozen Japanese artillery rounds within just two or three minutes. Four company commanders and seven enlisted men were killed and 35 were wounded. The battalion had to be withdrawn for reorganization [Smith, p. 150]. The loss of all four company commanders of the battalion was "perhaps the hardest single blow, materially and spiritually, suffered by the regiment during the entire campaign" [103rd Inf. History, p. 23]. These were the men of one of the three battalions that Wilber's artillery was supporting. Wilber never mentioned this tragic event in his letters, but did allude to it indirectly five days later in his letter of January 27.

x · o · ø · o · x

VICTORY AND HOMECOMING   PART II: FINAL BATTLES, LUZON

JAN. 26, 1945

Dear Norma + Children — It is evening of Friday. MacArthur has announced the divisions in Luzon so now you know where I am. All is still in good shape with the 152 + me. I haven't even been badly scared for several days and am sleeping nights again. The Japs have made several attempts on our batteries with the result that we have now official credit for two Jap officers and 29 Jap men killed by our men in defense of their guns. These were killed by machine gun and rifle fire. The Japs attack at night and we drive them off. Then, in the A.M., the attacked battery sends out a patrol that hunts them down and shoots them.

Today I saw a school in operation in one of the towns we have recovered. Probably the children don't appreciate our arrival. Good night, Loved Ones. Don't worry about me. I'm OK. — I love you all, Wilber

> MacArthur had probably announced which divisions were in Luzon shortly after the landings as Wilber had openly mentioned he was in the Philippines on January 16. As the combat slowed a bit, Wilber was able to write every day or two. It's also notable here, by inference, that he had not been "sleeping nights" these past two weeks.
>
> The Japanese, after attacking a battery position, would typically hide in nearby Filipino structures hoping to repeat the raid the following night; the Filipinos would then inform the Americans about their locations. It was unusual for (American) artillerymen to carry out such actions; it would usually be an infantryman's job. [152 FA Bn. Historical Report for period December 17, 1944 to February 15, 1945, para. 1-h-8 "Security"]

x · o · ø · o · x

JAN. 27, '45

Dear Wife — It's another evening and all is still well with me and the 152. Today I went up to the 3d Bn. [103rd Inf.] front line and gave them a little encouragement. My two officers and their parties seemed to be doing a good job. We ran into sniper and mortar and artillery fire. Waldo [Fish] was along and quite impressed. I don't think he liked it very much but of course he conducted himself all right.

> This mention of the 3rd battalion getting "a little encouragement" was a telling reference to the tragic losses of five days earlier. Wilber would often go to front-line infantry units to check on their situations and to give support to his artillery liaison and observer officers who were with the infantry.

But this visit appeared to have had the additional objective of providing a morale boost. Bringing along his executive officer (Fish) may have been part of that.

I had a good bath this evening and am feeling unusually clean. My boys have killed a total of 33 Japs so far that were trying to get into our gun positions. So far they haven't gotten in, but they keep trying. A good many heads have fallen [officers relieved] during the past weeks, but I am still in good standing. A Lt. Col. of FA was with us for five days. He said some very nice things about the Bn. and that he would be glad to serve under me. Since he was Reg[ular] Army I thought that pretty fine. It's raining, so love + goodbye. — XXXOOO Wilber

Wilber passed off the killing of "33 Japs" apparently without a thought other than pride that his men were protecting themselves and their howitzers. After all, "killing Japs" was their job.

On January 28, the 103rd Infantry Regiment began a period of less active combat, consolidating gains, and aggressively patrolling. Its infantry battalions were down to about half their usual strengths due to casualties (deaths, wounds, and illnesses). However, this phase of the fighting was not yet over.

x·o·ø·o·x

JAN. 29, 1945

Dear Wife — Today I'm writing about noon instead of in the evening. I've been down to my CP [command post] this morning and arranged for the planned fires for the day. A report just came in that a hill [probably Hill 355, northeast of Binday (Map 10)] we by-passed has been cleaned up. We have taken our objectives and are now in the "mopping-up" phase. That means my most urgent responsibility is to be prepared to knock out any enemy counter-attacks. We are working on that now.…

One of the Filipinos [who] has appointed himself as our Hq. officers mess boy without portfolio brought in a roast chicken. It was seasoned with garlic and ginger and was really something different and good. You may want to try it. He used quite a lot of ginger root (not powdered) and regretted the absence of one other spice, which was not available. I gathered it was possibly cloves, perhaps sage.… — Love, Wilber

x·o·ø·o·x

VICTORY AND HOMECOMING   PART II: FINAL BATTLES, LUZON

FEB. 3, 1945
Dear Wife — A letter dated Jan. 20 came from you today so I guess your mail is catching up. Other mail has apparently come by boat and has been correspondingly late. Things here have quieted down a lot recently and my personal hazards are reduced, not to what I like to consider normal, but to what is definitely better than a week ago.

Feb. 5 — Maybe I was wrong after all. I was shelled twice yesterday and again just now during breakfast. However so far I have been a fast man to a fox hole. The Nips really bracketed us this A.M. [with artillery fire]. Col. Devine had filled in my hole so I joined him, which so crowded the hole, we had to tremble in unison. My wire crew killed another Jap yesterday. They have done pretty well so far in that line and love it. I only hope they keep their luck and that no Jap catches them off balance....

News just came in that Manila was taken. We are on another part of the front where the publicity isn't so good but the fighting is still present. It seems pretty definite now that the 43d is credited with a pretty good job. The Corps (First) Commander [General Swift] sent us a very fine commendation. Tomorrow I have a Sixth Army inspection of areas, kitchens, uniforms and equipment while we are still firing. What a war! — It's dark, Lover, Good Night. I love all of you, Wilber

> How did we react to receiving these letters at home in Bangor, Maine? I for one just lived my teenage life and did not worry about his safety in combat. I just believed it would turn out all right and did not fret. But for Norma, did each frightening event he described bring new fear for his safety, or had his world become a distant and repetitious scene for her? Wilber had been in combat in 1943 (Solomons), 1944 (New Guinea), and now 1945 (Luzon). It was a continuing story. Nevertheless, his stories, amplified by her vivid imagination, must have had their impact during our Bangor winter.
>
> American troops entered Manila on this date, February 3, but the battle for different parts of the city continued until about March 3. The stubborn Japanese defense, even after being completely isolated, led to widespread destruction of the city. The 43rd Division was still busy fighting the Japanese far to the north.

x · o · ø · o · x

FEB. 6, 1945

Dear Nana — Two letters came from you today. One with a lot of clippings, cards, letters from friends and a Christ Church leaflet. It all was interesting and I enjoyed it but your letter was the best part of all. I can imagine the cold and discomfort of the winter is beginning (Feb. 7. The Japs again) [letter continued after an interruption] to get you pretty discouraged.... You may be right that we can't afford to keep a house and, if you think that is true, we should face the fact and get rid of it....

Some [Filipinos] work for us. One is a law graduate and he checks on all his countrymen who come near us. If they aren't known to be reliable he tells us + we move them on....

Remember Feb. is the worst month of the year in Maine. From now on the weather improves for you. I'm sorry I can't send some M.O.s but they don't pay us during combat periods. I love you and am sorry you have so many troubles. Someday maybe I can give you a little more of the "better" and less of the "worse." Anyway you are sweet. — Wilber

> Norma was depressed about her situation in Bangor, Maine. She was a de facto single mother in a society-minded town and was leery of gossip about herself. It was likely that none of her music or academic friends became close confidantes. She was also deeply unhappy about being separated from her baby Gale now 15 months old.

x·o·ø·o·x

EVE. FEB. 7, '45

Dear Sweet Wife — It is four in the afternoon and nearly time for Pistol Pete [Japanese gun] to open up on us. Our problem is to find him and silence him. The chief difficulty is that he is back in a cave somewhere in the mountains and uses a different gun each time. [The gun comes out of the cave just long enough to fire.] Whenever he fires, we get reports from all our observers, then try to out-shoot him. Eventually we always have but sometimes the first locations aren't the right ones, in which case much of our computing is done below ground [for protection from P.P.]. Tonight after studying his shell craters and other data, we have a battery laid on each of four P.P.s most likely (we hope) to shell us. If we have guessed right, he will receive our respects promptly + with interest. If we don't have the right ones we go thru the "try + try again" routine.

I'm afraid our correspondence so far as my writing [goes] hasn't been very interesting. It seems that I adapt myself to combat conditions for it doesn't make so vivid an impression on me as Munda [in the Solomons] did. Now I find the operations are more routine and nearly all days alike except those in which I'm badly scared. Those minutes stand out all right.

> Wilber had indeed begun treating combat more routinely. He was pacing himself more sensibly, probably with fewer long sleepless stretches than he had had in the Solomons.

We continue to do well and I am well pleased with the 152. So far our casualties have not been excessive and most of those slight. Yesterday a shell went thru one of our Peeps [Jeeps] just after the driver parked + left it. He is still allergic to Peeps.

> Another story Wilber told us later was about a cook who, after a shelling, came walking out from the kitchen area covered in "blood." Everyone thought he would drop dead at any instant, but he was smiling and OK. He had been lying low between high shelves of kitchen supplies when a shell fragment nicked a large can of ketchup high above him. He had not dared to move during the shelling, even as a steady stream of ketchup poured onto him.

I love you, Little Wife. Some of these days we can start over together again. Don't let things worry you too much. The willow that is adaptable stands against the storm better than the oak. You play willow and let me be oak.… — Wilber

x·o·ø·o·x

FEB. 12, 1945

Dear Nana — Again this is just a note to tell you I am OK and having a very pleasant time. The Japs + the 152 have had several artillery duels and the score is well in our favor. Also they have made numerous infantry efforts to get to our guns – result Jap dead is three officers and fifty men. One of ours has a scratch in his back of which he is very proud. We have been in the lines now five weeks, and the new men are all veterans now and very sure of themselves. Actually our landing and later operations involved many fewer casualties than I had anticipated. Halsey did a good job on the softening-up process, and Jap planes are rare.

Pop got decorated again [for the January 12 spotting on Hill 600]. This time it was a Silver Star based on an Infantry recommendation. I'm very proud of it but my inner conscience tells me I didn't really earn it. I'll send it as soon as it is presented which will probably be some time yet.

One of my Fort Sill friends showed up yesterday. I hadn't even known he was in the theatre. We had a short visit over a captured bottle of Jap Sake which tastes like a cheap Bordeaux wine.… — Love, Wilber

> This ended the first phase of combat on Luzon, which lasted a full six weeks. The 43rd Division deserved and got a bit of rest.

6

"Send along the blue letters and don't worry about them"

Guimba and Mabalacat
Rehabilitation and combat reserve
February–March, 1945

On February 13, the 43rd Division completed its first mission on Luzon. It, along with the rest of I Corps, had insured that the northern Japanese force (Shobu Group) could not plausibly attack southward and disrupt a drive on Manila by the XIV Corps. The 33rd Division relieved the 43rd Division on February 15. The 43rd reassembled in the vicinity of Santa Barbara (near Lingayen Gulf) to train replacement soldiers and to re-equip. The division was short 215 officers and 3,805 enlisted men from all causes. Some 40% of these officer positions and 65% of the enlisted slots were filled with replacements or the previously wounded returned to duty. The artillery was probably minimally affected by these personnel changes. During this period, Wilber's unit, the 152nd Field Artillery, was billeted at an estate in Guimba (Map 7), about 40 miles southeast of Lingayen Gulf. They moved there during the nights of February 14 and 15. Getting out of the combat area was not simple.

FEB. 15, 1945
[This letter was written on Japanese stationery.]
Dear Nana — This is the end of another of those busy days. I've probably traveled 200 miles in the past 24 hours, much of it over the same roads several times. Last night was one of those times when we had to displace under enemy shell fire. It is

a very interesting experience. I could silence the Jap guns but couldn't keep them silenced. He probably pulled them back in a cave after each round so my shells couldn't destroy his guns.

That meant that I tried to outguess him and fire just as he was getting ready himself. Also I wanted to be sure he didn't fire while my vehicles were in the danger area. So my driver and I sat in a ditch beside the road for six hours (10:00 P.M. to 4:00 A.M.) playing our little game. The uncomfortable part of the business was the fact that we had to be where the shells fell. It was a good deep ditch, two feet, and it sure seemed like home whenever we heard one coming our way. Luckily we could hear them before they arrived. It sounds very risky but really wasn't unless the rare chance of a direct hit occurred. However it was very impressive to hear the fragments whiz over our heads. The party was a success because we made our shift without any casualties.

Beginning tomorrow I get some rest from combat and so do the boys. It won't be a rest because the idea is to get equipment back into condition. It will however be a good change for the men to clean up, get away from the flies and out of helmets. I am fortunate in being able to find them a good bivouac in the gardens of an estate. There is a water system if we can repair the damage the Japs did and a nice house for the officers except for broken windows and one of the living rooms from which the Japs tore out the floor for fuel. However the roof is good, there is plenty of shade, and it will be better than a tent + fox hole.... — I love you, Wilber

x·o·ø·o·x

At Guimba, Wilber could now finally reengage with his family by responding to issues Norma had raised. Letters had not traveled freely between them since his departure from Aitape seven weeks earlier. She was managing the house and family and filling her mid-winter days with writing and piano practice. Valerie and I were making our way daily to and from our school along the three-quarter-mile often snow-covered Garland Street.

[REST AREA, GUIMBA] FEB. 18 '45
Dear Wife of Mine — At last I have time to start answering your letters. The earliest is dated Jan. 8 and the latest Feb. 4. One favor I would like to ask. When you write a critical or discouraged letter please don't apologize [in later letters] because I always get those letters first. By the time I've received two or three letters of that type I am convinced the worst is coming and am practically afraid to open my mail. Just send along the blue letters and don't worry about them afterward for they are always much less than I anticipate anyway.

CHAPTER 6   *Send along the blue letters and don't worry about them*

Thank you for all the birthday greetings. I'm hoping my 45th year [actually his 46th, which began Feb. 1] will see this job done and the family together again.…

Answering Jan. 12. – I'm glad the J. [Junior] League is really interested in a library for us. We will take care that it is protected and made available to every man. It is going to be the finest library in the whole 43d.… Yes I do think Hale might like the navy. If his grades are high enough, we might be able to send him to a "Prep" school for Annapolis. It is a three months course and one at least has never had a candidate fail to pass the entrance exams. However he may prefer other fields either before or after he graduates from Annapolis. Doesn't it seem odd to be thinking of college and a profession for our son already?

Re – Jan. 22. I do hope your Fantasy is just what Scribner's needs.…

You must be playing a lot lately. I'd like to see you at the piano again. At present I can't see sending either of the children to special schools. We might later fail to give them help on college because of too much expense now. I do think the year in N.J. was a fine thing but am a bit skeptical about private schools. Too many of their graduates don't know how to live with the average citizen. That shows up a lot in the army and is a heavy handicap. Teachers are usually better in private schools but the influence of the student group is less practical than in a public school. I'm glad you had a good N.Y. trip + certainly could have helped you have fun.…

> Norma had gotten away again, this time to New York and, we learn later (letter of March 17), also to Washington, D.C., to see (we surmise) little Gale. She may have created a new short work, "Fantasy," during her free hours in Bangor and hoped to interest the publisher Scribner's in it.

… We have moved to a less active area for a rest. At least these Japs can't reach us with artillery but we do have a few [Japanese] about nights. It's practically as safe for us as N.Y.C.… — Happy March Lion to H + V. Wilber

> Wilber again [letter 3/4/44] referred to the old idiom, "March comes in like a lion, and goes out like a lamb."

x · o · ø · o · x

> Wilber wrote to his sister Mary with many thoughts about his mother's recent widowhood, and gave an eloquent description of his feelings about previous misunderstandings between his family and Norma. He was fighting not only the Battle of Luzon, but also the battle of the Home Front, approaching the latter as a sensitive negotiator.

FEB. 18, 1945

Dear Sister — Although I'm still in combat, we have moved out of reach of enemy mortar and artillery shells. Those Japs in our vicinity are discouraged so we can rest the men. That is the cause for the shift. Things were hectic for a time and the boys earned their rest (?).

During the voyage here and during the combat, I've worried a lot about Mother. All the previous difficulties make me a bit doubtful about whether I will accomplish more by keeping quiet or by trying to urge decisions. In the first place I want to make clear that [my] being so far away, final action should be taken by you + Paul + Rex + Ruth.

It has always been my intent to try to have my own finances in shape to help Father + Mother when they most needed it. That is part of the cause for trouble, for they felt I was evading responsibility and not just postponing action....

While I was in Florida, I learned to like it there very much. It is possible (or was) to get nice living apartments or cottages on the seashore for a very reasonable rent. I believe Mother could live there and have a grand time. The few of us should be able to finance the plan with enough to keep her comfortable and give her a surplus for un-essentials too....

> Wilber's mother never left the Indiana farm.

Feb. 21 — ... So far as your comment that Norma is "jealous" of my family is concerned, that is hardly the case. You know of the unfortunate introduction she received to our family. She has been a lonely and fatherless girl who early learned she had to fight her own battles herself. Perhaps because of this she certainly, as we all do, has made mistakes and done things that have not helped the situation. On the other hand, I know she has been hungry, more than you + I can ever realize, for admission to our family. She and Evelyn have fought since childhood to keep themselves free of the [unfortunate] things they found in their own background and as a consequence look on our home pretty much as their ideal. Norma thought the world of Father and Grandmother [Wilber's paternal grandmother, Julia Seelinger].

Since I love both Mother and Norma, I can see where trouble has started and it is probably my fault that it did start. I do know and want you to know that any mistakes of this type Norma has made were because she is so completely loyal to me. She is my wife and has been a wonderful one and I love her dearly. I expect to stand by her whether she is right or not, just as I do not expect to judge whether mother is right or wrong. In other words I have a wife and a mother and to me those words answer any questions.... — Love, Wilber

> Wilber was facing the age-old problem of split loyalties towards wife and mother. Fortunately, neither was forcing him to make a hard choice. Would

CHAPTER 6   *Send along the blue letters and don't worry about them*

he be able to maintain his admirable stance—standing by Norma, right or wrong—upon his return home? It was to be a severe test for which he would not be well prepared.

x · o · ø · o · x

FEB. 21, 1945
Sweet Nana — I've just received a lot more delayed mail, mostly from my wife. Do you know her? She is that lovely lady who married me one evening out in Portland, Oregon....

No I'm not worried by your comments on Valerie. She is just a bit like a Sparlin and I like them....

[Re your letter of] Dec. 28 – I don't quite catch on to this sudden interest in [John] Adams [2nd president of U.S.] but am glad the old boy is still on the job as a paternal guide. Perhaps you are a descendant of [Adams's wife] Abigail. She is probably proud of you. I hope J.A. approves my fighting for his country. I'm really ashamed Valerie expects you to do her washings. She really is much more selfish than I knew. Perhaps I should stop her allowance. I'll wait until April, and if I haven't heard she does her full share about the home without haggling, I will stop it. I have no intention of letting my wife be a maid for a grown-up daughter of mine.

> Grown up? Valerie had not yet completed her twelfth year!

[Your letter of] Jan. 3 – The S.E.P. letter arrived and the [Saturday Evening] Posts [a weekly magazine] seem to be on the way again. Thank you for all the trouble you had for me. My "Oregonian" comes now too and I've your "Colliers" in which were lobster, cranberry sauce and tuna and OLIVES. It just happened we had a poor supper so [Sam] Pierson + I used some onions he brought and had tuna-onion-butter sandwiches. They were really good. Thank you. Yes Sam came back the day after we pulled out of the line for a rest, so he is resting too. He says it was hard to time his arrival so well but he waited for the artillery to stop, so he knew the 152 had relaxed. He looks fine, had a wonderful time, even spent one evening at home. His wife wrote a nice letter thanking me for giving him the chance.

I love you, Little Wife. Spring is on the way. Here are more voyage letters. — Love Wilber

> Wilber was finally forwarding to Norma the letters he had written en route to Luzon. Norma's interest in John Adams soon became focused on Adams's wife Abigail, whose letters to her husband are now legend. This

became a substantial research and writing project for her. She produced a play about Abigail, which, despite a number of attempts and revisions, was never published or performed. She was early to recognize Abigail's strong role as a wife responsible for home, family, and farm in wintery Massachusetts during John's long absences. Norma surely saw herself reflected in Abigail's experiences.

x · o · ∅ · o · x

The interplay between the newly liberated Filipinos and the Americans was interesting to Wilber, and to me. Heretofore there had been little time for Wilber to observe it.

FEB. 24, 1945
Dear Sweet — We've ended a phase of our work here and are out of the lines for reorganization and repair of our equipment [since Feb. 16]. Our bivouac area was designated in the rice plains where trees are as scarce as in the Palouse. However after a day's search we found a large hacienda with very large grounds. We received permission from the overseer to take over. The Japs hadn't asked him when they moved in and they had wrecked much of the house – one hardwood floor torn out for firewood, and doors smashed etc.

We tented the men in the grounds, which are well shaded and profuse with formal hedges and flower beds. They are really more comfortable than anywhere since the U.S. As soon as we began to repair the plumbing [and] the electric plant, the Filipinos who were former employees began to resurrect essential parts: faucets, light switches, carburetors, belts that they had hidden from the Japs. All at once we found we were employing two overseers, "the oldest employee who is too old to work," twelve house boys, four gardeners, two engineers, and a lawn mower operator. The last three mentioned drew "specialists" pay. When we tried to place two house boys in the officers' mess, the overseers said they weren't suitable and two additional men appeared the next morning as mess boys.

I inspect officers' quarters daily at nine and once rated a room as unsatisfactory because the officers hadn't put their things away. That [Filipino house] boy very sadly left by order of the head man that P.M. [afternoon]. Now when I criticize a room, I explain if the boy is or is not to blame.…

Washington's birthday is celebrated in the P.I.s and [a local attorney, José Dacquel] Dacquel invited some of our men to a dance. We sent 80 and they came home most enthusiastic about the hospitality. I think these people are more home people to our boys because of their American ways than the N.Z. [New Zealand] people ever were. Of course the Spanish background tends to a more natural hospitality than the British.

 The boys were a bit amazed too, when the people they had seen walking about barefooted in ragged clothes showed up at the fiesta with high heeled dancing slippers, evening gowns, and a knowledge of American dancing. They also agreed the orchestra was equal to top U.S. ones. All in all I was very glad, for now at last the men see something of what they are fighting for.… Here people they feel are our kind tell them in English what the Japs are like and what they did to the Filipinos.… — I love you Wilber

x · o · ø · o · x

 On the home front, I was enjoying the outdoor life of Bangor. My friend Bob Butler and I would take bicycle excursions to Pushaw Lake. In the winter, the ice on the lake was so thick that trucks could drive out onto it. We would take our rifles and shoot at crows on those trips. I was enamored of the new Mossberg .22 rifle that Mother allowed me to purchase, and I loved reading about hunting rifles. I was very conscious of firearm safety, and would never, ever point a gun in an unsafe direction even when I was "absolutely sure" it had no cartridge in it.

x · o · ø · o · x

 The 152nd Field Artillery Battalion was alerted February 25 to be prepared to move to a new position on March 1 [152nd FA Journal]. But first, Wilber was to write about friends and hospitality in the Guimba area.

FEB. 28, 1945
Dear Nana — Lover, today I mailed you a box of sundries as follows: three packages of seed rice for Hale; a fan for Valerie and a bag for you.… The rice is the result of a casual inquiry on my part about rice. It was the gift of the attorney of the estate we were living in. His name is José Dacquel.

 He and his wife had Waldo [Fish], McIntire and myself over for dinner one evening for one of the nicest evenings I have had for a long time. They took us over to call on their wealthy aunt Mrs. Martinez or Gonzales. She was ill so we only met members of the family. When we arrived a dance was in progress. I found one niece was a H.S. teacher in Manila and [I] confessed to being a teacher too, so out came the college annual. Next a nephew wearing a Lts. bar of the P.I. guerillas came over with his [college yearbook] showing that he graduated in civil engineering and another to say he graduated in agriculture. Another niece was playing the piano. We were served wine and visited a few minutes, then returned to the Dacquel home.

There after dinner we brought them to our movie, which has very poor sound, but was their first for four years. The next evening the townspeople brought over an orchestra and gave a combined native folk dance for the men of the Bn. and then a regular U.S.A. type of dance afterward....

Mr. + Mrs. Dacquel send you the bag. It is made locally and of hemp. They also gave me a camagong [kamagong wood, aka tiger ebony or ironwood] very beautifully carved cane. One of the Martinez daughters gave me the fan for Valerie, just because I mentioned it....

> Norma used that beautiful cane for many years until she died. I still have it. It is a light brown color with dark streaks and is quite dense.

Things have developed into an orgy of exchange of gifts with us on the defensive.... You will possibly hear from some of them as soon as mail is possible. Here are names and addresses: ...

This will give you a little picture of our "Rest period" we have had. Some day we will see them together for I do want us to come here someday. You would have so much fun with these people. I love you, Dearest. Don't ever think you are not my favorite girl. I am wearing your ring too. — Wilber

> Norma never got there, but I did in 1983. I searched out the addresses Wilber listed here, was able to connect with some of these families, and had a wonderful time. My story of that visit is in the following Interlude.

x·o·ø·o·x

On March 1, the 103rd RCT, with the 152nd Field Artillery Battalion (Wilber's unit), motored 60 miles southwest from Guimba to Mabalacat City, arriving at 5 p.m. This was roughly midway between Lingayen Gulf to the north and Manila 120 miles to the southeast. The 103rd RCT was to be division reserve during the 43rd Division's containment of the Japanese Kembu Group in the mountains to the west, in the Fort Stotsenburg Action. Otherwise, the Kembu Group would be a threat to the right flank of the XIV Corps, which was busy driving the last Japanese from Manila (Map 7). Wilber and his executive officer remained quite alone in Guimba that night.

CHAPTER 6   *Send along the blue letters and don't worry about them*

[HACIENDA; GUIMBA, MAR. 1, 1945]
Dear Sweet Nana — Today I hope it is warmer for you than your last letters described. This must be a real record breaking winter. I hope you don't get sick or fall on the ice and hurt yourself....

It is late, Dear, and I've been writing this letter all day between other items of business. I must get to bed now. This is my last night in the [Guimba] house with a bathroom, and Waldo [Fish] and I are alone with our two drivers. We expect to maintain a "close-in" defense tonight. Don't worry there is really no risk.

I love you. You are the only girl I've ever or ever will love. Be patient and wait for me. I'll try to be a good husband again some day. — XXXOOO Wilber

Mar. 2 [and now with his unit] — Still all is quiet. WB. I've pitched my tent under another tree, only for the first time since I left home, there is no tree. However it isn't too bad because there has been a good breeze most of the day.... I now have a "Number One Boy" on a salary of one peso a day. His name is Ignatius – and he wanted to come with me from our last area to help fight. His family lived in a town where the Japs massacred most of the people, so he doesn't know if they are alive. His valor may fade a little when the shells begin to come our way again, but in the meantime he is armed with a knife and takes good care of my things. I really do think you are wonderful. — XXXOOO Wilber

x·o·ø·o·x

Wilber's mother Elizabeth responded to Norma who had sent her a $50 check (about $600 today) and had evidently told Elizabeth, acknowledging their difficult history, that she could consider it as coming from Wilber, not from herself. Elizabeth wrote out a copy of her response for her daughter Mary. In forwarding it, she commented that it sounded "stiff." To me, it sounded gracious and warm, especially in the light of their past difficulties.

March 6, 1945
Dear Norma — I like to "consider" the letter you wrote to me on New Year's Eve as coming from you and the children rather than Wilber. It was a very thoughtful and unselfish thing you did in sending me a part of your [military] allowance.

I appreciate the spirit in which it was sent and I am returning it in the same spirit.

I have been able to pay most of the big bills and can pay the others before too long without using the money you need to pay for your home.

I am glad you and the children are together in that home and hope the time will soon come when Wilber will be there with you.

VICTORY AND HOMECOMING   PART II: FINAL BATTLES, LUZON

If any one of you feels like writing to me, I should be glad to hear from you. I am interested in all of you. — Lovingly yours, Elizabeth Bradt

This exhibited a remarkable change of attitude toward us on Elizabeth's part. Her husband's death may have prompted her to reexamine her viewpoints.

x·o·ø·o·x

On March 6, the 152nd Field Artillery Battalion was relieved of its reserve status and proceeded to the Wack Wack Country Club in the eastern outskirts of Manila. Resistance in Manila had ceased on March 3, and Wilber visited there "three days later" [letter 9/6/45]. Then on March 10, his unit moved to a position northeast of Taytay, another six miles farther east of Manila [152nd FA History]. It provided direct support to the 7th Cavalry Regiment and then, after one day, to the 103rd Infantry (3rd Battalion). Firing was limited to registrations (alignments) of the guns during these few days (March 10–12; 152nd FA History). The registration positions were in Japanese areas [letter 3/11/45].

x·o·ø·o·x

Wilber took time to catch up on correspondence with me. He shared with me "the most dangerous thing" he had done and what a "relief" combat was!

MARCH 10, 1945
Dear Son — Two of your letters, Dec. 31 and Jan. 28 have gone unanswered until today. They came while we were in the toughest of the fighting so I just read them and put them in my bag.... Your .22 [rifle] sounds interesting. I'll be wanting to see how it shoots. Do you work about the house quite a lot? A house sure makes work but it has its points. I'd sure like to have one again. I'm very proud of the showing you are making in reading the Lesson at church. I'd probably be scared.

... My big job is really to know what the infantry is going to do and to be ready to help them. Therefore probably the most dangerous thing I do is going around alone or with one man looking for new positions [to place my howitzers]. It was while on a trip of this kind that I did run into six [Japanese]. We are back in action again and it is really a relief to be just shot at instead of trying to do all the little things we do when not fighting. The Japs shelled us last night but as usual they shelled where we weren't. They also threw a few big rockets at us that came closer. However, I didn't get out of my cot so you know they weren't too close.

CHAPTER 6   *Send along the blue letters and don't worry about them*

I had always visualized Wilber as searching for new positions with a car (Jeep or command car) and driver. Here he suggested that he was sometimes truly "alone," perhaps on foot in relatively but not completely safe areas. He told us, I recall, how important it was that a driver have a good sense of direction when searching for artillery positions. Wilber would direct his driver to this site, then another site over there, and so on, until after a number of such moves, he would say "Take me home now." At this point it was important that the driver remember which way was "home," so he would not inadvertently drive into enemy territory.

I've seen Manila and it is really a desolate sight. I also talked with several of the released U.S. and British that the Japs had held in Bilibid Prison. They hadn't been treated as badly as those in other prisons. So far I've not found O'Day or Holloway Cook.

These were Washington State friends who were in the Philippines in 1942. Cook did not survive imprisonment.

It's time to stop. I planned to write Norma but the Doc has me doped with codeine for a cold and I can hardly hold the pen. I do enclose for her two or three items! I love all of you. — Wilber

x · o · ø · o · x

MAR. 11, 1945
Darling — Your letter of Feb. 22 just came and was really a bright spot in my day. I am still feeling pretty rocky but am much better than yesterday. In a day or so I expect to be much better and out on the [front?] lines again.… I'm writing this letter sitting just in front of Btry "B"s howitzers, and about every sentence they go "Blam" right over my head on the way to Japs over the next hill.

It is too bad mother didn't feel like acknowledging the $50.00 but I'm not surprised. In addition to the past difficulties she would always resent people expecting thanks. She said to me of Mary – that she was generous + thoughtful but always made her feel that she expected or insisted on thanks which she would have given much more comfortably if it weren't expected. I doubt if there is anyone quite like Mother, so don't let it worry you too much.

As noted earlier, Elizabeth did eventually acknowledge (and return) the gift.

… I'm really getting to enjoy certain aspects of combat and try to keep these things in mind. Must rest now. — XXXOOO Wilber

Wilber had come to "enjoy" the focused activity of combat in contrast to the bureaucracy of "rest" times, such as at Guimba. This may only have been posturing, but if true would imply that he would not be disappointed as the second major phase of combat on Luzon began in earnest. It included his most dramatic exploit of the entire Luzon campaign.

The B-29 raids on Japan were continuing with devastating fire raids on numerous cities. On the night of March 9–10, the city of Tokyo was firebombed. Sixteen square miles of city were destroyed by incendiaries dropped by over 300 B-29 bombers. Strong winds created a "firestorm" of destruction. Over 100,000 Japanese died that night.

7

"Things were tight for awhile"
Shimbu Line combat
MARCH–APRIL, 1945

On March 14, two regiments (103rd and 172nd) of the 43rd Division began an offensive east of Manila to push the left end of Japan's southern Shimbu Group out of its strong positions and deprive it of roads and waterways. Elements of the 103rd Infantry made a wide 25-mile sweep around Japanese positions in the vicinity of Teresa (Map 13) to assault them from the rear. Consolidation of these positions continued until about March 17. The 103rd then drove north and east from Teresa on March 20–21 to clear strong points at Mt. Balidbiran and along the Bosoboso River. This and other mopping-up actions lasted until about March 28. The 152nd Field Artillery provided the artillery support to the 103rd Infantry during this two-week period. It was a fast-moving action; Wilber marked a map with seven positions where his artillery had been placed during this time.

In Maine, Norma, Valerie, and I were emerging from winter in Bangor, and Norma was working at her writing, probably her Abigail Adams play, and practicing the piano. She may also have been re-assessing her decision to move us to Bangor. Her separation from little Gale—it appears from her subsequent actions—was becoming increasingly unbearable.

x·o·ø·o·x

MAR. 17, 1945

Dear Wife — Yours [your letter] of Feb. G.W. Day [George Washington's birthday, February 22] just came. A lot of your missing letters have come now. When we came to the P.I., mail was piled up somewhere until we had things in hand here. Then it was moved by ship until air mail was renewed for us. As a result your letters are like the continued stories in the Sat. Eve. Post – interestingly confused.…

We have been put into action to relieve a famous division [1st Cavalry], which needed a rest. We have made good progress since they pulled out. I am now behind a hill from which we can fire at the Japs and they cannot reach us. It is a lot better in that respect than it was farther north.…

When Valerie does baby things like walking barefoot on the linoleum while sick and says she hopes to get pneumonia, just let her be sick. I've no sympathy for such a person at all. I wouldn't even be interested in hearing a dope of that type sing. You baby her too much. Maybe she will decide to grow up some day. I surely hope so.

Your NY + Wash. [D.C.] trip must have been pleasant. It is too bad that we can't do these things together but perhaps we can soon. Your music and writing really is [sic] wonderful. I'm glad it is progressing to your satisfaction.…

It's time to stop now and get up front for a while. I am sorry to write so seldom, but in the evening I'm usually too tired and in the morning too rushed. Today I took time out and wrote first. You are still my beloved wife. Don't forget me. I'm the man you used to sleep with and the one who will be dropping by some of these days. I do love you.

Good Luck. Springtime is coming + so am I. — XXXOOO, Wilber

x·o·ø·o·x

A week later, Wilber wrote to "Sweet Valerie," having totally set aside his irritation with her behavior.

MAR. 25, 1945

Dear Sweet Valerie — It has been a long time since I have really had time to write and now I have just 30 minutes.

… The envelopes of funnies and candy and gum came about three days ago. I am hoping to get time to read them soon. One piece of candy went to a little Filipino boy and you should have seen him grin when he smelled it. His eyes just shone.

It is very hot and dusty here now, but we get along OK. A few generals have been inspecting the 152 lately. They seem to think we are pretty good. Yesterday I climbed to the top of a young mountain and watched some of the Japs fighting our men. We saw them run into some trees, and [we] put artillery fire on those trees – no more Japs.

CHAPTER 7 *Things were tight for awhile*

Again, here was Wilber's casual depersonalization of Japanese killed by his artillery. This was pretty heavy stuff for a 13-year old daughter, and was not the first time he had unloaded such sentiments on her. Recall the chilling, "Pretty soon, no more Japs," in his letter of August 5, 1943, (Book 2) to her. Under the guise of entertaining her, he could make light of events that were surely troubling to him at some level. Young Valerie would not call him on it.

I love you Sweet Heart and I'll get leave as soon as I can and come home for a month. Don't be impatient with me. The war will soon be over and you will probably think I want to stay home too much. Be a good girl. I was proud of the grades you made. Goodbye now. — XXXOOO Wilber

x · o · ø · o · x

The northern end of the Japanese Shimbu Line was in a much weakened state by the end of March, and the 103rd Infantry was given a new task, namely to drive east across the Jala Jala peninsula into the Santa Maria Valley (Map 14). On April 1, Easter morning, the 103 RCT had assembled in the vicinity of Pililla, and Tanay.

General wreckage in the town of Antipolo after it was taken by the 103rd Infantry, March 14, 1945. Wilber worked directly with the 103rd Infantry during most of the Luzon action.
[PHOTO: U.S. ARMY SIGNAL CORPS, SC 374456]

VICTORY AND HOMECOMING   PART II: FINAL BATTLES, LUZON

Observation post on Hill 600. Artillery observers of the 152nd Field Artillery Battalion direct fire on Mt. Tanauan prior to the attack and capture of this key peak by the 103rd Infantry, 43rd Division, March 19, 1945. [PHOTO: U.S. ARMY SIGNAL CORPS, SC 204234]

Japanese mortar gunner, captured by the 103rd Infantry, points out Japanese gun positions to General Wing, commander of the 43rd Division (center) and Colonel Cleland, commander of the 103rd Infantry, at 103rd Regiment Headquarters, Teresa, Rizal, Luzon, March 17, 1945. [PHOTO: U.S. ARMY SIGNAL CORPS, SC 264102]

CHAPTER 7   *Things were tight for awhile*

APRIL 1, 1945, EASTER SUNDAY
Dearest Wife — Happy Easter Sunday to you and the children. It is a beautiful Easter morning and I woke with the memory of you singing that pastoral the Cinci[nnati] Glee Club sang. Remember? We do have so much to thank God for this Easter. All of us are well and spring is coming to you and the end of the war approaches. The news from Europe is good and we seem to be doing all right here too.…

The other day General Wing [the division commander] came up front and pinned a bronze-star ribbon on Col. Cleland and myself. It is a sort of junior Legion of Merit. You will recall Whitney got one when I received my L. of M. I was surprised and very pleased because it came directly from Wing. Don't get the idea I am going around playing hero for I'm not. It is just a case of things that need to be done.…

I'm very [glad] you had a note from Mother. Maybe [it is] the beginning of the end to that trouble. It just showed that you were right to send that money even tho she didn't need it.… Yesterday I was out in the hills at noon so had lunch on someone at home – sardines [sent by Norma]. They were surely good too.… — XXXOOO Wilber – Apr. 2, '45 Everything still under control.

The citation for Wilber's Bronze Star reads:

[CITATION FOR BRONZE STAR, MARCH 26, 1945]
For exceptionally meritorious conduct in the performance of outstanding service as commanding officer of a field artillery battalion on Luzon, Philippine Islands from 9 January to 26 March 1945. (G.O. #52, Hq. 43rd Div., 26 March 1945)

Wilber's constant presence at the front and his constant pressing to get the best performance from his battalion in support of the infantry easily merited this relatively low-level medal.

x·o·ø·o·x

On the night of April 3–4, the troops of the 103rd Infantry assembled with great secrecy in the vicinity of San Miguel for the southeastward drive around the large lake of Laguna de Bay. They pushed off at 3 a.m. (Maps 7 and 14). An early objective was Mabitac, which was taken with little opposition. The more distant objective after the Santa Maria Valley was the bridge that crossed the Pagsanjan River at Lumban, some 18 miles to the south on the eastern shore of Laguna de Bay. Its capture before the Japanese destroyed it would allow the division to link up with the 1st Cavalry Division, which was driving up from the south. This would deprive the Japanese of main roads and force them into the hills, a major strategic goal.

VICTORY AND HOMECOMING   PART II: FINAL BATTLES, LUZON

Signal crew elevating communication wire above the "Tanay" sign on the shore of Laguna de Bay, 40 miles east of Manila at Tanay, Luzon, April 3, 1945. Their mascot monkey watches from the left end of the horizontal bar. Note the Japanese katakana characters for "Tanay" on the sign. Wilber visited a church in Tanay on Easter Sunday, April 1, 1945.
[PHOTO: U.S. ARMY SIGNAL CORPS, SC 205883]

A battalion of the 103rd Infantry with Wilber's artillery and some tanks moved rapidly down the lakeside road, encountering occasional resistance that was pushed aside so the drive could continue—though at some risk that the Japanese would reestablish roadblocks behind them (which they did). Wilber placed artillery at four different positions as they proceeded. When they reached the bridge, Wilber's vehicle was near the front of the column as was that of the regimental commander, Colonel Cleland. The final artillery position was back a few miles, from which the howitzers could fire in the vicinity of the bridge.

Wilber continued the story in this letter. It began with a brief pencil-scribbled note written on location, at the Japanese (southwest) end of the Lumban bridge, from a foxhole in the fading light of evening.

CHAPTER 7   *Things were tight for awhile*

Terrain over which men of the 1st Battalion, 103rd Infantry, marched for the night attack on Mabitac, which was seized on April 4, 1945. This photo was taken April 7. [PHOTO: U.S. ARMY SIGNAL CORPS, SC 374474]

Men of 103rd Infantry (K Co.) and a Sherman tank move up to clear a Japanese roadblock where a convoy of U.S. vehicles had been ambushed on the outskirts of San Juan, April 5, 1945. This probably was after Wilber and others had already passed by. San Juan was several miles north of the critical bridge at Lumban. Wilber placed Battery B of his battalion at San Juan so they could fire in the vicinity of the bridge. [PHOTO: U.S. ARMY SIGNAL CORPS, SC 266177]

APR. 5 '45 [EVENING; WRITTEN IN PENCIL]

Dear Wife — Just a note to tell you I am OK, in the trenches for the night. It is just like old times [at Munda in the Solomon Islands]. We have been using our artillery right over our shoulders again. As usual the Nips couldn't take it. Things were tight for a while.

It is getting dark so must stop. I do love you all so much

x·o·ø·o·x

He resumed the letter two days later.

APRIL 7, 1945 [WRITTEN IN INK]

Dearest Wife — Everything turned out OK the other night. I am back at the CP [command post] and have had a good night's rest. There are a lot of tall tales about now of Col Cleland's + my "Horatio at the Bridge" act. I'll give you the facts, not

CHAPTER 7   *Things were tight for awhile*

Letter begun in pencil by Wilber from "the trenches" while holding the Lumban bridge, P.I., as the sky darkened on April 5, 1945. He resumed the letter in pen two days later. Unrelated notations at top and side in pen are Norma's. [LETTER 4/5/45]

the stories altho they are much better. The 103d Combat Team had the mission [of] making contact with a neighboring division some fifty miles away. They were also trying to meet us. Our road for the last 20 miles ran between a shore line and a young mountain range. At each critical point we dropped off a few troops and pushed ahead. The [final] critical point was a long wooden bridge [at Lumban] over an unfordable river [Pagsanjan] in a deep gorge. If the Japs were able to burn or blow up the bridge we would be stopped for days.

 The deep gorge was not terribly deep, perhaps only 20 feet, but the river was definitely not fordable.

I moved one battery along just back of the head of the column and traveled with the point looking for positions. As soon as we reached a position in range of the bridge (5 miles) I put it [one of his batteries] in position. My [observation] plane had reported that the Japs were working around and under the bridge. We opened fire on the bridge on the theory that we preferred to damage it to having the Japs destroy it. The plane adjusted the fire and drove the Japs away.

> Battery B, consisting of four howitzers, was placed at San Juan at 11:00 a.m. [152nd FA Journal and Wilber's notations on Map 14]

In the mean time we were plugging on down the road. Just before we reached the bridge I lifted the artillery and we moved on the bridge. Just as Col. Cleland and myself, Maj. Colpitts (Inf.), and Capt. Averill with about ten men reached the other [side], the Japs hit the company just behind us with machine guns, anti-tank-guns and a whole lot of mortar. Obviously the company became very busy and we had a bridge to hold.

Just then Col. Cleland spotted the Japs on our side of the bridge coming back. He shot the first one with his pistol. Capt. Averill shot another and his driver Joe McCloud (Bangor, I think) still another. In fact about every one but yours truly was either hitting or missing Japs. I was flat on the ground radioing for artillery fire because there was a large group of Japs assembling about 300 yards away. Things looked pretty hot for a few minutes but the Dead Eye Dicks held out until I got the artillery in on the larger group.

Only then did we have time to see if the bridge was mined. It was and we cut the wires. The scrap lasted about three hours and we felt very lonesome part of that time. After the Japs were driven off the road and a company of infantry with tanks rolled across the bridge, everyone felt much relieved.

Col Cleland went back to his C.P. then and I decided to stay until artillery plans were complete. About half an hour later the Japs attacked again and established another road block behind us [north of the bridge] so I stayed all night. As a result, when I returned there were some more tall stories going on around [the] division. So if you hear them you will know what was behind them. Papa isn't a hero. He just seems to have a knack for getting into hot spots.

This morning a letter came from you saying you had received the list of the silver. I picked out the items myself with the idea you would have a good foundation for a set....

Did I tell you I went into a church [first] built in 1606 on Easter [April 1]. It was damaged and dirty and roof partly off, but someone had kept the light in front of the altar burning. I presume a priest was somewhere nearby. Anyway, I had a little Easter service all by myself and felt much better about it.

April 8, 1945 I love you. — XXXOOØ Wilber

CHAPTER 7   *Things were tight for awhile*

American tank and troops at the wooden bridge over the Pagsanjan River near Lumban, April 5, 1945. The bridge was captured by the 103rd Infantry with Wilber's artillery assistance on April 5. Wilber was stranded overnight on the far (Japanese) side of the river. The Japanese built this bridge with American prisoner laborers shortly after the surrender of Bataan in 1942. [PHOTO: U.S. ARMY SIGNAL CORPS, SC 205890]

During my 1983 trip to this area, I visited the bridge at Lumban and learned of its tragic earlier history during the Japanese occupation. I also found and visited the "1606 church" in Tanay (Map 14). [The 1945 capture of the Lumban Bridge is reported in: *43rd Div. Hist. Rpt. of Luzon*, p. 40; the 152nd FA Journal and History; and the *History of the 103rd Inf. Rgt.*, Luzon, p. 69–71.]

Wilber was awarded a second oak leaf cluster for his Silver Star for this action, in lieu of a third Silver Star. The citation reads:

[CITATION FOR SILVER STAR: LUMBAN BRIDGE ACTION, APRIL 5, 1945]
For gallantry in action against the enemy at Lumban, Luzon, Philippine Islands on 5 April 1945. Colonel Bradt, driving his own light truck equipped with a radio, advanced at the head of a column for the purpose of directing artillery fire in support of a fast-moving situation. Along with four other vehicles, he became separated from the rest of the column by a Jap road block. Two vehicles directly in

front of his were fired upon and disabled, thus blocking his way. In spite of the great danger involved, Colonel Bradt courageously pushed forward through enemy fire in order to secure a vitally important bridge. Knowing that enemy troops occupied the opposite bank, he raced his vehicle to the opposite bank and, with a handful of men, established a bridgehead and secured the bridge. With his group now cut off from the rear, with no prospective reinforcements, Colonel Bradt vitally assisted in repelling an enemy counterattack. Immediately after, with his radio he contacted and directed his cub plane pilot to request assistance from friendly troops advancing near the town. Due to the superior enemy forces and the tactical situation, the troops were not in position to render immediate assistance. Colonel then directed his pilot to land on a nearby road and offer artillery support to the friendly troops. Artillery fire destroyed the enemy forces and allowed our troops to advance. While directing the artillery fire, Colonel Bradt was fired upon by snipers from the rear. During this entire period of several hours, Colonel Bradt remained calm and cool, displayed outstanding traits of gallantry and utter disregard for danger and his own safety. (G.O. #311, Hq. 43rd Div., 12 June 1945)

Wilber surely was not "driving his own light truck," but would have had a driver and possibly a radio operator with him. The 103rd Infantry History described how Wilber used an artillery observation plane to relay communications to and from the 1st Cavalry Division. This allowed him to use his artillery to clear the way for them to join up with the 43rd Division, which they did the next day, April 6.

The rapid sweep down the east side of Laguna de Bay on April 4 and 5 was a masterstroke completely at odds with the usual American approach of daytime attacks and limited advances after massive artillery preparations. It totally surprised the Japanese and, with minimal loss of American lives, accomplished its objective of forcing the Japanese into the hills.

x·o·ø·o·x

For the rest of April, the 103rd Infantry, supported by Wilber's artillery, continued to ferret out Japanese pockets of resistance in the hills northeast of the Mabitac and east of Lumban. There was no further large-scale organized resistance in this area. The intensity of combat quickly diminished.

Headquarters Battery of the 152nd Field Artillery Battalion was located in Pakil (north of Lumban) from April 5 to 21. One of Wilber's most delightful encounters, written several weeks later to Valerie, occurred there. It involved two little Filipino girls who probably reminded him of his own daughter.

CHAPTER 7   *Things were tight for awhile*

Filipino guerillas guarding a group of pro-Japanese Filipinos (Makapilis). They are in the Pagsanjan town square on April 7, 1945, for questioning two days after the American capture of the city. The street is littered with worthless Japanese invasion currency. [PHOTO: U.S. ARMY SIGNAL CORPS, SC 265216]

JUNE 2, 1945

Dear Sweet Little Valerie — Or maybe you don't like to be called "little" now. You will always be my little girl until you are bigger than I am. I had chicken for dinner today so probably gained another pound. It sure is easy to eat too much. However out here where I have to climb a lot of hills I don't dare get fat or I couldn't do it. So my waist is 38 and my chest 42, which isn't being thin either.

Did I ever tell you about the two little Filipino girls, age about four and five years? It was at a little town called Pakil and happened several weeks ago. I was sitting in my tent beside a lake resting when [up came] two of the cutest little bright-eyed girls I had ever seen for a long time. They were as clean as could be, hair combed and dresses as neat and clean as the girls. They were barefooted.

They stood in silence looking me over very seriously to see if I would be cross. Then they said together, "Hi Joe." I answered "Hello! What is your name?" It developed one was Marguerita and the other _____. I next gave each a stick of gum. Each separately and very seriously said "Thank you very much," but didn't chew it then. They went out and held a conference in Tagalog [the native language] under the nearest tree and apparently decided the social amenities had been observed.

So they came back with a very business-like manner and said, "Soup please." After several repeats it finally dawned on me the poor little things were hungry, but I had no soup. So I opened my locker and found a Hershey bar and gave each a piece. They ate it after the "Thank you very much" then said, "Soup now?" I explained I had no soup and how sorry I was not to have soup for them, to come back some other time and maybe I would have some soup. So after they said, "We go now?" and I said "OK you go now."

They left with the air that Americans weren't quite up to their expectations and in about an hour were back. This time we went thru the usual salutations and one said, "Soup now." I said "No soup yet." So they retired to the tree and held another very serious conference then came back to me. One of them became very embarrassed and the other urged her to go and do something. Finally she held out to me a kind of radish they grow here in gardens. It was dirty and had obviously just been pulled. I took it, thanked them "Very much" and set it down on my table. Out they go for another very, very serious conference and having made a decision returned with the word I was to eat it.

I remembered all the precautions the army had taken about our eating root vegetables in the P.I., so stalled. I would eat it for dinner. No I should eat it now. It was very important to them so I scraped off some dirt and took a bite. They were just as happy as I ever saw anyone and I felt that if I had dysentery the rest of my life it would be worth seeing them so pleased.

Having broken bread with them so to speak, I set the radish down and thanked them "very much" a few more times, said it was good, etc. They then said with all the assurance in the world, "Soup now." I realized I had been trapped so I went to Sgt. Shippee and asked for some bread and butter or any suitable substitute for soup. All his food was in large cans so no luck there. The two little witches were waiting in my tent with the air that all was well in the world. My heart was bleeding. Why did I eat those oysters you sent? Why didn't I have some soup? I determined to write for all the soups there were.

Again I searched my things. No soup. I gave them some more gum, was "Thank you very much"ed again with the attitude that I was just leading up to the real gift.

Finally I had to admit still no soup. I was very sorry and wished I could give them some soup. They were terribly disappointed, my day was ruined, War was hell, and everything was wrong in the world that couldn't even give two hungry little girls the soup they had waited so long for the Americans to bring. I nearly cried.

Just as they left I gave them the half used bar of soap I had been using. They fairly danced with joy, eyes bright, said "Yes Soup! THANK YOU VERY MUCH, We go now?" I said, "yes you go now." They raced away thru the cocoanut grove holding hands. Americans were dumb but nice. I collapsed in my chair.

Later we set up a basis for business – two eggs, one "soup." … I had Sweet Heart, Palmolive, Ivory, Life Buoy and one or two other kinds. It was very difficult for them to decide which smelled and looked the best. They always took one cake, went out for their Tagalog conference, then came back and exchanged it for another ending up with Life Buoy.

It is pouring now outside; a leak in the tent is falling between my knees, another just off this page and another behind me. If I sit just right I'm dry. So good night Little Lover. Have a good summer & take good care of my family. — I love you and am Your Pop Wilber

In my brief half-hour visit to Pakil in 1983, I did not attempt to locate the two girls. I have since made queries without success. Wilber gave us very little to go on, but the story remains among the sweetest of all his adventures.

x · o · ø · o · x

On Thursday, April 12, 1945, President Roosevelt died of a cerebral hemorrhage. A friend told me about it; we were on our bicycles on a warm Bangor afternoon. I was stunned along with most of the nation. I had known no other President, having been barely two when he first took office. Wilber did not mention it in several subsequent letters. It was not until two weeks later, on the 29th, that he wrote Norma of his reaction: "It seems a very far away event to men who are living day by day."

On Saturday, April 14, and the following Sunday, Wilber found time to respond to Norma's queries.

APRIL 15 [14–15], 1945
Hello Beauty of Mine — Just a note from your dopey husband. I'm so glad you finally received your X-mas present and especially that you liked it.…

I've recommended my driver for a Bronze Star for helping move vehicles out of an area being heavily shelled, another Bangor man for helping to hold a bridge, another for saving a man by first aid while being shelled, another for leading a patrol that killed several Japs and captured their machine guns. Don't worry; I'm doing what I can to get recognition to the men who earn it.

It seemed that Norma had nudged him about this, perhaps because someone in Bangor had nudged her about a relative in Wilber's unit.

… You ask if I can or cannot come home.… I want to watch what happens after V–E [Victory in Europe] day. If it means Japan may also decide to sue for peace, I might better delay and come home with the assurance I would stay in the States. Still another factor is the possibility of my staying in the army as a profession without loss of rank. Don't breathe a word even to the children.... Life in the army might not be the most pleasant but it would be different. With you to help, we could see and do a lot. In the meantime it is almost dark.

> This was the second time Wilber had mentioned in letters that he was considering staying in the army after the war [letter 11/23/44]. It was far from clear though that such an opportunity would exist.

April 15, Sunday ... Don't worry about my decorations, I'm not taking any more risks than I consider advisable. Your letters come almost daily now and are such a help to me. You have no idea how interesting news of your house cleanings, sewing, scout problems, and the children is to me. Besides I look in each one and find you still love me and that is the important part....

> Norma had a great deal to write about during her stay in Bangor, unlike when she was hiding her whereabouts and activities during and after her pregnancy. Her life in Bangor was an open book, though the reasons for her visits to Washington were not. Norma must have felt emotionally well connected to Wilber if she was writing "almost daily." The act of writing would, in itself, reinforce that attachment. Indeed, they remained partners in this war.

Someone just opened up with his carbine. Probably [a] trigger happy [U.S. soldier or], possibly a Jap trying to get thru our perimeter. Definitely under control.
— XXXOOO Wilber

x · o · ø · o · x

> There was even time for a letter to his brother Rex. They served in the artillery together in the Indiana National Guard in the 1920s.

APRIL 15, 1945
Dear Rex and Gerrie — Thank you for the picture of Doug. He surely is a husky youngster and doesn't look too much like his father....

My battalion has quite a reputation for crowding the front lines. On two occasions technically they were in front of the infantry but not in danger more because of it. We also are the only battalion here whose positions have not been [successfully] raided by the Japs. They have tried it often enough for we have killed in a personal non-artillery manner over 75 who tried. Just three days ago two of my men stumbled into

CHAPTER 7   *Things were tight for awhile*

a group of about 50 Japs and killed seven before the Japs decided it was a major attack and beat it. It is a wonder they weren't both killed. You can see how much satisfaction I get from boys like those two. We really are getting on well....

Time to stop and go over to the infantry C.P. for the usual check up on what the arty. can do [for them]. — Love + Good Luck from Wilber

x·o·ø·o·x

On April 16, Wilber's Battery B moved north to Famy. On the 19th, the Sixth Army commander, General Krueger, was photographed by a signal corps photographer as he consulted with the 43rd Division commander, General Wing. On the 21st, Headquarters Battery of the 152nd Field Artillery Battalion (surely with Wilber) and Battery A moved northeast to Teresa (Map 13) while the other batteries moved to Tanay and Pililla. These moves were to support the 103rd Infantry in its mopping-up operations in the hills northeast of the main highway [152nd FA History]. The next day, Sunday, April 22, Wilber wrote to Norma.

General Wing, commander of the 43rd Division (left), and four-star Gen. Walter Krueger, commander of the Sixth Army, at 43rd Division Headquarters, Maybancal, Laguna, Luzon, April 19, 1945. [PHOTO: U.S. ARMY SIGNAL CORPS, SC 205910]

143

APR. 22, '45

Dear Wife of Mine — I've apparently been missing some of your letters for your April 3 mentions an infection in Hale's leg being drained as if I knew about it. Probably I'll get the details soon. I've had some of those things to deal with here too. Last month I had a bad one at the base of my thumbnail. The surgeon lanced it and used penicillin ointment on it. About five daily applications fixed it up OK. Another one I had been bothered with for several months was recently healed by sulfadiazine ointment. This last was a type of ringworm that I picked up in Munda and had never been able to cure before. Probably one of those two were [sic] used on Hale. At all events I assume he is OK again.…

Yes, we did go into a new action on the day you mentioned and went thru the Japs for three miles the first day. Since then we've had them off balance and have moved so fast they sometimes (forgot?) to fuse their tank and personnel mines which helps. Those were the ones I drove over then found [them] behind my car. Maybe you don't think that is a thrill. There was the other time when my car wheels went between two percussion fuses set in 100 lb. of TNT and Fish's car stopped with his front tire one foot short of and in line with a fuse. His driver took one look, said, "I feel sick," and laid down right there until he had recovered from the shock. There are special days and just days in combat. You can see this was one of the special ones.…

Papa has a new bath robe. It is the biggest I ever saw, made from Jap muslin. It is a "gorgeous" dark red with big (4-inch) light red and yellow flowers. The sleeves and pocket are light red with big yellow flowers. My name is embroidered on the pocket in script. You read we were in New Bosoboso in the New York Times so I can tell you it came from there. It is long enough to cover my ankles and loose enough to wrap around me (and you too). We'll have fun in it in front of the fireplace evenings. Maybe you won't let me wear it. I think it is the first time I just gave way to my repressed desire for loud pajamas + robe.

I love you my Darling. Am going to be dropping in someday for a date too. Please don't be too busy. I want you to sit by a mirror so I can see you twice. — XXXOOO Wilber

> Wilber told us in 1945 how the lady who made the bathrobe laughed and laughed as he explained how long he wanted it (down to the floor) and big enough to wrap comfortably around him one and a half times. After the war, I wore it for several years until it disappeared during one of the moves my parents made. Another historical artifact lost, but the story about it remains alive.

x · o · ø · o · x

CHAPTER 7 *Things were tight for awhile*

28 APR '45
Dearest Family — I'm lonesome tonight so will talk a little with you and then I won't be alone at all. My C.P. is in a lovely spot now [probably in Teresa] and my tent under a big mango tree overlooking a grassy slope as clean as our yard. It is so good to find a clean spot where there are no battle odors, few flies and at the same time no mud or dust. All around are clumps of bamboos and across the little valley a rocky cliff honeycombed with Jap caves. We killed over 300 in those caves before we (43d) "owned" that hill. It is all scarred where we blasted the entrances, but in the evening sun the scars disappear and it is a really lovely hill.

Thank you Hale for the picture of yourself, school and the house. The one of you is in my folder over my cot with Valerie's + Norma's. I'm proud of my family and the way you all keep my home until I can come back to it. I was thrilled to see the house – our home. It looked so good.

Apr. 29, 1945 — It got dark as usual too soon last night and interrupted this letter. This is Sunday A.M. and also the date the Japs here are supposed to counter-attack. We captured their orders so maybe the Japs missed getting theirs. Personally I don't think they can do much now.

> Emperor Hirohito's birthday, April 29, was an important day for the Japanese. An attack could well have been planned to honor it.

… The rainy season here is one month away now and we still have some scrapping [fighting] that needs to be done before then. May is the hottest dry month and is already pretty warm except for the fact that a breeze is usually blowing.

We listen to the news feverishly and it is all good: here, Okinawa, Burma, + Europe. I'm more optimistic about things than my reason tells me I should be. That "five years" we estimated might well be close. Just checking – I sent you about $600.00 some weeks ago. Has it arrived safely?

I love all of you very, very dearly and I can think only of how much I want to see each of you. — XXXOOO Wilber

> With its mission against the left end of the Shimbu line accomplished, the 43rd Division had played its role in rendering the Japanese incapable of organized action. The 43rd Division was relieved on April 30 and moved northward about 50 miles to the Santa Maria–Bulacan area. Thus ended the second phase of Luzon combat for the 152nd Field Artillery Battalion. The third and last was to begin within a week. There was no time for recuperation.

Okinawa, in the Ryukyu Islands, a mere 400 miles southwest of mainland Japan (Kyushu), had been invaded in force on April 1 and the fighting against the strong entrenched opposition carried on throughout April, May, and June while kamikaze attacks took a heavy toll on American ships. The island was finally declared secure on July 2. In Europe, Adolph Hitler committed suicide on April 30 in his Berlin bunker, and the German capitulation was only days away. Berlin fell on May 2, and a general unconditional surrender was signed on May 7 at Eisenhower's headquarters in Reims, France. German garrisons elsewhere were surrendering until May 11. May 8 was proclaimed "V-E Day"—Victory in Europe Day.

8

"We are in mud to our ears"

Ipo Dam combat
MAY 1945

The final task for the 43rd Division in Luzon was to undertake the capture of Ipo Dam. The dam, 25 miles northeast of Manila (Maps 7 and 15) in mountainous territory, provided about a third of Manila's water. The Japanese had closed the gates of the conduits to Manila and a severe water shortage was developing. The dam was in wooded hilly terrain with few roads and was strongly defended by the Japanese. Moderate forces had thus far failed to dislodge them. A rapid capture was necessary for several reasons: to reestablish the water supply, to prevent the Japanese from destroying the dam, and to avoid combat during the forthcoming (June) rainy season.

On April 30, Wilber, along with Majors Fish and Pierson, had gone on reconnaissance with parties from all batteries to locate new battalion positions in the vicinity of Santa Maria, about 15 miles west southwest of Ipo Dam. On May 1–3, the 152nd Field Artillery Battalion moved one battery at a time under cover of darkness in blackout condition (with only faint tail lights on each vehicle). Upon arriving at its new position, each battery immediately began registering its howitzers on likely target areas. Additional moves forward of the individual batteries took place in the subsequent days before the attack commenced.

On May 7, the attack on Ipo Dam began with one regiment (169th Infantry) attacking east against the main Japanese defenses on a high formidable ridge some four miles west of the dam. This was a diversionary tactic. The other two regiments of the 43rd Division (172nd and 103rd),

VICTORY AND HOMECOMING   PART II: FINAL BATTLES, LUZON

constituting the main effort, were to sweep in from the south over about ten miles of very difficult mountainous terrain in hopes of catching the Japanese off guard. Simultaneously, a regiment of Filipino guerrillas ("Marking's regiment") would approach from the north. Additional artillery units were attached to the 43rd Division and substantial air support was brought to bear. Dive-bombers would eliminate antiaircraft guns so the artillery-spotting cub planes could fly safely. Searchlights were employed to illuminate clouds that in turn illuminated the ground. This novel technique greatly hindered Japanese night movements and aided the removal of American casualties.

After initial rapid gains by the main southern force, U.S. forces encountered increasingly stiff Japanese resistance. Artillery followed close behind the infantry and engineers pushed through roads on which supplies could be brought forward and casualties removed. Japanese artillery fire was intense and well hidden, but air and ground surveillance could locate gun positions that could be destroyed by American "counter-battery" fire or bomber raids. Extensive use of napalm dropped by fighter-bombers exposed Japanese cave entrances. Progress was slow but steady.

Wilber marked the map of the operation to show 152nd Field Artillery emplacements at five locations in the 11 days (May 6–17) it took to capture Ipo Dam (Map 15). These emplacements were single batteries of four howitzers each. He leapfrogged them in order to provide continuous artillery support to the advance of the 103rd Infantry.

Meanwhile, in Bangor, springtime weather had finally arrived and morale was rising. Valerie and I were ending our school year in Garland Street Junior High School. Hundreds of teen bike riders crowded Garland Street at school commute times, taking care not to trip up on the trolley tracks. (That indeed had been my fate once, to my great embarrassment, while I was showing off at high speed for a group of cycling girls.)

x · o · ø · o · x

Wilber wrote the first extant letter during this campaign on the fifth day of the drive toward the dam. He had little time for letter writing.

MAY 12, 1945

Dearest Nana — The San Francisco radio says we are rapidly closing in on the Ipo dam so I assume it is safe to admit the radio is correct. We are still in active combat and things go well. I've been a good boy and haven't been out in front of the lines

CHAPTER 8   *We are in mud to our ears*

Colonel Marcus Agustin, Filipino guerilla battalion commander, briefs his officers prior to the drive on Ipo Dam, May 6, 1945. [PHOTO: U.S. ARMY SIGNAL CORPS, SC 199849]

An all-Filipino crew fires on Japanese defenses in the Ipo Dam operation on May 12, 1945. This 155-mm "Long Tom" gun, used by the Americans in the defense of Bataan in 1942, was captured by the Japanese and then recaptured in 1945 by the 43rd Division. [PHOTO: U.S. ARMY SIGNAL CORPS, SC 208328]

once in this action. Mostly I specialize in long hot hikes that are very dull and usually quite safe so far as battlefields go.

This is just between you and me. I have told Gen. Wing I would like assignment to the C + GS [Command and General Staff] school at Leavenworth at the same time that I get my leave. He said he was all for it but could make no promise for two reasons: 1st, the quota is not regular and 2d, a division commander never knows how long his tenure of office is....

> This was yet another of Wilber's mentions that one of his postwar options was staying in the army. He still had the option of returning to his position at the University of Maine.

Your comments about the house foundations agree with my picture of the situation. Some work needs to be done and it won't be too difficult when I get home. In the mean time we are making good progress by keeping the roof + paint in shape and making payments. If you want to rent it again, use your judgment. There is no way yet to decide what date I'll become a civilian....

> Norma had apparently broached the possibility that she would not stay in Bangor for another school year.

We just cleaned off all the Japs on Hill 1400 [en route to Ipo Dam] for the infantry. They walked up without a shot being fired at them. — I love you wife, XXXOOO Wilber

x·o·ø·o·x

> On the same day, Wilber wrote Valerie. Here we encounter a delightful story about the gum that Valerie had sent Wilber [see letter of 3/25/45]. It gives us another view of Wilber's activities in this action.

MAY 12, 1945

Darling Valerie — This is the day the Jap order said we were to be attacked. We captured the order and made our attack [toward Ipo Dam] a week ago. The Japs probably think we didn't play fair. Now I doubt if they can attack. However if they do, we will be all set.

I want to especially thank you for the big envelopes full of funnies. The little surprise gum or candy bar is nice too. Day before yesterday I was up in the front lines. It was a terribly hot day. The ground was muddy and the trail went up & down steep hill after steep hill. In the valleys I practically had to crawl thru brush and vines. On the slopes and hilltops the trail went thru cogan [cogon] grass, which is thick and taller than I am. I was plugging along wishing I had water, wishing I could find a breeze, wishing the war was over, wishing we had the dam we were after, and wishing I was home, when I found a pack of charcoal gum in my pocket. I put the whole big piece in my mouth and literally "chewed" my way up to the front lines, did some survey and told the infantry commander where he was, and then "chewed" my way back to my car and water. So you see how much your thoughtfulness helped me. It isn't the size of the gift or its cost that counts. I would not have sold that gum for ten dollars. The nicest part of all was the fact that I knew all that time my girl loved me. It was just like a holiday for me.... Goodbye now. — Love XXXOOO Wilber

> I do wonder, though, why the infantry commander needed the artillery commander to personally tell him where he was! Perhaps artillery surveys complemented the commander's knowledge of the terrain and his place in it. Wilber may have been simplifying the real story.

x · o · ø · o · x

On May 13, at 7 a.m., the rains began ahead of schedule. Sheets of rain turned roads into quagmires; trucks, tractors, and artillery were nearly immobilized. Progress was heartbreakingly slow. Supplies were brought in by Filipino work details and dropped by air. Casualties walked to the rear if they could. In spite of this, the troops pressed on and all three thrusts gradually made headway toward Ipo Dam. Wilber described the scene to me.

MAY 15, 1945
Dear Son — It has rained a lot for three days now and we are [in] mud to our ears. The roads we make are slippery and cars get stuck on each hill. Since it winds about thru hills, that means cars are having trouble everywhere. It is difficult for us to keep the ammunition up to the guns and then rain makes it hard to see where the enemy targets are. All in all, just now, it is a quite unpleasant war. The rainy season seems to be catching up with us.

However, the 152 is still in here firing. One gun slipped out of its position while firing so far we had to pull it back up a grade with a tractor. It had just kicked itself down the hill.

> The recoil of a howitzer when firing was substantial. Its "trails" had to be dug solidly into the earth to prevent it from rolling backwards.

I was quite impressed about your Scout exhibit [of war souvenirs]. It must have been really good. I would like to have seen it. It is too bad the Jap saber couldn't have been sent sooner. That saber isn't the officer's dress saber that everyone prizes so highly. This one is the enlisted cavalryman's saber. I've not seen many of these because we have not often been fighting Jap cavalry. I personally am feeling OK except for being rather generally tired. If combat eases off here during the rains, I'll soon get rested up.

> The exhibit of wartime souvenirs was a project I had conceived for our scout troop. We set the show up with great effort on large tables in the high school gym and bicycled all over town to collect souvenirs. Unfortunately, only five or six people attended that evening.

It seems good to know the war in Europe is over [on May 8] but it also seems a long way off. We didn't have any celebration because our attack here was just started. Since then we have realized it a little more. I'm certainly glad for it means a lot of boys will be home that would have died otherwise. Also it should discourage the Japs a bit. I think this war will be over in a year, perhaps sooner.

How do the yard and garden look? Have any of the fruit trees you and I planted survived the years? If so they should soon bear fruit. School must soon be over. What do you all plan to do this summer? I'm interested because it is still possible I might drop in next fall for a visit. I love you. — Your father, Wilber XXXOOO

x·o·ø·o·x

MAY 16, 1945

Dear Wife — It is evening again and we still are plugging hard. The worst enemy is mud and poor roads. One can shoot 2 1/2 tons of artillery ammunition in 90 seconds, but it takes a lot longer to get it into the battalion area over miles of mud.

Col. Cleland + I live in a tent and have mud underfoot but are lucky to have the tent for a lot of others are in holes full of water and mud with no roof over them. I have spent the day wading in the mud and working on roads and communications. When roads go bad and detours are being used, all telephone wires go out. [The bulldozers and trucks break the wires that are strung beside the road from tree to tree.] No communications means no artillery, so we have our problems. However we make progress and every man is working on getting artillery shells in front of our troops. It is funny what one does to win wars, and mud seems to always be present. It is like Munda except one doesn't get sniped at [shot at by hidden riflemen] so much as in Munda.

… I have a new Exec – Maj. [Franklin E.] Carpenter, and he is sure getting a rough initiation. Pierson [the Battalion S-3] is doing very well but of course I'm

Trucks in the rain and mud on the newly constructed road leading to Ipo Dam in the 103rd Infantry zone, May 18, 1945. [PHOTO: U.S. ARMY SIGNAL CORPS, SC 312642]

never satisfied, so both of them are sweating out their omissions and mistakes. In spite of all these items we still kill Japs and go ahead. – Here is my arm about you Beloved. — Your husband, Wilber

Here was Wilber's leadership in action: He was "never satisfied," even with officers of moderately high rank (majors) and lots of experience. Keeping the enterprise going in the rain and mud must have required superhuman efforts by all.

x·o·ø·o·x

Ipo Dam was captured by the Americans on May 17. Philippine guerrillas (Marking's regiment) reached the north end of the dam while the 103rd Infantry, supported by the 152nd Field Artillery, reached the south end where the vital hydraulic equipment was located. The dam had been prepared for destruction with tons of TNT, but the Japanese had failed to detonate it. Mopping-up actions in the 43rd's zone continued.

MAY 18, 1945

Dearest — Three letters postmarked May 7 came yesterday from you. Wonderful! It is like a four-hour rest to hear from you. You really take me home for a few minutes with each letter....

During this operation now we have been opposed by a lot of Jap artillery but now have, I'm sure, gained the upper hand. This combat team [103rd RCT] is now sitting on top of its objective [Ipo Dam]. Again we have made the end run and caught the Japs from behind. The early rains made it hard but we are now ready to go on to the final kill.

Yesterday I met [Gen.] Barker [Wilber's immediate superior] in a mudhole and had quite a talk after I had pulled him out of the mud.... All of this, coupled with a pretty high casualty rate in Bn. C.O.s during the past months, makes me the senior Lt Col in Div. Arty and second or third in the division. All of this coupled with the fact that Col. Cleland [commander, 103rd Infantry] has just become a B.G. [brigadier general] gives me food for thought. Two generals, Barker + Stark have suggested I take [command of] the regiment [103rd Infantry] and have said Wing is holding back only because I haven't said I would want it. I told Barker that the one thing I wanted was a leave to the U.S. during this rainy season. He said if it [were] at all possible he would support it. The understanding however is definite that I return here. At present I don't care to command a regiment. I'm a bit too tired just now and besides I really like artillery....

Don't forget that the "dream world" of the faculty is a more real world of progress than the war routine that has a temporary eclipse over the real progress in science, and humanities. Just because I turned into one of Halsey's "Swashbuckling Buccaneers" doesn't mean that something I taught at WSC was not more valuable.
— XXXOOO Wilber

[Note on side:] I'm so sorry about the Steinmetz boy [killed in action]. There are so many of these tragedies. Two of my friends this week here too. WB

> Wilber, admirably to my thinking, saw the larger picture, that the academic enterprise played the dominant role compared to wars in guiding human progress. He was trying to see the positive side of a return to academia despite feeling totally out of touch with it. The routines of research and teaching in academia, as he knew them, must have seemed insignificant compared to the combat responsibilities he was carrying.
>
> The two friends were Wilber's 43rd Division officer colleagues, Major Hugh Ryan and Lt. Col. Stephen Nichols, both of the 192nd Field Artillery, who were badly wounded in a jeep or command car when their driver's grenade accidently exploded. He had habitually kept several grenades for ready

CHAPTER 8   *We are in mud to our ears*

Japanese prisoners captured in the Ipo Dam sector enjoy a meal of army C-rations, May 18, 1945. [PHOTO: U.S. ARMY SIGNAL CORPS, SC 208622]

use in a small bag hanging from his seat and the jouncing of the vehicle must have dislodged a pin. [Barker, p. 238 and conversation with Howard Brown]. This was yet another instance of a "friendly incident" that killed or injured Wilber's friends. Ryan was photographed with Wilber in 1943 (Book 2, p. 82).

x·o·ø·o·x

Japanese "cave-home," possibly for officers, near the Ipo Dam sector, Luzon, May 18, 1945.
[PHOTO: U.S. ARMY SIGNAL CORPS, SC 208704]

Message center of the 43rd Division at Bulacan (40 miles west of Ipo Dam), May 31, 1945. Ipo Dam had been captured on May 17, but cleanup operations continued until June 25.
[PHOTO: U.S. ARMY SIGNAL CORPS, SC 236548-1]

CHAPTER 8   We are in mud to our ears

Aerial view of Ipo Dam and its mountainous surroundings, May 26, 1945. The dam had been captured by the Americans and Filipinos with its important hydropower facilities intact on May 17. [PHOTO: U.S. ARMY SIGNAL CORPS, SC 374505]

Then, as the third phase of combat on Luzon was winding down, Wilber was given a brand new assignment that was quite unusual for an artillery officer.

MAY 20, 1945
Dearest Nana — All the changes and promotions I mentioned in my last letter have finally been pretty well cleared up. Further, they have changed me from artillery to infantry. Gen. Wing called me in and asked, in fact almost told me, he was making me Exec. [second in command] of the 172d Inf. The Reg[imental]. C.O. is [Col.] Geo[rge E.] Bush, whom I supported in Arundel. He requested me from all the Div. Lt. Cols., which makes it nice for me.

Gen. Wing, after reminding me that plans in war are always subject to change, said he wanted me in line to take command of a regiment or to head his G-3 section. Either assignment would mean promotion to full colonel. He made it pretty strong and said he had wanted me to command a regiment for two years [since Munda] and that I was his first choice for G-3 whenever a vacancy occurs. Further he said he anticipated one or both of the vacancies might come in the next six months.

The G-3 section was responsible for operations of the division, a critical position.

I told him I did not feel it fair to me if I were to lose my chance for a leave and that Barker + I had planned for me to take leave during this coming rainy season. He said that as soon as Bush felt he could leave me in command that Bush would get his leave and then as soon as he returned I would have mine. That is about when Barker + I had planned it. I hope this means I can get home this fall but of course a lot of things could interfere. Wing also said that if prospects of my promotion faded, he would transfer me back to artillery.

I feel badly about leaving Barker for we have worked well together and I like him a great deal, profanity and all. He told several people that I was the only Bn. C.O. he had ever had that he never needed to check up on. He said also that if [a] promotion did not develop he would take me back in his Div. Arty even tho there is no vacancy. All in all I apparently have the good wishes of all three of the generals, Wing, Barker + Cleland, and the rest is up to me and the possibility of vacancies developing.

Cleland in answer to my comment that I didn't care too much about taking over the job of running around after three [infantry] battalions [i.e. an entire regiment], said that I had [already] been doing that in addition to taking care of an artillery battalion. I know you will worry about the possibility of an increase in my personal hazards. That is materially reduced for I will not be so near the front so often as now. Neither will I be running around alone in search of artillery positions. Altho I prefer artillery, having both branches on my record will help a lot if I do stay in the army after the war.

My address is still the same because no orders have been issued yet and there is always the possibility of a last minute change.

This appointment as executive officer of the 172nd Infantry Regiment was a lateral move to another lieutenant colonel position, but it opened the way toward regimental command, a full "bird" colonel position. (The insignia of a colonel is an eagle.) The 172nd Infantry, one of the three regiments of the 43rd Division, was a national guard unit from Vermont and the descendant of the Green Mountain Boys of Revolutionary War fame.

Wilber's experience "running around after" infantry battalions and possibly his earlier Washington State experience as an infantry officer qualified him for this unusual move. More important was his demonstrated performance as a commander. He was offered exactly this kind of lateral transfer after the Munda campaign almost two years earlier and had refused it. But this time, he would have little choice, though he probably felt more qualified for it now. In the letter of May 18 above, it was the prospect of becoming regimental commander, not executive officer, that had caused him to comment, "I'm a bit too tired just now." Nevertheless, he would soon be serving as regimental commander of the 172nd.

Yes, I knew Ernie Pyle quite well [at Indiana University] and had hoped to see him out here. He was doing a grand job....

> Ernie Pyle, a war correspondent widely known for his empathy for the ordinary soldier, was killed by a Japanese machine gun bullet on Ie Shima (or Iejima, near Okinawa) on April 18, 1945. He had gone to Indiana University and was in Wilber's class of only about 300 students.

I can see Hale is learning to let sprained ankles and "little colds" assume too much importance. He really should soon have a real job where he has an obligation to a time-clock.... If he could spend the summer with his grandmother really working on the [Indiana] farm, I will pay his fare there and fifty dollars a month for six days work a week except holidays. He could do a lot to make Mother more comfortable next winter and would learn a lot about farming from the friends I grew up with. I know there are a lot of objections to this idea but would really like him to go. With his allowance he should be able to save the entire salary each month toward his college expenses.

If you agree with me, send him on to Commonplace [his mother's name for their Versailles home on the farm] as soon as you can. It will be warm as toast there by June 1. June's the best month except for October. Don't wait to write and ask Mother. Send him and I know she will be glad [perhaps!]. I'll write her about the probability that he will come and why. The house needs work on it. No interior doors are in yet and the barn needs cleaning and a garden will need hoeing. I know he will like it and it will take a big worry off my mind. Rex + Mary + Ruth + Paul will probably be in + out during the summer and he will get to see his family. Please Nana. — I love you, Wilber XXXOOO

> I do not recall being so close to being exiled to the farm in Indiana. I probably had some pretty strong negative opinions about it, given my recent farming experiences at St. Bernard's School. It was possible that Norma did not want to see me go and never discussed it with me.

On June 8, with the capture of Mt. Oro, no Japanese could be found within about five miles of Ipo Dam. The third and last phase of combat on Luzon was essentially over, but mopping-up actions continued. The war was far from over and the Japanese homeland was still untouched by Allied boots. Wilber had not yet seen the last bullet come his way.

9

"[I] am again wearing the crossed rifles"
Wrap-up operations
MAY–JUNE, 1945

On May 21, Wilber was formally transferred to the 172nd Infantry Regiment as its executive officer. He soon had the much larger responsibility of commander with the departure of Col. Bush on leave. He would thus take the regiment through its final mopping-up operations, rehabilitation, and training for the forthcoming invasion of Japan proper. The war, it seemed, was far from being over for the 43rd Division.

MAY 23, 1945
Dearest Nana — This is my first day in the 172d Infantry. I've taken off the crossed cannons [of the artillery] and am again wearing the crossed rifles [of the infantry]. The new work is going to be largely administrative at least for a time. Most of the Division is quite thoroughly shocked because as they say, they have never heard of an artilleryman taking an infantry assignment.

In fact, many of them had indeed heard of this, because General Barker, artilleryman, had been the infantry division commander during the Baanga action in 1943.

Your books are rolling in every day now and they look fine. I have written to Troop 7 thanking them for their work + have told Maj. Carpenter (the new C.O.) [of the 152nd Field Artillery] to write the League as soon as it was apparent the books were all here, giving a report on those received. — Must Stop Now. But I still love you. Wilber

VICTORY AND HOMECOMING   PART II: FINAL BATTLES, LUZON

x·o·ø·o·x

    Wilber ruminated on his current position and on his future. He now favored remaining in the army. He was probably buoyed by his superiors' confidence in him.

MAY 23, 1945 [2ND LETTER; 6 P.M.]
Dearest Norma — I am sitting in the Regimental C.P. at six P.M. after my first day in the infantry. Ogden, my driver, and I reported this morning to our new job. Ogden had stayed with me and left the 152 to continue as my driver. He has been invaluable in the past and I am particularly glad he came with me.

    My C.O. is Col. Geo. [E.] Bush, Regular Army. I first met him in Arundel where the 169 [Field Artillery] supported the 27th Inf. He was Exec of the 27th then and we came to have a high regard for each other. He asked Wing for me this time. This work is going to be very different from my past two years and will be much like a rest because of the change. For example, I spent the afternoon at a desk studying current regulations and orders – and feel more relaxed than any time for a long while.

    This Ipo [Dam] operation is really over now and we are just mopping up caves and dugouts previously missed. The 43d has quite a reputation because of the speed with which we did the job [11 days]. Another division had tried it before and not done as well. [General] Krueger [commanding general of the Sixth Army] visited one of my batteries yesterday and we survived the ordeal. He said [to me], "Young Man, I know a lot more about the 152 Field Artillery than you think I do." Since I was in no position to contest the point we dropped the topic. He is, by the way, the only four-star general with whom I have shaken hands.

    Krueger may have been remembering the time that artillery fire, falsely attributed to the 152nd Field Artillery, had prevented his plane from landing at Tadji Airdrome, Aitape [letter 10/24/44].

    … It is quiet except for an occasional shot and a few artillery fires, which punctuate the silence and make it more noticeable.

    I love you, Sweet. Your picture sits on my box of books so you are an infantry-woman now. I hope you like it. I wrote you this morning but didn't really have time to tell you I loved you. You are the Darling of my Heart and the very favorite girl of my dreams. I dreamed of you last night too. Fun for Wilber. — Goodbye now, Wilber

x·o·ø·o·x

CHAPTER 9 *[I] am again wearing the crossed rifles*

In a letter to his sister Mary, Wilber wrote of his views on civilians in war and described his immediate environment at the infantry command post: carabao (a kind of water buffalo), little girls and boys, a naked soldier, a lost bar of soap, and a borrowed toothbrush.

HQ. 172 INF., APO 43, MAY 25, 1945
Dear Sister — Please notice my new address. I'm a Doughboy again.…

Mother wrote that you were anemic and should not give more blood.… It is more important to keep your health. Rex also has a tendency to overdo. He has mentioned that he is injuring his health by the work he has been doing. Maybe so but I think it is unnecessary. I'm possibly doing the same thing; but to me it is just being five years older. How this must bore you. It does me as I reread it.…

This would be lovely country to run about in, if the Japs weren't here. Some of the views are as beautiful as any I have seen. The people are nice and are friendly. It is interesting to watch them, especially the women carrying things on their heads. Even little three-year-old girls do it and the little boys ride carabao about and carry small machetes, most of the women smoke and are personally very modest but not at all disturbed by a bathing soldier. One of my boys lost his soap in a river and a woman who had been washing clothes downstream brought it up, soaped his back and gave it back to him. He was practically frozen by embarrassment but she gave him a nice smile and went to her washing. They are extremely clean in many ways. For example Col. Bush found one using his [Bush's] toothbrush once. Just once! — Love, Wilber

x · o · ø · o · x

The next day, he turned his attention back to Norma.

MAY 26, 1945
Dearest — … This day I have worked at the Hq. all day having conferences and checking on various details. Some things have been allowed to slide during the past months and I am gathering up the loose ends. Late this afternoon it stormed, and Col. Bush + I amused (?) ourselves in holding up the tent. However now it is cool and very comfortable. In fact I could use you for a little cuddling very well [sic].

We have a hen who survived the Japs and our fire too. She can fly like an expert. In fact she can make the top of a tree from a standing start. Just now she is going about with a speculative look in her eye picking a tree. Pretty soon she will take off and will light on a limb cackling nervously, then petulantly hop or fly from limb to limb until she decides the tree is entirely unsatisfactory. Then she will take a short hop of 20 yards to another tree and repeat the performance until it gets dusk then [she] quiets down.… — I love you. Wilber

x·o·ø·o·x

"Points" were awarded for service time, overseas time, medals (including the Purple Heart for wounds), and other items, and were used in establishing priority for redeployment to the United States. Many men with high points were "redeployed" to the U.S. unless they were considered "essential." General Barker had his own take on the point system.

JUNE 1, 1945
Darling — The old air mattress has given up the ghost. I've ordered a new one from [Fort] Sill but I don't expect it before Aug. In the meantime I blow it up and try to get to sleep before it deflates. I usually do.…

Barker told Waldo the same thing Wing told me about Redeployment only differently. Wing told me he considered me essential. Barker's remark was "Waldo you can stick those points up your ___ for all the good they will do you." What a man!

You remember the old correspondence lessons always used church steeples for aiming points and base points. Well, down here they are sometimes almost the only possible ones, in which case I always say "B.P. that church but adjust on a point to one side for I don't want to damage it." Sometimes I've detected a look of superiority in some of my young officers so I've repeated my orders not to damage it.

We [152nd Field Artillery] have only had three men killed in the entire campaign. On the other hand, Barker and staff moved into a church once and apparently didn't pay their rent for the Japs shelled it and killed Barker's chaplain [Capt. Barrett L. Tyler]. So you can take your choice, but I only shell a church when I know the Japs are fortified in it.

Your old man has been leading a very quiet life recently – all desk work. The Japs are getting scarce here now, altho a few still snipe at us now + then. Ogden and I were fired at from an ambush two nights ago as we drove along a rocky narrow road. However we operate on the theory that snipers miss and he didn't even come close. But all in all the rains are getting to be more important than the Japs here.… I love you Sweet Heart. Also H + V. — Your Husband, Wilber.

x·o·ø·o·x

In early June, the 172nd Infantry was moved north to the Sibul Springs-Laur region where it carried out active patrolling and established roadblocks in order to capture or destroy Japanese who had been driven from the Ipo Dam area. [172nd Inf. Ipo Phase Supplement]

JUNE 3, 1945
Dearest wife — Your May 21 letter came today and I loved every word.…

Your ideas on selling the house sound reasonable to me. Remember the agent's fee and don't sell for less than $6000.00 in your hand because you will have taxes and moving costs too. Don't take things that can be bought more cheaply than twice what they can be moved for. Be sure to keep things that cannot be bought.

I envy you living in the South [Washington, D.C.]. Maybe we can live there together sometime. (Don't forget you can get more for the house if people see it while your furniture is in it.) I always knew the house cost more than we should spend but I also had promised myself to give you three things – a large kitchen – a fireplace – a living room in which you could entertain. As you know, I prefer a smaller place with less work and no maid underfoot. Again don't worry about what to do about the house. Set a price, so you will be glad if someone takes it.…

We had raw sliced onions for supper today, and they were really good in sandwiches. The day was nice too and no rain. I really got quite a lot of work done. Yesterday I took a trip to the rainy season camp [in Cabanatuan, Map 7], total miles 150. A peep [jeep] isn't just the easiest vehicle either. When I get home it is trains and planes for me. No touring by auto.…

We have joked a lot here because in one of his orders Krueger stated the rainy season began June 1. Of course we all say, "By command of Gen. K," it did. Today it has rained three times and quite hard each time.…

The redeployment business has the lead in all conversations. Actually I don't know just how it would affect me. We have filled out a questionnaire answering that I do (do not) desire to leave the army before the end of the war. I answered that I did not. On points, the critical level is 85 and I have 156 with a probable additional decoration (5 points) in the mill. The other factor is a point factor based on officer efficiency. Mine being high is an additional argument for being sent back to the States.

Opposed to this is the General's desire that I stay with the division and my own interest in deferring a decision until the War Dept. specifies how I may or may not stay in the Service. Another factor is the fact that I am entitled to a leave in the US and am just Scotch enough to want it before I am out. Bush now expects to go July 1 and if he flies each way he could possibly be back Oct. 1 or before. Then comes my turn which should get me home by Nov. 1.

The situation is further confused by the possibility that GHQ will require that all persons with high scores be sent home shortly either on Leave or Redeployment.

There is some indication that this will be done; or that a stepped up tempo of the war might prevent or hurry my trip home....

> Wilber's planning was fruitless in this uncertain environment; Japan was still an active combatant, and the 43rd Division would most likely partake in the invasion of the Japanese homeland.

I'll miss our house and yard but am not sure I'll be sorry because it [the maintenance] did prevent a lot of rest and "pinpics" [children's lingo for "picnics"].... I hope you don't have too much grief in your move to the Sunny South and that you find a reasonable and nice home near good schools. Sweet Dreams, Lover. — Your, Wilber

> This letter made clear that Norma was selling the Bangor house and moving the family to Washington, D.C. Norma's need to be near her little girl (now 19 months) was understandable, but selling the Bangor house was puzzling because Wilber's position at the University of Maine still awaited him. He seemed remarkably unperturbed by her plans. His uncertainty about his own future, his ambivalence about returning to Maine, and the expense of maintaining that house seemed to have muted any negative reaction. Living arrangements could always be found if the family were to return to Maine.
>
> Also, by now, Wilber realized that he had to let Norma make the family decisions; by his long absence, he had essentially forfeited his right to make them. Was Norma also drawn to Washington because Monte was there? I am inclined to believe that she was primarily driven by her duty to her baby daughter. Norma was a duty-driven lady. She had decided to follow her instincts to care for little Gale and hope that some accommodation would be worked out when Wilber returned, if he survived the war.

x · o · ø · o · x

The 172nd Infantry was active in eliminating stragglers in the mountains east of Highway 5 during the period June 12–25.

JUNE 16, 1945
Dear Nana — ... We are still killing Japs but they are a little harder to find now than before. The rainy weather slows things too. We brought in two prisoners yesterday, one of whom had acted as interpreter when the Japs questioned American officers after Bataan. The Guerrillas that work with us killed a Jap Lt. Gen. here. I'll bet he was disgusted.

Wilber told me after his return home that one learned to think of the enemy as animals, like rats. This was the same Wilber who would release outdoors—not kill—a fly he had caught.

The orders just came thru giving me a second cluster on my Silver Star. This was for the bridge deal that I wrote you about some time ago. Since then I've lived a relatively quiet life. That gives me 161 points.

… I want to see the brown flecks in your eyes again and to walk in the snow with my arm about you. You see I do love you. Good Night Lovely Wife. — Wilber XXXOOO

x · o · ø · o · x

JUNE 21, 1945

Hello Dearest — This is a cleanup letter just for items you mentioned that I may not have answered.…

Here he responded to items in 11 letters dated May 6 to June 8. Several are presented here. I omitted a long exposition on international issues. He had proposed that to avoid wars one needed to acknowledge and make allowances for the economic interests of individual nations, even those one did not favor, such as Russia.

May 18 — … Mother writes that she now is very thin, weighs 120 or something like that. She likely is much healthier now.…

May 21 — Yes I was with the 103d in the Ipo deal. It was really a fascinating action and required a lot of push and new techniques. I did more hiking per day than for a long time. It was further complicated by heavy rains, which made ammunition delivery a real problem for the artillery. But we "do-ed" it, mostly by manpower. We just forgot everything except ammo, telephone wire, and firing for about a week. Trucks + tractors and dozers really tear out wire when the roads fail and they detour mud holes.

At one time (3 days) [about May 14] I had 25% of my men repairing and relaying wire. One of my men came up to me with tears in his eyes and his voice so broken he could hardly speak. He was about to drop with fatigue. (I didn't feel too peppy either.) It was pouring rain. He said, "Col. I've repaired the lines here seven times this morning and that dozer driver tore it out seven times. I asked him and told him to stop and he just said, 'To Hell with your wire, I have to build a road.' and went ahead thru my wire again." I know he expected me to go right over and shoot the dozer driver but all I could do was explain that he too was having trouble and had an important job too. I tried to let him see I knew just how hard he was trying to keep his lines in and how I thought he was doing a grand job, patted him on the back and went sloshing up the next hill. One feels pretty humble about commanding the American G.I.

Don't worry so much about selling the house. Just sell it.

> As he reassured Norma about selling the house, Wilber received disappointing news.

May 25 — The Command + Staff School is out because of my age. Don't worry about the [University] faculty. They are getting war nerves. I can stand combat but I don't know if I could do teaching during a war. This isn't more fun but it is a lot more interesting. I am still disgustingly healthy. It seems to agree with me. Two days ago I hiked up to one of our more distant outposts just in time to run into 24 Japs. Being a Doughboy [infantry] now, I took over, had a machine-gun set up + knocked off two before they ran. They don't fight now unless cornered....

Times here are quiet and under control. Bush leaves soon and I'll hope he makes good time so I can start about Oct. 1. — XXXOOO Wilber

> The firefight Wilber described here would qualify him for the Combat Infantryman's Badge, as he would learn shortly [letter 8/1/45].

x·o·ø·o·x

> On June 27, the 38th Division began its relief of the 43rd division, which, on July 1, was relieved of all combat responsibility on Luzon. It began its move to rainy-season camp near Cabanatuan.

JUNE 26, 1945
Darling Wife — The choir picture came and I definitely decided it was time for me to go home because I couldn't identify either Hale or Valerie – a sad state of affairs! However your picture still smiles at me from the end of my desk. It is restful to be at a desk job again.

June 27, 1945 — This is the third time I have started this letter and now I have only a few minutes. Today, Dearest, is the last day of this campaign for me. Tomorrow is the first day in the rainy season rehabilitation camp. Since Jan. 9 we have been out of active combat only ten days. I suppose that is one reason this division was pulled off the lines for this period. Of course we may be called out again without much warning, but I did want you to know I would be out of the front lines for a while now. Maybe you can sleep a bit better for knowing it.

CHAPTER 9 *[I] am again wearing the crossed rifles*

Guests at the dinner hosted by Col. Shih I. Sheng, commanding officer of the Chinese Volunteers in the Philippines on June 26, 1945. Attendees were Col. George E. Bush, C.O. 172nd Infantry, and his staff. Wilber identified the attendees as, from left, Majors Dan Carney and __ Levy, Sheng, Bradt, Bush, Chaplain __ Helsel, Maj. Jim Holden, Capt. Jim Ball, and Maj. Joe Snyder. Wilber's print of this photo is autographed "Your Friend, Shihisheng." [PHOTO: COLONEL SHENG]

Last night Col Bush + his staff [of the 172nd Infantry] were the guests of Col. [Shih I.] Sheng, the Chinese Colonel of whom I have written. He explained it was not a real banquet because many things were not available in P.I. We only had twelve courses and some of them consisted of only five or six different dishes. Even eating with chop sticks, I nearly foundered myself.

Some of the dishes were pieces of crab, shrimp, chicken, pork, fish, and other giblets fried in peanut oil. Also salads of leeks and other greens, pickled fruits, pickled vegetables. This was part of the first course. The dishes were set in the center of the table and we reached with chop sticks for the nearer ones, others were shifted and passed.

Soups included chicken and egg, birds nest, sharks fin, and two others. Other dishes were fried rice, squabs, chicken with garlic, pork with ginger, pigs feet, a large baked fish buried under a pickled salad, chow mein, noodles, and others of which I have only a hazy memory. Drinks were water, whiskey, Coca Cola, but no tea. I don't know if it isn't available or just not proper in this type of orgy....

Dearest I love you and can hardly wait to have you in my arms again. You had better start studying your safe periods for I expect to be taking advantage of them in two or three months. Wonderful Norma. My hand is lonely for the softness of you. Happy Dreams and happy day dreams too. I am very much your husband. — XXXOOO Wilber

    Wilber was again courting Norma at long distance with explicit sexual references; there had been relatively few of those of late. The distance, the routines and demands of war, and Norma's divided loyalties had removed some of the intimacy from their relationship, but here he was reaching out for it again.

    School for Valerie and me (7th and 9th grades respectively) ended in Bangor at about this time. We packed up our furniture and belongings in the Bangor house, which Norma had sold. She bought a home at 4421 Alton Place NW in Washington, D.C., near Tenley Circle. We could not move into it until August 1. So we rented a summer cottage at the shore in Bethany Beach, Delaware, for the month of July. We were to begin yet another phase of our lives.

    It would also be a new phase for Wilber as he was about to assume command of an entire regiment.

10

"Your old man now commands a regiment"

Camp La Croix, Cabanatuan
July–August, 1945

The rehabilitation camp at Camp La Croix, Cabanatuan (Map 7), featured extensive recreational facilities, but it wasn't all fun and games. The training and integration of replacement troops intensified throughout the month of July. The 43rd Division was being prepared for the invasion of Japan proper. Unfortunately for the division, but not for the men, many of its experienced personnel were entitled to return to the United States based on the point system and they did so. Wilber in his essential position could not yet take leave.

[CAMP LA CROIX, CABANATUAN] JULY 1, 1945
Dearest Mine — Your sweet letter of June 2 and one from Hale + Valerie came a day or so ago. I'm glad the saber came thru OK. Did Valerie like the chest? Perhaps she hasn't seen it yet. It is a field chemical and bacteriological laboratory kit. I picked it up in a large Jap supply dump at New Bosoboso. There were microscopes, surgeons' instruments, dental tools and other interesting things, which were turned in to U.S. Salvage. Optical equipment cannot be sent home as souvenirs.

> For many years, I had a Japanese field microscope that Wilber had sent or brought home. My daughter used it in the early years of her veterinary practice.

Col. Bush is hoping to start [home] any day now. He may come to Washington [D.C.] with his wife, Helen, and if so will call you at Paul's address. I do hope you see him for he is as fine a friend as one could ever have. I liked him in Arundel where he gave me my first silver leaf – one of his only two. Since I have come here he has been wonderful and most helpful.

We are now pretty well moved into our rainy season quarters. He + I live together in a floored hut which is paneled with woven bamboo matting called suali(?) [sawali] and has a thatched roof. It is really comfortable and cool but inclined to harbor bugs. We spray frequently and sleep under netting. Since my new air mattress came today ($23.20) I expect a really good sleep. The other has been leaky for several weeks.

It is still in the plan for me to come home this fall. I dream about it nights and think about it days. To be with you + the children again will be the most wonderful thing I could have given me.

July 2 — … You needn't try to explain that I am so important that I cannot be spared. I probably am of little importance in the big picture. The main factor as I diagnose myself is a feeling that I cannot come home with Japs still killing and causing suffering until I can feel that I could not do so well as another [person]. When that time comes, I'll gladly come home to stay, for then I can feel I did what I could when the opportunity was here to serve my country. Possibly the reason I feel this way is entirely selfish. I may just love the life but I don't think so. If I felt now I could face my conscience while my friends go ashore in the next landing, I would come home at once and love it. Anyway my cheek is on your shoulder and my arms are about you, My Lover and I love you more today than a year ago but not so much as I shall next year.

> What introspection! Wilber may already have known or suspected the unit was slated for future combat landings and was examining his motives for wanting to stay for those. He saw the defeat of Japan as his mission, and he did not want to let his friends down. On the other hand, he did find satisfaction, it seems to me, in his military competence. Of course, because General Wing considered him "essential," the choice was not really in Wilber's hands. If Wilber had indicated a strong desire to leave the battlefront—either vocally or on the "questionnaire" [letter 6/3/45]—as many probably did, he would immediately have been considered less essential. General Wing did not need ambivalent commanders. A determined and positive attitude was mandatory.

I appreciate your news comments even tho I didn't fully agree. What do you think of the S.F. [San Francisco] results now? I hope it is a step ahead, but if it is,

CHAPTER 10   *Your old man now commands a regiment*

Wilber as executive officer of the 172nd Infantry, May or June 1945, probably in front of his and Col. Bush's tent, Luzon, P.I. [PHOTO: COURTESY OF GEN. GEORGE E. BUSH, 1986]

the people still will be the only means of making it work. People not paper must do the planning and accomplishment. I pray that we do it well.

The United Nations Charter was signed by 50 nations in San Francisco on June 26.

Goodnight Sweet Heart. I'll see you when the leaves turn if it is at all possible. Love to you from me. — Wilber

x·o·ø·o·x

On or close to this date, July 1, Norma, Valerie, and I moved to Bethany Beach, Delaware. We took along a beautiful little blond girl, Norma's baby Gale, aged one year and eight months. I vividly remember first meeting her a day or two earlier as Norma took us into her bedroom in Monte's Q Street home, where she had been napping. She stood up in her crib, with sleepy

Little Gale at about 20 months when I first met her. [PHOTO: BRADT-BOURJAILY FAMILY]

CHAPTER 10 *Your old man now commands a regiment*

eyes, and reached out to Norma, saying "Mama, Mama." I did not pick up on that, but Norma, years later, told me she thought that that had given away the game.

Gale was described to Valerie and me as the daughter of Monte and a third wife who had since left him, a Swedish woman named Marta Lindstrom who is listed in Monte's entry in the 1946–47 Marquis "Who's Who in America." I believe this person and the marriage were totally fictitious and were invented solely to explain the blond baby. Mother obviously cared for this poor "motherless" child, and we were to take her to Bethany Beach for the month of July. Valerie (age 13) became the de facto live-in baby sitter and felt greatly put upon by this little girl who, while cute as could be, had been raised almost solely the past year by her grandmother Terkman (Monte's mother) and was, understandably, quite spoiled in our teenage eyes. Grandmothers are softies, easily manipulated by two-year olds.

That month at Bethany Beach was memorable. Our rental was a small house one or two blocks from the beach. I spent a lot of time in the water and learned that Delaware is chicken country. I soon knew how to gut a freshly killed chicken and took a try at working in one of the chicken-processing plants some dozen miles away. After one day's work, I demurred; the work (simple labor, carrying boxes, and so on) was boring, and it was a long hot day away from the beach. Some of the laborers there were German prisoners of war. One was avoiding work by peacefully napping in an out-of-the-way corner, and no one was disturbing him.

The prime entertainment in town was the bowling alley. However, there was a camp for prisoners of war (POWs) on the outskirts of the village, and films were shown some evenings for the prisoners; they were American films with German subtitles. We kids could go and watch from the very back of the rudimentary hut in which they were shown. The German prisoners got the best seats!

Not far away, American fighter planes out over the ocean a mile or more would practice shooting at target sleeves towed by another plane. Due to the travel time of sound, the pow-pow-pow of the machine guns would reach us five or more seconds after the plane had pulled up from its diving pass at the target. One day, we woke to a continuous loud roar coming from the sea. Dozens of navy landing craft were approaching the beach, a drill for the forthcoming invasion of Japan.

Norma attempted to keep me busy; I helped a repairman do odd jobs for the cottage renters for a while, but was not of much use. Most of all, though, as a 14-year-old in that warm summery environment, I remember yearning for a girl my age at the beach, though I never mustered the nerve for a "date." I also yearned mightily to become the owner of an army Jeep.

This idyllic life was occasionally punctuated by conflict between little Gale and her caretakers, 13-year-old Valerie and Norma. Norma seemed to have lost the knack for dealing with young children. She tended to argue on a two-year-old level, and on that basis, the two-year old always won! Did I help with her care? Possibly, but I surely could have done more; in those days, childcare wasn't a man's job. I did wash a lot of dishes and gut quite a few chickens, though.

x · o · ø · o · x

JULY 7, 1945

Darling Nana — … Your Old Man now commands a regiment. Of course it is only while Col. Bush is away, but just the same it goes on the record. I hope I do well, and I'll sure try.…

Times are sure rushing. This isn't a rest camp. It is just a preparation period and a rainy season. My thatch roof seems to be weather proof and is really cool. I'm putting in a ceiling of white cloth to make it brighter inside. Did the bamboo case for the saber come thru in good shape? I thought you would like to give it to someone.

I love you. Do you recall a woods in Indiana? You were wearing a blue lace dress and had gold flecks in your eyes and other things too. That is one of the most wonderful days I've known. — XXXOOO Wilber

> Wilber was probably recalling their lovemaking in the woods of the Versailles farm, out of sight of Wilber's parents.

x · o · ø · o · x

JULY 9, 1945

Dearest wife — You surely got rid of the house in a hurry, didn't you? It looks as if we made a profit on that deal. Actually I am very relieved that it is sold. It was really too big for us and I knew it but bought it because you had always wanted some of the things it offered. I always planned to sell it altho not so soon. I hope you didn't make a mistake in letting the range + refrig. go. It may be some time yet before they can be bought.

CHAPTER 10   *Your old man now commands a regiment*

Generals Wing (center) and Barker (right), commanders respectively of the 43rd Division and the 43rd Division Artillery, on July 8, 1945, shortly after the division moved to "rainy-season-camp" near Cabanatuan. The 43rd Division would shortly begin preparations for the invasion of Japan. [PHOTO: U.S. ARMY SIGNAL CORPS, SC 395883]

You have my hearty approval on the children's activities in working. I hope they are saving their money for college. They must not count on our being able to give it to them but must be able to pay a good share of it themselves. I'm sure we will be able to help them but it could happen differently....

Rent in Washington must be very high. I can't see why you picked that place to live. You must have done a lot of adapting to live in the places I've taken you to live. I'm sure it would be nice to be there with you, but if I picked a place with the whole country to choose from, it wouldn't be at Washington, D.C. I must have hermit's blood in me. Crowds of people only look good to me when they are quiet. That is pretty seldom. I've been reading Thoreau's "Walden." He built a house for $28.15 and considered it cheaper than renting. Of course, mine here is cheaper than that but all the plumbing is primitive.

… I love you, dream of you, want you, and expect to be with you this fall. I pray each day it will really happen. — Your husband. Yep! That's me. Wilber

Our move to Washington, D.C., was puzzling to Wilber. I should have been puzzled too but wasn't. Beforehand, I was unaware of "Monte's baby" and afterward did not see her as a motive for our move. I accepted without question whatever reason Norma gave.

x · o · ø · o · x

Wilber next turned to Valerie with news of two American admirals and a Japanese general.

JULY 19, 1945
Dear Valerie — The other day I looked at the picture of the choir and – Surprise! – there you were smiling at me as plain as day. When it came I looked and looked for you and Hale and couldn't identify either one of you. Now I feel much better about it because at least I know I can still recognize each of your and Hale's faces.

Mister Nimitz and Mr. Halsey have just been dropping a few 16-inch shells eight miles from Tokyo. That must have embarrassed the Mikado. Gen. Yamashita [senior Japanese general in the Philippines] is supposedly still hiding in some gully in Luzon. He is probably trying to remember how Geo. Washington got out of Valley Forge. Gen. Y. was the one who published an order that his troops should fight a delaying action, but that when the time was right he would give the word to counterattack – even if it was 20 years from now. I'll bet his feet are wet today.…

It is very rainy here now. In fact it rains several times every day now. The men get soaked while training but we ignore the rain and keep going. However they do have dry tents and are comfortable in them.

I liked your drawing of the chest and rug. It made me lonesome to be home. The chair on your card too was a very nice invitation. I'm thinking seriously of dropping in on you some of these days.… — Love from Pop

x · o · ø · o · x

Wilber did his best to calm Norma who felt put upon by Wilber's brothers Paul and Rex and even by Wilber himself. Her comments may have dated from our arrival in Washington, where Paul lived, prior to our going to Bethany Beach. She was in a sensitive mood, probably due in part to her risky role-playing with baby Gale.

CHAPTER 10   *Your old man now commands a regiment*

JULY 20, 1945

My Dearest Sweet Wife — Yesterday I wrote to Valerie and Col. Bush. In a day or so I'll be writing to Hale for I have a bigger pile of unanswered mail from him than I realized. Our new home sounds just fine. I know you will make me feel very much at home there too. You must have been very tired when you finally reached your beach. I would dread moving all our furniture anywhere. Did it suffer much during the move? …

Re the Bradts – Don't let them bother you. Don't try to tell me what is wrong with us. I know all our peculiarities and bigotedness, and all I can say is to please just be immune. I'm sorry Paul + Rex have been critical and unpleasant to you, but we are a poor sort in many ways – mostly, I hope, the little things. Essentially I believe my brothers + sisters are OK. Most of their intentions are fair. They just feel that "family" means license to be cruel and unpleasant.…

What [are] you going to do with our savings? Remember this isn't a time to buy. I don't want a house in Washington, D.C., at all. Did you contact Mrs. Cleland? I hope so, for Joe is in the U.S. now and will probably be in D.C. soon. Did I ever tell you he is the "Silver Fox" because of his white hair? Don't be fooled. He is three years my junior.

> In fact, I believe Norma had already bought the Alton Place property.

…. Don't be so touchy about my "cracks." I don't make "cracks" to you. I know you write and I should have remembered not to say mail came "occasionally." Neither did I ever think you were "going out" with men. If you did, I'd know it was OK and I don't know what I said but it must have been bad. Please don't be cross with me Nana. It is lonely here too.

> Wilber may have made comments in jest that had inadvertently cut close to the bone, but I found no letter that would so qualify.

Today I sat on two general courts [military trials], made an inspection, spent an hour on paper work and the rest of the time on plans for next week. I also invested in a haircut. For supper we had a can of lobster I've been hoarding since X-mas. The cook made a stew but not so good as in Bangor.

Yes, I do love you. Also Hale + Valerie. I really am still the same guy you married once and I'm still glad. — XXXOOO Wilber

x · o · ø · o · x

Two days later, Wilber was in a blue, contemplative, poetic mood. He was acutely aware that he was "depressed" and was immersing himself in sadness, with poignant thoughts. Such immersion can sometimes help one feel better.

JULY 22, 1945
Nana Dearest — It is late Sunday evening and I am lonely for you. Today you have been in my mind all the time. I've been remembering all the sweet dear minutes we have shared and I do so need them again. It is all right to talk about the nearing of the end of this war, but it would be heavenly to know it had been won. I know it has seemed long to you and that it has been hard for you and I shouldn't write a blue letter. I try not to feel discouraged but it has been so long away from you and home and the real people. I keep telling myself that again we can live and think and be safe together, but of course I know it really will never be. If I can just be with you that would be enough without the other things.…

How is my boy that I so wanted to walk with thru these years? These were the years I most wanted to be with him. When we could talk together and he could teach me the things boys teach their fathers. And I hardly dare think of my "Little Tumblebug" [Valerie] who is now so grown and hardly knows her Daddy. It has been so long a war and so many people are tired.

Don't misunderstand me. This is just a blue day … I want again to be able to plan and work for those plans – not just orders and orders and still more orders. If one could just always keep one's perspective they wouldn't be so wearying but they are so omnipresent and all encompassing. They cover shirt and shaves, drills and drains, flies and tanks, machine guns and malaria but always in some way you (or rather me).

I'm so afraid to count on my promised leave. It is so important to me that I can not really believe it could happen.… Tonight I would so love to hear you play [piano] – perhaps something by Schumann or Chopin, or some of the little light Polish dances. I should like to see a (no, my) flower in your hair again instead of knowing the smell of battlefields. I wish again and again for one of our evenings above the Ohio [River], for a walk in the snow of Broadway [in Bangor] with you, and for a stairway to carry my lover up in my arms, or a sunny mountain top to share with you.

Beloved, enough of this, I just love you more each day and that is all I'm really saying. I know we will go on together after this war so why should I be so depressed? I won't be any more.

… I must write to the mother of Heidelberger for he was killed in August [1943] and I want her to know I remember too. I thank God that this action didn't take any of my officers except as wounded and only two of my men killed in six months fighting. The Lord was kind to the 152 and to me. Good night, my lovely dream wife. I love you so much it hurts. — XXXOOO Wilber

CHAPTER 10   *Your old man now commands a regiment*

What had brought on this blue mood? It might have been his memory of his junior officers lost on Munda—in particular Lt. Norbert Heidelberger—darkly tinted by the perpetual tropical rains and the forthcoming invasion of Japan, an ominous undertaking. He may simply have been bone-tired. Norma's own blue letter, to which Wilber referred above, may also have been a factor.

x·o·ø·o·x

Wilber's outfit, the 172nd Infantry, was not yet free of all combat. On July 23, the 172nd was ordered to provide one battalion to intercept Japanese stragglers in the Dingalan Bay and other areas who were raiding Filipino homes and gardens as they tried to reach General Yamashita's forces in the Cagayan Valley. The regiment also provided a platoon to cover the town of Papaya. These operations were successful and would last until August 15. There was no indication that Wilber was personally involved in these actions, but they did require his attention. The rest of the regiment continued intensive training at Camp La Croix.

Five days after writing his blue letter to Norma, Wilber had clearly shed his blue funk.

JULY 27, 1945
Dearest Mine — Do you realize that some eighteen years ago you + I were just newly engaged and Dean Kimbrough approved? I've been thinking how wonderful it was to find you that summer. I never knew until then that being in love was anything but a mental strain on the people concerned. Then with you I found it was all flowers, and sunshine and moonlight on snow and lovely music and everything from which dreams are made. It is still as wonderful today. You are really something very special to me....

I'm so glad to know something about your play [probably that about Abigail Adams]. Monte has surely helped and I think he is fine. I am impressed just to think Helen Hayes [famous actress] will see it. This should be the time for you, Beloved. You have worked so hard and so honestly that I know you will succeed in your writing. It should be this year, the fifth year of the independence of Norma....

The 172 had a decoration ceremony this week, and Gen. Wing gave me my Silver Star among many others who had done more than I.

July 28 — This is a Saturday and Wing spent most of the morning inspecting us. He seemed quite well pleased with what he saw. This was his old regiment and he does a lot of visiting with men. He really likes this regiment to be the best.

General Leonard Wing (left) presents Wilber with the Silver Star medal, July 25, 1945.
[PHOTO: U.S. ARMY SIGNAL CORPS]

I have your letter of the 18th and also have signed the deed [of the Bangor house]. However before you sign it, you must insist that an additional limitation be added, in that we do not warrant the property against claims arising from any rights that may have accrued as a result of the joint use of our driveway by the neighboring property owner.... so I am sending the deed to you instead of to him.

> Wilber still helped with small but important details of the family life. It kept him connected to us.

Thanks for paying French. I mailed my Silver Star [medal] yesterday. It is as hot here now as anywhere in the Islands. I mean hot. Love again. — XXXOOO Wilber

> On this date, July 28, 1945, the division received "Alert Plans" [Barker p. 230] for Operation Olympic, the invasion of the Japanese homeland on the southern part of the island of Kyushu (Map 17) slated for November 1, 1945. The 43rd Division would be one of three divisions in the XI Corps. After the capture of Japanese airfields in southern Kyushu, the plains of

Tokyo on the main island of Honshu would be invaded on March 1, 1946 (Operation Coronet). The overall plan was called Operation Downfall. Judging from the Japanese defenses of islands close to the homeland— specifically Iwo Jima and Okinawa—it would be a bloodbath. The pressure of preparations was increasing both outwardly and inwardly.

x · o · ø · o · x

AUG. 1, 1945
Dearest Wife of Mine — Life as C.O. [of the] 172 [Regiment] is a bit hectic but interesting. I haven't found much time to write anyone but there is still ample time to look at the pictures of the very special people in my world. I am very proud of my family. It is still a common thing for officers to remark about my two daughters being so pretty.

During the past week we have had both our [Sixth] Army [Krueger] and our [XI] Corps commander [Charles P. Hall] in the area. They seemed well satisfied and spoke highly of our (43d) past record. It seems the 43d can point with pride. I hope we can say the same after the next job. Lt. Gen Hall seemed quite interested in the fact that I am an artillery officer. Maybe [he] has his doubts.

Did I tell you I still hold my artillery commission and am "detailed to the infantry" [by order on Aug. 9; WB journal]. I wear the infantry insignia while so detailed and still retain my good standing as an artilleryman. Did I also tell you I've been awarded the "Combat Infantryman's badge"? To earn it, one must function in actual infantry combat while in the infantry. After I had been in a little brush with 24 Japs [June 19] and had taken charge of our group + done a little of what we are paid for, Col. Bush announced I had now earned it. I'm glad about it for artillerymen cannot earn it.

We are in the Jap business again in a rabbit-hunting sort of way [e.g., in Dingalan Bay]. Many are surrendering but a few want to fight and do. One prisoner was delivered literally to my door today. He saluted all U.S. soldiers [even enlisted men] and seemed to be all thru with war. Most of these Japs raid barrios for food and we get calls for help and go out to run them down. We also set ambushes and catch quite a few that way. Their morale is very low and many are low on food, without arms and in rags. Their fun is all over now, and their chief worry is the fact that Filipinos still think that a Jap head is good proof he is a dead Jap. These Filipino reports [of killed Japanese] are often exaggerated so we often cross examine quite thoroughly. Occasionally some guerrilla will very proudly prove our suspicions unfounded by producing the evidence. It is quite convincing.

Aug 2. If you like Wash. D.C. and Paul hasn't spoiled it for you, I'm all for it myself. Love you a lot. — Wilber

On or about this date, August 1, our stay at Bethany Beach came to an end, and we moved into the Washington, D.C., house at 4421 Alton Place, NW. There, I began a job as messenger for the Chestnut Farms Dairy in downtown Washington on Pennsylvania Avenue, a few blocks from the White House. I believe little Gale returned to her Q Street home under the daily care of her grandmother, in accord with the continuing fiction that Norma was not her mother.

x·o·ø·o·x

This is only the second extant letter from Wilber to his mother after his father died in December 1944, though he had apparently been writing monthly. This letter had been forwarded to Rex and was in his packet of Wilber's letters. It gave no indication she was responding to Wilber, but elsewhere we saw that she was. [letters: Elizabeth 1/9/45, WB 5/25/45 & 6/21/45].

AUG. 2, 1945

Dear Mother — Another month has gone by since I last wrote you. As you have undoubtedly noticed I do write at the first of the month except when Gen. McA. [MacArthur] has other ideas. This time his ideas do not include me.

We are in a camp on Luzon training new men what we think they should know before the next scrap. At the same time as a sort of secondary effort, we still kill Japs. For example I arrived just one minute too late today. A guerrilla had just shot a Jap that I might have persuaded to surrender if I had been there sooner. However so it goes. He is dead + perhaps I'm alive just because I did arrive one minute later. Such things occur so often that one isn't particularly impressed even with the idea of [one's] own death. The Jap actually looked relieved and as if his worries were gone. It really is a pity that more of them won't surrender. They have been thoroughly taught not to do so and are just like children when they find we feed them + treat them well. They seem to have no loyalty to each other, for a prisoner will frequently guide us to his former comrades and advise how best to destroy them. They are queer people and I'll be glad to see the last of them....

I excised here a detailed description of the planting and tending of rice fields, which reflected Wilber's and his mother's common interest in farming.

I wrote Ewing [a neighbor in Versailles?] asking for suggestions for ways I might help get you better set for the winter.... Mary painted me a pretty rigorous picture of things there in winter. If you want to stay there, I want you to do just that, but I do want to make things as comfortable as I can. Please let me help and tell me what needs to be done that I can do from here.

I haven't told Norma or the children yet but my chances of a leave this year are growing pretty slim. I may get two weeks instead of the 45 days allowed. It is very disappointing for I had promises but a promise in war even by a general is just a statement of intention, so I'm not complaining. Fifty-four months away from home is a long time and so is 34 months overseas a long time. Maybe we should hurry up and win this war too.

It is late and I must stop. I love you and hope things go well with you. — Your son, Wilber.

> The rapidly approaching invasion date (November 1) precluded a longer leave. Wilber's awareness of his own vulnerability in the coming invasion would surely have heightened his interest in seeing his family before then.

x · o · ø · o · x

AUG. 7 [6?], 1945 [EVENING]
Sweet Wife of Mine — Sunday I wrote you a letter but it got in the waste paper before I could finish it, so all I can say is that I did think of my family on Sunday. Tonight I am just back from a school on use of air support as it will be available in this theater. Very interesting and I'm glad the subject wasn't "How the Japs will use their Air Force." Thanks to Halsey and a few assistants we are past that phase.

… If I get home, I'll possibly stop for a day or so with Mother then come on to you. I don't want to lose the time to travel both ways for I'll almost surely only get a short leave and I know I'd never give up the last days from [with] you. Perhaps we should decide the Orono idea later, altho I probably must go even if only for a day or two. Good night lover. My light is due to go out. I love you. — Wilber.

> Wilber must have been aware by this time that the invasion plans for Kyushu would most likely prevent him from obtaining leave, but he was still hoping that a short one would be possible.
>
> All this changed on the morning of Monday, August 6! An atomic bomb was dropped on Hiroshima, Japan, at 8:15 a.m. (Japanese time) that day (7:15 a.m. in the Philippines), and was announced by President Harry Truman at 11 p.m. (Philippine time) that evening.
>
> It appeared that Wilber had not heard of the Hiroshima bombing on the

VICTORY AND HOMECOMING   PART II: FINAL BATTLES, LUZON

evening of the next day unless this letter was misdated and was written on Monday evening, the 6th. His reference to not writing Sunday could have implied that he was writing the next evening, Monday, before the announcement.

It was also possible, although less likely, that Wilber had seen the bomb as a continuation of the fire bombings of Japanese cities that had been going on for some time but had not brought the war to an end. Thus, the atomic bomb may not have seemed to the troops like the epochal event that it was to Americans at home. General Barker, in his book [p. 230], did not mention the atomic bomb, only the first Japanese peace initiative (and he misdates it).

─────────────────────────────

On August 9, the Soviets entered the war against Japan by invading Manchuria. Later that day, a second atomic bomb was dropped on Nagasaki. This prompted intense debate in Japan between those wishing to fight on and those pushing for acceptance of the Allied unconditional-surrender demand in the Potsdam Declaration of July 26. The emperor was asked, early on the 10th, to choose between the two positions and came down sadly but firmly in favor of acceptance. This acceptance was passed to the Allies later that day with the proviso that the emperor would retain his "prerogatives." The Allies responded on the 12th that the emperor and Japanese government would be subject to a supreme allied commander. How to respond to this occasioned more debate and the emperor was again consulted, with the same result. He prepared a recording of a surrender announcement for his people, and an unsuccessful military coup failed to find and destroy it. On the 14th, the Allies received word that Japan had accepted the Potsdam terms, and at noon on the 15th, Japanese time, the emperor's message was broadcast to his people. [Morison, v. XIV, p. 336ff]

─────────────────────────────

On these tense anticipatory days during my lunch hour, I would walk the few blocks down Pennsylvania Avenue from the dairy where I worked to the White House. I would stand silently watching, with other bystanders, the limousines arriving and departing. Would the Japanese overture lead to peace or not? Everything depended on the nuances of the Allied and Japanese responses to each other's messages. I was acutely aware that I was at the geographic epicenter of the entire world's attention!

x·o·ø·o·x

> As he wrote this letter to Norma, Wilber knew of the initial Japanese message on the 10th, and possibly also of the Allied response on the 12th. It was a significant moment for him.

AUG. 12, 1945
Darling of Mine — Today may be the last day of the war. I can realize how you and the children must be feeling. Here we aren't much excited because everyone feels it so strongly. We can't yet realize even that it may so soon be over. Church attendances were very high and I think we were all thinking the same things.

Now I must tell you that my leave has been cancelled. It is one of the hardest things I could be writing for I had been almost down to the day-counting stage. Now I can't begin to say how disappointed I am and how sorry I am to have raised your hopes. There is however, Darling, this bright side to the situation. If the peace comes, I will be home to stay before too long.... This should make a lot of boys from Europe pretty happy – that we finished our own war before they had to help us.

> The cancellation of Wilber's leave was due to the impending November 1 invasion of Kyushu, Japan, as Wilber later explained [letter 8/16/45]. It had nothing to do with the ongoing peace overtures.

So far as the plan for staying in the army is concerned, no way whereby that is possible has developed yet....

Of course, Lover, I am really too happy that I may never again have to send men into places where I expect them to die. For that I could wait a while longer to see you. The thought that the end of the fighting may be here seems unbelievable to me. I keep saying to myself that maybe there won't be any next battle, that no shells will be going by too close again. In a way I'll miss the thrill of wondering if I can wiggle out of tight places, but my intellectual self reminds me not to be regretful. All I can think is how much I love you, how now at last I can really feel that I will be home with you again....

> So for Wilber, there was indeed a certain "thrill" to "wiggling out of tight places"! He went on to give his family some of the credit for his survival. It still seems a miracle that he did survive, given all those close calls.

You, Dearest, have also won your war. Our home, thanks to you, still is complete and perfect. You have helped the children and I'll never repay you for all the letters that meant so much to me. Each hour I've known you and the children were my partners and it meant more to me than anything else in the world. We will be walking together again before too long and I hope never to be parted.

VICTORY AND HOMECOMING   PART II: FINAL BATTLES, LUZON

… Cleland is back but I've not seen him yet. I'm thrilled that I may have finished the war commanding a regiment. I never expected that to happen. We finish our most recent tactical mission Wednesday [at Dingalan Bay and elsewhere] with quite a few more Japs to our credit. I'm glad it's over and really hope it is the last time I'll ever have to order men out to be killed.…

Yes, I definitely agree that you + Hale made the right decision about Indiana. I'm always meddling because I do want to still be a father and husband.

How goes the play? I'll tell Barker what you said. He has really had a hard time and feels badly about going home without a promotion. I told him that we who served with him knew how much better he had functioned than other artillery commanders we have seen. He received the Air medal yesterday. His artillery has never failed to make a superior showing and he does feel good about that. He says his wife has been pretty fine about his being away. Many wives are making things pretty hard for officers here.…

> Gen. Barker had led the divisional artillery through the entire war, with superb results. Unfortunately, that meant he had held the same rank, brigadier general, the entire time while many others were rapidly advancing.

We built a bamboo officers' club where the officers can loaf and drink cokes, "rum and coke," or water. Not much choice but we do have ice and limes so I drink a lot of lime cokes. It is sure good for my morale.

It is evening and I've been in and out of this letter nearly all P.M. No news yet from Japan, but I'm not much worried because they are pretty smart and know when they are through. Who is this Senator Stewart who wants us to keep fighting to the last Jap? There are regulations that prevent me from now saying what is in my heart about that.

I do love you, my Dove of Peace. It won't be so long now. — XXXOOO Wilber

> This was Wilber's last letter before the cessation of hostilities. He was now being abruptly diverted into a new worldview. No longer would he face combat and possible death on Japanese shores, but rather a new and uncertain peacetime future in America.

11

"So it's over. Well! I think I'll go sit under that tree"

Camp La Croix
AUGUST–SEPTEMBER, 1945

On August 14, Japan accepted the Allied Unconditional Surrender terms and on the 15th all U.S. offensive action against Japan ceased. The relief, of course, was huge, both in Luzon and for us in Washington, D.C.

At the end of the war (August 15), Yamashita's Shobu group still had about 65,000 troops of which about 52,000 comprised an organized defensive force. The original number in the Shobu group had been 150,000. The force had been contained by the Americans to a small region of Luzon (the Asin Valley), but had not been effectively destroyed as General Krueger thought. Yamashita believed he could hold off the Americans for another month or so. At war's end, some 50,000 Japanese, including Yamashita himself, exited the mountains of northern Luzon. Yamashita had effectively carried out his planned delaying action for more than seven months. His efforts may have spared by several months the home islands from Allied invasion. [Smith, Triumph, p 579.]

x·o·ø·o·x

Wilber wrote his first letter home after the cessation of combat. He deemed it to be as "historic" as the one he had written on December 7, 1941, during the attack on Pearl Harbor. It was addressed to all of us.

Wilber's letter to his family at the end of World War II, August 16, 1945.

CHAPTER 11   *So it's over. Well! I think I'll go sit under that tree*

AUG. 16, 1945

Dear Family, All Three of You — Congratulations to each of you for being well and fine all thru the war. You have each done your share in the winning of this war just as much as if you were fighting. Your letters to me, your care of each other and your sympathy and goodness have been the only things that made my stay here possible.

The war is over. The peace is here. That doesn't mean all the things you have been needing will all at once be here. It does mean, however, that most of those away from home can come home alive. The dirt and danger and tiredness will be much less. You can sleep better, worry less and be proud of a job you have done well.

I am thankful to have lived to see the end of the war. In fact I'm rather pleasantly surprised to be here considering the times I considered the odds against it. There is no question in my mind but that your prayers and the prayers of your friends [were] a great help and protection to me in the past years. I do thank you and them from the bottom of my heart. I'm sure we all thank God for the care He has given us during these times and will try to be worthy.

As you know, my leave was cancelled, and it is OK now to tell you the reason was that the next battle was almost here. I was to be (and am now) the combat commander and was very busy with plans for the landing and action. It looked like a real job and you can be sure it is a relief to not be facing it. Now I will not ask for leave but will stay until the urgent need for me is past and then request release. Just how soon that will be, I do not know, but it may be as much as six months. I wish it might be now but it cannot be so soon. I don't know what plans are being prepared for us but have no doubt the radio will be announcing things much more freely before long. Ruhlin is back with us. He looks fine, and I was really glad to see him. He had come by our house in Bangor to see you, but you were already gone....

Do you know I'm very proud to have ended the war in command of a regiment? That is something I never expected. Now if, when I can retire, I am still in good standing, everything will be OK here. Gen. Cleland is back here now. He said he talked with you but couldn't find time to see you. I'm sorry for you would like him....

We are having a heavy storm just now. My grass roof is streaming water all around the eaves. Incidentally it leaks in the center but not seriously. The lightning really cracks around here, and the water and wind combined make quite a picture. I don't know now if Col. Bush will return or not. Probably many now on leave who have been here a long time will be held in the States. He was not due to start back until the end of this month.

I should like your advice about when I should try to come home.... I'm about ready to retire as one of Uncle Sam's boys and to start being a private again. (Private citizen would be a real promotion.) [This is a play on the word Private, the lowest rank in the army.] ...

VICTORY AND HOMECOMING   PART II: FINAL BATTLES, LUZON

The 43d didn't do any noisy celebrating. No promiscuous firing, no one hurt and no regrets. I was proud after reading the news of the hysteria elsewhere. This is really a fine division and I'll always be glad I stayed with it.

I love all of you. I am coming home just as soon as seems possible and wise and it is going to [be] just wonderful to be with you again. For now, Good Night! — XXXOOO Wilber

Had Wilber really been set to command an entire regimental combat team in the Kyushu invasion or was he to be executive officer under Colonel Bush? This would have been a major difference in responsibility. As commander the full burden of command would have been his. As executive officer, he would have been responsible only for the management of the regiment in accord with the commander's wishes. He was quite clear in the above letter when he stated that he "was to be (and am now) the combat commander." See also his letter of September 6, 1945: "In fact for the invasion I was to command over forty-five hundred men."

High competence as a combat commander was a much sought-after trait in the face of the expected fanatical Japanese defenders of their homeland. Placing top people in the most critical positions would have been a priority. Since Colonel Bush was also of high repute and had commanded a regimental combat team in the Luzon action, he may well have been slated for a higher command or one as commander of another regiment in need of a strong, experienced leader. Bush was clearly expected to return to the division [letter 8/21/45], though in the end he did not.

I contacted Bush in the 1980s, and he told me that as far as he had known, he would have returned to his old command, the 172nd Infantry before the invasion, but did not know what other plans his superiors may have had for him. Wilber had been in a position to know this, having been intensively involved in the planning with those superiors. Wilber would thus have faced the huge task of leading an entire regimental combat team in the invasion of the Japanese homeland. It would have contained almost ten times the manpower of his former battalion commands, 4,500 versus 500 men.

x·o·ø·o·x

In this letter to Norma, Wilber noted their upcoming wedding anniversary and revealed his thoughts, hopes, and concerns.

CHAPTER 11   *So it's over. Well! I think I'll go sit under that tree*

AUG. 21, 1945

Hello Anniversary Wife — Maybe this letter will arrive on our [18th] anniversary [Aug. 28]. I hope so for I've no gift on the way [with which] to tell you I love you. This is the letter for telling you I do love you. A week from today we start another year together. I am reminded that each of the past years has been a wonderful soul satisfying experience. I am particularly joyful this time for I now know most of this year we will be together again. If you know how much I love you, you will appreciate my thoughts about our reunion. It is a dream that I can expect to be fulfilled. I do know so many sweet things we will find in that dream and can hardly wait for it.

There are so many things to think about now that I have very little time to write. As soon as MacArthur's plans for the various armies here are announced, we can do a little personal planning. In the meantime this is what is in my mind now. If Col. Bush returns from his leave, I can expect to be released here within three months if I desire. I do. If he does not return and I continue as regimental commander, my release might be delayed another three months. I should like a month for rest before going back to work and then should be ready to take over at Maine again for the second semester.

If I am not needed at Maine before July '46, I would probably study during that semester or go to Maine and do research for a second choice. I'm writing to [Dean] Cloke stating the possible fact that I may be available for the spring semester and asking if they want me back then. In this connection I have just received a very fine letter from Hauck [president of the University of Maine] approving my decision to see the war thru and re-stating his eagerness for my return.

So far as my staying in the army is concerned, I am not planning on that. If legislation is passed, I will consider it carefully. It will need to be really favorable, however, to convince me of the need for further separation from my family. There is also the possibility that I might fail the physical requirements and be left unemployed on short notice. So far all examinations show me in fine shape, but it is true I am having trouble with one shoulder. It may be arthritis, or a nerve injury or a torn ligament. The MDs don't seem to know just what causes the pain. X-rays show no injury and other specialist check-ups seem to establish just that my shoulder pains me. I probably pain it.

Before I am released I'll have another session in the hospital to make a more thorough investigation. In the meantime, it doesn't disable me at all, is just annoying, and has been so all thru the Luzon campaign. This is to be considered in future plans, you see. Probably if I get a month's rest, a good many tensions and minor ailments will disappear. I was pretty run down after Ipo [the Ipo Dam action] but have been improving steadily since the middle of July.

So Dearest, my anniversary gift to you is just a loving husband who expects very shortly to be delivered physically on your doorstep. It will be so good to be home again. When this final job is done, I'll present my points to Wing and say my speech. Since I have a good many more [points] than anyone else in the division, I'm sure he will listen to me.... [no closing]

There was an ebb and flow to Wilber's plans for the future. He seemed reconciled to returning to Maine, but the army still beckoned if it would have him. Unfortunately, his high number of points would probably not help with this; it would depend more on army postwar policy. He had been in the division for its entire overseas service and had been awarded seven medals (Legion of Merit, Purple Heart with cluster, Silver Star with two clusters, and Bronze Star). According to him, this gave him more points than anyone else in the division, an impressive record indeed.

x·o·ø·o·x

[AUG. 28, 1945] ANNIVERSARY DAY!

Hello Lovely Bride of Mine — About this time a very short time ago, I stood watching you walk down the aisle of a church in Portland [Oregon]. You were lovely, my Darling. Your dress was beautiful and you were graceful and sweet and I knew I would love you forever. When you came to me I was so happy that there was love and certainty in your eyes and I knew life with you would always be a joy and a dream of perfection mixed with sunshine and flowers and music and blue sky....

Now the war is done and we start our nineteenth year with peace. It must be a glorious year because it will bring us together again. After that anything will be likely to happen and I know it will be fun and wonderful and exciting. I do love you so much more than last year and the years before. I know now how perfect a home can be, how fine children can be, and I can hardly wait until I am with all of you.

It is late now, Nana, and I've been up until 2:00 A.M. for two nights, so here is dreaming at you. — XXXOOO Wilber H.H.P.P. (Happy husband + Proud Pop)

Norma's response to this must have been a mixture of elation and dread. She would surely have shared the widespread euphoria that the war was finally and successfully over, and she could take pride in having played her role as morale builder in helping Wilber survive it. On the other hand, she likely had no idea how her competing loyalties to little Gale and Wilber would play out when he returned home. Were she and Monte fearful that

CHAPTER 11   *So it's over. Well! I think I'll go sit under that tree*

harm could come to them or to Wilber if he came to realize the truth? Or, did they naively expect their lie about Gale's parentage to remain viable in the long term?

x · o · ø · o · x

On this date, September 2, on the battleship USS Missouri in Tokyo Bay, the surrender documents were signed by General MacArthur and Admiral Nimitz, a representative for each Allied country, and by Japanese officials. The war was officially over.

By this time, Wilber would have been pressed with preparations for the move of the regiment into Japan as an occupation force. Entirely new plans were now required and in a hurry. Nevertheless, he found time to write to me.

SEPT. 2. 1945

My dear Son — Yesterday I told Valerie hers was my last letter for a time, but now I find a few minutes that I had not counted on having. It is a very busy time handling an infantry regiment and it seems this one has a reputation for activity. We are always getting involved in things. Tomorrow it is the dedication of a monument to the Dead of the 43rd at Ipo Dam. I must get up early and bump myself over four hours of rough road before 1030. By the time I get there my rump will be exactly the shape of a Jeep seat. You wrote me once about Jeeps. So far as my personal use of them is concerned, they are wonderful – for the Spanish Inquisition. I could think of nothing more fitting than to sentence Goering [Nazi German air marshal] to 500 miles a day in a Jeep until dead. When I get home I'm going to specialize in comfortable sitting.

It is cool today. A typhoon is due tomorrow, and it has been rainy and windy today. Maybe we will be picking up tents tomorrow. It has happened before. General Cleland came over today and visited an hour or so. We really have a good time together. If we were back in combat, I'd like to be with him again. Life was always interesting around him, because he was always getting worked up about things, especially enemy artillery.…

Did mother mail my other uniforms? I hope so for I wanted them to be well ahead of the Christmas mail rush. My stuff from Pat French [Bangor uniform dealer] never came, so I would like the following ribbons bought, cellophane-covered and assembled on bars of three, three and two. Please air Mail.

1 Silver Star with 2 clusters, 1 Bronze Star, 1 Legion of Merit, 1 Purple Heart with 1 cluster, 1 Asiatic-Pacific with four stars and one arrowhead, 1 Infantry Combat Badge, 1 World War campaign, 1 American Defense, 1 Philippine Liberation with 1 star and 1 arrowhead.

VICTORY AND HOMECOMING   PART II: FINAL BATTLES, LUZON

Show this to the Officer Uniform Company for authorization to buy. I am authorized to wear each of the above. — Your father, Wilber Bradt, Lt. Col.

I love you and can hardly believe the war is really over and that I may be home before too long. We don't earn decorations now. We wear them. WB

> A cluster on a medal ribbon indicates a second decoration. A star on a campaign ribbon represents a particular "campaign" or battle in that theater. The four battle stars on the Asiatic-Pacific ribbon were for Guadalcanal, Northern Solomons, New Guinea, and Luzon. The (duplicative) battle star on the Philippine Liberation medal was independently merited. An arrowhead indicates an amphibious landing. Wilber wrote in his log that his "assault landings" were New Georgia, Baanga, and Luzon. Only one arrowhead is allowed per campaign ribbon.
>
> These ribbons symbolize Wilber's war as a series of icons. Norma successfully carried her family through the conflict and her war service could well have been recognized with ribbons for parenting, soldier support, childbirth, Manhattan, Bangor (Maine), and Washington, D.C. The icons in either case, real or imagined, left much unsaid.

x · o · ø · o · x

SEPT. 5, 1945
Dearest Wife — A very, very short note because I have just been told censorship is lifted. If so, this will be mailed. We sail for Tokio [sic] day after tomorrow and will be part of the occupation forces in that area. I'm combat team commander (5 ships + 4,000 men) and have been very busy these past weeks planning first the attack which was to have been next month and more recently this unopposed landing. It is a welcome change. I do love you and am on my last, I hope, job. Then HOME and you. — XXXOOO Wilber

> Wilber was developing an almost boyish enthusiasm for getting home. He too must have been having some misgivings about how his relationship with Norma would fare after the long separation. And there was, as well, his uncertainty about his future employment.

x · o · ø · o · x

CHAPTER 11   *So it's over. Well! I think I'll go sit under that tree*

SEPT. 6, 1945, [U.S.S. MONROVIA, MANILA HARBOR]
Dearest Wife — Last night I came aboard the USS Monrovia and found a long letter waiting from you. Don't worry about the house being ready for me. Any place where you are will be to my liking. And as for Washington, if you like it there, it is the place for you. I should not mind the heat after three years in the tropics.…

We are sitting in the harbor and I am astounded at the change since I first saw it. That was only three days after the 37th had captured Manila [on March 3] and the harbor was full of Jap wrecks. No U.S. ships were in yet because of mines and the fact that Fort Drum was still Jap held. Now I can see hundreds of U.S. vessels. The wharves are crowded and busy. We have certainly moved in. I eat with the Commodore (Tyler from Maine). He is regular navy and seems very pleasant. Gen. Barker and Col. [Wm. B.] McCormick [Barker's executive] will come aboard tomorrow.…

> Fort Drum was a fortified island at the mouth of Manila Harbor south of Corregidor. Corregidor was the famed last major American bastion to fall to the Japanese in May 1942. On the return of the Americans in 1945, Corregidor was secured on February 26, 1945, after a ten-day battle. The Japanese held Fort Drum until mid-April.

I love you, Darling. Don't forget it and please don't worry or work too hard. — Wilber Bradt

[Note in margin:] I bought a camera last week. The little one went by the board somewhere. This takes 120 film, and I think will be a good one. WB

> I used this very camera all through high school. It was an Argus Argoflex.

x · o · ø · o · x

> The 43rd Division sailed for Japan on September 7. Wilber was on the USS Monrovia, commanding the 172nd Regimental Combat Team. This was to be an unopposed landing under peacetime conditions. Nevertheless, the reaction of the Japanese to the forthcoming occupation was not yet known.

x · o · ø · o · x

> Accounts of the planned invasion of Kyushu (Operation Olympic) are chilling. The 43rd Division was to land on the southern end of the beaches of Shibushi Bay (Ariake Wan) on the southeast coast of Kyushu (Map 18) in order to capture nearby Japanese airfields in the vicinity of Shibushi. There

197

were to have been numerous other simultaneous landings on Shibushi Bay and elsewhere on southern Kyushu. The Japanese had anticipated correctly that the first Allied landings would be on southern Kyushu and were building up their forces there. Thousands of planes were available, but there was a deficiency of trained combat pilots. With minimally trained pilots, they were planning on overwhelming kamikaze (suicide) attacks on the transports carrying the American troops. Estimates of potential casualties at this stage reached beyond 30%, along with huge anticipated losses in the subsequent combat. Success was far from guaranteed. [Drea, p. 74].

I visited the nearby Japanese rocket launching facility, Kagoshima (now known as Uchinoura Space Center), on two occasions in 1983. On one such trip, I visited the beach where the 172nd Infantry would have landed. The mountainous terrain surrounding the beaches was frightening in the context of 1945. An artillery map (Map 18) in Barker's book shows that the 43rd Division artillery shells could have reached the small town of Uchinoura, in which I stayed. I had a copy of that map with me. The proprietors and guests in my ryokan (inn) were more than a little interested in it.

Before moving on to Japan with Wilber, let me describe my 1983 visit to the battle sites and the people Wilber knew in Luzon.

PART III

INTERLUDE 1983

LUZON, PHILIPPINE ISLANDS

MAY, 1983

★ ★ ★

12

Laguna de Bay and Corregidor
May 1–6, 1983

In May 1983, I visited the Philippines en route from Japan to an astronomical observing run (session) in Australia. (I was in the midst of a six-month sabbatical in Japan.) On that same trip I also visited the Solomon Islands. I described in Book 2 of this work the latter visit, as well as my 1984 visit to New Zealand. In the Philippines, it was my intention to find the people Wilber had met and to visit the places he had been. I wanted to have a more visceral sense of his experiences there.

Wilber, ever the scientist, documented his letters with the names and addresses of the people he had met. I wrote ahead to several of them, hoping the ancient addresses would suffice. I received one response, from Emma Peralto, the wife of a protégé of Judge José Dacquel—Dacquel was an attorney Wilber had met when his battalion was at Guimba for a ten-day respite from combat. I had only one short week in Luzon to explore Wilber's diverse activities over six months, so the efficient use of my time was essential. Ms. Peralto had arranged for a young relative, Boysie Florendo, to help me out.

x·o·ø·o·x

My journal (with excisions and edits) continues the story. I wrote this entry in Cuyapo, a town north of Manila, a few days after my arrival.

Trip around Laguna de Bay – Sunday, May 1
My first day in Manila, I was met by young (35-year-old) finance officer, Boysie Florendo, who drove me all around Laguna de Bay, counter-clockwise, the direction opposite that of the 103rd Infantry in April 1945.

We drove first to Pagsanjan and then north a mile or two to the Lumban bridge, which Wilber had helped capture and hold from the Japanese side of the bridge. It was a relatively placid river, 30 to 50 yards wide with banks no more than about five yards high, hardly the deep gorge described in official histories and Wilber's letter. We found there an iron "old fashioned bridge," built in 1949 according to the plaque mounted on it. Adjacent to it, just upstream, one could see remnants of the wooden pilings of the old bridge barely protruding above the water. It was the end of the dry season and the river was very low.

I could not believe I was walking the very same grounds upon which Wilber and some 15 others had hunkered down to defend the bridge they had just crossed. To modern-day Filipinos there, it was just ordinary ground, but to me it seemed sacred.

We talked to an old man at a bus stop there and to a middle–aged man at the police station in the town of Lumban. From them both, the following story emerged. In late 1941, the retreating Americans, or possibly the Filipino guerrillas, blew up the original bridge. The Japanese then constructed a wooden one with the labor of 150 American prisoners of war. Lumban was a sleepy village with small houses, a very old church, and a theater where the prisoners were housed. The local Filipinos

Southwest end of the bridge over the Pagsanjan River at Lumban, Luzon, and me, May 1983. [PHOTO: HALE BRADT]

CHAPTER 12   *Laguna de Bay and Corregidor*

Boysie Florendo interviewing an elderly man at the bus stop at the Lumban bridge, May 1983. [PHOTO: HALE BRADT]

Two wooden pilings of the 1942 bridge at Lumban barely showing above the water surface at seasonal low water, May 1983. [PHOTO: HALE BRADT]

helped by "giving the prisoners cigarette butts" when they could. It was this wooden bridge that was being used when the Americans (including Wilber) arrived in 1945. The 1945 capture of the bridge by the Americans was not a big deal in the eyes of the townspeople. The building of the bridge by the captured Americans in 1942 had made a much greater impression.

I later happened upon the story of the building of the Lumban bridge in Donald Knox's *Death March*. The 150 American prisoners had built the wooden bridge in about six weeks beginning just after Corregidor fell on May 6, 1942. At one point, Filipino guerrillas raided the town, killing several Japanese guards and telling the prisoners, who were quartered in the theater, they could escape with them. (Most of the Japanese were in a camp outside town.) Only one chose to go with them. The next day, the Japanese, as they had threatened, executed ten American prisoners as retribution for the one who had escaped.

I contacted the three survivors quoted in the book; others contacted me when I expressed an interest in the Bataan survivors' newsletter, *The Quan*. The horror of those tense moments during which the ten men were selected, as the jittery, upset Japanese trained their rifles and machine guns on the entire contingent, was graphically described by several of these men in letters to me. One soldier saw his brother executed. The Lumban Bridge seemed to have been the most vivid experience in their entire three years of captivity. One called the bridge the "structure of tears."

North of Lumban, the road went over a [small] hill and down into the village of San Juan. This was the hill over which the forward elements of the 103rd Infantry (including Wilber) raced toward the bridge hoping to prevent its being blown up. We went by San Juan too fast for me to pick out where near the town Battery B of the 152nd FA might have been placed.

The Laguna de Bay is a huge lake about 30 miles across, east of Manila. It is crisscrossed with fish pens. Much of the fresh fish one can eat in Manila is from there. As we drove north along the eastern side, we next came to Paete and then to Pakil. Pakil is where the two little girls wanted soap, but Wilber thought they meant "soup," so we decided to drive into Pakil. A very narrow street led into the square from the "highway." A truck coming out made us wonder if we could go on in, but he cooperated (practically climbing the side of a house) and in we went. There was some kind of festival going on this week so there were some stalls and people and cars around, but not too many as it was early. Some boys were playing basketball and festival (rock) music was playing at a deafening level. This was hardly in keeping with the spirit of the ancient plaza or my 1945 reveries.

CHAPTER 12   *Laguna de Bay and Corregidor*

Jeepneys at Cuyapo, Luzon, decorated with bold colorful painted designs, May 1983.
[PHOTO HALE BRADT]

We had the driver of a Jeepney take a picture of us in front of his highly decorated (gaudy), Jeepney and the cathedral, but he seemed to point the camera off to the left somewhere. (Maybe his girl friend was over there?) We thought of looking up Margarita [the little girl who wanted soap], but since the only clue I had was her age in 1945, we didn't try, but went on.

Jeepneys were then and still are ubiquitous in the Philippines. Originally they were WWII Jeeps converted to mini-buses. They were and still are wildly decorated with colored figures, extra lights, and sundry other adornments.

After my return to the U.S., I made a photo-foraging trip to the U.S. Defense Department photo archives in Washington, D.C., where I found a photo of lots of people on the steps of a public building or church in Pakil. General Wing (43rd Division commander) and Colonel Cleland (103rd Infantry commander) were prominently visible in the front row. Soldiers and many women in fancy dresses were in the photo, which was taken during the celebration of the town's liberation. When I received the enlarged print at home a couple of months later, I found my father in one of the back

Celebration of the liberation of Pakil, P.I., April 9, 1945. Wilber is at left rear in helmet (see enlargement to left), General Wing (commander, 43rd Infantry Division) is front center with lei, and Colonel Cleland (commander, 103rd Infantry Regiment) is at right with hat in hand. [PHOTO: U.S. ARMY SIGNAL CORPS, SC 266243]

rows. He had uncharacteristically joined the group for the photograph and was looking directly at me with a grin from under a helmet; he was the only person with a helmet. It was almost as if I had found him there in Pakil!

I have since then been in touch with a Pakil native, who is a teacher here in the U.S. He and his relatives in Pakil have succeeded in identifying most

CHAPTER 12   Laguna de Bay and Corregidor

of the people in the photo, discovering with pleasure that his mother and grandmother were among them! I recently conducted a class in astronomy at his Arizona school, via Skype from Boston. Positive effects of the war ripple on decades later.

We then drove by Pangil, Siniloan, and Mabitac, but did not look into them; the highway now bypasses the village centers. The highway was two lanes total, one each way, like the typical highway in the U.S. in the 1930s and 1940s. As we drove along I was following the day-by-day progress, in reverse, of the 103rd Infantry on the aforementioned map in Barker's book. We then followed the road up the mountains to San Miguel where the 103rd Regimental Combat Team (RCT) assembled under cover of darkness in preparation for the attack into the valley the next day. We came down to the lake again at Pililla, which was celebrating its 400th anniversary! We then drove the about 1 mile into Tanay.

I saw a big church there and suggested we see if it might be the "damaged" church "built in 1606" that Wilber visited on Easter 1945 – all alone – a rather touching recollection [letter 4/7/45]. The plaque on the church gave 1606 as the date of the original church, 1783 as the completion date of the current church, and 1939 as the installation date of the plaque, so the plaque was there in 1945. I concluded therefore that this must be the church Wilber visited. It is San Ildefonso Parish Church. I spent a moment visualizing Wilber's solitary Easter visit and photographed the plaque and the inside of the church.

Plaque giving the history of San Ildefonso, May 1983. The original parish church, possibly located elsewhere, was built in 1606. The present church was completed in 1783, and this plaque was installed in 1939. [PHOTO: HALE BRADT]

Exterior and interior of San Idelfonso de Toledo Church in Tanay, May 1983. Wilber had visited this church 38 years earlier, on Easter Sunday, April 1, 1945. [PHOTO: HALE BRADT]

We then proceeded on into and around Manila including the oldest part and the lovely large park on the waterfront where everyone was enjoying Sunday. There I bought tickets for the Corregidor tour the next day (Monday).

Then, we went to a great continental restaurant "Mario's" where I had lots of cold beer; did it ever taste good after that long hot day. I then went back to my hotel from which I could see Manila Bay. Some sight: I had known of the Bay since my boyhood and here I was really seeing it!

So ended my first day in the Philippines – some day!!

The next day, I would step outside Wilber's direct experiences and visit the famed island of Corregidor. I was still writing these entries at Cuyapo, on May 3.

x · o · ⌀ · o · x

Visit to Corregidor; Monday, May 2

The trip Monday, to Corregidor, on May 2, was fascinating. Many of the original U.S. Army concrete buildings are still standing but are heavily damaged and in ruins from the heavy shelling by the Japanese in 1942 and the Americans in 1945. Corregidor, an island in the mouth of Manila Bay was the last bastion of the American defense when the Japanese conquered the Philippines in 1942 (Map 16). It fell on May 6, a full five months after the beginning of the war and about one month after the surrender of the American troops on nearby Bataan Peninsula. The Bataan surrender led to the infamous Bataan death march of American prisoners. Soldiers who fell behind were savagely executed by the Japanese.

There are still guns and mortars there, many damaged in the 1942 battle. The huge (10-ton) mortars that were tossed about like matchsticks when an ammo magazine took a direct hit are still lying where they fell. The explosion shook the island to its core. The famed Malinta tunnel is open; the tour bus goes through it, and one can peer (and go into I am told) the side tunnels where President Quezon lived and Gen. MacArthur had his headquarters. One can see the façade of the old base theater, the North Dock from which MacArthur left the island, and the South Dock from which Pres. Quezon left, both looking like they did in 1942 (according to photos I saw). Cute children of island staff sold postcards and other souvenirs. There is a monument on the topmost location where the old Headquarters and parade ground were. It was a living island with a formal, permanent military base until the hell of 1942 and 1945 ravished it. I was reliving those days every moment. The protected isolation of Corregidor preserves its artifacts well. It is a rare historic place.

Ruins of the base theater, Corregidor, May 1983. [PHOTO: HALE BRADT]

American 12-inch coastal gun, Corregidor, for the defense against naval threats from the west. May 1983. [PHOTO: HALE BRADT]

CHAPTER 12   *Laguna de Bay and Corregidor*

Malinta tunnel on Corregidor Island, May 1983. It was used for storage, shelter, a hospital, the headquarters for the U.S. Far East command (Gen. Douglas MacArthur commander), and the government seat of the Commonwealth of the Philippines (Manuel Quezon, president) during the Japanese siege in 1942. [PHOTO: HALE BRADT]

We visitors toured the island for about two hours by bus with lots of stops. The trip out there and back was on a hovercraft, which floats above the water on a cushion of air and can travel very fast, up to about 25 MPH. It took an hour from Manila. On the way back, it was initially quite rough but then it quieted down for the sunset ride into Manila. The sun was at our backs shining onto Manila, a beautiful sight.

That evening (Monday) Boysie met me and he took me to a Philippine restaurant, the Tito Rey. They have washbasins out in the open so you will wash thoroughly before eating with your fingers—from all the seven or eight serving dishes—many types of seafood, some hot and spicy, all good. It was "finger-licking good"!

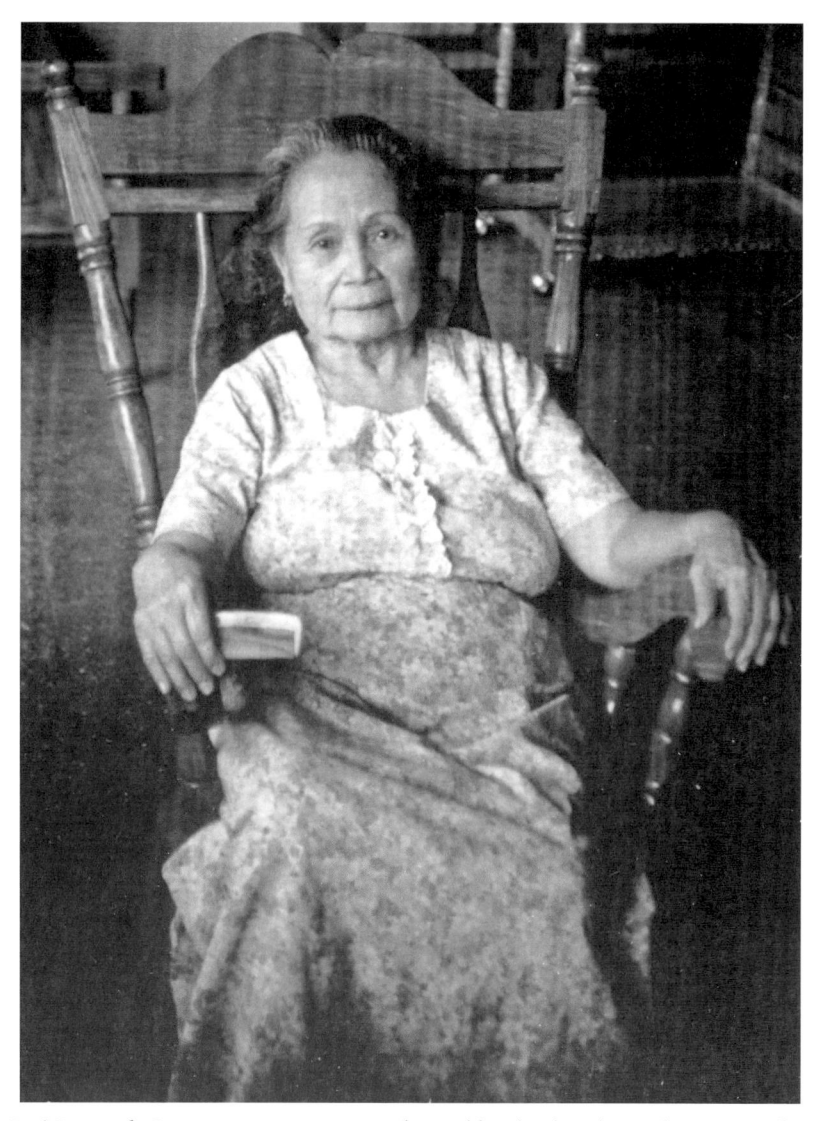

Mrs. José Dacquel, Cuyapo, P.I., May 1983. She and her husband were hosts to Wilber's unit when they were recuperating at nearby Guimba. [PHOTO: HALE BRADT]

13

Hacienda Cinco, San Fabian, and American Cemetery
May 3–6, 1983

The next day, Tuesday, May 3, I met Emma Peralta who took me by bus up to Cuyapo where I spent the next two nights. Cuyapo is near Guimba where Wilber's unit had had two weeks of "recuperation," and it was not far from Lingayen Gulf where the landings took place. I was met at my Manila hotel by a relative of Boysie's and taken to the bus station where I met Emma. The bus ride to Cuyapo provided yet another view of Philippine life. My journal continues the story.

Cuyapo, Mrs. Dacquel, Hacienda Cinco; Tuesday, May 3

Right now, I'm sitting in the home of Mrs. José Dacquel in Cuyapo, Luzon, about 100 miles north of Manila. It is a modest contemporary "modern" home which replaced the one Wilber knew, after a fire. The late Judge Dacquel and his wife, my hostess, were the gracious hosts of my father and his battalion. The battalion was in rest camp near here (Guimba) after the first five weeks of fighting in Luzon. I am sitting in a bedroom with two walls open to the outside (large louvered windows) through which I can see palm trees, get an occasional breeze, and hear cocks crow, see people, bikes, and an occasional moped with side cart (the local taxi). It is hot, dry, and lazy. Most of the breeze on me is from a fan. I just had a bath in the bathroom, which lacks sink and running water. I used a scooper to scoop water from a very large bucket to wash myself and to flush the toilet, and to shave. Primitive, but very refreshing!

Here in the rocker (as I write this), I was brought little green balls (Caramay fruit) to eat with sugar or salt. These were good in the heat: juicy and tart when you bite into them. I was given the choice of slippers to wear, one set for the house and another set for the bathroom. They had gone to the store to buy them; I reimbursed them. I had shown up with only my oxfords and jogging shoes, and they were deemed to be neither comfortable nor sanitary.

The bus coming here was Express, 3rd class, no air conditioning, 3 hours duration, and breezy with open windows. The driver was very skillful dodging others, little motorcycles, jeepneys, etc. We drove through lots of rice fields and fresh vegetable fields too. Cuyapo is right in the middle of large fields or former estates called "Haciendas." Many of these have been broken up by land reform.

Mrs. Dacquel is 77 years old, chunky, and very spry. She doesn't remember Wilber, but does remember entertaining a lot. Foolishly, I had failed to bring a reasonable photo. I read to them (about five people) Wilber's 1945 letter about the hospitality they gave him, and they were quite touched by it. I asked them about their experiences in the war, and learned the following:

(1) Cuyapo was pretty isolated and therefore pretty much left alone by the Japanese during the occupation. They did tell, though, of a hooded (to hide his identity) collaborator (Filipino working with Japanese) pointing out to the Japanese people who were guerrillas. Those so identified would be taken to Guimba, a nearby (larger) town, for questioning. They heard of terrible tortures, but did not see such happenings here in Cuyapo.

(2) The hacienda where the 152nd FA Bn. (Wilber's unit) stayed was, I am told, surely the deSantos's hacienda; it was tremendous in size (possibly 9,000 hectares or 22,000 acres). It has since been broken up due to land reform. The house where the officers lived is no longer there, torn down, they said. Boysie had told me he remembered seeing only the porch pillars standing, some time ago.

The next day (May 4), I continued the story of May 3.

Yesterday after my arrival here, Edgar José, a young college grad, took us to Guimba. We saw the ruins of the main home of the hacienda where the 152nd FA Bn. officers stayed. The building was not completely demolished; the Corinthian pillars of its formerly elegant facade were still standing. A son of the owner had a small hut there and was digging in the foundation for "treasure" the Japanese said they left there "under the stairs." He showed me some small bones which he claimed were human (I couldn't tell). He is very poor now.

He suggested we talk to the ex-driver of the deSantos family who lived nearby, Eugenio Gabres. We looked him up. He remembered that the "156th Infantry" was there and said it was the only unit to stay there for two full weeks. This agreed well enough with the facts (152nd Field Artillery for two weeks). He served as a barber for the unit, he said. About twelve local people joined us and some told of the danc-

ing parties on the lawn that Wilber had also described. Many of the local people had not been in Guimba then; they were off at "evacuation centers." These were villages in the mountains organized by the Filipinos so they would be far from the fighting and the Japanese.

After the visit, we drove down to the town of Guimba, and then returned to Cuyapo. On the way down to the hacienda and back to Cuyapo, we drove by many small villages, small houses, children playing in yards, all very, very poor and rural, dirt common areas without grass, rather flimsy houses, all very communal and close-knit. On our return in the evening, the houses were lit and one could see a bit of evening life, which included the open, circular huts alongside the road where people gathered to gossip and where someone is always on watch for "undesirable elements," e.g., cattle thieves.

The hacienda where the 152nd FA stayed was Hacienda Cinco, Lenned Guimba, N.E. It was one of five estates established by Isidor deSantos for his five children (by breaking up the original estate). Hacienda Cinco consisted of 1,800 hectares (4,450 acres), had 365 tenants, and encompassed parts of five towns. Everyone agrees that the house and grounds were beautiful in 1945 and thereafter. The house was a very imposing structure of ten rooms. The hacienda consisted of rice fields as far as the eye could see.

Portico of the main home of the Hacienda Cinco, May 1983. The 152nd Field Artillery Battalion had a two-week respite from combat here in March 1943. [PHOTO: HALE BRADT]

Lingayen gulf and Manaoag; Wednesday, May 4

The next day, Edgar drove us in his car to Manaoag and San Fabian, towns Wilber had gone through after landing on the beaches of Lingayen Gulf. I wrote about the trip upon returning that same day.

Well, the highlight of stupidity today was the drive to the beautiful white sand beaches at San Fabian, Lingayen Gulf, without a bathing suit. And was I hot when we arrived there after an hour's drive in the boiling Philippine sun at about 1 p.m.! Now, I am back in my well-ventilated bedroom in Cuyapo sitting with the fan on me after a refreshing bath.

The San Fabian beach where the 152nd FA Bn. landed (with the 103rd Regimental Combat Team) is a beach with lots of vacation houses, which I understand were not there in 1945. Lots of people and children were swimming; I should have gone swimming in my shorts. I did spend some moments contemplating the scene there on Jan. 9, 1945. The town of San Fabian, where the 152 landed, was, on my visit, just another sleepy town with lots of tricycle taxis (motorized) and Jeepneys.

Our first stop on the way to San Fabian was Manaoag where Wilber rescued the wounded Filipino guerrilla by using his artillery on Japanese machine gunners. We talked to the clerk (Mayor's secretary) of the Town (who wasn't there at the time but was in the guerrillas elsewhere) and several at the "Camp Manaoag," now called Camp Lt. Tito B. Abat, which has been an army camp since before WWII. It is on "Hill 200," a rolling set of ridges north and east of Manaoag, which the Japanese defended and the 103rd Infantry had difficulty taking. We ate our lunch in the officers' little bamboo straw-roofed, cool hut while we chatted and read Wilber's letters. They were quite interested in the guerrilla rescue story, but could not identify the place. Our minimal efforts failed to find the place or anyone who remembered the incident.

Manaoag is a pilgrimage town – Miraculous Virgin – and many people go there in May to pay homage. We visited the church and saw two funeral processions. One group carried the coffin and everyone else walked slowly behind. The women carried colorful umbrellas as shields against the sun. In one case we saw the children and family all lining up to be photographed behind the open coffin as a memento.

Life and death go on and on. I was immersed in the events of 1945 and these people were losing loved ones in 1983. Most probably, those loved ones carried memories of the war to their graves. Such memories survive in the minds of fewer and fewer of the living as time goes on, until, finally, the story will live on only in written histories and artifacts.

CHAPTER 13 *Hacienda Cinco, San Fabian, and American Cemetery*

The drive to Manaoag from Cuyapo had taken about 1.5 hours through rice fields, all of which are dry now, and the drive further north to San Fabian took another hour. We drove on dirt, unpaved roads and other times on "fancy" highways, one lane each way, but paved! One high point on the way to San Fabian was our getting stopped by the police who didn't think Edgar's penciled license plate saying "Road Test" was quite up to par. They said they would have to impound the car. But Emma talked with them, mentioned a local (big shot) relative and the "fine" came down from 500 to 200 pesos ($50 to $20), which I gratefully paid (it was a long walk back), and we were on our way.

At a Coke break a little later, in a fly-ridden lunch place (Emma suggested we not eat the meat dishes), Edgar made beautiful cardboard hand lettered license plates (front and rear) which said "Registered but No Plate Available." This modification to the plate had been kindly suggested by the troopers who had stopped us! I was wondering how many times I would have to pay 200 pesos before we made it back home. However, that was the only time. I also paid for gas we bought, $10 + $10, and gave Edgar another $20 to help support his 1969 Ford Mustang which was fire-engine red with a good stereo system. You should have seen us rumbling over dirt roads with western guitar songs playing loudly, just like an old movie.

x · o · ø · o · x

Manila and American Military Cemetery; May 5–6

On Thursday, May 5, I took the bus with Emma back to Manila. My time in the Philippines was growing short—I was to fly out the following evening. In Manila I was back in the Silahia Hotel. And very soon, the various relatives of Wilber's Cuyapo acquaintances, the Dacquels and deLeons, many of whom are still in Manila, began to get word of my presence, and I became even busier!

After the three-hour bus ride with Emma Peralta, I treated myself to lunch and a much-needed refreshing swim in the outdoor pool of the hotel. I had made some brief notes about the two days in Manila as they occurred and wrote them up two weeks later during a cloudy night of an astronomical observing run in Australia.

Upon my return to Manila on May 5, I was promptly adopted by two daughters of the deLeons and their families. They had been in their late teens or early 20s in 1945 and remembered well the dance at Hacienda Cinco. Several army truckloads of girls were brought down for the dance (the few miles from Cuyapo to Guimba), but only the upper-class girls could dance with the officers. They did not remember specifically Wilber.

The first evening, I was taken (I paid) to another gourmet Philippine restaurant [the Sinagbo] by one deLeon daughter (Lusita Javier), her husband and two adult children, and Emma. Afterward, I was taken to see another deLeon daughter at about 10 p.m., then back to the hotel.

The next morning (May 6, Friday), I was picked up by another deLeon daughter and husband and taken to their home for breakfast with her family. Lunch was at a Chinese restaurant with Lusita and her husband, after which they took me to the Manila American (military) Cemetery. These meals were all festive, familial gatherings with wonderful tasty dishes. The Filipinos enjoy their food and their families, and they know how to entertain their guests.

The cemetery was beautiful, much like Arlington National Cemetery, but in a way even prettier. Most of the graves had simple white marble crosses while a few had Stars of David, rather than the simple headstones of Arlington National Cemetery. The rows of crosses are more striking, especially with their sharp shadows in neat rows in the hot Philippine sun. All the Pacific military dead of WWII were brought here unless their families requested they be returned to the U.S. Earlier, these bodies had been buried in military cemeteries in the combat areas.

It occurred to me that I might find the graves of the officers Wilber had lost in the Solomon Islands. Indeed I found them: Lts. Malone, Payne, and Heidelberg, the three forward observers for the 169th FA Bn. who were lost in the Munda/Baanga battles and about whom I knew so much: Norbert Heidelberger, died 8/15/43, grave A–3–71; Earl M. Payne, 7/13/43, F–11–30; Arthur Malone, 7/28/43, A–12–115.

Lieutenant Norbert J. Heidelberger as an army private in 1941 or 1942. He was a forward observer of the 169th Field Artillery Battalion and was killed on Baanga Island in August 1943, a loss that Wilber felt deeply. [PHOTO: HEIDELBERGER FAMILY]

CHAPTER 13   *Hacienda Cinco, San Fabian, and American Cemetery*

Manila American Cemetery, May 1983. The remains of servicemen who died in the Pacific Theater were brought here or were returned to their homes after the war. The three forward observers Wilber lost in the Solomons were interred here. Lt. Norbert Heidelberger's grave is the second from the camera, with my pen leaning against it as a marker. [PHOTO: HALE BRADT]

Grave of Lt. Norbert Heidelberger and me at the Manila American Cemetery, May 1983. The text on the cross reads: "Norbert J. Heidelberger; 1 Lt 169 FA Bn 43 Div; New York Aug 15 1943." I also located the graves of Wilber's two other forward observers who were killed in the Munda action, Lieutenants Earl Payne and Arthur Malone. [PHOTO: HALE BRADT]

VICTORY AND HOMECOMING   PART III: INTERLUDE 1983

As I walked the rows of crosses I could see other 43rd Division casualties. Each stone gave rank, name, unit (division and regiment or battalion), and date of death (no birth date). From the date I knew, most probably, just where the casualty occurred. It was a series of friezes of the 43rd Division's advance through the Pacific that touched me deeply. One grave of a private of the 103rd Infantry from Maine had died April 5, 1945. This was the day Wilber, working with the 103rd Infantry, helped capture the Lumban bridge. Was he there with Wilber or further back along the road when he was killed? That gravestone lent some harsh reality to the story of that day.

So ended my stay on Luzon. That evening (Friday, May 6), with several small gifts in hand from my Filipino friends, I was on a plane bound for Australia and the astronomical work I was being paid to do.

My visit was rich in impressions of places and people and long-ago events. It has now been more than 30 years since that trip. Another generation has passed on, and a new one has grown to adulthood. I have not maintained contact with these wonderful people and sadly contemplate how the events of the 1940s are fading from their collective memory. Does anyone know or even care that the 152nd Field Artillery Battalion from Maine spent two weeks recuperating in Guimba in February 1945, or that on George Washington's birthday there was a wonderful moonlit dance at the deSantos's hacienda with an orchestra "equal to the top U.S. ones"?

Other than the photographs I took, my only memento of the visit that I still have is a simple brass letter opener I was given as I left. I still use it regularly and it brings back memories of that visit. I will never forget the warm generous hospitality of the Filipinos I met through Wilber's friends. But of course, I also have Wilber's letters and that beautiful walking cane of kamagong wood given to Wilber by the Dacquels [letter 2/28/45]. They are reminders of the same kind of hospitality he had received in 1945.

x · o · ø · o · x

After my Australian astronomical observing run and a week in the Solomon Islands, my month in the Pacific was coming to an end, and I was returning to Japan from Port Moresby in a jet airplane. In the previous 30 days, I had experienced my own adventures in many corners of that great ocean. I had canoed (with motor) around the Munda waters of the Solomon Islands with Alfred, my guide; found disintegrating planes, tanks, trucks, and helmets; contemplated the dark waters of Blackett Strait between

CHAPTER 13   *Hacienda Cinco, San Fabian, and American Cemetery*

Kolombangara and Arundel under the full moon; stood on the same ground that Wilber had at the Lumban Bridge; walked the Lingayen beach at San Fabian where he landed amid exploding shells and aerial machine-gun strafing; and visited (see next chapter) the beach in Kyushu, Japan, where he would have landed on November 1, 1945, for the combat he did not expect to survive [letter 9/20/45]. I had relived my father's 1100-day Pacific odyssey during my own 30-day mini-odyssey.

As I was winging my way back to Japan, so too had Wilber been heading there in 1945, but much more slowly on the USS Monrovia. I fully expected a safe arrival, but he surely felt some uncertainty about the reception his troops would receive as they set foot on the Japanese homeland.

PART IV

JAPAN AND HOME

SEPTEMBER—DECEMBER, 1945

★ ★ ★

14

"Tokyo and Yokohama are ruins"

Kumagaya, Japan
September 1945

With the war officially ended, Wilber faced a new challenge: the occupation of Japan. He would also face the challenge of coming home and moving back into civilian life again. At the same time, it would be a change of scene for Norma, Valerie, and me. Perhaps we would be moving back to Maine again? We did not know, and frankly at age 14, I didn't even think about it. Norma also had to face the implications of her attachments to both Wilber and little Gale, now almost two.

Wilber's September 1945 departure for Japan coincided with the beginning of the school year for Valerie and me. Valerie was in eighth grade at Alice Deal Jr. High School and I in tenth grade at Woodrow Wilson High School, both public schools in Washington, D.C. and both within walking distance of our Alton Place home. The transition had not been difficult for us; we were used to changing schools, having sat in diverse classrooms in New York, New Jersey, and Maine during the war years. I took up a paper route delivering the *Washington Post*. Rising before dawn, I would deliver 40 or so papers in the neighborhood by bicycle. I learned how to fold the paper so I could fling it toward the front door from the sidewalk, with only rare irretrievable landings on a roof. The job provided good spending money.

After preparing us for school and settling us in the Washington house, Norma had her writing (the Abigail Adams play) and piano practicing to keep her busy. She also contributed to the care of baby Gale, who lived with Monte at his Q Street home, four miles south of us.

VICTORY AND HOMECOMING   PART 1V: JAPAN AND HOME

x·o·ø·o·x

The USS Monrovia (APA-31) with Wilber and part of the 172nd Regimental Combat Team left Luzon on September 7. They were destined for the port of Yokohama in Tokyo Bay. They would debark in Yokohama on the 13th, only 11 days after the peace treaty had been signed. This was Wilber's tenth overnight voyage (Map 2) since departing San Francisco on October 1, 1942. Wilber wrote Norma the day after their departure.

[USS MONROVIA] SEPT. 8, 1945
Dearest Wife — We are just leaving the shelter of Luzon and starting thru the Luzon Straits between that island and Formosa. So far the weather is good and the sea smooth, but it is reported we will see rougher water beyond the Straits. The sun does not come up like thunder in the China Sea and I'm very disappointed. However K. [Kipling] was right about the flying fishes [in his poem "On the Road to Mandalay;" see commentary on letter 1/6/45]. I saw three sharks too that he missed.

Tonight for the first time overseas we sail with the lights on and the portholes open. There is nothing so hot as the hold of a ship with all ports closed. This is the first convincing indication to us that the war is over. I hope for more evidence soon.

> There was still concern that some Japanese would try to resist the American landings, so the division remained equipped and prepared for combat. [e.g., Krueger, p. 344]

I am really hoping to start home by X-mas. It is all a matter of replacements arriving here and I'm pretty sure some Regular Army Lt. Col. who wants his eagles [promotion to Colonel] will suddenly have a yen to leave his desk, come out here and command a regiment. If I'm right, he can have my job any time. Barker is on this ship too, and he also says he is ready as soon as his original officers are on the way home. I am the last of the 152 regiment and only a few of the other artillery old timers remain.

> Wilber was the very last of the officers of the original 152nd Maine Regiment still with the 43rd Division. He had truly made finishing the war his own project, and he was determined to see it through to the end. An eminent Australian historian and veteran of World War II emphasized to me how far Wilber was from the norm, because, he said, most soldiers wanted to get out of combat areas as soon as possible while still alive and uninjured. This opinion is not popular today nor was it then, as we honor our military for their courage and devotion to their country. But surely there is truth in the historian's assessment.

CHAPTER 14   *Tokyo and Yokohama are ruins*

Don't worry about my research work. What I must do first is get myself re-educated in chemistry. If we live in Orono and don't have a big house to take care of, I'll get the research done and the study too. If we go to school for a while first before going to the U. of Me., I'll do it that way. One thing I'm sure is more important to me is time to spend with my family. If I stay in the army, it will be solely for financial reasons, not for any love of the profession. There are more little bickerings, petty matters, back bitings in the army in a month than in a year of teaching. I could find worthwhile things during combat, but couldn't be too interested in peacetime. No more National Guard now for me. That is a job for younger men now.

With no car we should live in Orono because it would take too long getting back + forth to Bangor. Later if we find we can afford it, I suppose a car will be required. I wrote Cloke I'd take a month vacation before going back to the U. no matter when I was released. I don't care if your house is fixed or not. It will be home to me. I'll try hard to be there Feb. 1 for a combined X-mas and birthday [Wilber's birthday was February 1]. In the meantime I love you more than I can ever write. I'll tell you someday soon all about it. — Your Loving Husband, XXXOOO, Wilber

> Wilber seemed more focused on returning to the University of Maine, but had a rather grim view of a spartan life there because of a shortage of money.

x · o · ø · o · x

> As was typical of him, Wilber, in a period of less activity, began to contemplate what he had been through, namely the buildup to the invasion of Japan. He shared his thoughts about that with his brother Rex and his wife. He felt he could be completely honest with them.

SEPT. 8, 1945 [ON USS MONROVIA]
Dear Rex and Gerry — I'm sitting on the deck of the USS Monrovia on the way to Tokyo. It is good to have a little less on my mind than I expected to have on my trip to Japan. Incidentally plans were well completed on that job. I knew which hills I was to take and what some of the difficulties were. All in all it is a relief to hope the next landing will be unopposed. We were to be a "spearhead" division again, and I never did care for the term.

I wrote Ruth that we didn't have a celebration nor feel like it. One soldier said, "So it's over. Well! I think I'll go sit under that tree," and he had a rather typical reaction. However we didn't sit under a tree, for the attack plans were changed to occupation plans, and we have been rushing on them until yesterday. Yesterday we sailed, and I've slept since [then] more than in three days before.

VICTORY AND HOMECOMING   PART 1V: JAPAN AND HOME

Sitting "under that tree" was a metaphor for the quiet relief many felt about the war's end. The forthcoming but now canceled invasion of Japan had meant that the men of the 43rd Division had been, in effect, on death row, but were now suddenly released into the open countryside, free to pursue the lives of their dreams.

I ended the war in command of the 172 Inf. [Regiment] and am taking the regimental combat team to Japan. That is the biggest job I'll do in the army, and having done that and having actually reached Japan, I am ready to call the job done so far as I'm concerned. I'm very tired but find myself in good physical and mental condition except for a bad case of homesickness. Since this is my 36th month overseas, I've no complaint at all about my own condition.

Actually I have hopes of being home for a late Christmas-Birthday party and have told Norma not to send presents to me here. I've been away too many Christmas days so am going to have the next at home even if it is too late....

The China Sea is smooth now but a typhoon is predicted so we may get splashed. A water spout went past the ship yesterday, but I missed it. — Goodbye and good luck, Wilber

x·o·ø·o·x

He now turned his attention to Norma. He was on his first peacetime voyage.

SEPT. 10, 1945
Hello Darling — I've been thinking of you and wondering how soon I can be with you again. The main idea is replacement. I hope the army gets something on the way [here] besides lieutenants pretty soon. Probably I'll need to run this job for two or three more paydays, then I should spend a couple of weeks in a hospital check-up, then I'll be really unreasonable about getting home. It seems odd to be really planning to get home [to] stay. Maybe it is still just a dream.

The lights are left on the ships at night now. That was the most convincing end of war event to me. I stood at the rail a long time watching them remembering how many nights I'd done the same thing watching for submarines. Some night I want us to stand at a rail just watching the moon on the waves and knowing we are together. Officers still marvel at my young wife and speak of your beauty. I'll speak of it too some of these days.

I've done a lot of sleeping on board and quite a lot of reading. It is really a good rest and I find I need it. In fact if I can come home on a good ship instead of by air, I may do it for the rest. Air travel here hasn't reached [the] luxury phase yet.

CHAPTER 14   Tokyo and Yokohama are ruins

Another reason we know the war is ended is that ships will now stop to pick up a man who falls overboard. Before they didn't dare stop so the poor fellow was left. All in all things are improving. I'm ashamed at the food we get when I know you are short. We are getting the eggs + ham + steak you are not having. I wish I knew how to share with you.

I love you, Wife of Mine. You have done a wonderful job in keeping our family well and together and training them the right way. I hope I can share your burdens soon and let peace come to you too. I do so want you beside me again. I'm glad you like Washington. It must be nice if you like it. I'm sorry I said I wouldn't prefer it, for I'm sure if you were there I'd be content. Good cheer, Lovely Wife. I'll hold you so tight when I get home, you'll never get out of my sight. I love you. — Wilber

[Note in margin:] Sept. 15. Am just outside Tokyo and as busy as can be now. No trouble. Am OK. Will write as soon as possible. Tokyo + Yokohama are ruins. WB

x · o · ø · o · x

The 172nd Infantry arrived in Yokohama on September 13 and were debarking dockside at 6:30 a.m. the next day [WEB Journal]; there was no longer any need to climb down nets into small landing craft. The unit moved immediately to the Kumagaya airbase, 45 miles northwest of Tokyo. Their occupation duties were to keep order and to collect weapons. Although Wilber did not know it yet, after a mere 14 days in Japan, the 43rd Division would be boarding ships for America. In this letter to me, he told about Japanese soldiers and the reactions of Japanese civilians who had never seen an American soldier.

[VICINITY KUMAGAYA, JAPAN] SEPT. 17, 1945
Dear Son Hale — Your especially nice letter of Aug. 14 came today and I am sitting down to answer it right away. Your work at the dairy must be interesting. It is amazing to me that you should earn so much. Did I ever tell you that when I graduated from the University some of my classmates took jobs at $85.00 a month and none were as high as your pay. Of course money bought more then. You can see what is meant by inflation by this if you consider what goods or food your pay will buy as compared to what it would have bought twenty years ago.

It must be interesting to be in Washington [D.C.] while all the peace rumors and messages are flying.

There are some Jap soldiers all around me now. They are sweeping out the Hq. bldg. We use them to do all kinds of work such as digging ditches, latrines, cleaning up areas, handling heavy equipment. They work well but one can't tell what they are thinking. I suspect they aren't at all except what the Emperor tells them.

Day before yesterday I was driving thru some country where no Americans had been yet. It was interesting to see the Jap reactions. Many women would dash inside their houses, others would hold their hands over their children's eyes, some boys were very formally turning their backs, other saluted, still others just gawked. Many men would fold their arms and bow very formally or salute, or take off their hats. They were very helpful as to directions whenever my Nisei (U.S. Jap) asked them questions.

The country near Tokyo and 75 miles away is almost all little gardens, which I presume they consider fields. Tile roofs on houses are common. The shrines and temples are very interesting from the outside but we are not allowed inside.…

> This spoke well of the U.S. military's sensitivity to Japanese customs. The American occupation was to be paternal, not intrusive or oppressive.

I am very proud of your job and of you. You have done a fine share in this war. — Love, Wilber

x · o · ø · o · x

> The 43rd Division next received VERY big news.

SEPT. 19, 1945
Dear Darling Wife — Today is the big day. We have just received orders for the 43d to return to U.S. as a division and soon. I have real hope of being with you, not for X-mas, but for Thanksgiving. Dearest I'm so happy. The sun would be shining for me even if it were pouring. I don't know how or when we will be released in the U.S. There may be some parade obligations. Neither do I know which port we will enter thru, but you can be sure I'll send a wire as soon as I can.

Today I wrote Cloke asking to be put back on the payroll for the second semester. I told him to write me at your address for letters would only follow me now. To you also I say, don't write, for I won't be here by that time. I may be on the water (but not moving) by the time you read this. Isn't that hard to realize.

We are beginning to be settled here in a temporary way. Day before yesterday we had a typhoon and so spent yesterday picking up pieces. One of the hangars we live in was bombed and I can't imagine who would have done it. There is surely a big leak in that roof.

Goodbye now Lover and Hale + Valerie. I love you all more than I can ever say. — Wilber

Up to this time, Wilber expected that individual soldiers would be deployed back to the states, but not the entire division. The 43rd Division began to take in "high-point" soldiers from other units and to transfer out "low-point" personnel, in preparation for shipment to the States. With his huge number of points (161), Wilber would remain with the 43rd Division and thus also as commanding officer of the 172nd Infantry; he would return to the United States in that position.

It was probably on this day that, listening to the student-read daily news over the school PA system, I heard that "The 43rd Division will be returning home from Japan." I let out a little yelp of pleasure, which attracted only a brief questioning glance from the presiding teacher. No further note was made of the announcement; the classroom reverted to its atmosphere of quiet industry. I was probably the only one in that entire high school so directly affected by that momentous news.

x·o·ø·o·x

Here again, Wilber shared with his brother Rex some of his darker thoughts about the planned invasion, including the presumed likelihood of his not surviving it.

SEPT. 20, 1945
Dear Rex + Gerry + Connie Lou — Your nice letter came today. And today we are in process of leaving Japan for the States. There is a lot to be done so we are very busy taking over Jap installations, counting or rather estimating the equipment they surrender, and at the same time prepar[ing] to sail.

I'm very proud of the work you have been doing on the A.B. [atomic bomb]. We had already made plans for the landing on Japan and there would have been many casualties. In fact I didn't expect to come thru that one alive. Your work very definitely was a major factor in bringing the war to an end before we did move in. The 43rd was one of the assault divisions in the landing and my regiment was given the point considered most critical to the success of the division action. That meant we couldn't take our time but would have to drive thru anything we met the costly way. So I thank you and Daniels not only as a commander but [also] for myself. It is good to be coming home.

I do plan to see you before I go back to the Univ. but of course can make no plans now. I hope you + Gerry have a good winter and that everything is well with the children. Personally I could do with a bit of rest and I imagine you too. — Love, Wilber

VICTORY AND HOMECOMING   PART IV: JAPAN AND HOME

"The costly way," not expecting "to come through that one alive," and "given the point considered most critical" vividly expressed his view of the invasion.

Why had Wilber's regiment been assigned the "critical point"? Given his history, he may well have volunteered his unit for that position. Was this overreaching or simply his or his superiors' belief that his men would perform better than the other regiments in that position? During my sabbatical trip to Japan in 1983, I visited the beach where the 172nd Infantry was to have landed. It was overlooked by mountains to the south reaching to 2600 feet. They had surely been defensively tunneled for Japanese troops and guns and would have been a threat to the entire division's landing area. The 172nd Infantry, according to a map dated August 5, 1945 [Barker, p. 231], was responsible for the taking of those positions.

The Japanese had deduced the likely landing sites and were rapidly building up troops on Kyushu hoping to make the landings so costly that the Allies would be willing to negotiate favorable peace terms. An abundance of airplanes with minimally trained kamikaze pilots were available and were

The beach at Shibushi Bay, looking south, May 1983, with me and overlooking mountains reaching to almost 3000 feet. The 172nd Infantry, Wilber's unit, would have landed at this southern end of the beach on November 1, 1945. They had been given "the point considered most critical." [PHOTO: HALE BRADT]

expected to exact a heavy toll on the transports even before the landings. In addition, civilians including women and children were being armed with simple weapons such as sharpened bamboo stakes; this could have made every Japanese civilian into a combatant. The resulting loss of life on both sides could have been horrific [Atill, Part 3].

After the war, it was found that Japanese preparations for the landings were greatly delayed. This, the ineffective weapons in the hands of civilians, and the limited training of, and limited supplies for, the available troops led to a postwar assessment that the XI Corps most likely would have been able to fulfill its objectives, namely to drive west through to Kagoshima Bay and to link up with I Corps in the north (Map 17), though possibly on a delayed time scale and with an unstated number of casualties [Antill, Part 4].

x · o · ø · o · x

All was now "orderly confusion" as the regiment prepared for departure. In the midst of it Wilber exhibited some boyish enthusiasm for the return home.

[NO DATE, ABOUT SEPT. 23, 1945]
Darling Wife — We "progress." Everything is all orderly(?) confusion while we transfer all the low point personnel to divisions remaining here and receive those with high points. We count and recount everything from shirts to trucks, rush supplies here and yon and build tent camps for the regiment that is to relieve us. But it is fun. Our date for boarding ship now is the 27th. Sailing date may be later but probably only a few days. It is rumored [wrongly] that we go to Fort Lewis for initial processing. I'll wire you on arrival in U.S. After the division is processed, I'll probably be shipped to [Fort] Meade [Maryland] and will call you from there if your phone is listed. If not, I'll taxi.

My efforts to get warm uniforms out here has caused you a lot of trouble and successfully taken them out of circulation but who cares? I'll be getting into civies [civilian clothes] as soon as possible. The one wool uniform I have here will get me home OK – probably slightly unpressed [that is, wrinkled]. The ribbons came yesterday and were fine. Hale surely acted promptly on that matter. I doubt if many other officers get theirs before we sail.

Anything sent to Wilber would not find him in Japan. He had requested the ribbons in his letter of September 2.

Just now it is pouring rain and I'm glad to be under a roof. It is hard to realize my tenting days are practically over. Every hour or so, I feel good realizing we didn't have to fight our way ashore and to Tokyo. We earthquaked last night – no thrill!

I can't think of anything to mention or write about because I'm coming home, I'm coming home. I'm really coming home. I love all of you so much and have dreamed of this so long that I really am almost delirious. I agree that, if Valerie's teeth aren't straight now, you should get treatment started without delay. We probably have more cash now than we will a year from now. I love you. — Wilber XXXOOO

x·o·ø·o·x

After hectic preparations, the move to Tokyo and their shipment home was at hand. The preparations, both for the regiment and his own personal affairs, kept Wilber very busy. This was his last overseas letter, except for one written en route home. In five days he would have been outside the continental U.S. for a full three years.

SEPT. 26, 1945

Hello Star of My Life — Tomorrow we go aboard ship! These past days have been as hectic as combat. It is times like this that I am thankful for a good staff. They really are a fine lot and I am saved a great many details and much work. We have been at Kumagaya north of Tokyo about fifty miles. I haven't seen Tokyo yet, but will try to spend an hour or so there on the way to the dock.

It promises to be a good ship altho personalities make a lot of difference in the way things are done. The troops who came over on her weren't too happy, but the direction of travel [to Japan] may have been a factor. It is a long way home and I don't know when we sail, but tomorrow at 9:00 A.M., I start the return trip. I can hardly believe it is really here. The return won't be a rest for I'll have about five thousand men and officers and that means a lot of organization because they come from three divisions [regiments?]. However being the senior commander on ship, I'll have the only stateroom for one person that is intended for generals. It should be comfortable. I may see Joy but am not sure. You could send a letter there if you like.

Joy Cook was a friend in Washington State. Her husband Holloway did not survive Japanese imprisonment.

I am shipping a box, which may arrive ahead of me. It is mostly equipment such as shoes, denims, and books but don't let the children open it. There are one or two things in it I intend for X-mas and I'd like to keep them as surprises. If my footlocker arrives ahead of me or my bedroll, they may open the bed roll but not the foot locker. There is a little present for each of you in it [the bed roll] for your birthday and Hale's and Valerie's birthday[s] and you might as well have them now. You can decide which is for [whom] and select one each. Nana is final authority between H. + V. and one yellow item is for Nana herself. I have a present for me in the roll too (gloves).

> The metal footlocker was full of souvenir Japanese pistols.

My present intentions include at least a month's rest, which may be on a "Leave" status or after release and a session in the hospital to clarify my physical condition. My shoulder and back have improved steadily since I had a special seat put in my Jeep and my dysentery has disappeared but I want to be sure I'm cleaned of any of the tropical bugs I may have accumulated. Don't let all this worry you for I undoubtedly am as well as if I had lived in the U.S. these past three years. This is insurance against any delayed action trouble that might cost me a lot.…

I'm completely at a loss for things to say now. There is just one thing in my mind. I'm so thankful to be coming home to you and the children and do love each of you so much. This is my last overseas letter. I hope it isn't too long before you have my first U.S. telegram. I know you won't have a phone so it will be a wire [telegram]. Better buy a very, very cute nightie too. I've been imagining you in one for a long time. — XXXOOO Wilber

> Wilber was planning his homecoming, and romance was definitely on his agenda.
> On the 27th, the regiment moved to Tokyo and boarded the USS General John Pope (AP-110), a large transport ship named after a Civil War (Union) general. Loading the 172nd Infantry and the 2nd and 3rd Battalions of the 169th Infantry was complete by 5 p.m.
> Nine years later, in June 1954, I boarded her sister ship, the USS Gen. George M. Randall, in Tokyo. I too was a military passenger, though I was definitely not the senior officer aboard. I had left my own U.S. Navy cargo ship in Japan because my two-year stint in the navy was nearing an end. The Randall was loaded with troops who had been in Japan and Korea, many for extended periods. The departure was very festive, with a band playing and colored ribbons running between ship and shore, most unlike the many routine, unnoticed departures I had experienced on the navy cargo ship on which I had served, the USS Diphda (AKA-59). The joy all around was catching; it gave me goose pimples!

Was Wilber's departure similarly joyful or was it a quiet departure with a sober sense of relief on the part of each departing soldier? I would guess the latter. His ship was probably the first departure for the U.S. from Japan with U.S. troops, and peacetime customs may have been slow to unfold. A western social community did not yet exist in Tokyo. As my ship pulled away from the dock and those colorful ribbons began to break, I was replaying Wilber's departure, but was probably not then conscious of it. Now, I feel it poignantly.

15

"My heart rests in your dear hands"

At sea and Washington, D.C.
September–December, 1945

The USS General Pope left Tokyo at 9 a.m. on September 29, 1945 [WEB Journal]. Wilber was the senior officer aboard. He apparently wrote only one letter to Norma during the voyage, and it was an outpouring of gratitude for her support and love during the long war. But, it closed on a note with darker overtones.

USS GEN. POPE IN NORTH PACIFIC, OCT. 5, 1945
My Dearest Lovely Wife — There is little point to writing this letter for I hope to tell you all the thoughts of it with your hand in mine. Darling my duties are nearly over in the army. Anytime that I have had trouble, it has meant so much to me to know you were waiting with confidence in me. You have helped me to show patience with those whose performance was poor. You have been beside me in lonely spots and have shown me faith and love to shorten long days and hours.

It has been memory of you and your sweetness and beauty that has held my love and desires. I have been true to you and have touched no other woman. This has been hard thru the long months but I knew you too were needing caresses and denying yourself. You have always been so clean, so true, so fastidious, so much the perfect mate, that I could not leave your love even for an hour.

There have been times when I lacked the courage to continue the pace I had set for myself, when it was a temptation [to] not go into dangerous places that day. On those days you have reassured me and led me thru the hard places. Your days have been lonely. You have worked too hard. You have been ill away from me and have done many things I ought to have done. Yet your letters have been brave and sweet and loving until I could not but adore you. These hard days are nearly past. Others will perhaps come but we know, you and I, that the real victory is that our love has stood the test and will stand all others. My Princess, your love is all that is important to me. You give me courage, sympathy, understanding, and yourself. I know of nothing more any man could desire than these treasures you have brought into my life.

Neither do I forget the two fine children you bore me. Your love brought joy to my life when you gave me those dear little mites. Under your guidance they have followed the right road. All these things and many more have you given me. I will always need them and you. I shall love you and cherish you thru eternity. My life will be yours to use. My heart rests in your dear hands. Never try to leave me, Beloved, for I can never let you free. — Your Husband, Wilber

> He had such an idealistic, wonderful view of Norma, but it was all based on her role in providing support to him and the children. Sadly, he could not see the complexities of her feelings and life, in part because Norma could not bring herself to share them with him. That ending, "Never try to leave me, Beloved, for I can never let you free," was probably meant to be a positive statement about their bond, but in retrospect it was chillingly ominous.

x·o·ø·o·x

The 172nd RCT arrived in San Francisco October 8, 1945, three years and one week after Wilber had departed San Francisco. This may have been San Francisco's first view of returning troops after the war's end. I learned only recently of photos of its arrival in San Francisco harbor that day, taken by a newspaper photographer, in the archives of the Bancroft Library of the University of California, Berkeley. They showed hundreds if not thousands of happy soldiers lining the decks, some brandishing captured Japanese flags.

One of these photos was a shipboard interior shot of Wilber and another officer, probably taken because Wilber was the senior officer aboard. He had a big grin, unlike most other photos of him. His Eisenhower jacket was only modestly adorned (no ribbons) but proudly showed the crossed rifle insignia (of the infantry) and the Combat Infantryman's Badge. This photo is unique in that there are no other photos taken of him after his return. There was no rush; he would be around a long time, we thought. It was a joy for me to find this one of him on board the USS General Pope the day of his return.

The 43rd Division was deactivated from federal service at Camp Stoneman, Pittsburg, CA, which lies off the northern end of San Francisco Bay on the San Joaquin River. Wilber's unit, the 172nd Infantry was formally

CHAPTER 15 *My heart rests in your dear hands*

USS General John Pope (APA-110) returning 5,000 troops home to America from the Pacific Theater, San Francisco Harbor, October 8, 1945. Wilber was the senior army officer aboard. [PHOTO: BRK00012312_24A, *SAN FRANCISCO NEWS-CALL BULLETIN* NEWSPAPER ARCHIVES, COURTESY BANCROFT LIBRARY, U. OF CALIFORNIA, BERKELEY]

Soldiers returning to San Francisco on the USS General John Pope after lengthy war service in the Pacific Theater, October 8, 1945. [PHOTO: BRK00012314_24A; *SAN FRANCISCO NEWS-CALL BULLETIN* NEWSPAPER ARCHIVES, COURTESY BANCROFT LIBRARY, UNIV. OF CALIFORNIA, BERKELEY]

VICTORY AND HOMECOMING   PART IV: JAPAN AND HOME

Wilber (left) and Capt. Wood Reddy on board the USS General Pope on the day of their return to San Francisco, October 8, 1945. Wilber was the senior army officer on board.
[PHOTO: BRK00012315_24A; SAN FRANCISCO NEWS-CALL BULLETIN NEWSPAPER ARCHIVES, COURTESY BANCROFT LIBRARY, UNIV. OF CALIFORNIA, BERKELEY]

CHAPTER 15   *My heart rests in your dear hands*

General Leonard F. Wing, commanding general of the 43rd "Winged Victory" Division. This photograph was in Wilber's papers and was inscribed, "To Lt. Col. "Bill" Bradt with admiration for a fine and gallant soldier. Leonard F. Wing, Maj. Gen., U.S.A." One of two national guardsmen to have commanded a division in World War II, he returned home to Vermont after demobilization early in November 1945. He died there, at 52, of a heart attack the next month on December 19, 1945. [PHOTO: U.S. ARMY SIGNAL CORPS]

VICTORY AND HOMECOMING   PART IV: JAPAN AND HOME

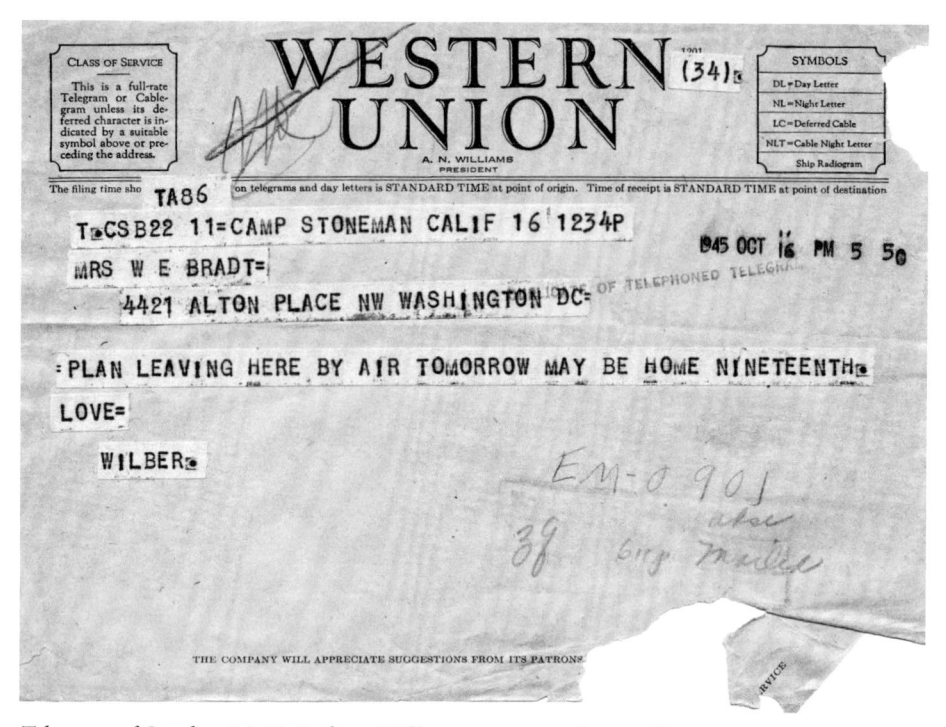

Telegram of October 16, 1945, from Wilber announcing his trip home to Washington, D.C., from Camp Stoneman, California. He had been in the United States since October 8.

deactivated on October 13, 1945. It may have been at this occasion that the division commander, General Wing, inscribed a photo of himself for Wilber: "To Lt. Col. "Bill" Bradt with admiration for a fine and gallant soldier." The deactivation of the 43rd Division was completed on November 1 as its headquarters was released from federal service.

From Stoneman, each man was sent to an army separation center near his home. For Wilber, this was Fort Meade, Maryland. He departed California on October 17, after sending a telegram home. He crossed the country on a government transport plane. He later told of his difficulty sleeping during the long flight given the noise, hard floor, and cold of the cargo bay; his head wound bothered him a great deal, he said. Upon arrival, in the Washington, D.C., area, he checked into Fort Meade, and arrived at our home on the evening of Friday, October 19.

We heard a knock on the door, I opened it, and there he was in full dress uniform. I immediately received a one-armed hug; his valpack (military folding suitcase) was in the other. Mother screamed happily from the kitchen and there were hugs and smiles all around. I do not remember more of that evening, except that he advised us, with a grin, not to be alarmed if we saw him wandering around in the back yard at night, as he was not accustomed to indoor bathrooms.

x · o · ø · o · x

Valerie recalled his return and time with us:

Daddy's return
Valerie Bradt Hymes (2011)
I was 13. My strongest memory of my father's return is one of ineffable joy. I seemed to be suspended in air, just happy to be in his presence, enjoying the sound of his voice, not always understanding what he was saying but not really caring. I loved the way he smelled like he did before he went away to war.

The only specific event that I remember before learning he was gone was when he took me to an orthodontist to find out how much it would cost to have my front teeth straightened. I remember the dentist because he was in a wheelchair, a victim of polio. I remember his office was on I Street, and that it was spelled EYE Street. Unfortunately, the cost was too high and I remember daddy saying it would have to wait.

After his death, the dentist saw the news story in the Washington Star and called us to say he would fix my teeth at no cost.

x · o · ø · o · x

Two days after Wilber came home, on Sunday, October 21, he and I went to see the famous concert violinist, Fritz Kreisler, in a recital at Constitution Hall [*Washington Post*, October 21, 1945]. Mother must already have had the tickets for me and herself, so we decided that Wilber and I would go instead. I was studying violin, so it was considered important that I attend, and he was a lover of classical music. Unfortunately, we forgot to take the tickets with us, but we talked our way into the hall. We did not remember the seat numbers, but knew the section (far left near the front). As the concert was about to begin, there remained two pairs of empty seats in that section, but Wilber did not want us to sit in either lest it be the wrong pair and the rightful ticket holders arrive at the last minute. Thus we stood just inside an entrance door throughout the entire first half of the concert watching and listening to Kreisler. When I complained about my hurting feet, Wilber replied that I should not complain but rather think about how

Kreisler's feet felt, as he had to stand throughout the entire concert. Fortunately, we were able to sit during the second half.

I remembered this event well but not its date and was unsure who the performing artist was. It was only recently that I found a notice of the concert in the *Washington Post* online archives and learned that it occurred only two days after Wilber's return and that indeed the artist was the legendary Fritz Kreisler. This was one of the only two father-son outings we had after his return.

x · o · ø · o · x

Norma, Valerie, and I had been in Washington for only about 11 weeks when Wilber arrived home and thus our acquaintances were few. Wilber was a complete stranger to the area. There was no influx of visitors and friends to see him, which probably would have been his preference anyway. His one close contact in Washington was his brother Paul, who lived four miles away. He and his family were away during the weekend Wilber arrived, but they came to see him Monday evening. Josephine, Paul's wife, told the story in a letter to Elizabeth, her mother-in-law.

x · o · ø · o · x

[Wash. D.C.] October 25, 1945
Dear Mother — … Monday night, that is, the 22nd, we went over to see Wilber. He had gotten in town Friday morning [actually evening] and had been calling us regularly since then [while we were away]. When Paul talked to him, he was so excited. (Paul, I mean.) We had been eating and Paul got up from the table to call and see if Wilber was at home [i.e. had arrived from San Francisco yet] and he rushed back and said, "Hurry up, I've got to change my clothes and we'll go over right away." And I said, "Paul, can't I even put some of this food in the ice box?" and he said, "No, we haven't got time!! Anyway, when he wasn't looking, I put some things away and got Alan [their 11-month-old son] together and over we went.

Wilber looked very tired when we got there so we thought we'd only stay awhile, but he got more and more animated and interested the more he talked, and pretty soon it was 10:30 and we couldn't believe it.

Norma is well but also has a case of "battle fatigue," I think. The kids [Hale and Valerie] looked fine and are doing well at school.… We love you a great deal, Josephine
P.S. Norma just called to say that Wilber, who is now stationed at Ft. George

CHAPTER 15   *My heart rests in your dear hands*

Meade, near here, has entered the hospital there for a general checkup before he is discharged. He has picked up a tropical bug that he is gradually getting rid of and in one engagement a splinter of a shell struck him on the left eye (I think) [actually the right eyebrow] and pushed the bone down against the eye. This bothers him quite a little and he wants to have it taken care of before he is discharged because he has no desire to end up in one of these veteran's hospitals where they take so long to do anything. He says he's afraid to get out of their jurisdiction because he'll have to wait there and he wants things over so that he can do anything he wants as soon as he is out. When he sees you will depend on how long they will take to clean up these small things wrong with him.

Wilber's journal gave Wednesday, October 24, as the date he checked into the Fort Meade Hospital.

I think he is right about taking care of himself now because the longer a little thing is left, the bigger it becomes and the harder to take care of. [Josephine had been a nurse.]

You must be proud of Wilber, mother. He is a fine man! I meant to tell you that Hale [your grandson] is serving a morning paper and is studying violin under the concertmaster of the symphony orchestra here in Washington. He has impressed them so much with his ability that he has a partial scholarship for study. He's doing very well by the name of Hale, don't you think, for one so young? We all love you. — Jo

[Note added by Paul:] P.S. Wilber would have stopped at [the] farm to see you if he hadn't been shipped by air freight to Washington. I love you too, Paul.

I remember that evening well. Wilber told the entire Baanga story in detail, the story he had never written up because it was "a depressing and unfortunate affair in several ways" [letter 10/22/43]. His enthusiasm may have stemmed in part from Paul's being an interested and knowledgeable listener. They had served together in the field artillery of the Indiana National Guard. How I wish I had a recording of that evening.

x · o · ø · o · x

As for the shrapnel in Wilber's eyebrow, Norma told me at the time that there were risks to both removing it and leaving it in place. He was still on malarial medication and was seeing a psychiatrist. During all or most of this period, he was a patient at the Fort Meade Hospital, but would come home weekends and sometimes more often. I do not remember his being or acting depressed; he appeared fully communicative to me, though as a

VICTORY AND HOMECOMING   PART IV: JAPAN AND HOME

14-year-old, I might not have picked up any alarming signals. My memories of those six weeks include the following:

— Wilber discussed my new *Washington Post* paper route with me. It got me up before dawn so the 40 or so papers could be folded and delivered before breakfast and school. He suggested it might interfere with my studies, and that I drop the route; if I did, he and Mother would provide enough allowance for my necessary expenses, to which I acquiesced. I was a high school sophomore.

— Upon leaving a movie theater, I saw that Wilber hesitated and stared intently back at a man in the lobby. He thought that the person looked Japanese and wanted another look. His sensitivities were still heightened: it had been important in the jungle to make instant identifications!

— I went to Fort Meade with Wilber one day. It must have been on a weekend when I did not have school. We took the trolley to the bus station near Lafayette Park opposite the White House. He was dressed in his uniform, with its three rows of ribbons, the Combat Infantryman's Badge, six gold hash marks signifying three years overseas, and the Lt. Col. silver oak-leaf insignia; it made quite an impression on me and, I noticed, on others. Very few soldiers had had a full three years overseas. We sat in the park for quite awhile waiting for the bus and had a long chat the content of which I have forgotten now except for one major item I describe below. The bus to Fort Meade, a trip of perhaps 40 minutes or so, was crowded with many standees. I had a seat but Wilber did not; he stood with one foot on the low step next to the front door. He said later that it felt like his spine was being pounded into his skull.

— In that conversation in Lafayette Park, he told me that Mother wanted to separate from him. He told me this in a matter-of-fact way without any particular emotion. I got the sense that it was a problem to be solved, not a family disaster. I was not particularly jolted by it, nor did I worry much about it. (I tend to take on a responsibility if no one else is likely to do so, but not to worry if the ball is in someone else's court.) I figured they would work it out. A few days later, at home, the radio was playing in the background and it suddenly began broadcasting an argumentative scene between a man and his wife. Upon hearing that argument, I hesitated to turn it off, as that might reveal that I knew about the family trouble. My dilemma was solved when one of my parents asked me to turn it off, which I promptly did.

Years later, when I asked Norma about her desire to separate from Wilber, she said that she had planned it to be only temporary and that she would have moved to a room in a nearby home and still kept house for our family. This was her plausible intention. I discount the more extreme possibility that she had told Wilber she was leaving him for Monte and Gale. His equanimity would hardly have fit that scenario.

– Valerie and I had bought a dozen or more baby chicks to raise, which was a total failure, as they died one after another. There were still a few alive when Wilber came home. He said that he would take care of those left, whose prospects were dim. Later that day, as I was passing the outside basement door, I glanced in and saw him fling a living chick into the furnace onto the burning coal. I thought it rather cruel, but also recognized its efficiency.

– That furnace needed coal twice a day, which was mostly my task. The hot water for the house was heated by a gas burner in the basement. The hot water was stored in a cylindrical tank about a foot in diameter and five feet tall. The gas valve had to be turned on and off by hand. We would run the burner for an hour or so a couple of times a day, or when we knew we would be needing hot water. One day, after it had been agreed that I would be responsible for turning off the burner, I left the house without doing so. Later on, Wilber also left without checking on it.

When I returned hours later to an empty house, there were ominous sounds from the basement. I quickly went down there and found steam spouting from mini-holes in the tank. I immediately turned off the gas and returned to the kitchen and opened the hot water faucet to release the steam pressure. I should have done these two things in reverse order; the tank could have exploded with me next to it. Wilber's comment to me later was simple: "You said you would turn it off." In the Pacific, he had written that he had to give his junior officers the opportunity to learn from their mistakes. I had just received a vivid lesson on just how that worked!

– On that same day, Wilber had taken a long walk alone for many miles out Wisconsin Avenue to Bethesda and possibly beyond, and then back again, reminiscent of his long excursions in New Caledonia and on Pavuvu in the Russell Islands. He was surely trying to work off his frustration and worry over the situation at home, his health, and his employment choices.

What did I learn from Norma about this period in later years? She told me that she had needed "courting" before being taken sexually, and that Wilber had not sufficiently appreciated that need, though his courting in his letters had been very compelling, she said. She admitted that things had been tense between them, and that he had slept with his pistol (loaded I presume) under his pillow. His military colleagues told me this was not so far-fetched because they had always done this in combat areas. She also said that once, when she was leaving the bedroom after a tense discussion, he had said, chillingly, "One more step and you will be sorry," which truly frightened her.

Norma also told me that when she had gone with him to Fort Meade to see the psychiatrist, she was told she had to be more sexually receptive to him. As she told it, the psychologist gave no acknowledgment of her position and feelings. Norma could make self-serving statements, but surely there were elements of truth in these recollections.

In the last years of her life when Norma had finally been able to share the story of Gale's birth with us (see the Epilog below), I asked her if she and Wilber had ever talked frankly about their intimacy issues, and she answered me by saying: "One day when he was sitting at the dining room table, I came up behind him and put my hands on his shoulders, whereupon he said 'Why do you do that if you don't love me?'" I truly believe (or want to believe) that Norma wanted the marriage to work out, but she was torn by the unspeakable truth of Gale's birth. It is possible that neither of them could muster the courage to speak of it.

Gale's existence had not been a secret since we had met her in Washington the previous summer and had taken her to Bethany Beach with us. Wilber would have known through our letters that she was with us and that she was Monte's daughter by the departed wife. I surmise that Wilber had deduced by now the possibility that Norma was Gale's mother. The dates of Gale's birth and infanthood matched the period in which Norma had been on her own—Valerie and I were at camp and then boarding school—and had been so uncommunicative about her activities and whereabouts (See Book 2).

x·o·ø·o·x

Here, Wilber's mother Elizabeth writes to her daughter Mary and quotes an excerpt from a letter she had written to Wilber. It could not have sat very well with him and might even have discouraged him from contacting her.

Nov. 16, 1945

[To Wilber from his mother:] "You wrote of bringing Norma here with you. You may, if she wants to come. The members of your family haven't been very popular with her while you were gone. I wish she had not written to Hale about trying to influence your vote. It was so near the time he had his heart attack. That was Nov. 11th. I'm trying not to live it all over again these days, but it isn't easy."

CHAPTER 15   *My heart rests in your dear hands*

Dear Mary — The above is a verbatim copy of what I wrote to Wilber. That is <u>all</u> I said about her. (It was in about the middle of a long letter.) I wrote a long letter to him and made it as nice as I could.

Later – Nov. 19. I think yours is a nice note to him....

x · o · ø · o · x

During these last weeks of his life, Wilber wrote several letters to family members who were not in Washington, D.C., and to colleagues at the University of Maine. We also have a few of his letters that were saved by other family members.

Wilber wrote to his sister Mary on November 20, but did not mail the letter; it was found on his desk after he died and forwarded to Mary. A handwritten copy was in the collection of letters I received from Wilber's brother Rex. Mary had sent the original (now lost) to their mother and made a copy for Rex, which she mailed to him on January 12, 1946.

20 NOV. 1945 [TUESDAY]

Dear Little Sister [Mary] — Your "welcome home" letter came to me at the hospital today and was duly appreciated. Yes, I'm still at the hospital being rehabilitated by the army. I anticipate being released soon, however, so suggest you write me next at 4421 Alton Place, Washington 16, D.C.

I don't know just what I will be doing yet, but am pretty sure I won't spend the first winter in the north part of the country. Michigan U. sounds fine, but I nearly freeze here, so I regretfully decline your hospitable offer. Thanks anyway. Paul and Jo were over the other day, and it was surely good to see them. The children are so big that I can hardly believe they are mine. I keep calling Hale "Paul" for he looks a lot like him and is taller than I am.

Paul and Josephine had apparently visited our home the previous weekend, November 17–18. This was most likely their first visit after the October visit. Wilber was at Fort Meade during the week, and there were only three weekends between Paul's two visits. There would be lots of time for visits later, it seemed.

Don't be over-impressed by my being in the hospital. There is nothing wrong with me except I'm tired, and I'm getting rested. After I've had some more of it, I can get back on the job. Rex seems to have had one [a job] lined up for me, but I had to dodge it for I am a little too tired yet and don't want to disgrace him. It was sure good tho to know he had thought of me.

… All in all, I've no complaints about my luck when I think how many friends are still [buried] out there. In the meantime, Happy Thanksgiving. — I love you, Wilber

x·o·ø·o·x

On Thanksgiving Day, Thursday November 22, we Bradts invited the Bourjailys to join us for dinner at 4421 Alton Place. Wilber had met Monte before going overseas and was well aware he and his family were supportive friends of our family [letter 1/30/44, Book 2]. As noted above, he would also have known that Monte and his mother were now caring for a motherless daughter of Monte's.

Present were the four Bradts, with Wilber in his dress uniform, complete with ribbons, insignia, and overseas hash marks. The Bourjailys included Monte, little Gale, Monte's mother Terkman, and his sister Alice, an army nurse. Alice and Terkman were helping Mother in the kitchen. Gale remembers Wilber's dress uniform and sitting on his lap; his uniform greatly impressed her. She was one month past her second birthday. This was probably the first time Wilber had seen her.

At one point, Norma, who was in the kitchen with the women, gave a little cry, and Wilber called out, asking if there was a problem. Receiving no answer, he took it to mean she was okay. In fact, Norma had spilled grease and had burned her leg rather badly, though it only briefly interrupted the festivities.

It may have been while she was on his lap that Wilber—according to a story Norma told us much later—put his hand on Gale's head, pulling her hair clear of her high rounded forehead and commented that it "sure looked like a Sparlin forehead." This gathering could well have stood as an unspoken test of whether the two families could move forward under the fiction that Gale was Monte's child by a third wife. There was hardly space for the proverbial elephant in that small crowded living room.

x·o·ø·o·x

On the evening of Thanksgiving, Elizabeth wrote to Wilber, her son, but decided not to send the letter. Instead she sent it to Mary with notes in the margins. Elizabeth was 70 years old.

Dillsboro, Indiana, Thurs. night. Nov. 22, 1945

[Note to Mary in the top margin:] Friday A.M. I decided not to send this to Wilber. That reference to Norma might lead to trouble. I don't owe him a letter.

CHAPTER 15   *My heart rests in your dear hands*

Begins to look as if Norma were getting in her "dirty work." … I'm not afraid to write anything to you.

"Dear Son — There seems to be some secrecy as to why you are in the hospital. It makes me wonder if there isn't something serious the matter. The last paragraph of your last letter was dated October first and you [said] that you were nearing the Aleutians. Yet the letter was not mailed until 8 p.m., Oct. 29th. Were you unable to mail your letter when you reached this country? I've had letters from others mentioning your "back," a "bug you've picked up," a "fragment of a shell," and "resting." No explanation of any of them. I am not frail nor am I unable to take things as they come. I'd rather [hear the truth] than be kept in the dark.

"I'm not surprised at your being in the hospital. I've been proud of the constitution that would take you safely thru so much. Not many could have done it.

… [No conclusion, Elizabeth Bradt]"

[Note to Mary at end:] Mary: Don't say anything to the others about Wilber not writing to me. Most boys [would] tell their mothers they are at home [after a long absence] even when they are married. Maybe this is like his wedding [of which he did not inform us beforehand]! I'll wait awhile before I judge. Wrote [to] tell him to discontinue his $25 [checks] now, and I'll pay back when I could. Told him it had been very welcome and appreciated.

I find it remarkable and almost unbelievable that Wilber had not written to his mother in the five weeks that he had been back in the U.S. Perhaps he had called her, but this letter makes it seem that he had not. He had written from the ship, but had long delayed mailing it. Perhaps he was simply tired of being the peacemaker between Norma and his mother, and, with no definite plan for his future, he might not have been inclined to face his mother. Her comments regarding Norma in her letter of November 16 (above) would also have been a damper. She seems to think his not writing might be due to Norma's "dirty tricks."

This unsent letter to Wilber continued on with news of friends, visitors, and of Elizabeth's doings on the farm, including walking to town and back, a challenging endeavor of several miles and steep hills for a 70-year-old. She also told of getting a recalcitrant cow to stand still for her milking. The only other reference to Norma was quite benign.

x·o·ø·o·x

The following letter from Wilber to his brother Rex was located in Fort Meade Hospital after Wilber died and was forwarded to Rex by Norma.

VICTORY AND HOMECOMING   PART IV: JAPAN AND HOME

It was given to me in the 1980s by Rex's son, Douglas. It had been the only extant letter written by Wilber after his arrival in the U.S. until I more recently found the few (presented here) in the Mary-Elizabeth-Rex correspondence. Wilber's openness about his state of mind and body was about as frank as one could get.

27 NOV. 1945 [TUESDAY]

Dear Rex — You have no idea how much I appreciated your thoughtfulness in presenting my name for the job you wrote Paul about. Also your confidence in my ability was indeed encouraging particularly since it came just at the time I was and am wondering if I have any ability as a chemist. It was necessary to explain just why I couldn't be interested at the time. In the first place I had no idea how long I would be kept in the hospital and in the second place I was too tired to even talk with anyone about a job.

The situation with me is pretty well clarified now. I've been quite thoroughly examined and several things of a minor nature cleared up and others treated. I'm free of an intestinal parasitic infection, have malaria but have successfully gotten off malaria [medications], teeth OK, a fragment of steel in my right forehead has been located and will probably be left alone, a back injury is apparently going to entitle me to a good cane for they can't find anything by X-ray. However it doesn't bother me enough to matter.

> The "fragment of steel in my right forehead" is the only concrete evidence I have that a piece of shrapnel was actually there, in his eyebrow. The autopsy of his body did not mention it.

The reason I'm still being held here is simply combat fatigue. I'm just plain tired, so tired that at first writing was difficult and enunciation poor and I tended to be hysterical [teary?]. It seems that when I relinquished my command and was told officially I was tired, I just all at once realized and admitted it to myself and then was tired. I am much improved after a month here mainly due to a lot of sleep and freedom from responsibility so will likely be released soon. I've avoided many outside contacts largely because of the above reasons but now I hope to get organized on the matter of a job. I don't know if I will go back to Maine or not. The schools there aren't as good as I want for the children and frankly the winter there doesn't appeal to me now. Some job farther south where there were good schools would interest me a lot. I may look around this part of the country while I'm here and will consider industry as well as university work. Also I've a lot of study to do, some I've already started.

> One of the fictions of World War II was that combat fatigue, now known as Post Traumatic Stress Disorder (PTSD), was not officially recognized as

CHAPTER 15   *My heart rests in your dear hands*

2

have successfully gotten off malaria, teeth OK, a fragment of steel in my right forehead has been located and will probably be left alone, a back injury is apparently going to entitle me to a good cane for they can't find anything by X-ray. However it doesn't bother me enough to matter. The reason I'm still being held here is simply combat fatigue. I'm just plain tired, so tired that at first writing was difficult and enunciation poor and I tended to be hysterical. It seems that when I relinquished my command and was told officially I was tired, I just all at once realized and admitted it to myself and then was tired. I am much improved after a month here mainly due to a lot of sleep and freedom from responsibility so will likely be released soon. I've avoided many outside contacts largely because of the above reasons but now I hope to

Second page of Wilber's letter of November 27, 1945, to his brother Rex describing his weariness.

a disorder. Its prevalence and long-term effects may not have been fully appreciated, but it had been well known as a post-war condition ever since the "shell-shock" cases of World War I.

Paul + Jo [brother and his wife] were out to see me, and Paul surely looked good. He and Hale look so much alike that I've trouble to keep from calling Hale "Paul." The children are well and make good records at school. They have certainly proven that the presence of a father is of little consequence.

> "Of little consequence." It might have seemed that way as Valerie and I continued our daily schooling and activities with only nominal attention to our parents, like most teen-agers. In fact, Valerie and I strongly felt his presence all through his absence through his prewar influence on us and through his letters. As for confusing faces and names, during Wilber's absence, I myself had had trouble distinguishing him and Paul in my mind's eye, because the two brothers looked so much alike!

It seems odd to be back where there are pavements, street lights and show windows and people that don't look afraid. I think I'll like it.

I don't know if I ever gave you a resume of my activities of the war so here it is in chronological order: … It was a lot of water and a lot of perspiration but interesting and I'm back in much better shape than I expected.

We had a good Thanksgiving [Nov. 22] together at home and I hope you all had the same. I'm sorry I couldn't stop on the way to see [7-year old] Connie Lou but the army flew me thru the southern route without any stopovers. However, I'm still wanting that date with her some of these days. — Best of luck and love to each of you, Wilber

> The calm mention of Thanksgiving seems to signify that it had not been a defining event for him. Wilber had some time earlier, probably on her birthday, written to Connie Lou promising to take her out on a "date."

x·o·ø·o·x

A letter from Mary to Rex dated January 12, 1946, included the following copy in Mary's hand of a letter that Wilber had drafted but not mailed. It was addressed to Dean Paul Cloke, dean of the School of Science and Engineering at the University of Maine; he had been Wilber's immediate superior at the university. Wilber still held, but was on leave from, his position as the head of the Department of Chemistry and Chemical Engineering. The draft was dated November 30, the day before Wilber died.

NOV. 30 [1945] [DRAFT LETTER, NOT SENT]

Dear Paul [Cloke] — I arrived in the States early in Oct. and after a couple of weeks in California was sent to Ft. Meade, Md., for separation. On Oct. 24, I was placed in the Regional Hospital for checks and recuperation and am still there [five weeks later]. The general findings indicate a rather complete condition of fatigue, which has already shown considerable improvement. However, it is rather definite now that I should not try to go back to work in February. Consequently in view of your statement that a July return would be acceptable to the University, I would appreciate that privilege.

There are other factors, which I have considered carefully these past weeks, which suggest to me that I should not return to the University. One of these is the fact that I would like better schools for the children than those available in Orono or Bangor. Another is the fact that if I can find suitable opportunity in industrial work, either on a full-time or part-time basis for a while, it would improve my teaching value. Frankly, I have felt at Maine on the defensive on that basis. A third factor is that I find Norma had a pretty hard struggle against the weather last winter and that she much prefers living in a milder climate. The fact that I have just come from the tropics perhaps makes me more than usually understanding of her viewpoint. The fact that I am apparently at the maximum possible salary has also concerned me. My 1939 contract … was $3700.00 [per year] only temporarily reduced. There are one or two other personal matters concerning my father's death and my family responsibilities which would be facilitated by a less remote location than Maine.

> Wilber's starting salary in 1936 had been $4,000 per year. His pay as a lieutenant colonel had been much greater, perhaps about $8,000. He seemed to believe that his family life would continue despite Norma's intent to separate, possibly only temporarily.

Perhaps I should not have bothered you with such details, but I am anxious to be perfectly frank and fair with you in this matter. What I am requesting is the opportunity to re-orient myself professionally [and] to have a reasonable time to consider other position opportunities. If you can agree on whatever date you suggest, I will either resign or will definitely plan to continue at Maine. As it looks now, I will be in the army on terminal leave at least until late March. My finances will require that I be employed by July, so I should expect to have reached a decision before the end of March.

You will have noticed that none of the factors mentioned are singly of undue importance. To counteract all of these, I will remember the pleasure of working at Maine and particularly that of working with you and Pres. Hauck. That has been and would be a major reason for a decision to stay at the U. of Me. You may be sure that if I do return, it will be whole-heartedly and gladly. Perhaps I am still a bit too tired to have a proper perspective on any job.

Will you please discuss this letter with Pres. Hauck and write me about your decision. I will be very grateful for any consideration you can give me in this matter. It had been my plan to come promptly to Orono [for a visit], but this hospitalization has delayed me. I must spend some time with my Mother in Ind[iana] as soon as possible and will see you as soon after as I can.

Please write me at 4421 Alton Pl. NW, Washington, D.C. I am able to be home at least once a week. Norma and the children are well and it's wonderful to be even almost home. — W.E.B.

Wilber was giving Cloke fair notice that he might not return to Maine. He was "too tired" to consider "any job." He was unusually open about his thinking for a man of his era.

x·o·ø·o·x

On Friday evening, November 30, 1945, the entire family went to my high school, Woodrow Wilson, to see the fall musical put on by the students, Gilbert and Sullivan's *Trial by Jury*. An archived news announcement [*Washington Post*, November 25] gave me the date, which I had forgotten. (I did not perform in it but did in later musicals.) We walked to the school, perhaps a 15-minute trip, as we had no car at the time. On the way back about a block from home, it was raining lightly and a cab driver came by and offered to drive us. My father said simply, "Thank you," meaning "No, thank you." The cab driver was puzzled, as was I, and asked again, receiving the same answer. Eventually the confusion was resolved and we continued our walk home. I was struck then by the different environments in which we had been living these past years; our languages seemed to have diverged!

It may have been on this occasion that Norma desperately wanted to go to Monte's house to take care of Gale who was sick, but Wilber insisted she stick with the family. I don't remember the details, but for Norma, this stood out as a painful memory of those days. She was torn between two obligations and probably could still not discuss with Wilber what he likely already knew.

This day, November 30, was Norma's 40th birthday. I remember no celebration but we probably took note of it with a candle-lit cake at supper before going up to the high school.

CHAPTER 15   *My heart rests in your dear hands*

x · o · ø · o · x

The following morning, Saturday, December 1, 1945, Wilber did not return to Fort Meade as planned because he was suffering from a recurrence of malarial symptoms—chills and a fever. He had recently been taken off malarial medicines. Valerie and I left the house early for our respective dance and violin lessons. Norma called to us as we headed out, "Don't forget to say goodbye to your father," which we then dutifully and off-handedly did. After we left, Wilber went down to the basement to sort out souvenirs for Christmas presents. His notebook had a list he had probably written that morning:

X-mas
Mother - jacket
Rex - saber
Jack - pistol
Connie Lou - 43rd insignia ornament (plastic)
Evelyn (Miss) - parachute

Rex was his brother and Connie Lou his niece (Rex's daughter). She would turn eight on December 28. Evelyn was "Little Evelyn," Norma's niece (Milton's daughter), who was 22 and about to be married. The parachute was to be for her wedding dress.

According to Norma, the door to the basement was open and she and Wilber had spoken back and forth to each other a couple of times about the Christmas presents. At about 9:15 a.m., Norma heard a loud bang from the basement. She ran out the front door into the street screaming for help.

Washington Sunday Star 12-2-45

Fatal Shooting of Colonel, Pacific Hero, Probed by Army

Officer Is Found Dead in Basement Trophy Room

Washington police and Coroner A. Magruder MacDonald are awaiting completion of an Army investigation of the circumstances surrounding the gunshot death of Lt. Col. Wilber E. Bradt, 45, Pacific war hero and former college professor, who was found in a weapon-filled basement trophy room at his home yesterday morning with a gaping wound in his chest.

Walter Reed Hospital authorities, who assumed charge of the investigation immediately after a neighbor found the often-decorated officer's body in the Bradt home at 4421 Alton place N.W., are expected to conduct an autopsy today. Meanwhile, Walter Reed officials have requested Fort Meade authorities to make Col. Bradt's medical history available for scrutiny in the inquiry.

Col. Bradt, according to members of the family, was on sick leave from his post at the Meade Separation Center. Asked for details of Col. Bradt's illness, his sister-in-law, Mrs. Paul Bradt, said, "The same thing that seems to be wrong with most of the men when they first come back from overseas."

Neighbor Finds Body.

The body of the recently returned officer was discovered by a neighbor, L. E. Mattingly, 4425 Alton place, a Treasury Procurement employe, who

LT. COL. WILBER E. BRADT.

of authority in the case as permitted by co-operation on my part."

Classmate of Ernie Pyle.

Col. Bradt, a native of Bangor, Me., was a classmate of Ernie Pyle at the University of Indiana. He was head of the chemistry department at the University of Maine and a captain in the Maine National Guard in March, 1941, when he entered active service.

He served at Camp Blanding, Fla., and Camp Selby, Miss., before going overseas in October, 1942, with the 43d "Winged Victory" Infantry Division. He was a field artillery commander in the Solomon Islands and New Guinea campaigns and landed

Treasury Procurement employe, who rushed into the basement at approximately 8:45 a.m. in response to the screams of the officer's wife, Mrs. Norma S. Bradt. The widow told police she was washing breakfast dishes after sending the two young Bradt children off to take their dancing lessons, when her husband went into the cellar trophy room.

Mrs. Bradt said she carried on a brief conversation with her husband from the head of the stairs while he prepared to pack up some firearms for Christmas presents to his two brothers. A few minutes later —at about 8:40 a.m.—she told investigators, she heard a loud explosion.

Startled by the noise, she ran into the street where Mr. Mattingly and his wife, Ida Mattingly, were attracted by her screams. Mr. Mattingly went into the trophy room alone, he told reporters, and found Col. Bradt lying on his back with his arms folded across his chest. A .45 caliber Army pistol lay two inches from the body. Mr. Mattingly said the body had no pulse and appeared "cold and stiff."

Mr. Mattingly then telephoned Walter Reed Hospital. Capt. William M. White, a medical officer at the hospital, arrived on the scene soon afterwards and pronounced Col. Bradt dead. The body was taken to the District Morgue where Dr. MacDonald conducted a thorough examination.

The coroner said the shot passed entirely through the body, piercing the heart. He said there were numerous powder burns and evidences of explosive action on the chest, indicating the shot was fired at extremely close range.

An Army summary court will render an opinion following the post mortem examinations, on which Dr. MacDonald will issue a certificate. He described the Army's assumption

mander in the Solomon Islands and New Guinea campaigns and landed in the first wave at the invasion of Luzon at the Lingayen Gulf.

When the Japanese surrendered, Col. Bradt took a regimental combat team of the 43d Division into Japan. He returned to the United States in October, 1945, and was ordered to duty at Fort Meade. Mrs. Bradt, a native of Spokane, Wash., moved into the Alton place residence in August and Col. Bradt joined her there about six weeks ago, the family said.

Col. Bradt holds the Legion of Merit, three Silver Star medals, the Bronze Star Medal and a Purple Heart with cluster for two wounds receieved in action against the enemy.

There are two children, Hale, 14, and Valerie, 13. Col. Bradt also is survived by his mother, Mrs. Hale Bradt, of Versailles, Ind.; two brothers, Rexford and Paul Bradt, 6626 First street N.W.; two sisters, Mary E. Bradt, Ann Arbor, Mich., and Mrs. Ruth Bradt Wilson, Burlington, Wis.

Burial will be in Arlington National Cemetery, probably Tuesday, according to members of the family.

News story of Wilber's death in the Washington, D.C., Sunday Star of December 2, 1945.
[WASHINGTON (D.C.) STAR, P. A6]

PART V

EPILOG

1945–2014

★ ★ ★

16

"I have never known such deep despair and ill health"

Washington, D.C.
December 1945–June 1947

On the Saturday he died, Wilber was 45 years old, exactly two months shy of his 46th birthday. Valerie was 13, I was six days short of my 15th birthday, and Norma had turned 40 the day before. There were several trunks and boxes in the basement containing Wilber's belongings and souvenirs. A metal footlocker held many Japanese pistols; my recollection is that there was no ammunition for them and that many were rusty and inoperable.

Norma told me that when she heard the gunshot, her first impulse had been to run to the basement door but was stopped by a vision of Valerie and me blocking her way. She remembered, and I also recall, that Wilber had either written or said that he felt he had the will power to live long enough to shoot any enemy soldier who had just shot him. So she ran out to the street instead. Valerie remembers Norma's story a little differently: that the basement door was closed and as she ran toward it, she believed she saw, written in blood on the door, our names, Hale and Valerie. This prompted her to run into the street. Preserving her life for the sake of her children was uppermost in her mind in either version. Were the discrepancies in these stories creative constructions of our youthful minds or did Norma tell us different stories at different times? We suspect the latter; her thoughts at that moment were surely confused and complex.

Wilber had suffered a gunshot wound to his chest from his personal .45 caliber Colt pistol, the one given him in 1936 as a departure gift by his Washington State military colleagues when we moved to Maine. It probably was already in the basement with the other souvenirs. An autopsy performed at the army's Walter Reed General Hospital on Sunday, December 2, confirmed the coroner's statement to the Washington Star that the bullet had perforated his heart and passed completely through his chest. His death was ruled a suicide, based in part on powder burns on his chest. Members of Wilber's family thought that Norma might have shot him, but that, to my mind, is preposterous, as she had had absolutely no experience with firearms, much less with a Colt .45, nor would she have had the presence of mind to do such a thing.

Valerie and I returned home separately, heard the news of the "accident," as described in the Prologue to Book 1 of this work, and reacted very differently. I remember that I did not suffer painful grief, but rather was shocked into a complete absence of feeling; I simply went numb. Did the fact that Wilber had been away so long mitigate the pain? Or was I suppressing it? Thirteen-year-old Valerie responded with a quiet anger; she collected her necessities in a paper bag and fled to a neighbor's home. I remained at home.

On Sunday, the newspapers carried the story. The *Washington Post* heading (without photo) at the bottom of the front page, read, "Professor Turned Hero Found Dead of Gunshot Wound Here." The *Washington Star* heading on page A-6 (with photo) was, "Fatal Shooting of Colonel, Pacific Hero, Probed by Army."

That morning, a young navy medical corpsman from Minnesota saw the story; he had been attending the navy's deep-sea diving school at the Washington Navy Yard. He realized that the story involved his half-sister Norma. They were both children of Stonewall Jackson Sparlin, but had not been in touch for a long time, so neither was aware of the other's presence in Washington. His name was Stonewall Emerson Sparlin, or "Stoney," age 22. He had previously served with the Fourth Marine Raider Battalion as a medical corpsman on New Georgia Island at the same time Wilber had been there, but neither man had realized it. He immediately got in touch with us, and Norma made our home his home for the next several months while he was stationed in Washington. He was a levelheaded, good-natured, handsome fellow who became a tower of strength to all of us in those stressful days. He was like a big brother to Valerie and me.

On Monday, I went to school and had a pretty typical day. I did not volunteer the fact of my dad's death to my friends, though some may have

CHAPTER 16   *I have never known such deep despair and ill health*

Stonewall "Stoney" Sparlin, Norma's half-brother, about 1945, in his navy uniform. He was a pharmacists mate first class and had served with the marines as a medic in the Solomon Islands. While on duty at the navy's Deep Sea Diving School, he made our home in Washington, D.C., his home after Wilber died. [PHOTO: COURTESY OF GAIL SPARLIN].

been aware of it from the newspapers. At most I might have received a quiet acknowledgment from an empathizing teacher that I don't recall now. At the end of the day, I told my friend Archie Beard that I would not be at school the following day, Tuesday. He asked me why, and I, with an embarrassed grin (!) as I delivered the blockbuster news, told him I was going to my dad's funeral. That painful self-conscious moment is permanently burned into my brain.

That evening (Monday) we went by car to the funeral home. There were no visitation hours or wake. Mother went into the funeral home accompanied by either Stoney or Monte, or one of Monte's sons. I remained in the car. She returned saying she had kissed Wilber's lips. Even today, I can hardly bear to imagine the anguish she must have felt.

On Tuesday, Wilber was buried at Arlington National Cemetery. It was cold and cloudy with a light rain. Our funeral party was small: Wilber's brother Paul and his wife Jo were there, as were Wilber's other brother Rex, Stoney, and General Cleland, Wilber's associate in Luzon, who escorted Mother. Monte was there with his army-nurse sister Alice and probably his mother Terkman. I was there, but Valerie had refused to go. There was a brief service in the cemetery chapel. The burial immediately followed under a small tent over the gravesite. There were the customary prayers, the playing of taps, the rifle salute, the removal of the U.S. flag from the coffin, the ritual folding of the flag, and the presentation of the flag to the widow.

The burial plot is Section 10, number 10599 RH. The standard simple tombstone erected shortly thereafter carried the wrong birthdate, February 2, 1900; the correct date is February 1. The light-hearted joke Wilber had endured his entire life about his birthday being (almost) on Groundhog Day (February 2) persisted even after his death. He would have appreciated the humor in that. Some years later, the tombstone was replaced with one inscribed with the correct date.

On Wednesday, I was back in school and so was Valerie. Norma was intent on keeping our lives on as even a keel as possible; resuming our normal routines seemed the best way to do that.

x·o·ø·o·x

All who knew Wilber were, of course, stunned by his sudden and unexpected death after his survival through so much combat. There are some extant letters that revealed some of these feelings. A few weeks after Wilber's death, Norma wrote to Wilber's brother Rex and his wife Gerry.

DEC. 22, 1945
Dearest Rex and Gerry — Your goodness and kindness have remained with us comfortingly. I could not properly express my appreciation of your having come to us, and of all your attentions to Hale and Valerie, to our home and to Wilber and myself. Your letter was wonderful. You don't know what it meant – your words about the atmosphere of our home, etc. I know how tired you must have been when you returned. Your invitation is appreciated, but we cannot travel due to funds, high school, etc. I would love to talk to Gerry, as I think I know her particular kind of strain and shock, which produced her miscarriage that time.

There was no way for me to get away from it, either, and last Saturday [Dec. 15] night I collapsed, miscarried (6 wks. pr.) here at home, hemorrhaged, and was taken to the hospital close to a nervous breakdown. I was kept under sedatives until

CHAPTER 16   *I have never known such deep despair and ill health*

Monday, when they operated, and also quite asleep all week. I had seen Paul + Jo on Sat. a.m. and did not want them to leave, somehow. I understood they were going away for the weekend so friends and neighbors took the children, and Hale returned daily to fix the fire. My brother Stoney is now here on 5-day leave and helping us. He has already fixed the basement.

Stoney had cleaned up the basement, which had brown bloodstains on the linoleum still remaining from the initial cleaning.

Don't worry about my not crying. I did a lot both before + after you left. I am getting better, though Gerry will understand how my back feels (like crumpled paper). — Lots of love and do make a good Christmas, Norma

x·o·ø·o·x

The same day, December 22, Josephine, Paul's wife, wrote to her mother-in-law, Elizabeth. Only the fifth and sixth pages remain. It expressed a deep anger toward Norma, the source of which was partially revealed in a later letter to Mary on January 18.

[**Dec. 22, 1945**]
[Dear Mother] — … I wrote you a letter about Norma the other day in the heat of anger (it was really heat too; I was burned up.), but I'm not going to send it. I can tell you better when we see you later on. Besides it wasn't a nice Xmas letter and I don't want you to think I feel that way about Xmas. However, I'm going to give you a slight warning. If Norma writes you a lot of stuff, take it all with a great deal of salt before you believe it. A word to the wise is sufficient. Tell Mary this too, if you wish because Norma's getting all the sympathy and more than she needs.
Mother, if you haven't already, could you send on my letter about Wilber to Ruth. She asked us to write her about it, and I thought we'd see you and send it on then, so I told her we'd do that, but now it will be later and she might like to know a little more than she already does.
I hope you are having not such bad weather and that the cows, calves, cats and chickens are able to stand everything as well as you have done. — We all love you, Jo

The "lot of stuff" might have been Norma presenting Gale as Monte's baby by a third wife, a story that Jo probably could see through quite easily. And, of course, seeing this would have made Norma an adulteress and totally undeserving of sympathy in the eyes of Josephine and the Midwestern Bradts.

x · o · ⌀ · o · x

I have no recollection of that Christmas, but we surely celebrated it in some manner, probably quite low key. Norma would have been intent on maintaining some sense of normalcy for Valerie, Gale, and me, so we probably had a tree and presents. Stoney used Norma's typewriter to write his mother the next day. Our home offered him a welcoming environment.

x · o · ⌀ · o · x

A few weeks later, there was an outpouring of anger toward Norma about Wilber's death from Josephine and Paul Bradt in a letter to Paul's sister Mary. Paul and Jo lived in Washington, D.C., as we did, and thus were more familiar with our family's circumstances than others would have been. The bitterness and anger toward my mother was an atypical outburst from these, the gentlest and nicest of all the Bradts. For this reason, the existence of this letter was kept from me until 1984 when Wilber's other sister Ruth passed it on to me. It gives some insight into Norma's actions the day Wilber died.

Washington 12, D.C., January 18, 1946
Dear Mary — … Mary, I have now joined the ranks of the sissy sisters-in-law. (I didn't quite spend Jan. 20, my birthday, in bed, but I almost did). I had a miscarriage last Monday, Jan. 14, 1946 and today is my first day up.…

Jan. 22 — I told Paul that maybe this was a visitation on me because of the way I felt about Norma. Right at present, Mary, my opinion of Norma is so low that I can't express it. Ever since Wilber's accident she has bobbed up with things that have infuriated me so that I couldn't even express myself – except by sputtering – (as you call it). I wouldn't say anything til I was so worked up that I'd sit down and write a letter either to mother or her and then I'd tear it up and throw it in the wastebasket so to date, i.e., until this letter, no one but Paul knows how I feel about her. I did allow myself to say in one letter to mother that "at present Norma was getting all the sympathy she needed and to take anything she said with a great big handful of salt before she answered." In her return letter mother said that she would be careful and I had hoped that that would be all that needed to be said.…

In the first few hours of her [Norma's] supposedly great sorrow she told me a number of things which I am sure she never intended to tell anyone, and she mistakenly thinks that as soon as I get a chance I'm going to tell the whole family. Paul doesn't even know all that she said, and as far as I am concerned (I worked in

CHAPTER 16   *I have never known such deep despair and ill health*

```
          U. S. NAVAL RECEIVING STATION
            NAVY YARD, WASHINGTON, D. C.
                                  26 December 1945
```

Dear Mom.
   Well Mom, another Christmas has come and gone. Hope you had a wonderful one and many more to come. Maybe I'll be able to spend the next one at home and also I'll be able to buy you the kind of xmas present that is deserving of you. Give your husband my best regards and hope he is well and happy.
   Had a very nice Christmas and guess who I was with. Well you never would but I am at Norma Sparlins home or Norma Bradt as you would remember. You see it was only by accident that I found her. Her husband who was a Lt. Col. in the Army and just back from overseas accidentally killed himself and one Sunday while in the barracks reading the paper, I came upon this article about his death. I immediately called Norma and have been staying at her house most of my off time and liberty hours. In fact she wants this to be my home and so I am moving in part of my things and when I get off work at the diving school at 4:30 I come right over here and stay all night and help out. I've been studying and it is so much quieter over here and she has a wonderful library and this typewriter here to work with.
   She is wonderful person and has been more than good to me. She has two wonderful Children, Hale, who is 15 and Valerie the girl who is 13 and they are perfect as far as I am concerned. We get along swell and they call me uncle. They want to know if they can call you grandmother. I wish you would write to norma at her address and you can also write me at her address if you like. It is Norma S. Bradt, 4421 Alton Place NW, Washington,16, D. C. I know that she wants to hear from you and now in the grief over Wilbur I know a letter would help. I have also located all the rest of the Sparlins and must soon write to them all.
   Well Mom. for now I must close. Hope I hear from you very soon.

                                  Loads of Love,
                                     Stoney

Letter of December 26, 1945, from Stonewall "Stoney" Sparlin, Norma's half-brother, to his mother. He was attending the U.S. Navy Deep Sea Diving School in Washington, D.C., at the time. The letter gives some insight into our home life at that difficult time, 25 days after Wilber's death. [LETTER: COURTESY OF GAIL SPARLIN] *a medical office 8 years and listened to many tales of broken lives, etc.), if she doesn't know by now that what she told me is her business and not mine then there is no use telling her.*

It appears she did tell Paul most or all of it; see his addendum below.

Hale came over to see us Xmas week and he and Paul were having such a good time together and she called up three times to tell him to come home. I answered the phone 2x and Paul the last time. Hale had overstayed his time but if he doesn't know at 14 (after having lived in New York City and gone all around there by himself) how to care for himself here, then he is mentally deficient. (He is far from that, and I am afraid that Paul and I both told some falsehoods for him so that he wouldn't be punished.)

I would typically bicycle the 5.5 miles through Washington's Rock Creek Park to their home on the trusty one-speed bike I had bought in Hattiesburg Mississippi in 1942. Mother, quite reasonably, was probably concerned about my returning after dark. She never punished me and rarely if ever chastised me. Her disappointment about unsatisfactory behavior was sufficient restraint.

Mary, I don't believe any of Norma's stories. That tale about a miscarriage after some of the things she told me is a cover up for her own feelings of guiltiness in the whole matter. She is intent on how the world looks at her, not on what effect she has on Wilber's loved family or her own children.…

I believe Norma really did have a miscarriage shortly after Wilber died; I remember her being taken to the hospital and being told it was a miscarriage. It was not surprising given her history of miscarriages after Valerie's birth, possibly due to Rh blood factor incompatibility. That event is vivid in my memory; it was not a product of her imagination. It also suggests that my parents did have sexual relations after Wilber's return from the Pacific.

Now to be a little more cheerful. We're all returning to normal from last week. The sun is beautiful today, tho' the wind is blowing hard. Alan [her young son] and I haven't been out yet but think we will go out tomorrow.…

I hope this letter will not make you feel too blue but you must know, since things have been said, what goes on. We love you very much and want to hear from you. — Your sister, Josephine

The letter was continued by Paul.

CHAPTER 16   *I have never known such deep despair and ill health*

Dear Mary — I guess after reading Jo's letter that it is better to tell all one knows and be done with it. That would be easier to one's face than on paper.

Wilber was in every respect, as far as I know, fine. Norma's mother, I take it, taught Norma that men couldn't be true; just as it seems Norma is teaching Valerie. At least during the war, Norma put out rumors that Wilber had another girl and wouldn't come back. Perhaps she knew he would be wise to so do. After he came back, and we visited them, Wilber told tales beautifully of the land, the experience of battles, the strategy he had used for certain gains, etc. But their children, Norma had sent to bed or upstairs to study! Twice when Wilber had occasion to mention the native women – how they carried their groceries on their heads, and at another time of some humorous answers they had given – Norma interrupted to say that Wilber always had seemed to get along fine with the women! Can you imagine a man thrown for years almost exclusively with men being blamed for remembering such incidents? Could you imagine being blamed for noticing or remembering a few incidents involving men, if you had been limited to feminine company for five years?

Wilber was undoubtedly discouraged at having forgotten his chemistry during the war. It was inevitable. Jo and I sent him blanks for some post-doctorate fellowships. Rex tried to get him in as vice pres. of a big industrial firm. He took neither suggestion. What he needed was a wife and love. He had dreamed all these years of returning to all of the blessings of home in a free country. His wife's nagging and other faults had grown to seem small and he yearned for her again.

But she apparently was not yearning for him. She was resolving that after the war she would make the decisions. When he wanted to caress her she withdrew. She wouldn't have him sexually. She dominated the children. The hospital psychiatrist told her that they could do Wilber no good until she gave him sexual relief.

He should have given her a good beating and left her. Instead he stayed and took punishment no one of us knew he was getting. It all seemed finally so discouraging that, while he was cleaning his pistol just after a quarrel, the fancy took him to press the muzzle against his heart and pull the trigger. He did.

Mary, Rex doesn't know all of this, nor did I until after I got home from the funeral. Norma, in her first feeling of guilt confessed it all to Josephine while Jo tried to comfort her. A few hours later the story was all getting a new color as it was touched up for telling. She hadn't quarreled with Wilber, it had been Hale and Valerie quarrelling. She hadn't failed to go to Wilber's side because she was afraid he'd shoot her too; it had been because she was afraid she'd faint until help would be too late, etc. Probably the [story of the] miscarriage and jungle fever were [meant] to prove her faithfulness.

Don't try to do anything to or for Norma. It will do no good. Valerie is insincere by training. I think Hale will come around OK. Norma used to be the suppressed *genius, the artistic temperament, the chained butterfly. She talks confidently of seasonal tours at $100 per night.*

Now she is free. I fear she seems a little piqued when I ask her how her practice [of the piano] is progressing. Isn't music the greatest sympathy in sorrow?

Mary, you live your life anyway you please. You are honest, and you're generous; and you're heart is right. It is these unnatural scheming egotistic, dishonest people that hurt. They are ugly at any age when you know them. — We love you, Paul

Wow, what an outburst of anger and emotion! It seems utterly out of proportion to Norma's shortcomings as portrayed here. I attribute the disconnect either to the fact that Paul wasn't "telling all" by omitting his knowledge of Gale's origin—it was perhaps too shocking to put in writing—or to their extreme guilt at not having done more for Wilber. Paul was his blood brother, and in those six weeks Wilber was home, it is likely they visited him only twice. The self-anger could have been huge and Norma may have amplified it with impolitic comments. All these factors were likely in play.

Was Norma really the ogre portrayed here? I don't think so. She would have been highly defensive in the face of Wilber's devastating action and may well have adjusted her stories because of it. If there had been a quarrel before Wilber went downstairs—as seems likely to me from this letter —it was probably a carryover of the argument of the night before about Norma's concern over Gale's illness. That she did not go immediately into the basement could well have been a fear of being shot. That was implicit in her stories to Valerie and me; she had to live to care for us. She may have later realized that such a fear might not play well with others. Reconstructing her thoughts in those horrible first moments would have been well nigh impossible.

I never found Norma overbearing as a parent. On the contrary, she gave me enough free rein to establish my own self-confidence. She allowed me to commute to school alone as a 12-year-old in New York City, let me buy and use a rifle in Bangor at age 14, and, as a high school student in Washington, D.C., let me bicycle (and later drive) all over the city. She did not press me regarding my academics or which girls to date. With me, she kept her counsel, sensing that pressure would be counterproductive. She was more sensitive with Valerie and would react strongly and often counterproductively to perceived threats to Valerie's well-being.

After Wilber's death, Norma found comfort in the Catholic priests at the neighboring St. Ann's Church. The priests assured her, charitably, that God would decide Wilber's spiritual fate with compassion even though suicide is a grave sin in Catholic theology. By contrast, the local Episcopalian minister

CHAPTER 16   *I have never known such deep despair and ill health*

was very non-committal on this matter and this offended her. Thus began her lifelong devotion to the Catholic Church. She was soon attending instructional lectures by Bishop Fulton Sheen, later of TV fame, and some years later joined the Franciscans as a lay (Third Order) member.

x·o·ø·o·x

At some time during the next months, Monte and Gale moved into our home. Monte's mother Terkman was also with us for a time until she moved to a home in Virginia with her brother. Monte had left government service by then and was attempting to start a new business, the Globe (newspaper) Syndicate, featuring political columnists and comic strips. He promoted several well-known commentators as his writers. This entailed much stuffing of envelopes for mailings to newspapers, as well as

Me and my little half-sister Gale, summer 1946, in the back yard of our Alton Place home in Washington, D.C. We have been pals ever since. [PHOTO: BRADT FAMILY]

VICTORY AND HOMECOMING   PART V: EPILOG

Page 274: Monte Bourjaily and Gale, early 1946 in Washington DC. She was two and he 52. Monte was the only father she knew. [PHOTO: BRADT-BOURJAILY FAMILY]

Gale (age about three) and her Lebanese grandmother, Terkman Bourjaily. Washington, D.C., 1946. Terkman lived with us in Washington at the time. She died in 1950. [PHOTO: BRADT-BOURJAILY FAMILY]

Gale and me when she was perhaps two and I was 15. She feels today that I played an important fatherly role for her. I am wearing Wilber's army fatigue jacket. [PHOTO: BRADT-BOURJAILY FAMILY]

This page: Gale in front of our Alton Place home at age about three, Washington, D.C., 1946. [PHOTO: BRADT-BOURJAILY FAMILY]

travels to visit editors. We all helped, and Norma, with her clerical skills, assisted with correspondence and writing. I did not know the financial arrangements, but I am sure Monte's rent money and possibly a salary paid to Norma saved her from having to seek out a night-club job as a pianist or to do clerical work. It is amazing that we all could fit in that little house on Alton Place. I do not remember the sleeping arrangements, but I am sure they were quite circumspect. Little Gale quickly became a treasured member of our family.

Norma took the $10,000 insurance payment she received from the U.S. government and placed it in irrevocable trusts for Valerie's and my college educations at $5,000 each. She did this quite early when her prospects for income were nebulous at best. Ten thousand dollars was a lot of money, equivalent to about $130,000 today. Putting this beyond her own reach for our benefit was admirable and, for her, the beginning of a long self-imposed penance.

x·o·ø·o·x

How did I fare after my father's death? I recall no great grief or depression, but rather a numbness. I had not had a father at home the preceding five years, so this felt like a continuation of the status quo. I was a sophomore in high school and had not yet connected to school activities. Later that winter, I was serving as a messenger for the school's front office before school started and was sent to a classroom with a message. There I found a room full of singers rehearsing some wonderful classical work; music filled the room. This sent a thrill through me, resonating strongly with my earlier experience as a (soprano) choirboy at Grace Church in New York City. I immediately joined the chorus, as a bass, and attended its before-school rehearsals. That group became a home for me in that large school.

Another "home" was the contingent of students I encountered in the more challenging classes. I chose the classes voluntarily, but had to work hard to get good grades in them. I was back into Latin having taken it in fifth and sixth grades at Grace Church School. During the school day, I plugged along doing my academics and music (chorus and later orchestra), and did little in athletics or school politics. I was a quiet, studious person. Outside of school, my studies kept me quite busy but I found time for biking and photography, often with one or two friends. Guns in the house were forbidden, of course, so my shooting career was over.

On Sundays, I would often go rock climbing with the group my Uncle Paul had helped found (Rock Climbing Branch of the Appalachian Trail Club of Washington, D.C.). They were first-rate climbers. I became only moderately competent, but it was great outdoors experience. In the summers of 1946 and 1947, I returned to Grace Boys Camp in New York State, which I had attended in 1943, first as a senior camper and then at age 16 as a junior counselor. I specialized in taking the campers out on hiking-camping trips, a responsibility that served me well.

x·o·ø·o·x

CHAPTER 16   *I have never known such deep despair and ill health*

A posed picture of me and campers making believe we were heading out for an overnight camping trip, at Grace Boys Camp, summer 1947. We would typically hike about eight miles to a shelter, cook supper and breakfast, and return the next day. I am wearing Wilber's army fatigue jacket. [PHOTO: GRACE BOYS CAMP]

Valerie had a hard time with the new family arrangement, and the tensions would sometimes run high. At age 13, she was not happy. Monte's authoritarianism would have been anathema to any 13-year old and were especially so to strong-willed Valerie as she coped with the loss of her father. Furthermore, she was not happy at Alice Deal Junior High School. Here she describes her high-school years.

ANNAPOLIS, MARYLAND, 2010

My memories of being at St. John Baptist School in New Jersey in the 6th grade had been good, so when it was suggested that I return there in the ninth grade, I did not argue. But when the tenth grade came along and I knew Hale would be in the same public school at home, I decided to try it.

Alice Deal Junior High in the 8th grade had been horrible – my worst memories were (1) seeing my father's face and violent death on display in both large Washington newspapers, and (2) having nobody to eat lunch with and taking my sandwich out onto the field where I sat among weeds and condoms.

At Woodrow Wilson High School, there was Hale and things seemed better. I think I even played piano—the song "Brazil"—for some musical he was in. But the daily challenge of trying to figure out what to wear at a time when the Gibson girl look was "in" was too much for me. So, I fled back to the convent school with its shapeless uniforms, nuns and comfortable routines.

Valerie finished high school at St. John Baptist School, graduating in 1950. The school provided both the order and the freedom Valerie needed to grow into a fine young woman, wife, mother, and productive journalist.

x·o·ø·o·x

A year after Wilber's death, Norma wrote our cousin Connie Lou and her parents (Rex and Gerry) about the past year and her future plans.

[POSTMARK JAN. 5, 1947]
Dearest Connie Lou and HER PARENTS — My, but were we showered with gifts! I had wanted your address, to wish you MERRY CHRISTMAS and HAPPY NEW YEAR and before I had got around to it, here came your wonderful box! Those earrings are simply stunning, and the kitchen reminder pad is really a necessity for me. Those earrings really impress me – I should have had them for the reception for the Arabian Prince here, to which I was invited. I am beginning to go out a little, and also attended an affair celebrating the Independence Day of Lebanon. It was given by the Lebanese President, Dr. Malik, who used to be a professor at Beirut University. The Bradt cousins (Gordon A. Bradt) in Evanston could tell you all about that, as they used to visit there with their missionary father.

You don't know how we appreciated your thoughtfulness about the box, and also how doubly dear all of you have become to me this past year. Rex's coming [for the funeral] was a great blessing, and his courage and sweetness have been a wonderful example, I feel that the love which Wilber had for all of you has been transferred to me to use toward you, and now I feel more truly "Bradt" than I ever did during his lifetime, and will always, even though in the distant future I should change my name, for any reason.

Rex, what would you think if I should become engaged to Monte Bourjaily whom you met here. He lost his sister, my friend, Alice, the Army Nurse, who was right beside us at Wilber's services (remember?). She is buried close to Wilber in Arlington, and had requested the same ceremony. This mutual sorrow has brought us together, and leaves no one to care for his motherless child (Gale). (He said if he had had a boy, he would have been named Dale). [Rex's first son Dale had died in a traffic accident at age seven in 1940.] Hale + Valerie have not had a father, except for weeks during six long years. Monte is devoted to them, and is happy to accept the responsibility. Valerie has four more years of high school (Hale 2) before their college fund (W's insurance) is available. — Love and Many Thanks, Norma

Please tell none of the rest of the family now, [do] write your reaction!

P.S. It has been a terrible year. I have never known such deep despair and ill health. Only in the last two months have I been on my feet for any length of time. And I did not know it was possible to grieve so much for anyone. If I had not had our children (and Gale), I do not know what would have happened to me. I felt too much attracted to the space at Wilber's side [in the cemetery], reserved for me, and life seemed to hold no charms. Frankly, the doctor thinks my only chance to pull out of this is to try to interest myself in rebuilding a normal family life. Monte understands and has seen me through my worst times. — Love N.B.

Norma's grief and pain surely ran very deep in inexpressible ways. I was insensitive to any outer signs of this and recall no period of her being incapacitated except during the hospital stay after her miscarriage. Like all of us, she carried on with her daily tasks, supporting the family along with Monte's syndicate business. She continued with most of the routine household duties, though I remember washing lots of dinner dishes. Monte was very old-school in such matters, but he was a determined, hard worker; after supper he would invariably return to his syndicate work.

x · o · ø · o · x

Five months later, Norma wrote again to Rex, describing how our lives were evolving a year and a half after Wilber's death.

June 4, 1947

Dear Rex — … We went to Arlington [Cemetery] on Memorial Day (we are there often of course) and covered the grave with a blanket of crimson roses from our yard. It looked so beautiful. The Scouts had been there early and put a flag on each soldier's grave, also a large poppy and a few pink roses. The services by the veterans' organizations in the Amphitheater were impressive. I often wish that some of Wilber's family could be here to go with us to these observances. Some time, if possible, I would hope we could have an anniversary and those who want to, could meet there together.…

The city of Bangor recently dedicated a Book of Honor of all their [Bangor's] war dead. We were invited but could not go, and they sent us a duplicate of Wilber's page. The book will be in the Bangor library in an illuminated case, and a page will be turned each day forever, God willing. We have the other mementoes, the scroll from the War Dept. and the medals, and so we are mailing this page copy (it is beautiful) to [Wilber's mother on] the farm [in Indiana]. It says "Died of Accident" although they are familiar with the details. I would rather they said "Died of Wounds" which they say on our certificates and is the purely honest statement, or rather " … as a result of wounds inflicted in the Pacific campaigns."

The library in Bangor still displays that book under glass and still turns it to a new page nearly daily. They have another copy they can pull out to show any page of interest to a visitor.

We are not going to write there [to the farm] as our letters are not welcome, so perhaps you can explain this large page when you get there.

St. John's Episcopal Church in Bangor has recently dedicated a large stained glass window to the four boys [from the church] who lost their lives in service, and Wilber's name is incorporated there. Some day you may want to go and see this window.…

I hope that you will pass along these pieces of news to the family as you see them. Hale sees Paul quite often but they talk of [rock] climbing, hiking, etc., … — Kindest regards, Norma

Wilber's name in the church window is there today because Norma made a huge issue of it. The minister, Mr. Furrer, did not want to include it on the grounds that the death did not occur in combat or in wartime. And, of course, she was right in arguing that, in effect, it very much had.

17

"I think we might grow to love each other. Don't you?"

Midwest and East Coast
1947–1984

Norma and Monte Bourjaily were married September 6, 1947, by Bishop Basie of the Antiochian Orthodox Christian Church in Brooklyn, New York. Monte's two divorces precluded marriage in the Roman Catholic Church. He was 53 and she 41. Monte meshed into the family, although his temper, when provoked, could be a problem. On one occasion, I had slapped Gale when she was being frustratingly recalcitrant, and Monte absolutely blew up, nearly assaulting me. With time he mellowed, and of course I had learned my lesson. He took his new family seriously and treated Valerie and me as his own children.

Was the Norma-Monte marriage a love match or a way to do the "right thing?" Monte and Norma had grown accustomed to each other as they joined forces to raise the combined family after Wilber's death. Marriage two years later must have seemed the natural thing to do. It ensured that Gale would have her father's presence as she grew up. It gave Monte another chance at fatherhood, which he felt he had not handled well with the three boys from his first marriage. As a World War I veteran, he surely must have suffered grave shock and guilt about the role his own actions might have played in Wilber's death. Perhaps he considered marrying Norma his duty. His womanizing days certainly were over. As Norma wrote, the two of them were lonely and in grief; this was enough in itself to bring them together. However, the marriage was not a sham; as the years passed, they became true companions in the deepest sense. And there was intimacy: on March 21, 1950, Norma, at age 44, gave birth to another daughter, Dale Anne.

Monte continued to pursue his newspaper syndication business at which he was so very talented. Over the years, it evolved into primarily an editorial service; he wrote daily editorials that could be used without attribution by editors of the subscribing papers. Every day, he would read the *New York Times* from cover to cover and then write commentary on several current topics. The pieces would then be sent to subscribing newspapers, possibly as many as 40 or 50 in the best of times.

It was not an easy existence; syndicated features were not in demand during wartime because there was plenty of live news. The Korean War (1950–53) thus nearly killed Monte's syndicate. In response, Monte sold the elegant Connecticut waterfront home he had optimistically bought in 1949 but could no longer afford. It had been our family home for two years. With cash from the sale, he leased and later bought the *Grafton Sentinel* daily newspaper in the hills of northern West Virginia and moved the family with the two younger girls there in 1951. (Valerie and I were both away in college by then.)

Monte, with Norma's involvement, immersed himself in the nitty-gritty hands-on work of running a newspaper in the bustling railroad town of Grafton, West Virginia. Valerie and I, on our school holiday visits, were recruited to help with circulation and advertising. In 1954, Monte resurrected the Bangor, Maine, afternoon newspaper, which he called the *Bangor Patriot*. This took the family to Bangor, our old home city, for a few years. After a few years, when it was on the verge of profitability, Monte's backers pulled out, and the paper was shut down. In 1958, they established a home in Spring Lake, New Jersey. From there for many years, Monte and Norma managed the Grafton paper and Monte continued writing his daily editorials until very late in his life. For several years, they also lived in New York City to facilitate Dale Anne's studies there.

Elizabeth, Wilber's mother and our grandmother, was still living on the Versailles farm through the 1950s, having stayed on after her husband's death in 1944. Norma did not intrude on Wilber's family, but ensured that Valerie and I stayed in contact with our only living grandparent, Elizabeth Bradt, and also with our Bradt aunts and uncles. Later, on my own, I visited Elizabeth there several times prior to her death in 1961.

On one such visit, as I came into the kitchen in the morning, Grandmother asked me how many eggs I wanted for breakfast. I responded that two would be fine. She was crestfallen and explained that she had lots and

CHAPTER 17 *I think we might grow to love each other. Don't you?*

Studio photo of the six Bradt-Bourjailys in Grafton, West Virginia, early January 1952. Valerie and I, in the rear, were home from college for the holidays. Monte, Dale Anne, Norma, and Gale are in front. [PHOTOGRAPHER: UNKNOWN]

lots of eggs that were laid daily by all those hens in the coop by the porch entrance. Hadn't I noticed? I then allowed that five or six eggs would be fine and that greatly brightened her mood. A few years later on my next visit, I was greeted with the same question in the morning. I naturally responded that five or six would be fine; again she looked crestfallen. She explained that she no longer had chickens (hadn't I noticed?), and that she had very few eggs. I then allowed as how two would be just fine.

x·o·ø·o·x

Gale's parentage remained a puzzle to Valerie and me as well as to Gale herself, throughout her youth and early adulthood. The half-true story that she was Monte's daughter by a (non-existent) third wife would soon become awkward because Gale had always believed that Norma was her mother.

283

The "true" story presented to Valerie and me in 1950 was yet another half-truth: Gale was the daughter of Norma and Wilber, in accord with her birth certificate. Norma told us that Wilber had returned briefly to the West Coast in early 1943 to make arrangements for his division related to the sinking of the SS Coolidge (Book 2), and she had met him there. The justification for the earlier story, Norma said, had been that when she wrote Wilber of her pregnancy, he did not believe the baby was his, and in despair she had given the baby to Monte who had always wanted a daughter. It was a creative story that served moderately well for a few decades into the future.

It may have been a year later (1951) when a family friend suggested to Valerie and me—we were in our late teens—that half of each story was the truth and that Gale's biological parents were, in fact, Monte and Norma. This placed the scarlet letter in my own family! I was taken aback by this idea and recall telling this shocking possibility to a few friends upon my return to college. My reaction was to not probe further. Norma's story was not implausible, so for the next 30 years, I chose to live with the ambiguity that Gale's father could be either Monte or Wilber. I simply did not know. I came to understand that the Indiana Bradts were convinced Monte was the father and that Norma had been unfaithful, but I discounted that because the Bradts had already been so prone to thinking ill of Norma.

To resolve any uncertainty in her own mind, Elizabeth had written her congressman requesting the dates of Wilber's overseas service: the answer, obtained from the army, was that Wilber had been overseas from October 1942 to October 1945. I knew of this letter but did not consider it definitive; the army records might not have recorded a brief official visit to the West Coast.

In 1953 when Gale was ten years old and the family was living in West Virginia, Monte formally adopted Gale. A new birth certificate was issued with Monte listed as the father, Norma as the mother, and the child's name as Abigail Therese Bourjaily. In those days the adoptive parents were documented as if they were the biological parents, in many cases to hide the disgrace of an illegitimate birth. In Gale's case, this could have led to awkward questions because Gale's birth had taken place in 1943, four years before her "parents" (Monte and Norma) were married in 1947. Although few would likely have noticed this discrepancy, Norma and Monte nevertheless went to court in 1954, to close this possible window on the truth.

At their request, the court issued a Supplemental Adoption Decree, which stipulated that Monte was the adoptive father (that is, not the natural father). The decree stated that the child "was born in lawful wedlock to Wilber ...

and his wife, Norma," and that Wilber "was the natural father of said child." Explaining this fiction as truth to a lawyer and a judge required some chutzpah. (I myself might simply have let sleeping dogs lie.) Their understandable motivation in the culture of the 1950s was to shield Gale in later life from the awkward truth about her parentage. It was a tangled web indeed.

Several years later, to further "rectify" matters—and possibly because she wanted to become a Third Order Franciscan—Norma went about having her marriage sanctified in the Roman Catholic Church, as distinct from the Antiochian Orthodox church in which she and Monte had been married. This required that Monte's two previous marriages be annulled, even though the first had produced three sons. We children were led to believe that they undertook this successfully, but with great effort, and then took new marriage vows in St. Catharine's Church in Spring Lake, New Jersey, in the early 1960s, a service Abigail remembers attending.

About this time, Norma told me and others in the family that she and Monte had forsworn sexual relations. She would have been about 55 and he about 66. We, her adult children, considered this action and its notification to us unnecessary and rather bizarre. Obviously, her wartime actions were still haunting her, and she felt compelled to "cleanse" herself in her children's eyes.

Did Monte subscribe to all this? He had also become a dedicated Catholic and quite conservative in outlook. He was willing to follow Norma's lead, but I wonder about the celibacy bit. Perhaps his interest had dissipated. He was grateful to be in a stable marriage and would go out of his way to support Norma in endeavors that would make her more comfortable with herself. Tolerating all these machinations may have been, in his mind, penance for his wartime transgression.

I have been unable to find, after considerable effort, any church record of a formal remarriage or of marriage annulments, or of Norma's baptism as a Roman Catholic as an infant (Book 1). I thus am left with some doubt about these matters, though to Norma they were quite real. The ceremony Abigail remembers may in fact have been a simple renewal of marriage vows.

Such readjustments were only one aspect of Norma's and Monte's lives during their productive 32-year marriage. Their journalistic enterprises, her music, and their parenting, were all-encompassing and dominated their lives for the three decades of their marriage.

After Gale's 1953 adoption, we all began to call her by her new name, Abigail or Abby, as was her preference. The name doubtless came from Norma's fascination with Abigail Adams, wife of the American President, John Adams. Abigail grew into adulthood believing the family dogma that

Norma was her mother and that Wilber, the deceased war hero, was her father. As an adult she became aware of her ambiguous paternity, but never gave it serious consideration.

At some time after Abby was married (in 1965), her husband Tom had looked Monte in the eye and asked him if he was Abby's father, "Please tell me; she wants to know!" and Monte had looked away and responded simply and unconvincingly, "She's Wilber's baby." He continued protecting his wife's honor to his dying day. Sadly, he died in 1979 at age 85 with his paternity not yet recognized by his own daughter who was then 35.

Abby herself was not to know the true story until my research came to fruition several years later.

x · o · ø · o · x

Wilber's mother eventually accepted Abby as a family member. They had met once or twice when Abby was quite young and Elizabeth was quite charmed by her. Monte and Norma, when traveling in Indiana on a sales trip, would drop off Valerie and me and sometimes Abby at the farm to meet our grandmother and would return a few hours later to pick us up. They did not impose themselves on Elizabeth. Past history still loomed large.

Many years later, when Gale was 15, she initiated a correspondence with her "grandmother Bradt." Elizabeth was 83, and none of Abby's biological grandparents were alive at that time. It probably took Elizabeth aback to receive Gale's letter, and she might well have thought ill of Norma for allowing or encouraging Gale to write. To her credit, Elizabeth rose above such considerations and responded warmly.

These letters painted vivid scenes of Elizabeth's later years. In the first, she told about her love of bug hunting and her maternal grandmother, some of which appeared in Book 1 of this series. Her letters were written at the Versailles, Indiana, farm, but were on a postal route out of Dillsboro (the adjacent town).

DILLSBORO, IND., FEBRUARY 5, 1959

Dear Abigail — Your Christmas card should have been acknowledged weeks ago but I find a first letter so hard to start. Once I'm started, I'll not know when to stop. I thank you for your Christmas card. It was a surprise. I was pleased with your grades. Hope you keep them among the top ranks.

I wish I might have studied Biology. It was not offered when I was in High School. Ruth took it at Indiana University and I enjoyed helping her find her

CHAPTER 17   *I think we might grow to love each other. Don't you?*

specimens. We hunted all over pastures and byroads around Bloomington but never did find any "Granddaddy long legs" or "tumble bugs." I'd enjoyed playing with them when I was a child. Ruth left the farm [in Versailles] when she was three, so she never knew them. You likely do not either. Some time, if you should come to visit me, we will try again to find some – if you are interested in bug hunting. I still am....

Didn't I tell you I'd not know when to stop, once I started? Next time – if you survive this letter – I'll tell you how Grandpa thought Grandma tried to "pizen" [poison] him.

I hope there will be a "next time" for I think we might grow to love each other. Don't you? — Elizabeth Bradt

Elizabeth did have her soft side. I myself never did learn how Grandpa thought Grandma had tried to poison him.

x · o · ø · o · x

Two years later, Elizabeth noted that Abigail was graduating from high school and I from graduate school.

Dillsboro, Indiana, June 12 [1961]
Dear Abigail — Yesterday was your [graduation] day and I thought of you often. Hale and Dottie [my wife] were sure to say you were the prettiest girl graduate and it doesn't take any stretch of the imagination to believe they were right. Now, the thing to do is to prepare for school again on a much larger scale....

Were Dale Anne's grades "away up there" again this semester? I hope so.

When is Hale's commencement? A graduate from M.I.T. is something for which to be proud, but a Ph.D. is a lot more. Williys [Elizabeth's daughter Mary's husband] and I both crow a lot [about him]. He never had a child and is so proud of Hale, he struts when we talk of him. Confidentially, I feel like strutting about him, too. — Much love, Elizabeth Bradt

It pleases me still that my grandmother felt this way.

x · o · ø · o · x

Elizabeth died on July 20, 1961 at age 86 in her bed in the house my grandfather Hale had built on their farm. Mary wrote Abby, now 18, about it.

Me (the driver) in my beloved Model A 1930 Ford in Grafton, West Virginia, June 1952, after my college graduation. I am about to depart for the West Coast for navy duty with a Dutch exchange student, Toby Swelheim. The rumble seat was packed full of our baggage with a poncho covering it. Another college friend, John Hayes is at left. John also owned a Model A roadster and is giving me last-minute advice. [PHOTO: HALE BRADT]

FORT WAYNE, IND., JULY 30, 1961
Dear Abby — As you already know, Mother will never be able to answer your good letter received four hours after her death. Though I have never had a gift for writing letters, that was such a good letter and most surely deserves an answer. You must already know that Mother was very fond of you, and your letters were a source of much pleasure for her. She asked me to read several of them, and at the time of her death more than one of them was on her dresser in her bedroom, for re-reading no doubt.... — Love, Mary Bradt Higgins

Elizabeth's first great-grandchild, my own daughter Elizabeth who was her namesake, had been born 18 months earlier. Unfortunately, I had not taken her to Versailles to see her great-grandmother. During my grandmother's final illness, I proposed such a visit, but my uncles and aunts discouraged me; my grandmother, they said, would probably not be aware of her. I heard later that Elizabeth seemed nearly comatose those last days in the presence of her children. However, when a visiting grandchild was

CHAPTER 17   I think we might grow to love each other. Don't you?

Me in Wilber's army fatigue pants, my grandmother Elizabeth, my Model A, the old Bradt log house (background), and the original barn (behind house) on the Bradt Versailles farm in 1952. This was my first stop on my cross-country trip after leaving Grafton. I was 21 and she was 77. She lived nine more years, until 1961. [PHOTO: HALE BRADT]

alone with her, she would liven up considerably. Seeing her namesake (baby Elizabeth) might have been an appreciated gift.

x·o·ø·o·x

Elizabeth left the Versailles farm to her children or their heirs, giving her daughter Mary Higgins a life interest so she could live there during the balance of her life. Mary did so almost to the end, 26 years later, and became a much-admired local legend in her own right. She was the Versailles "grandmother" of my girls. Like her mother, she could make her wishes very well known. For example, it was definitely not wise to knock on her door during the Saturday afternoon Metropolitan Opera radio broadcast, as you would not be kindly received.

Mary and Abby kept the correspondence going off and on over the next decades of Mary's life. When Abby was 26, she received this letter.

[DILLSBORO, IND.], 11 JANUARY, 1970
Dear Abigail — It was a pleasant surprise to get a Christmas card and especially to get the long note and the picture of your daughter. She and I celebrate our birthdays on the same day. [Jan. 8; Mary in 1903 and Corinne in 1969] She may be interested in this later as I was always interested in the fact that I was born on my great grandmother's birthday, and my great grandmother was born on the day that Andy Jackson fought the battle of New Orleans after the end of the war of 1812. This always made the remembering of that historical date especially easy for me. But then, historical dates were always easy for me to remember….
— Love, Mary

x · o · ø · o · x

Paul Bradt, Wilber's brother, was living with Mary in the Versailles farmhouse when he died on April 5, 1978. This letter from Mary, a month later, to Abby and her husband Tom, told of my visit and offered Abby an important reassurance.

9 MAY 1978, SUNNY
Dear Abby and Tommy — … We [Mary and Hale] have always loved opera together and he [Hale] came to be with me a day after Paul's death, bless him. You have a wonderful brother. After he had gone back to Boston, I mailed him opera glasses, which Wilber had bought for me at a pawn shop when he was on the Indiana University swimming team. He was a plunger [a diver], and the team went to Chicago on one of its trips. It was there that he bought the glasses for me.

… Rex mentioned that you were worried about whether or not you were blood kin of ours. Do not worry about that; you want to be a Bradt and we Bradts want you to be one of us. Is not that enough? How much better to be wanted and one of us than to be a member of [a] family who was never mentioned nor admitted to the family circle. In fact, if you want us, it is mutual, and so it is settled; you are one of us. Both Rex and Ruth in her letter to me spoke of how charming you both were.…

Such a lot of reminiscing. I promise not to repeat this performance. Fewer flowers, more cats, dust and disorder here. — Love, Mary

CHAPTER 17   *I think we might grow to love each other. Don't you?*

x·o·ø·o·x

Late in their lives, Wilber's youngest sister Ruth Wilson wrote to Norma. Norma was 74 and Ruth 64. Here again was some reconciliation, understanding, and reassurance.

Aug. 25th, 1980, Burlington, Wisc. 53105
Dear Norma — … One of the reasons I am so glad to hear from you – I was glad to know I was no longer bitter about Wilber's death. I'm ashamed to say I was at the time. I realize it was much harder on you than me. Such things are so hard to understand – I guess no one really can. You and Monte certainly did a good job raising your family to be so nice and deserve a lot of credit. — Hope all is well with you, Ruth Wilson

x·o·ø·o·x

Two years later, Ruth wrote to Abby, who was then 38. Ruth was able to look inward at her own feelings and generously express them to Abby.

May 15, 1982
Dear Abby — For some time, I've wanted to write to you but the garden and yard work are too temping and demanding this time of the year.…

I want to thank you and Norma for letting me get acquainted with you. I will admit I was bitter after my brother's death. I suppose I felt Norma had betrayed my trust in her. Because Wilber had loved her so much, I did also. I believe it was the last letter I received from him in which he said how very tired he felt – that when he went to war he had tried to leave things as if he would never return and that he could hardly believe he was really coming home. I've thought of that many times and it helped me understand things I believe. Maybe it will help you also.

Norma could have kept you, Hale, and Valerie away from us. It probably would have been easier for her to have done that. However, knowing you three has made the pain much less. I am no longer bitter but appreciate her patience with me.

… I hope you will always consider me your Aunt. — Love, Ruth Wilson

That Wilber's sisters could express their acceptance of both Norma and Abby late in life is very heartwarming for me. I never heard such sentiments from the brothers, but being men, perhaps their reticence about expressing feelings is understandable. But my sense, from their warm interactions with us, was that they accepted the realities more easily than did their sisters. Each of the Bradts would warmly welcome me whenever I dropped in, which I often did in my academic travels. Norma and Abby were more painful reminders for them; their acceptance by the family was more difficult and thus even more admirable when it came.

x·o·ø·o·x

This is a letter written to my wife Dottie and me by Nobuko Ohashi, the wife of a Japanese colleague of mine, a professor at Tokyo Metropolitan University. She at age about 27 was visiting the U.S. with her husband in April 1984. The Ohashis knew the story of my father and of my inquiries and interviews about him during my sabbatical in Japan the previous year. Here she told of her visit to Wilber's grave in Arlington National Cemetery.

MAY 16, 1984
Dear Mr. and Mrs. Bradt — ... On the last day of Washington, D.C., I visited your father's grave in Arlington Cemetery. It was such a nice spring day, there was no cloud in the sky. No tourist bus was running around, no people, no cars. I was alone on the bright fresh grass. Your father's grave appeared out of sudden (I don't think graves are arranged by numbers.) I knelt down before the grave thinking what to say – Long time ago – before I was born, your father was fighting against our old people. And now, I'm here in front of him. I was at a loss what to say. I only remembered his smiles on the photos you showed us. Very strange feeling captured me. I felt tears on my cheeks.

It was such a nice spring day – indeed!!

Thank you again for your kindness [during our visit to Boston]. — (Takaya and) Nobuko Ohashi

I found this to be deeply touching. Reconciliation between the two wartime opponents is a continuing, multigenerational process.

18

Reflections

Salem, Massachusetts

2014

Life continued on for all of us. I finished high school in 1948 and went on to Princeton University where I majored in music and then served two years in the U.S. Navy during and after the Korean conflict. As navigator on my ship, I plotted our course right past Shibushi Bay on Kyushu, Japan, some half-dozen times without realizing that Wilber would have landed there in the planned invasion of Japan. I returned to Princeton for a year of physics courses and then earned my PhD in physics at MIT. I was fortunate in being able to stay on as a faculty member for a long career there. My research specialty was x-ray astronomy, which we carried out from NASA satellites. I was deeply involved in the experiments on the SAS-3, HEAO-1, and RXTE missions. I retired from MIT in 2001 and now live in Salem, Massachusetts. I have been married since 1958 to Dorothy, a special education teacher and mother of our two daughters. One daughter has two young-adult children.

My sister Abigail spent her later pre-college years in Spring Lake, New Jersey. She attended Manhattanville College in Purchase, New York, married a dentist and, with him, has become a superb home designer and expert in classic cars. She often serves as a judge at Rolls Royce rallies. They are the parents of three children and now live in Maryland. Our youngest sister Dale Anne lives in Europe. She has worked in government and private agencies dealing with sustainable farming and other environmental issues on an international scale. She has four children.

Valerie, after graduating from St. John Baptist School in 1950, went on to college at Barnard and Columbia University, married, and became a prominent journalist in Maryland. She covered Maryland for WTOP, the dominant Washington, D.C., news radio station, and covered Capitol Hill for the Eyewitness News television stations. She reported on the Governor Agnew scandal in 1973, and her live reporting of the Governor Wallace shooting in Laurel, MD in 1972 was broadcast around the world. She is now deeply committed to supporting the prison ministry of the Episcopal diocese of Maryland. In 2009, she looked back on the origins of her career in an essay entitled "My Career as a Journalist."

Annapolis, Maryland, 2009

My stepfather, Monte Bourjaily, when general manager of United Features Syndicate, persuaded Eleanor [Roosevelt] to write her column, "My Day." It was a big coup in the newspaper world.

He also persuaded me to write a teen column called "Among Us Teens by Val" when I was 16 years old. Eleanor's column was published in hundreds of newspapers; mine was published in eight – but three of them were the Washington Star, *the* Buffalo News *and* Grit. *Cannot remember the others.*

I wrote it six days a week for two years. My friends and I would sit around and make up fads. I even had fan mail. But what I hated the most was that my mother would edit the column and put in things like, "Teens find making friends with their parents a good move."

It was a real chore, but it paid off when I applied to Barnard College at Columbia. I got a scholarship and was cited in its news release about the freshman class having a "syndicated columnist." Which I was, but in only eight newspapers. After two years of Barnard, I transferred to Columbia University, and won a job as an editorial assistant at the Alumni News. *That led to a long career as a journalist so I won't complain.*

x·o·ø·o·x

Toward the ends of their lives, Monte and Norma enjoyed visits to St. Petersburg, Florida. In 1978, they sold their large New Jersey home and moved to Florida where they purchased a condominium. Monte had already had one or more strokes, but was still quite mobile. He died in St. Petersburg on May 6, 1979, and was buried there.

I began my immersion into Wilber's letters late the following year on my 50th birthday. My research finally made it abundantly clear that Wilber had

CHAPTER 18   *Reflections*

The Bradt-Bourjailys about 1978 in Spring Lake, New Jersey. Norma and Monte are seated in front, and standing (left to right) are Valerie, Abby, me, and Dale Anne. Monte had suffered one or more strokes by this time. He died in 1979. [PHOTO: BRADT-BOURJAILY FAMILY]

not returned to the United States during his three years of overseas duty, a fact that definitively resolved the ambiguity of Abby's parentage. Before I could call her with this epochal information, she had gone, unbeknownst to me, to Florida and interviewed Norma about her long life. When she got to the war years, she begged Norma to tell the story of her birth. Norma still did not admit to Abby directly that she was Monte's baby. Rather she told a story that made it clear. My news then, a few weeks later, was no surprise to Abby.

I had heard Norma tell the story in other contexts that did not, however, carry the import of this telling. Here is Norma's story as Abby told it to me:

In Washington State, Wilber and I occasionally ate in a Chinese restaurant with friends [probably Charlie's Place; letter 2/22/43]. Charlie, the owner, had a wife who still resided in China. On several occasions over the years, he greeted his customers with cigars and the happy announcement that he was the father of a new baby boy or girl, born to his wife in China. When asked how this could possibly be since he never went to China, he answered, "I have a very good friend in China."

Thus Norma was aware in her last years that we all knew who fathered Abby. I think she felt that if we had learned earlier of her infidelity, we would have blamed her for Wilber's death and despised her for it. I think her avid religiosity and her extreme sensitivity to sexual matters revealed a deep-seated anxiety and guilt. Later she was assiduous in personally caring for Monte in his last invalid years, at great effort and inconvenience and possibly at the cost of her own health. When Abby once asked her, at the time, why she did this rather than hiring caretakers, her response was, "This is my penance."

During Norma's widowhood and my WWII researches, I would occasionally call her and tell her how good and conscientious a mother she had been during the war years. On hearing this, she would begin to cry. She could not believe that this was true.

It must have been a great relief to Norma to learn that her children could absorb the true story without hating her. We didn't hate her and we knew that Wilber's suicide had had many causal components: the reoccurrence of malaria that morning, his depression, his forehead wound, his reluctance to return to the University of Maine, and his forgotten chemistry. Then in the background were the "special days" (Wilber's words) of combat, the killing, and the loss of close friends in battle and by friendly fire. Most of all, we couldn't hate Norma because, after all, she was our mother.

Norma continued to live in her Florida condominium after Monte's 1979 death. In 1985, after she had suffered several strokes, we moved her to a nursing home in New Jersey, a mile from Abby's home. A few months later, on February 17, 1986, she died of heart failure at age 80 in the nearby hospital in Neptune. She was buried in St. Catharine's cemetery in Spring Lake, and Monte's body was moved from Florida to be beside her there, at Norma's request. She could have been buried next to Wilber at Arlington National Cemetery, but that possibility did not interest her after 31 years of marriage to Monte and a quarter-century attending St. Catharine Church.

With Norma gone, the Wilber-Norma-Monte story came to an end. But the impact of their lives carried on in their surviving siblings, children, and grandchildren. Three of Wilber's siblings were still living at the time of Norma's death. Mary died the next year, on October 9, 1987, Rex on February 5, 2001, and Ruth on September 7, 2006. Norma's last living sibling, Evelyn, who was on that memorable 1931 cross country car trip (Book 1),

CHAPTER 18   *Reflections*

Norma at the piano in a New Jersey nursing home, 1985. She could only play a few halting chords in this, the last year of her life. In my mind, I can still hear Beethoven's Waldstein Sonata reverberating through our Bangor and Washington, D.C., homes in the 1940s.
[PHOTO: HALE BRADT]

Norma and Valerie at Norma's 80th birthday, November 30, 1985, at Abigail's home in Allenwood, New Jersey. Norma died 11 weeks later on February 17, 1986. [PHOTO: HALE BRADT]

VICTORY AND HOMECOMING   PART V: EPILOG

Wilber's sister Mary Bradt Higgins in her retirement community apartment in Versailles, Indiana, in 1987. She died later that year. That little grin often followed a pithy comment. She was a wonderful font of family history. [PHOTO: HALE BRADT]

Wilber's three surviving siblings in 1987: Mary, Ruth, and Rex. They died in 1987, 2006, and 2001, respectively. Ruth's husband Jack Wilson still carries on at age 93 at this writing (2014). [PHOTO: HALE BRADT]

CHAPTER 18 *Reflections*

My Aunt Mary Higgins and me in front of the covered bridge over Loughery Creek, Versailles, Indiana, 1987. This was the route Wilber and his family took from the farm to town during his boyhood. [PHOTO: HALE BRADT]

died at 98 in Spokane, Washington, on August 6, 2008, after a long bout with Alzheimer's. With the exception of Ruth's husband, Jack Wilson (b. 1920), who remains alert and mobile at 93 (in 2014), that entire generation of the family is now gone.

I had become quite interested in the Versailles farm as I was probing Wilber's story in the 1980s and had grown quite close to Mary. In 1987, I purchased my relatives' interests in the farm, and after Mary died, managed it from afar (Belmont, Massachusetts) as best I could. The fields and house were rented out and the old barn was refurbished. I relished my occasional visits there, as they connected me to Bradt family friends and the land and home of my grandparents. In 1993 a twister took down the barn, and later I took down the asphalt-shingled house my grandfather Hale had built in 1939. In 2001, the farm, then with no buildings, was deeded to the State of Indiana (Department of Natural Resources) to become a part of the adjacent Versailles State Park. A part of the proceeds of that transaction now annually benefits the media center of the Versailles school system in which my grandfather Hale, as a young man, had taught a century earlier.

x · o · ø · o · x

We are left wondering why Wilber chose such a self-destructive act.

It is, of course, impossible to know because the act itself is illogical. In his depression, he may not have been able to see a credible path forward for his life. He may also have thought, impulsively and tragically in error, that he could solve a sticky family problem simply by removing himself from the scene. Sadly, he didn't realize that life was not as cheap as he had been forced to think in order to tolerate the combat losses of friends, unknown Japanese soldiers, and even himself in the planned Kyushu invasion. It really wasn't so "simple," and the ultimate cost was greater than he could possibly have imagined.

How can we assess Norma's role in the story? My view is that she was a victim of her own aspirations. Choosing to leave the tight society of Bangor, Maine, in 1941 in an attempt to advance her artistic skills in New York City, she became vulnerable to her own need for attention and affection. This led to years of anguish, guilt, cover-up, and lies. Her anxieties and actions were probably rooted in an insecure and abusive childhood (Book 1). Nevertheless, her strengths and convictions had shone through in her continuing creativity, her devotion and attention to Wilber and her children throughout the war, and subsequently in her commitment to her postwar family and second marriage. She was a survivor when Wilber was not. He was a hero, but so was she a heroine. Her decision not to seek an abortion in 1943 was truly courageous. This led to the creation of another life, baby Gale, now Abigail, who was a joy to the family and who grew to be a wonderful creative woman.

Of course, there would have been no such story if Wilber had not chosen to enter the military in 1941, and it would have been a very different story indeed had he not chosen to take his own life. Norma's decision to take her family to New York and Monte's willingness to befriend a family strange to the city were also choices that drove the story. But when viewed in the light of their previous experiences and the circumstances forced on them

CHAPTER 18   *Reflections*

by a world war, their choices seemed limited or nearly nonexistent. How could Norma, with her musical and literary ambitions, not have sought her fortune in New York City? And how could Wilber not have entered the service after years of paid training as a national guardsman, and in fact what choices had he perceived to be open to him on that fateful day in 1945?

x · o · ø · o · x

The unions of Wilber, Norma, and Monte resulted in seven children, the four borne to Norma and the three boys by Monte's first marriage. Their progeny number 23, and 21 of them are still living in 2014. Regrettably, Wilber did not live to know the fine people Valerie and I married, nor our children, his grandchildren; but his spirit lives on through them, and also through the descendants of his university students and the men he led through their dramatic Pacific odyssey.

On my solo 4,700-mile auto trip through the eastern and central U.S. in 2012, I had rewarding visits with numerous Bradts, Sparlins, and Bourjailys. They were in all walks of life from medical research, motel management, blues singing, and university and high school teaching. The Bourjailys, my step-relatives, enriched that trip as indeed they have throughout my entire life. I still love the Lebanese food that Terkman Bourjaily and my mother would cook, and I still think of yogurt by its Arabic name, leban. That trip brought me to another level of acceptance of my parents' story.

Clint Eastwood's 2006 movie, *Letters from Iwo Jima,* portrays the story of the battle for Iwo Jima from the Japanese perspective. At the close, the favorably portrayed Japanese commander takes his own life with a bullet in the chest with his personal .45 Colt pistol, which had been given him as a gift by his American army colleagues at the end of an exchange visit to the U.S. in the 1930s. I saw it alone in the small theater near my home. The parallel to Wilber's death in these details brought me to tears. I cried and cried and, later at home, continued to cry. I had never before cried for Wilber. Or perhaps I was crying for all those soldiers, American and Japanese, lost in the Pacific, or for what might have been had Wilber lived. Or, maybe they were tears of gratitude for what we have today, much of which can be traced to Wilber and Norma, and yes, also to Monte.

★

VICTORY AND HOMECOMING   PART V: EPILOG

My two daughters, Elizabeth and Dorothy, Christmas 1964. [PHOTO: HALE BRADT]

Valerie's children (Wilber's grandsons), from left, Dale, Scott, and Gary Hymes, 1966. Wilber had five grandchildren in all and sadly knew none of them. [PHOTO: DONALD HYMES]

Acknowledgments

I have been pursuing the story of my father Wilber and mother Norma for nearly 34 years and have been aided by so many individuals and organizations that it is not possible to properly acknowledge them all, but I will do my best.

First and foremost, my sisters Abigail and Valerie deserve my utmost gratitude for letting me tell our family's story and for moral support throughout. Abigail's husband Tom has been an enthusiastic supporter, and Donald, Valerie's husband, has provided sage editorial advice.

This work could not exist but for those who husbanded my father's letters for the 35 years it took me to wake up to their existence and intrinsic value, namely my mother, my Bradt grandmother, and my cousin Alan, all of whom are now deceased. My aunt, Wilber's sister Mary Higgins, chose to give me a collection of letters between Wilber's mother and father written in the 1910s and 1920s, and between Mary and her mother in later decades. These shed important light on the familial relationships that were so influential in my father's life.

In the early 1980s, I hired students and secretaries—Trish Dobson, Pam Gibbs, Brenda Parsons, and Nancy Ferreira—to type Wilber's letters into a primitive stand-alone word processor. They were persevering, patient souls who took a serious personal interest in the story. I used those files to create the volume *World War Two Letters of Wilber E. Bradt* (by Hale Bradt, 1986), a complete compilation of Wilber's letters of which I created only 40 copies, mostly for relatives. The current work is, as described in the Prologue, a distillation of the complete letters with much more supportive material.

General Harold R. Barker, Wilber's immediate superior in the 43rd Division, wrote his *History of the 43rd Division Artillery*, which is rich in technical detail—operation orders, maps, and rosters of officers, medal winners, wounded, and killed. It pertains directly to the units Wilber commanded. This, along with other published histories and documentation in Wilber's papers, provides context for the events Wilber describes. At my request in 1981 when she was 75 and still quite alert, my mother typed an eight-page

VICTORY AND HOMECOMING

summary of her life that was a valuable view of her life as she then, perhaps somewhat wishfully, remembered it.

Conversations and correspondence with Wilber's military and civilian associates and his siblings in the 1980s materially enriched this story. Especially helpful were Howard Brown, Waldo Fish, and others of the Rhode Island National Guard; Donald Downen of the Washington State National Guard; Irwin Douglass of the University of Maine; and Robert Patenge, formerly of the 169th Field Artillery Battalion. My 1983 conversation with Japanese Colonel Seishu Kinoshita, who fought opposite Wilber on Arundel was an emotional highlight for both of us. Howard Brown died this year (2014); the others long before. My aunt Mary Bradt Higgins was especially helpful with her wonderful memory and facility with the typewriter. Her sister Ruth and brother Rex were also generous with their recollections and so were my mother's relatives, especially her sister Evelyn and Evelyn's daughters, Jane and Julie. My Bourjaily stepbrother, Paul Webb, and the former wife of his brother Vance, Tina Bourjaily, were helpfully responsive to my queries.

My visits in 1983 and 1984 to the Pacific sites of Wilber's odyssey (Solomon Islands, Philippine Islands, New Zealand, and Japan), and my meetings with the people he had encountered added important dimensions and perspective. In New Zealand, Olive Madsen, Minnie and Sidney Smith, and Dawn Jones Penney were most helpful. In the Solomons, my guide Alfred Basili got me around efficiently in his motorized canoe, Liz and Ian Warne provided hospitality on Kolombangara, and Claude Colomer took photos for me after I had immersed my camera in seawater, and so did the Warnes. In the Philippines, Mrs. José Dacquel whom Wilber had known, Emma Peralto, Boysie Florendo, and the deLeon family made my visit most fruitful. Boysie spent a day driving me to sites on the Laguna de Bay, and young Edgar José drove us to Lingayen Gulf in his 1969 Ford Mustang with the music playing loudly as we cruised down roads reminiscent of the U.S. in the 1930s. These Pacific visits were facilitated by my residence in Japan while on sabbatical leave in 1983 at the Japanese Institute of Space and Astronautical Science. I remain grateful for its generous support of my scientific endeavors.

I was fortunate to have started this project when many of my informants were still living. In recent years, I have been in contact with families of soldiers and in one case a sailor who served with Wilber, namely the families of Charles D'Avanzo, Robert Patenge, Donald Mushik, Lawrence Palmer, Saul Shocket, and Marshall Dann. Their recollections and generous sharing of memories and photographs further added to the story.

Acknowledgments

Faculty, archivists, and librarians at the universities Wilber and Norma attended or taught at (Washington State University, Indiana University, University of Cincinnati, University of Maine) helped flesh out those aspects of their lives. Staff at the National Archives in Suitland, Maryland, Washington, D.C., and College Park, Maryland, on my half dozen visits over the years were expert at finding needed documents. Also helpful were librarians and archivists in New Zealand (Auckland, Christchurch, and Wellington), and at the City of Nouméa, New Caledonia; Bancroft Library of the University of California, Berkeley; Columbia University; Tacoma Public Library, Washington; Seattle Museum of History and Industry; U.S. Army Center for Military History; Japanese Center for Military History of the National Institute of Defense Studies (IDS); and elsewhere. It was Dr. Hishashi Takahashi of IDS who put me in touch with Col. Kinoshita.

I am most grateful to Robin Bourjaily, Maura Henry, and Richard Feyl for readings and editorial comments on near-final drafts. Frances King did heroic service as editor and manager of the final phases of this work, and Lisa Carta's attention to detail and superb design sense created a most attractive set of books. Suzanne Fox, Richard Margulis, Kate Hannisian, and Michael Sperling contributed much appreciated marketing advice.

The many Bradts, Sparlins, and Bourjailys I have queried and visited over the years have helped create this story. In many respects, it is their story too. Many friends and colleagues have suffered my recounting parts of the story to them over these past decades. My daughters, Elizabeth and Dorothy, and my wife, Dorothy, have borne the burden more than most, and they did so with grace.

I, of course, take sole responsibility for errors and misrepresentations herein.

Bibliography

The following references have been particularly helpful to me in creating the Wilber's War Trilogy. They do not by any means comprise a comprehensive list of World War II Pacific Theater sources. Many of these volumes and documents are now available on the Internet.

Official military journals, histories, and operations reports of the following units during World War II, U.S. National Archives and Records Administration (NARA):

172nd, 103rd, and 169th Infantry Regiments of the 43rd Infantry Division.

152nd, 169th, 103rd, and 192nd Field Artillery Battalions of the 43rd Infantry Division.

27th, 145th, 148th, and 161st Infantry Regiments; see also Karolevitz reference below.

43rd Infantry Division Historical Report, Luzon Campaign, 1945.

History of the 103rd Infantry Regiment, 43rd Division, January 1, 1945 – May 31, 1945. [Detailed narrative history of the entire Luzon campaign for the regimental combat team that included Wilber's artillery battalion]

Logs of naval units:

LCI-65

LCI (L) Group 14

Histories sponsored by the U.S. military:

United States Army in World War II, The War in the Pacific Series. Sponsored by the U.S. Army Chief of Military History, U.S. Government Printing Office, 1949–1962:

Morton, Louis. *Strategy and Command: The First Two Years.*

Morton, Louis. *The Fall of the Philippines.* [1941–42]

Miller, John, Jr. *Guadalcanal, The First Offensive.* [Guadalcanal campaign, 1942–43]

Miller, John, Jr. *Cartwheel, the Reduction of Rabaul.* [New Georgia campaign, 1943]

Miller, Samuel. *Victory in Papua.* [Eastern New Guinea campaign, 1942]

Smith, Robert Ross. *Approach to the Philippines.* [Northern New Guinea campaign, 1944]

Cannon, M. Hamlin. *Leyte: The Return to the Philippines.* [Leyte campaign, 1944]

Smith, Robert Ross. *Triumph in the Philippines*. [Luzon campaign, 1945]

Williams, Mary. *Chronology 1941–1945*. [World War II events]

MacArthur, Gen. Douglas, *The Campaigns of MacArthur in the Pacific, Reports of General MacArthur, Volume 1*, U.S. Army Center for Military History, CMH Pub 13-3, 1994.

Morison, Samuel Eliot. *History of the U.S. Naval Operations in World War II*. New York: Atlantic, Little, Brown, 1948–60:

Vol. III, The Rising Sun in the Pacific.

Vol. V, The Struggle for Guadalcanal.

Vol. VI, Breaking the Bismarck Barrier.

Vol. VIII, New Guinea and the Marianas.

Vol. XII, Leyte.

Vol. XIII, The Liberation of the Philippines.

Memoirs and histories by participants:

Barker, Harold R. *History of the 43rd Division Artillery*. Providence RI: John F. Greene Printer, 1961.

Eichelberger, Robert L. *Our Jungle Road to Tokyo*. Rockville MD: Zenger Publishing Company, 1949.

Halsey, William F. and J. Bryan III. *Admiral Halsey's Story*. Rockville MD: Zenger, Publishing Company, 1947.

Krueger, Walter. *From Down Under to Nippon*. Rockville MD: Zenger Publishing Company, 1953.

Ockenden, Edward. *The Ghosts of Company G*. Infinity, 2011. [The TED Force in New Guinea]

Sledge, E. B. *With the Old Breed*. New York: Ballantine Books, 1981.

Zimmer, Joseph E. *History of the 43rd Infantry Division 1941–1945*. Baton Rouge, LA: The Army and Navy Publishing Company, undated, probably late 1940s.

Other histories and memoirs:

Bauer, K. Jack and Alan C. Coox. "Olympic vs. Ketsu-go," *Marine Corps Gazette*, August 1965, v. 49, No. 8.

Bourjaily, Vance. "My Father's Life," *Esquire Magazine*, March 1984, p. 98.

Donovan, Robert. *PT 10*. New York: McGraw-Hill, 1961.

Drea, Edward J. "Previews of Hell." *Quarterly Journal of Military History*, vol. 7, no. 3, p. 74. Aston, PA: Weider History, 1995. [Planned invasion of Kyushu]

Drea, Edward J. *Defending the Driniumor: Covering Force Operations in New Guinea, 1944*, Leavenworth Papers No. 9, Combat Studies Institute, 1984.

Estes, Kenneth W. *Marines Under Armor*. Annapolis MD: Naval Institute Press, 2000.

Bibliography

Goodwin, Doris Kearns. *No Ordinary Time.* New York: Touchstone, Simon & Schuster, 1994.

Hammel, Eric. *Munda Trail.* London: Orion Press, 1989.

Hasegawa, Tsuyoshi (Ed.) *The End of the Pacific War, Reappraisals.* Stanford, CA: Stanford University Press, 2007.

Keegan, John. *The Second World War.* New York: Viking Press, 1989.

Knox, Donald. *Death March.* New York: Harcourt, Brace, Jovanovich, 1981, pp. 181–184, 227. [The Lumban bridge story]

Karolevitz, R. F. (Ed.) *History of the 25th Infantry Division in World War II.* Nashville, TN: Battery Press, 1946, 1995. [Actions of the 27th and 161st Infantry Regiments]

Larrabee, Eric. *Commander in Chief.* New York: Simon & Schuster, 1987.

Paull, Raymond. *Retreat from Kokoda.* Australia: Wm. Heinemann Press, 1958.

Potter, E. B. *Nimitz.* Annapolis MD: Naval Institute Press, 1976.

Skates, John R. *The Invasion of Japan.* University of California Press, 1994.

The Official History of the Washington National Guard, Vol. 6, Washington National Guard in World War II. State of Washington: Office of the Adjutant General. [Also contains WW I and the 1935 strike duty]

Unpublished or self-published documents:

Antill, Peter, *Operation Downfall: The Planned Assault on Japan, Parts 1–4,* http://www.historyofwar.org/articles/wars_downfall1.html (1996).

Bourjaily, Monte F., "Re: Monte Ferris Bourjaily," 1936. [Résumé with references]

Bradt, Hale V. *Story of the Bradt Fund, the F. Hale Bradt Family, and their Versailles, Indiana Farm (1906–2001).* Self-published, 2004. [Early years of Wilber Bradt's life]

Bradt, Hale V. *The World War II Letters of Wilber E. Bradt.* Self-published 1986. [The nearly complete letters, transcribed and privately bound and distributed]

Bradt, Norma S. *Memoir, 1981.* [Eight page self-typed document]

Bradt, Wilber E. *Personal Journal (1941–45).* [Five handwritten notebook pages of dates, places, incidents]

Fushak, K. Graham. *The 43rd Infantry Division, Unit Cohesion and Neuropsychiatric Casualties.* Thesis, U.S. Command and General Staff College, 1999.

Higgins, John J. *A History of the First Connecticut Regiment, 169th Infantry 1672–1963.* Unpublished, 1963.

Patenge, Robert. *Memories of Wilber E. Bradt,* 1997. [Patenge was a survey officer in the 169th Field Artillery Battalion under Wilber Bradt in the Munda campaign, World War II, and later served with the 103rd Field Artillery Battalion.]

Saillant, Richard. *Journal of Richard L. Saillant.* Transcribed by Joseph Carey. [Saillant was an officer in the 118th Engineers of the 43rd Division until April 1944. The Munda campaign is vividly described.]

Zimmer, Joseph E. *Letters from Col. Joseph E. Zimmer to his wife, Maude Files Zimmer 1942–1945*. Transcribed by Maude Zimmer. [Zimmer was an infantry officer in the 43rd Division who served in the 169th Infantry, 103rd Infantry, and other elements of the 43rd Division from 1941 until May 1945.]

Newspaper archives, 1941–45:

Bangor (Maine) *Daily News*

New York Times

Wellington (New Zealand) *Evening Post*

Washington (D.C.) *Post*

Washington (D.C.) *Star*

Notable conversations with 43rd Division participants and one Japanese officer:

Howard Brown (1981 through 2012)

Warren Covill (1981)

Seishu Kinoshita, Kyushu, Japan (1983)

Albert Merck (1984, 2009)

William Naylor (1984)

Robert Patenge (1997)

INDEX Book 3

Bold page numbers indicate a chapter or, if a page range is given, a part.
Italic page numbers indicate a photograph or map.
WB — Wilber Bradt; "Hale" is Wilber's son; "F. Hale" is Wilber's father

18th Army, Japanese
   attacked across Driniumor R., 9
   on New Guinea, 5
   retreat and surrender, 18
43rd Infantry Division
   actions in Luzon, *xxviii*
   left Luzon for Japan, 196
   message center, May 1945, *156*
   ordered to U.S., 230
   organization of 1944, *xx*
   relieved after first Luzon action, 115
   relieved at Aitape, 47
   relieved of all combat, Luzon, 168
103rd Infantry Regiment
   four company commanders killed, 107
   supported by 152nd FA Bn., 15
126th Infantry Regiment of 32nd Div.
   supported by 152nd FA Bn., 15
152nd Field Artillery Battalion
   arrived Aitape, 10
   crowds front lines, 142
   displacing under fire, 115
   en route Aitape, 5
   en route Luzon, 70
   headquarters at Teresa, 143
   moved to Driniumor River, 14
   offense vs. Shimbu group, 127
   Wilber commands, 6
161st Infantry Regiment
   coffee pitcher rescued by WB, 34
   from Wash. State, in reserve, 79
169th Field Artillery Battalion
   René DeBlois commanded, 6
   Service Battery notoriety, Aitape, 33
172nd Infantry Regiment
   de-activated 10/13/45, 238
   given critical point, Kyushu, 231
   WB commander of, 176
   WB exec. of, 157

Adachi, Lt. Gen. Hatazo
   commanded 18th Japanese Army, 9
   retreat, surrender, suicide, 18
Adams, Abigail
   as namesake, 285
   Norma wrote play about, 119
Agustin, Col. Marcus
   Filipino guerilla commander, *149*
airplane
   for artillery observation, 19
   Gen. Barker learned to fly, 32
   kamikaze (suicidal air attack), 36
   WB learned to identify, 86
Aitape, New Guinea
   beauty of beach in evening, 48
   beauty of ocean at night, 39
   howitzer firing, *26*
   intensive training at, 23
   map of coastline, *xxv*
   operation declared over, 18
amphibious landings, Luzon, P.I.
   aerial view, *93*
   boat schedule, 73
   Bombardment Force, 82
   early actions planned, 78
   early landing, advantages of, 77
   first day's advances, *xxxi*
   LCVPs heading for beach, *93*
   maps, *xxix, xxx*
   overall organization, 82
   practice for, at Aitape, *74*
   Task Force 78, 75
   Task Force 79, 82
   unloading supplies, *94*
   Wilber's equipment, 89
amtrac shielding soldiers, *98*
Antipolo, Luzon, P.I., damage to, *129*
Arlington National Cemetery
   Alice Bourjaily interred at, 278

simple headstones, 218
WB burial, 265
artillery, Japanese
    12-inch gun, Luzon, 107
    152nd can outshoot, 88
    at Ipo Dam, 154
    Pistol Pete hard to locate, 111
atomic bomb, 185
atrocities, responsibility for, 46
Averill, Capt. Roger L.
    at Lumban bridge, 136
    battery commander, 97

Baanga action, story of, told, 245
Bangor, Maine
    Book of Honor, 279
    discomfort of winter, 111
    family returned to, 3
    house sold, 176
    memorial window, St. John's Ch., 280
Barbey, Vice Adm. Daniel E., commander, Task Force 78, 75, 82
Barker, Brig. Gen. Harold R.
    at review, Cabanatuan, *177*
    explained value of points, 164
    in mudhole and conversation, 154
    in rage about training, 58
    learned to fly, 32
    without promotion, 188
    wrote Valerie, 12
Battle of the Bulge, 66
Bedford, Indiana, inf. commander from, 20
belt, combat for Luzon landing, *89*
Bethany Beach, Delaware
    family at, August 1945, 170
    German prisoners at, 175
bicycle
    delivered papers with, 225
    Maine, 4, 141
    Washington, D.C., 270, *273*
Bombardment Group
    arrived Lingayen Gulf, 87
    mission, Luzon, 70
books for 152nd
    arrived, 161
    Junior League was to send, 117
    requested from Jr. League, 62
Bourjaily, Alice (sister of Monte)
    at Thanskgiving dinner, 250
    interred at Arlington Cemetery, 278
Bourjaily, Dale Anne (daughter of Monte)
    birth of 1950, *282*

photo of, with family 1952, *283*
photo of, with family ca. 1978, *295*
Bourjaily, Gale aka Abigail
    at Bethany Beach, 175
    corresponded with Eliz. Bradt, 286
    corresponded with Mary Bradt, 290
    half-truths about, 284
    photograph of
        family 1952, *283*
        family ca. 1978, *295*
        in chair at about 20 months, *174*
        in yard, running 1946, *273*
        standing with smile 1946, *275*
        upside down with Hale ca. 1946, *274*
        with father Monte ca. 1946, *274*
        with grandmother Terkman, *274*
Bourjaily, Monte F.
    family 1952, *283*
    family ca. 1978, *295*
    helped Norma with play, 181
    holding little Gale ca. 1946, *274*
    married Norma Sept. 1947, 281
    Norma engaged to, 278
Bourjaily, Terkman (mother of Monte)
    at Thanksgiving dinner, 250
    Lebanese cooking, 301
    lived with us, Wash. D.C., 273
    raised baby Gale, 175
Bradt, Elizabeth P. (mother of WB)
    corresponded with Abigail, 286
    died 1961, 288
    eggs for grandson, 282
    life as a widow, 52
    lived on Versailles farm, 19
    returned check graciously, 123
    with Hale and Model A 1952, *289*
    wrote Wilber, 106
Bradt, F. Hale (father of WB)
    critically ill, 45
    died Dec. 3, 1944, 47
    retired in Versailles, Indiana, 19
Bradt, Hale V. (son of WB)
    .22 rifle, 121
    advice on dating from WB, 30
    date with girl, Bangor, 4
    intimate conversations, 27
    job at dairy in Wash., D.C., 184
    life in Bangor, 4
    not sent to Versailles, 159
    photograph of
        at Lumban bridge, *202*
        bicycle and Gale 1946, *273*

camp counselor 1947, *277*
family 1952, *283*
family ca. 1978, *295*
grandmother 1952, *289*
Heidelberger grave, *219*
Model A, *288*
playing with Gale ca. 1946, *274*
portrait Hattiesburg 1942, *50*
Shibushi Bay, Kyushu, Japan, *232*
splashing in lake 1944, *24*
with Aunt Mary 1987, *299*
scouting in Bangor, Maine, 152
visit to Luzon, 1983, 199
Woodrow Wilson HS, 10th grade, 225
yearned for a Jeep, 176
Bradt, Mary (sister of WB)
corresponded with Abigail, 290
photo of 1987, *298*, *299*
photo of with Ruth and Rex, *298*
reassured Abigail, 290
Bradt, Norma Sparlin (wife of WB)
became a Catholic, 272
concerned about her privacy, 17
defense of Wilber to Rex, 55
engaged to Monte Bourjaily, 278
home Washington, D.C., 1945, 225
in Indiana woods, 176
insisted on her independence, 13
interest in Abigail Adams, 119
married Monte Bourjaily, 281
miscarriage Dec. 1945, 266
photograph of
at piano 1985, *297*
family 1952, *283*
family ca. 1978, *295*
portrait 1944, *49*
splashing in lake 1944, *24*
with Valerie 1985, *297*
portrait of, arrived, 48
returned to Bangor, xiv
sent blue letters, 116
Third Order Franciscan, 285
visited Washington, D.C., 17, 128
war service, 196
Wilber's "Dove of Peace", 188
Bradt, Paul (brother of WB) & Josephine
address used by WB, 172
anguished letter to Mary, 268
Hale rock climbing with, 276
visited Wilber, 244
Bradt, Rex H. (brother of WB)
job contact for Wilber, 249

photo of 1987, *298*
WB shares thoughts with, 227
WB's last letter to, 251
Bradt, Valerie E. (daughter of WB)
Alice Deal school 8th grade, 225
asking, "Is I is or is I ain't", 53
expects Norma to do washings, 119
face in photo recognized by WB, 178
hopes to get pneumonia, 128
photograph of
family 1952, *283*
family ca. 1978, *295*
portrait Hattiesburg 1942, *50*
splashing in lake 1944, *24*
with Norma 1985, *297*
sent WB funnies and gum, 128
St. John Baptist School, 277
wrote General Barker, 12
Bradt, Wilber E.
academic world is real, 154
army career postwar considered, 43, 142
arrived home, 242
at Aitape, 10
bathrobe, new Filipino, 144
Bronze Star awarded to, 131
C.O. of RCT, Operation Olympic, 191
Combat Infantryman's Badge earned, 183
combat more routine, 112
commands 152nd FA Bn., 6
commands 172nd Inf. Rgt., 176
death by gunshot, 264
depressed, 180
directed firefight, 168
discouragement, 85
en route Aitape, 5
executive of 172nd Inf., 157
father, last letter to, 51
firefight with six Japanese, 105, 124
funeral, 265
general command school, requested, 150
generally tired, 152
grandchildren, *302*
has hermit's blood, 177
Hill 600 guns silenced, 105
I'm coming home, 234
intoxicated on USS Fayette, 47
leave cancelled, 187
loves mother & wife, 118
motives for staying with division, 172
mottled-gray attitude, 54
never satisfied, 153
no escape from responsibility, 43

photograph of
    as executive of 172nd Inf. 1945, *173*
    at Pakil celebration 1945, *206*
    awarded Silver Star 1945, *182*
    Col. Sheng dinner 1945, *169*
    on USS Gen. Pope 1945, *240*
    with Capt. Burns, Aitape 1944, *25*
planned for leave home, 185
plea to his mother, 61
premarital chastity, 31
rescue of Filipino, 97
searches for positions alone, 124
Silver Star presented to, 181
some minutes are worth more, 73
thoughts about postwar, 193
will miss the thrill, 187
Bronze Star awarded to WB, 131
Burns, Capt. Frank J., 25
Bush, Col. George E.
    at Col. Sheng dinner, *169*
    C.O. of 172nd Inf., 157
    requested WB as his executive, 162
    role for Kyushu invasion, 192

camera, purchased by WB, 197
cane, kamagong, 122
Carpenter, Maj. Franklin E.
    commander of 152 FA Bn., 161
    new exec. of 152nd FA, 152
chapel
    Aitape, 38
    Arlington, WB service in, 266
    truck parked in, 54
Chestnut Farms Dairy, Wash., D.C., 184
Christmas 1944, 64
Cleland, Col. Joseph P.
    at Lumban bridge, 136
    at Pakil celebration, 205
    at WB funeral, 266
    called Silver Fox, 179
    commander, 103rd Inf. Rgt., 53
    gets worked up re enemy artillery, 195
    on USS Fayette with WB, 72
    photograph of
        at Pakil celebration, *206*
        with Japanese prisoner, *130*
    planned Luzon landings, 77
    played with medicine ball, 75
    promoted to brig. general, 154
    WB shared tent with, 152
Cloke, Paul, Dean at U. of Maine
    WB wrote to, re return, 230

WB wrote to, re vacation, 227
combat
    Luzon, **67–198**
    New Guinea, **1–66**
Combat Infantryman's Badge for WB, 183
commendation
    for 152 FA Bn., Aitape, 20
    for 43rd Div., Luzon, 110
convoy, track en route Luzon, *xxvi*
cook bloodied with ketchup, 112
Cook, Holloway
    not found among prisoners, 125
    WB may see wife Joy, 234
Corregidor Island 1983
    base theater, *210*
    coastal gun, *210*
    Hale visited, 209
    Malinta tunnel, *211*
Covill, Capt. Warren K.
    harangue from Barker, 59
    SS President Coolidge sunk, 59
Cuyapo, Luzon, Hale visited, 213

Dacquel, José
    attorney, hosted dance, 120
    gift of rice, 121
    photo of Mrs. Dacquel 1983, *212*
    visit at home of, 121
dating, advice for Hale from WB, 30
DeBlois, Lt. Col. René L.
    commanded 169 FA Bn., 6
    Service Battery his problem, 33
    wounded, 13
Devine, Lt. Col. James "Wally"
    executive officer of 103rd Inf. Rgt., 47
    rescue of Filipino, 100
Dewey, Thomas, presidential candidate, 8
DeWolfe, Capt. Thomas A.
    fractured vertebra, 17
    visit to front lines, 16
Douglass, Prof. Irwin
    acting head, U. Maine chem. dept., 54
    shared WB correspondence file, 54
Driniumor River
    Japanese attacked across, 9
    move to, 14
    training at, 28

Epilog, **261–301**

facsimile
    clipping re WB death, *258*
    combat belt, Luzon landing, *89*

Index

first WB letter from Luzon, 97
guerilla rescue, sketch of, *101*
knife made for WB, *42*
list of gifts, notebook, *257*
shipboard menu, *80*
Stoney letter to mother, *269*
telegram Oct. 16, 1945, *242*
WB letter at Lumban bridge, *135*
WB letter of 11/27/45, *253*
WB letter, end of war, *190*
Family trees, *xix*
Filipino contacts 1983
    Dacquel, Mrs. José, 214
    Florendo, Boysie, 201
    Javier, Lucita, 218
    Peralto, Emma, 201
Filipinos
    guerilla commander, Col. Agustin, *149*
    guerilla rescued, 97, *101*
    manning 155-mm howitzer, *149*
    mess boy brought chicken, with ginger, 109
    two girls wanted soap, 139
    work for Americans, 111
Fish, Maj. Waldo H.
    at Guimba with only WB, 123
    captured Japanese prisoner, 16
    car stopped short of road mine, 144
    dinner on USS Fayette with WB, 47
    New Zealand relationship, 40
    up to front lines with WB, 108
fishing in surf, Aitape, 26
Florendo, Boysie, Lumban, P.I., *203*
Fort Meade Hospital, 245
forward observers, memorandum on, 39
foxhole, fast man into & trembling in unison, 110

gambling on ship, 6
garden, hibiscus and fireflies, 41
Gilbert Islands, *xv*
Grace Boys Camp
    Hale and campers hiking, *277*
    Hale at, 1946 and 1947, *276*
Griswold, Lt. Gen. Oscar W.
    commander, XIV Corps, 78
Guam captured, *xv*
Guimba, Hacienda Cinco
    close-in defense, 123
    dance for men, 120
    described, 116, 120
    Hale visited, 214
    portico of old home, *215*
gum, chewed on way to front, 150

Halsey, Adm. William F., Jr.
    commander, Third Fleet, 82
    WB his Swashbuckling Buccaneer, 154
Hattiesburg, Mississippi
    Norma remembered at, by WB, 10
    one-speed bicycles from, 270
Hauck, Arthur A., president, U. of Maine
    approved WB plans, 193
    mentioned in WB draft letter, 255
Hayes, John K. M., Model A, *288*
Heidelberger, Norbert J.
    Hale visited grave, 218, *219*
    photograph of, as private, *218*
    WB wrote mother of, 180
hen, flies like expert, 163
Henderson, Chester, farmed cropland, 52
Hill 200
    attack on Pozorrubio from, *xxxiii*
    enveloped by 103rd RCT, *xxxii*
    first day's objective, 96
    secured Jan. 17, 103
Hill 355 taken, 109
Hill 600
    artillery observation post on, *130*
    important difficult objective, 105
    Silver Star for WB, 105
Hiroshima, atomic bombing of, 185
Hollandia, New Guinea, landings at, 5
howitzer
    105-mm at Aitape, *26*
    155-mm Long Tom at Ipo, *149*
    Japanese 12-inch, Luzon, *107*
Hussey, Capt. Robert S., battery commander, 97

insurance payment, into trusts, 275
Interlude, Luzon, **199–221**
Ipo Dam
    after capture, *157*
    captured, 153
    Hill 1400 cleared, 150
    map of drives toward, *xxxvi*
    operation began, 147

Japan, occupation, **223–57**
Japanese
    areas of Pacific controlled by, *xxii*
    artillery difficult to locate, 107, 111
    attacked across Driniumor River, 9
    attacks on batteries, 108
    defensive zones, Luzon, *xxvii*
    Filipino guerrillas decapitate, 183
    guide Americans to comrades, 184

VICTORY AND HOMECOMING

killed by 152nd boys, 109, 112
officers' underground shelter, 156
prisoners eating C-rations, *155*
ran into trees, 128
reactions to occupation troops, 230
resources on Luzon, 95
retreat from Aitape, 18
Jeep
    also called Peep, 112
    good for torture, 195
    Hale yearned for, 176
    shell through, 112
    went 150 miles in, not easy, 165
jungle road mysterious, 39

kamikaze attacks
    in Lingayen Gulf, 87
    initiated at Leyte Gulf, 36
    threat during voyage to Luzon, 70
knife
    made for Wilber, 42
    razor sharp for Luzon landing, 89
Kreisler, Fritz, recital by, 243
Krueger, Gen. Walter
    commanded rain to start, 165
    commander, Sixth Army, Luzon, 79
    conferring with Gen. Wing, *143*
    declared Aitape operation over, 18
    knew about 152nd FA, 162
Kumagaya airbase, Japan, 229
Kyushu, invasion of
    planned, *xxxviii*, 191
    Shibushi Bay and Hale, 232

La Croix, Camp, Luzon, P.I., 171
Lester, Capt. J. C.
    entertained WB on USS Fayette, 47
    Skipper of USS Fayette, 72
Letters from Iwo Jima, parallels to WB death, 301
Leyte Gulf entered by TF 78, 84
Leyte, Philippine Islands
    invasion of, Oct. 20, 1944, 23
    landings at Ormoc Dec. 7, 1944, 44
Lingayen Gulf
    American landings at, *xxix, xxx,* 91
    Hale visited, 216
Lucerne, Maine, vacation at, 24
Lumban bridge
    capture by Americans, 132
    Hale visited, 202
    iron structure 1983, *202*

Japanese roadblock north of, *134*
map, approach to, *xxxv*
photograph of 1945, *137*
pilings exposed 1983, *203*
Luzon, Philippine Islands
    actions of 43rd Division, *xxviii*
    battles, **67–198**
    Cabanatuan, **171**
    Central Plains, **95**
    Guimba & Mabalacat, **115**
    Interlude 1983, **199–221**
    Ipo Dam, **147**
    Japanese defensive zones, *xxvii*
    Shimbu action, **127**

Mabalacat City, 152nd FA motored to, 122
Mabitac, Luzon, after night attack, *133*
MacArthur, Gen. Douglas
    announced divisions in Luzon, 108
    commander SW Pacific Area, 5
    directed to take Leyte, 23
    on USS Boise, 87
    planned occupation of Japan, 193
    signed surrender documents, 195
Malone, Arthur, Hale visited grave, 218
Manaoag, Luzon, P.I.
    Hale visited, 216
    wounded guerilla rescued, 97
Manila
    captured March 3, 110
    harbor described, 197
    map, Manila Bay, *xxxvii*
    visited by WB, 125
Manila American Cemetery
    Hale visited, 218
    Heidelberger grave, *219*
    rows of crosses, *219*
maps
    actions of 43rd Division, Luzon, *xxviii*
    Aitape coastline, *xxv*
    areas controlled by Japanese, *xxii*
    beaches, 43rd Div., Lingayen Gulf, *xxx*
    beaches, Sixth Army, Lingayen Gulf, *xxix*
    capture of Pozorrubio, *xxxiii*
    convoy track en route Luzon, *xxvi*
    drive to Lumban, *xxxv*
    Eastern New Guinea, *xxiv*
    first day's advances, Luzon, *xxxi*
    Hill 200 enveloped by 103rd RCT, *xxxii*
    Ipo Dam, attack plan, *xxxvi*
    Japanese defensive zones, Luzon, *xxvii*
    Kyushu Olympic landings, *xxxviii*

Manila Bay, *xxxvii*
Pacific Areas with WB voyages, *xxiii*
Shibushi Bay, artillery plan, *xxxix*
Teresa-Bosoboso River region, *xxxiv*
Mariana Islands
   landings, xv
   turkey shoot, xv
Marshall Islands landings, xv
menu, shipboard, *80*
mines in road, 144
Model A Ford roadster
   Grafton, West Virginia, *288*
   Versailles, Indiana, *289*
mortar fire
   dud exploded, 35
   during hike with Maj. Fish, 108
   Hill 600, Luzon, 106
   Lumban bridge, 136
   results of, at Corregidor, 209
   scared by own, 14
   TED force casualties, 18
Mushik, Capt. Donald L.
   father died, taking leave, 46
   organized ship's mess lines, 6
   visit to front lines, 16

native choir, Aitape, *60*
New Guinea
   combat, **1–66**
   map of eastern part, *xxiv*
Nichols, Lt. Col. Stephen L.
   wounded by driver's grenade, 154
Normandy landings, xv

Ohashi, Nobuko, visited WB grave, 292
Oldendorf, Vice Adm. Jesse B., commander, Bombardment Force, 82
Operation Coronet, invasion of Honshu, 183
Operation Downfall, invasion of Japan, 183
Operation Olympic, invasion of Kyushu
   43rd Division alerted for, 182
   landing sites, *xxxviii, xxxix*
   planned, 197
   WB a RCT commander for, 191
   WB did not expect to survive, 231
orchestra equal to top U.S. ones, 121
Oseth, Col. I. M.
   of War Dept., on USS Fayette, 72
   photograph of, at Manaoag, *102*
   rescue of wounded Filipino, 100
   WB most intelligent, 104

Pacific Areas, map of, *xxiii*
Pagsanjan, Luzon, Makapili prisoners, *139*
Pakil, Luzon, P.I.
   celebration of liberation, *206*
   girls wanted soap, 138
   Hale visited, 204
Paris, entered by Allies, 21
Payne, Earl M., Hale visited grave, 218
Pierson, Maj. Samuel F.
   grabbed log in river, 29
   misses voyage to Luzon, 71
   returned to unit, 119
   S-3 of 152nd FA Bn., 18
   suggested sign on tree, 17
   sweating out his mistakes, 152
point system
   161 points for WB, 167
   43rd Div. transferring personnel, 231
   85 required for return to U.S., 165
poisonous gas anticipated, 83
pontoon bridge, Aitape, *29*
Pozorrubio, Philippines, 103
prisoners of war
   American, building bridge, 1942, 202
   Bataan death march, 209
   Germans, in Delaware, 175
   guide Americans to comrades, 184
   Holloway Cook died as, 125
   Japanese delivered to WB, 183
   Maj. Fish captured Japanese, 16
   two Japanese brought in, 166
Pushaw Lake, bicycle trips to, 121
Pyle, Ernest "Ernie," killed, WB knew at Indiana U., 159

Raihu River, Aitape, 10
rain
   172nd trains in, 178
   artillery firing during, 152
   by command of Gen. Krueger, 165
   howitzer recoiled down hill, 151
   lineman & dozer driver, 167
   season began, 151
rat trap yields, 25
ribbons, campaign
   arrived, 233
   requested, 195
rifle, .22 in Bangor, 4
Roosevelt, Pres. Franklin D.
   died, 141
   elected to fourth term, 38
   running for 4th term, 8

VICTORY AND HOMECOMING

Ryan, Maj. Hugh E.
    wounded by driver's grenade, 154

Saipan secured, xv
San Fabian, Luzon, P.I.
    Hale visited, 216
    landing site, 78
    municipal hall, 99
    soldiers fording stream, 98
San Ildefonso church, Tanay
    Hale visited, 207
    photographs of, *208*
    plaque of history, *207*
    WB visited, Easter, 136
schools, private, a handicap, 117
scouting in Bangor, 4
segregation in U.S. Navy, 72
Sheng, Col. Shih I., hosted feast, 169
Shibushi Bay, landing sites, *xxxix*
ships
    Hinoki, Japanese destroyer escort, 91
    lights left on after war, 228
    SS President Coolidge, sunk 1942, 59
    USAT Sea Devil to Aitape, 5
    USS Diphda, AKA-59, Hale served on, 235
    USS Fayette, APA-43, to Luzon, 47, *71*
    USS Gen. George M. Randall, AP-115, Hale on 1954, 235
    USS Gen. John Pope (AP-110)
        arrived San Francisco., 239
        soldiers and flags, *239*
        to U.S.A., 235
        WB and Capt. Reddy, *240*
    USS Monrovia (APA-31) to Japan, 197
shower oil drum described, 59
Silver Star
    cluster for WB, Filipino rescue, 97
    Hill 600 action, 105, 112
    presented to WB by Gen. Wing, 181, *182*
    second cluster for Lumban bridge, 137
silverware
    on USS Fayette, 79
    sterling, gift for Norma, 79
Sixth Army
    commanded by Gen. Walter Krueger, 18
    inspection by, 28
sniper fire
    at Lumban bridge, 138
    missed moving targets, 164
    ran into with Fish, 108

soap
    Filipino girls asked for, 139
    retrieved by woman for soldier, 163
souvenirs
    captured at Aitape, 33
    scout exhibit of, 152
    sent from Japan, 235
    sent from Luzon, 171
Sparlin, Norma. *See* Bradt, Norma Sparlin
Sparlin, Stonewall E. "Stoney"
    joined our family, 264
    letter to his mother, 268, *269*
    photo of, ca. 1945, *265*
St. Petersburg, Florida, condo at, 294
Stark, Gen. Alexander, asst. commander, 43rd Div., 72
stationery, gift from Hale, 14, *15*
sulfadiazine for ringworm, 144
surrender
    by Japan, 186
    documents signed, Tokyo harbor, 195
    soldier's response, 227
    unconditional demanded by Allies, xv
Swift, Lt. Gen. Innis P.
    commander, I Corps, 79
    commendation for 43rd Div., 110
    conferring with Gen. Wing, 99

Tadji Plantation, 10
Tanay, Luzon, P.I.
    San Ildefonso church, *208*
    signal crew, *132*
TED force, friendly-fire deaths, 19
telegram, WB sent Oct. 16, 1945, *242*
Teresa, P.I., 152nd headquarters at, 143
Third Fleet
    Adm. Halsey commanded, 82
    covered Japanese airfields, 88
Tinian captured, xv
Tokyo, Japan, bombed from Marianas, 44
training
    amphibious at Aitape, 28
    at Driniumor River, 28
    for invasion of Japan, 161
    Gen. Barker in rage about, 58
    rain soaks men during, 178
Tyler, Father Barrett L.
    killed in shelled church, 164
    mad about truck in chapel, 54

USSR at war vs. Japan, 186

V-E Day (Victory in Europe), 146
vehicles. *See also* Jeep
    at Lumban bridge, 137
    blackout condition, 147
    how to load onto landing craft, 69
    in rain, Ipo action, *153*
    jeepneys in Cuyapo, *205*
    moved out under fire, 116
    on and off ships, 28
    truck caught in river, Aitape, *29*
    truck stolen, Service Battery, Aitape, 33
voyages, map of, *xxiii*

Washington, D.C., **223–57**
    family moved to, 165
Wilkinson, Vice Adm. Theodore S.,
    commander, Task Force 79, 82
Wilson, Ruth (sister of WB)
    gave WB holster, 25
    kind words for Abigail, 291
    kind words for Norma, 291
    photo of with siblings 1987, *298*
    shared anguished letter, 268
Wing, Maj. Gen. Leonard F.
    at Pakil celebration, 205
    Bronze Star for WB & Cleland, 131
    conversation re WB prospects, 157
    inscribed photo for WB, 242
    inspected by, 25
    party with bagpipes, 70
    photograph of
        at Pakil celebration, *206*
        conferring with Gen. Krueger, *143*
        conferring with Gen. Swift, *99*
        military review at Cabanatuan, *177*
        portrait presented to WB, *241*
        presenting Silver Star to WB, *182*
        with Japanese prisoner, *130*
    relieved regimental commander, 103
Woodrow Wilson HS, Wash., D.C.
    Hale in 10th grade, 225
    news report of 43rd Division, 231
    Trial by Jury, 256
    Valerie attended, 278
World War II
    Germany surrenders, 146
    Japan surrendered, 186
    landings in Normandy, xv
    Luzon invaded by Allies, 95
    WB letter at end of, *190*

Yakamul, New Guinea, WB visited, 26
Yamashita, Gen. Tomoyuki
    C.O., Japanese 14th Area Army, 95
    hiding in gully, 178
    Shobu Group survivors, 189

★ ★ ★

UNITED STATES MARINES

Jan. 12, 1945

Dearest,

Am in the Philippines, Am well, and having a real time. The Bn is doing a fine job. Don't worry about me. Tell Mrs. Averill that Roger is OK, also Bob Hussey — Both are doing a magnificent job.

Love,
Wilber